MW01193593

Cover photo by Dominik Keller

A TEXTBOOK
OF
OARSMANSHIP

A Classic of Rowing Technical Literature

A TEXTBOOK
OF
OARSMANSHIP

A Classic of Rowing Technical Literature

BY

GILBERT C. BOURNE

Secretary of the Oxford University Boat Club 1884 and 1885

Sport Books Publisher, Toronto, Canada

Acknowledgement To Stephen Orova, the head rowing coach of Drexel University, who provided his personal copy of Bourne's original publication, and to Oxford University Press, for granting permission to reprint. *Publisher.*

Canadian Cataloguing in Publication Data

Bourne, Gilbert C. (Gilbert Charles), 1861-1933.
A text-book of oarsmanship
Originally published: London: H. Milford, 1925.
ISBN 0-920905-12-9

1. Rowing. 2. Exercise. I. Title.

GV791.B68 1987 797.1'23 C87-095070-3

Distribution in Canada and world wide by
Sport Books Publisher
278 Robert Street
Toronto, Canada M5S 2K8

Printed in the United States

FOREWORD

A thorough study of early classics in any discipline is a valuable and essential exercise for understanding past developments as well as for gaining solid knowledge as a foundation for future research and technical modifications. In rowing, a number of such works come to mind, including F.S. Kelly's *Essay on Sculling,* R.C. Lehmann's *The Complete Oarsman,* Steve Fairbairn's works and Richard Burnell's work in the 1950s and 1960s on rowing and sculling. But the classic of classics for the rowing world is Gilbert Bourne's *A Textbook of Oarsmanship.*

The book is a masterpiece written by a Renaissance man — Bourne, the writer, Bourne, the coach, Bourne, the anatomist, and Bourne, the artist. The book also represents the culmination of a brilliant life, being published in 1925, exactly 40 years after Bourne's tenure as secretary of the Oxford University Boat Club in 1885.

In designing the content of the book Bourne seemed to harmonize the text with the execution of a single stroke cycle — simplicity is paramount. The main parts of the book identify and represent the key components of rowing: i.e., The Theory of Rowing, The Art of Rowing, Oars and Boats, On Coaching and On Muscular Action in Rowing. This careful layout of Bourne's master plan subtly recognizes the scientific undergirding of the sport, the ballet or ideal movement patterns of the sport, the mechanics and tools utilized by the athlete, the importance of a skilled mentor and, finally, the recognition of the internal mechanics of the athlete's body.

The first three chapters are a must for any student of rowing who is seeking both scientific and practical foundations for future investigations. Bourne's work should be read in conjunction with modern works by Herberger and Korner. In particular the theory of boat moving (chapter 1) is still relevant and has excellent diagrams on the speed curves of boats and stroke patterns of the oar. The second chapter on ideal movement patterns is an excellent complement to the theories of chapter 1. Again Bourne has drawn exact descriptions of proper and improper body positions that are still relevant today. His stick figure (Fig. 29, page 139) predates the modern computerized wizardry of the American researcher, Gideon Ariel, by 52 years.

The chapters on oars and boats provide excellent diagrams on the effects of various rigs. These chapters have provided the basis for much of the current literature on this particular subject. Finally, we come to the concluding chapter on muscular action in rowing. Contemporary coaches might argue that Bourne's ideal is a little stiff and postured but they will still derive tremendous benefits from a careful study of this chapter, which provides direction in the coaching of sound body movements. It cannot be emphasized enough that a coach must be thoroughly versed in how the body is structured and how that structure moves ideally, and the chapter on rhythm covers this topic extremely well.

The republishing of this seminal piece of work in our sport is timely, as we are becoming more aware in sport of the wisdom of the body and body movements. Bourne's brilliant *A Textbook of Oarsmanship* is excellent companion reading to current sport and rowing literature.

JIM JOY
Technical Director
Canadian Amateur Rowing Association

CONTENTS

LIST OF ILLUSTRATIONS

PREFACE

More than forty years ago, when still an undergraduate at Oxford and full of the glorious confidence of youth, I wrote in manuscript and illustrated some 'Notes on Rowing and Muscular Action in Rowing' for the use of the New College Boat Club. This early effort had a certain measure of success. At any rate it was read and re-read by successive generations of New College oarsmen until, in the course of years, the note-book fell to pieces and its pages were scattered and lost. Thereupon I began to collect materials for a book which was to follow the lines of my ephemeral essay. But pressure of other and more serious work prevented my undertaking the proposed task until I left Oxford in 1921. Since then the work has progressed slowly, and has grown until it has reached its present dimensions. If I have treated the theory and art of rowing at great length and often in repulsively minute detail, it is because others have made contributions to the subject too weighty to be dismissed in a few lines. Colonel A. G. Shortt, Messrs. F. H. Alexander, A. Cruickshank, E. McGruer, R. W. Blakeley, and others have dealt, at greater or less length, with the theory of the stroke. Sir Theodore Cook, in his volume entitled *Rowing at Henley*, has propounded innumerable questions relating to boats and oars. I must express my obligation to all of them for calling my attention to a number of questions which, in my earlier rowing and coaching days, I had never thought of.

I am only too well aware that, in attempting to elaborate the work of my predecessors, I am exposing myself singlehanded to the criticisms of some of the most censorious persons in the world. I tremble to think what Mathematicians, Naval Architects, Anatomists, and Oarsmen will have to say to my lucubrations. With some of these, if they disagree with me, I am confident that I can speak boldly in the gate. From others I can only hope to escape with a not too merciless castigation. But if they will do me the honour to use their whips on me I shall have achieved my object. For I wish to provoke the interest of oarsmen who are also mathematicians in the numerous problems relating to the propulsion of racing-boats, to oars, and to boat-design, which I have propounded and discussed, but do not pretend to have solved. It is, to my way of thinking, intolerable that a Wrangler should row in a University boat and not bother himself to inquire into the principles on which his oarsmanship depends.

The chapters on muscular action are the outcome of studies and observations extending over a number of years. If open to criticism in detail, I believe that the principles laid down are sound. The anatomical illustrations are so far original that they nearly all represent the subject in a rowing position instead of in the conventional attitudes adopted for descriptive purposes by anatomists. I have to thank Messrs. Geo. Bell & Sons and Mr. James M. Dunlop for permission to copy figs. 63 and 64 from the latter's excellent *Anatomical Diagrams for the Use of Art Students.* My special thanks are also due to Professor Arthur Thomson of Oxford for much advice and assistance in making photographs in his laboratory, and to his skilled assistant, Mr. W. Chesterman, who took the photographs on which many of the anatomical illustrations are founded. Even more I am indebted to Mr. P. C. Mallam, without whose very practical help the anatomical drawings could not have been made. I must also express my thanks to Professor H. H. Turner, F.R.S., and to the Rev. J. Kenneth Best of Cheltenham College for steering me through certain mathematical eddies in which I was very nearly engulfed. Also to Mr. E. W. Powell and Mr. C. A. Gladstone for helpful advice and criticism on Chapters IV and V. I cannot too fully express my obligation to Sir John E. Thornycroft for the unvarying kindness and courtesy with which he has placed all kinds of technical apparatus and illustration at my disposal. The frontispiece is reproduced by the kind permission of Messrs. Hills & Saunders of Eton. Finally, I hope I have made it sufficiently clear throughout this book how much I owe to the teaching of the late Provost of Eton, Dr. Edmond Warre, from whom I, no less than many other generations of oarsmen, learned nearly everything that I know about rowing. My attempt to push the analysis of the stroke to the farthest limits of which I am capable has resulted in a complete vindication of the principles which he laid down for the guidance of all future generations of oarsmen.

GILBERT C. BOURNE.

TWYNING MANOR,
TEWKESBURY.
April 27, 1925.

Photo by Hills & Saunders, Eton

THE ETON EIGHT, 1881

Bow. W. K. Hardacre. 2. F. I. Pitman. 3. T. M. Babington. 4. D. H. McLean
5. F. E. Churchill. 6. St. C. Donaldson. 7. G. C. Bourne. *Str.* J. Baring. *Cox.* O. W. Rayner

CHAPTER I

THE THEORY OF ROWING

MAINLY HISTORICAL

It was one of the Duke of Wellington's generals who, when importuned by a young officer for advice as to how he might best learn the duties of a soldier, answered: 'By fighting, Sir, and plenty of it.' Similarly I would answer to the aspiring oarsman who asks how he may best learn the art of oarsmanship: 'By rowing, Sir, and plenty of it.' For of this much I am convinced, that oarsmanship, like many other things of greater or less importance that are taught at the present day, suffers from too much teaching, and would be improved by less learning and more practice. An excellent reason why I should not do what I am setting out to do, to write a book on the theory and art of rowing. I can only plead, in extenuation of the offence of adding yet another to the already too numerous works on the subject, that I have been asked to do it and that, after going into the matter with much more thoroughness than seemed necessary at the outset, I am satisfied that so much false doctrine has found its way into print that there is room for an exposition of the true and only faith of oarsmanship. No doubt about it there is a true doctrine, and wherever oarsmen are gathered together in this country they unite, with singular unanimity, in doing reverence to it. It is the traditional English style with its long body-swing, its quick 'catch at the beginning', its rapid recovery of the oar with the wrists, followed by a prolonged and balanced swing forward. That is the right way, the only way: all oarsmen, young and old, are agreed upon it. But then differences of opinion begin to creep in. The older school of oarsmen who learned and practised the art of rowing on fixed seats—their number, alas, is rapidly diminishing—refuse to recognize the traditional style in modern oarsmanship. The style of rowing, they say, has changed and changed for the worse, nor is the change altogether attributable to the introduction of sliding-seats. For at Oxford and Cambridge, in the Torpids and the Lent races, where most of the oarsmen engaged have never rowed on anything but fixed seats, the oarsmanship is very much inferior to what it used to be. Though I have kept abreast with modern developments of rowing and am far from being a *laudator temporis acti*, I am bound to add my testimony, that the style of fixed-seat oarsmanship of to-day shows a lamentable falling off from what it was forty and even five and twenty years ago. The art of rowing on a fixed seat is nearly extinct. It seems clear, then, that the traditional style of English oarsmanship, to which we all do lip-service, is held in some sort of ancestral reverence but is not generally practised to-day. If our practice is at variance with our professions there can be no settled and accepted theory of oarsmanship. If there is no definite theory we are aiming at something that we are not likely to achieve, for we cannot have any precise notion of what we are aiming at. That our notions are, to say the least of it, indistinct is obvious from the discussions of oarsmen, which almost invariably end in anecdotes of the prowess of individual oarsmen who have distinguished themselves at Henley and elsewhere. These individuals are esteemed, not so much for the theoretical excellence of their oarsmanship as for their successes, and it is conveniently ignored that they rowed in all kinds of different shapes. I am far from wishing to suggest that all oarsmen should row in the same shape. Individuals differ so much in proportion of limbs and body that a good deal of liberty must be conceded to every man in a crew if the whole is to be welded together in harmonious action. For action, be it observed, is not the same thing as posture or shape, though unthinking coaches are prone to confuse the two. But after due allowance is made for idiosyncrasies there can hardly be a doubt that, in such an art as that of oarsmanship, there must be, for any given type of boat, some one method of propulsion which is the best, both for obtaining speed and for sparing the oarsmen from unnecessary labour and exhaustion. The qualification 'for any given type of boat' is important, for the best method for propelling the light hulls of racing-boats is assuredly not the best for heavy craft such as a tub-four or a tub-pair, and an experienced oarsman will always modify his action and therefore his 'style' to suit the particular kind of craft he is rowing in. Coaches, I am afraid, are not always so discriminating, and much harm is done by insistence, in clinker-built boats, on methods only applicable to light carvel-built racing craft. For present purposes we need only consider the best method of propelling racing-boats. These, whether they be eights, fours, pair-oars, or sculling-boats, are of the same type and differ only in the number of men and therefore the load that they are designed to carry.

To many oarsmen it will seem unnecessary and even absurd to embark on a long and somewhat tedious inquiry into the best method of propelling racing craft. It has been proved, they will say, over and over again by experience; the best method is the accepted style of English oarsmanship which has come down to us from Warre and Morrison and Woodgate and has been preserved through the decades by Darbishire, Willan and Tinné, by Goldie and Rhodes, by Marriott, Edwards-Moss and West, and more recently by Muttlebury, Fletcher, Gold, and a score and more of more recent oarsmen. Yes, but what is this traditional English style? and has it been handed down intact but for the modifications necessarily introduced by the use of sixteen-inch sliding-seats? Dr. Warre and Mr. Woodgate looked with sorrow and something approaching contempt on the oarsmanship they witnessed in their declining years, and such oarsmen as Mr. T. C. Edwards-Moss, Judge Gurdon, and Mr. L. R. West would, I venture to say, be singularly unhappy if they could, by a miracle, be included in even a good class modern crew. I could, however, pick out here and there a crew, and always a winning crew, of recent years in which they could have rowed without any departure from their accustomed style, sixteen-inch slides notwithstanding. Methods, and with methods style, have changed a great deal within the last forty years, and in my opinion have changed very much for the worse since somewhere about the beginning of the present century, though from time to time a crew has appeared which has harked back to the old principles and has shown an overwhelming superiority over all its opponents. Such, to mention only four instances, were the Magdalen College crew of 1910; the Leander eight and the New College four of 1913; and the Third Trinity (or Eton Vikings) four of 1922, 1923, and 1924.

It may be said, with some measure of truth, that these crews differed from others solely in this, that they achieved what others were aiming at and that the underlying theory of good oarsmanship was the same for all. I take leave to object that this is not the case, for the good reason that there is not and never has been in the last century a complete theory of oarsmanship. There has been a practice of good oarsmanship, founded upon a number of maxims learned by experience, but that is quite another thing.

How far we are from a true theory of oarsmanship is shown by the fact that up to quite recently all oarsmen believed that a boat travels faster when the blades are in the water and slower when the blades are on the feather. For the boat, they said, must lose way between the strokes. More recently Mr. Alexander has maintained, with a wealth of mathematical and mechanical demonstration, that a boat travels at greater speed during the feather than during the stroke, and for bad oarsmanship he seems to have proved his case. I shall sustain the thesis that with the best oarsmanship the mean speed of the boat is the same during the stroke and during what I shall henceforth call the 'run' between the strokes. This single instance is sufficient to show what important differences of opinion may exist on a cardinal point in the theory of oarsmanship.

A complete theory must take into account many things relating to the boat, the oars, and, most important of all, to the man. But whatever the views set forth on these points, the theory, if it is to be of any value whatever, must be conformable to experience and must be competent to give a rational explanation of many things that are puzzling and apparently paradoxical in rowing. It may be useful to give examples of these paradoxes.

There is the gentleman whom I am wont to refer to as a ' stopper '. He has long been a puzzle to me. As a rule he is a powerfully built man and rows in apparently correct form. His work is not at fault, for his effort at every stroke is apparent, and he sends down a great swirl of water from his blade. His ' beginning ' is to the eye at least as good as that of his comrades. His length of swing is irreproachable and his pluck and endurance beyond all cavil, for he will go on working to the very end of a hard race when defeat is certain and the rest of the crew have thrown up the sponge. He generally enjoys the reputation of being a hard worker and a good stayer and as such readily finds a seat in a College and sometimes even in a University crew. It is hard to find fault with him, yet a little experience tells one that for the purpose of winning races he is better out of the boat than in it. Sometimes a College, as the result of erroneous teaching, puts on a whole crew of ' stoppers ' and its descent in the bumping races is swift and sure. I shall hope in the following pages to give a reasonable explanation of the mystery of the ' stopper '.

It is no less a mystery that a heavy and powerful crew rowing with good length, in orthodox style, and at a faster rate of stroke, is often completely outclassed by a lighter crew rowing at a slower stroke with no apparent effort. I recall two races, the Belgians against Trinity Hall in the final heat for the Grand Challenge Cup in 1906 and the Sydney Rowing Club against New College, Oxford, in the fourth heat of the Grand Challenge Cup in 1912. In both races the English College crew rowed much the longer stroke and evidently put forth much the greater effort, yet the visiting crew, conspicuous for the shortness of its swing, went ahead easily at a slower rate of stroke, and for the greater part of the course maintained and improved its advantage without any apparent effort at all. It would be interesting to know the difference between the expenditure of energy in foot-pounds in the winning and the losing crew in each of these races.

I followed both and am sure that the expenditure was far less in the winning crew. I could give many other instances, but these two have stuck in my memory because the English crews were swinging out in the orthodox English style and should on that account have had an advantage over their opponents, but it was obvious that their great labour was wasted and that in rowing speed is not so much a consequence of the amount of horse-power developed as the manner in which the power is applied.

In both these races the foreign or colonial crew had a better ' beginning ' than its English opponents. It is a truism in the rowing world that a quick catch of the water at the beginning of the stroke is essential to sustained speed over a course of any length. Not necessarily to speed, for crews without any true beginning have, by means of a hard thrust of the legs in the middle of the stroke, shown a surprising turn of speed for a short distance. But such a crew cannot keep up the pace, and if pressed by a crew having a good beginning and fast enough to prevent its taking a prolonged ' breather ', breaks up and collapses before the end of the course is reached. But what is this ' beginning ' ? It is a most elusive thing ; the despair of many an aspirant to rowing honours. I venture to say that it is not what nine-tenths of those who talk about it believe it to be. It certainly is not attained by a violent and spasmodic effort, nor by throwing back the head and shoulders, nor by any similar artificial tricks taught by second-rate coaches in the vain hope that their pupils will thereby get the real thing. It is in many respects paradoxical, for the oarsman who succeeds in quickly moving his shoulders and body through a considerable angle has certainly missed his beginning, but the oarsman who has got it cannot, because of the resistance he encounters, move back very fast. Yet great quickness of movement is essential to getting hold of the water at the beginning. It is a thing to be striven for, yet, if the oarsman strives too hard, he is sure to miss his aim. I call to mind three very effective oarsmen who had a complete mastery over the ' beginning '—Mr. R. S. de Havilland, Mr. J. A. Ford, and

Mr. G. O. C. Edwards. Mr. Ford was an upright and shapely oarsman ; Mr. de Havilland round-backed, rough and vigorous ; Mr. Edwards seemingly careless to the point of sloppiness. All three had this feature in common : that they came forward easily and confidently and then, without any marked uplift of the hands or any marked display of energy in throwing back the body, in the twinkling of an eye the blade of the oar was covered to its full depth and instantly a mass of green water was piled up against it. For the rest of the stroke this solid-looking mass of water was swept back with unfaltering precision and at the finish the blade of the oar left the water as it had entered it, without flurry or splash, and the mass of water swirled away with scarcely a bubble round the edge of the vortex which the movement of the blade had set up. I have not seen another ' blade ' exactly like these, and there can be no doubt that each of the three oarsmen named was master of the art of boat propulsion. What I want to call attention to at the moment is that the thing was done with the utmost economy of effort. That is the mystery of the beginning : that it must be caught in an instant and caught firmly, yet without hurry and without undue effort.

It is another paradox in rowing that, as the oar enters the water, the speed of the hull is checked by the pressure exerted by the oarsmen on the stretcher and that the speed increases as the blades leave the water. So the boat should progress in a series of leaps, and most racing-boats undoubtedly do progress in this fashion. Yet in all the crews I have had to do with that have developed exceptional speed the boat does not travel by jumps, but holds its way so steadily that the variations in speed, which must accompany the method of propulsion by oars, are inappreciable to the eye. I have often observed this in watching crews rowing past the Green Bank above the Gut at Oxford where, in summer time, vertical stems of the rushes afford a good measure of the progress of the boat. Whenever I have seen the nose of the boat move steadily and at apparently uniform speed past those rushes I have known that I had a winner, whatever the strength of the crews opposed to it. Nor have my expectations ever been disappointed. It is worthy of remark that whenever a boat does move like this the crew seems to be sending it along without any obvious effort. A notable example was the Cambridge crew of 1888, without a doubt one of the finest crews ever sent by either University to Putney. The boat travelled so smoothly and the oarsmen seemed to be exerting themselves so little, that it was difficult to believe that it was going as fast or the oarsmen were working as hard as they actually did.

I may conclude this introductory matter by reference to the vexed question of the proper angle that the oar should make with the boat at the beginning of the stroke, or to put it in another way, whether men should ‘ slide up to their work ’ or be set back three or more inches from it. Certain assumptions being granted, it is easy to demonstrate on mechanical principles that, the efficiency of the oar regarded as a lever of the first order being greatest when it is at right angles to the boat, the most effective stroke is one that begins and ends at equal angular distances from the right angle. The whole angular movement of the oar being taken at 80° (there are valid reasons for not exceeding this limit), this would mean that the stroke should begin at 50° and end at 130°, and that would involve placing the men at least six inches away from their work. But even the most fanatical adherents of the doctrine of ‘ pinching the boat ’ make the concession that the oar should begin at 45° and end at about 125°, the men being placed about three inches away from their work. I will only say here that I have again and again tried the experiment of putting men three inches or more away from their work and have never obtained any advantage from it, but rather the contrary, and this is the common experience of both oarsmen and coaches. When practice is so much at variance with theory it is certain that the latter has failed to take all the factors into account. I shall offer what I hope will be accepted as a reasonable solution of this vexed question in the following pages.

As soon as I began to write about the theory of oarsmanship I realized that the task on which I had entered light-heartedly was going to be far from easy. The more I have grappled with it the more difficult it has become, and I soon arrived at this safe but not very helpful conclusion : that there is no settled theory of oarsmanship that can guide both coaches and oarsmen, because the subject is so inherently difficult that it requires a much profounder study than has hitherto been thought worth while to give to it. A complete solution involves the study of the interaction of a number of variables, and this, it need hardly be said, means the use of elaborate methods of mathematical analysis. The mathematician who undertakes this analysis should himself be an experienced oarsman of an observant turn of mind, otherwise he will leave out of account factors which are of importance to a correct solution of the problem. I am quite incompetent to undertake any such analysis, and if I were competent should not think of publishing it in a book intended to be of practical value to oarsmen and coaches. Mathematical reasoning expressed in symbolic form is for the elect and not for the multitude. But a good deal has already been done, and I will endeavour to put it together and present it in a simple and intelligible form.

It was a surprise to me to learn on the authority of Mr. F. H. Alexander, that the theory of rowing was subjected to mathematical treatment by no less a person than Léonard Euler, the great Swiss mathematician of the eighteenth century, in his *Théorie complète de la Construction et de la Manœuvre des Vaisseaux*, published in St. Petersburg in 1773. It need hardly be said that the essentials of the problem were grasped and accurately worked out by so acute a mind, but his solution is of less interest to us because he did not deal with the problem as it affects light racing-boats and modern types of oar, for the very good reason that they did not then exist. I know of no other important contribution to the subject until the two papers of Mr. E. Cuthbert Atkinson, published in 1896 and 1898.[1]

[1] E. Cuthbert Atkinson, ' A Rowing Indicator ', *Natural Science*, vol. viii, no. 49, March 1896. Ibid., ' Some More Rowing Experiments ', *Natural Science*, August 1898.

He invented a rowing indicator which recorded, in a series of curves, not only the type of stroke rowed by individual oarsmen but also the amount of work done at every part of the stroke. By means of this indicator Mr. Atkinson obtained a number of valuable data, almost the only ones of their kind existing. It is to be regretted that on his leaving Oxford in 1897 Mr. Atkinson was unable to continue his valuable experiments. It is also to be regretted that nearly all his experiments were made in a tub-pair, and with College oarsmen whose proficiency was not more than moderate. He obtained a few tracings from a Torpid eight early in practice, but none from a light eight, therefore his results must be read with due allowance for the conditions under which they were obtained. It is an interesting commentary on this that in the autumn of 1895 I persuaded two 'Varsity oarsmen (the late Sir W. E. Crum and Mr. C. K. Philips) to come out in a tub-pair with Mr. Atkinson and myself to try the indicator. It was his earlier and unimproved pattern. First one and then another of us took the stroke-seat, to the thowl of which the indicator was attached. Mr. Crum registered a greatest pull of 174 lb. and 602 foot-pounds of work during the stroke, but the indicator had not been designed to record such pressure and the instrument was completely closed during part of the stroke, so that Mr. Crum's work was really in excess of what was indicated. I then took my turn and registered a greatest pull of 166 lb. and 498 foot-pounds of work during the stroke. The diagram of my stroke was republished as *K* in Mr. Atkinson's second paper, and has since been republished and commented on as an abnormal stroke of great power but short amplitude. Well, I was 34 years old, my rowing weight was below 10 st. 10 lb., and I was out of practice and condition when I rowed that stroke, though I had made my final appearance at the Henley Regatta in the preceding summer. The power, of course, was a good deal less than Mr. Crum's and the stroke is deficient in length, the curve suggesting that I had put all my strength into the first part of the stroke, had found that, in the heavy tub-pair with two passengers in the stern, I had 'bitten off more than

I could chew ' and therefore curtailed the finish. But I am of the opinion that the type of stroke was more nearly representative of that of the 'Varsity oarsmen of those days than the ' normal ' diagrams registered by the College oarsmen. Lastly, Mr. C. K. Philips took the stroke-oar and, when given the word to ' row ', put in such a mighty effort that he threw the instrument out of gear and the experiment came to an end without his stroke being registered at all. Mr. Atkinson's improved indicator was designed to register a maximum pull of 220 lb. and over, but unfortunately the opportunity of testing it with ' blues ' at the oar did not recur before he left Oxford. As far as the single experiment went the difference in the power developed by first-rate and second-rate oarsmen was sufficiently startling, but it must be remembered that on that November afternoon there were two men seated in the stern and on all other occasions only one. The additional weight probably called forth a correspondingly greater effort on the part of the oarsmen.

An even more important contribution to the theory of rowing was Mr. Atkinson's inquiry into the efficiency of propulsion by oars. In this connexion he pointed out that ' since the rowlock is moving forwards and the tip of the blade backwards, some point between these is neither moving backwards or forwards. This point may be called the Turning Point.' After showing that the turning-point must change its position during the stroke, Mr. Atkinson attempted to ascertain the mean position and the excursions of the turning-point with exactness by taking a rapid series of photographs of an oar in motion, on the same plate, from a point vertically above the boat. As always happens in the case of a single experiment, circumstances intervened which prevented the attainment of a perfectly accurate result : nevertheless Mr. Atkinson was able to construct a diagram which shows sufficiently faithfully, not only the movements during the stroke of points marked at various places on the length of the oar, but also the distances travelled by the boat at intervals of about 0·07 of a second. In fig. 6 of his second paper is shown graphically, I think for the first time, the marked retardation of the speed of the boat as the blade enters the water and the considerable acceleration during the first part of the swing forward. Again it is to be regretted that these results were obtained from a photograph of a heavy slow-moving tub-pair and not from a racing-boat moving at high speed. But it is notoriously difficult to get oarsmen training for a race to subject themselves to observations and experiments of any kind. They might consent to be experimented upon by their coach, but coaches seldom have the requisite training and imagination to carry out a series of exact experiments.

Mr. Atkinson's observations and conclusions, published in a rather obscure and short-lived scientific periodical, not likely to be consulted by oarsmen, did not attract the attention they deserved, and for the matter of that, oarsmen of that period were sceptical of the value of scientific inquiries into the art of rowing. They thought they knew all about it and shortly afterwards elaborated sundry erroneous theories which led to a sad deterioration of English oarsmanship.

The next experiments of which I have any record were made in France by MM. les Docteurs Lefeuvre et Palliotte.[1] They remained unknown in England until brought to light a short time ago by Mr. F. H. Alexander. The French experimentalists used a light sculling-boat and were very thorough in their methods, taking simultaneous records of the speed of the boat, the pressures on the starboard and port rowlocks, the pressures on the stretcher, and the movement of the sliding-seat. Furthermore, to bring out more clearly the results which follow the oarsman's movements, they sculled in a variety of styles, some of them very incorrect styles, and gave figures illustrating the curves obtained in each experiment. Unfortunately the scale of these figures is so cramped that they are not as useful as they might be. But they demonstrate clearly that as soon as the oar enters the water, down goes the speed of the boat and, contrariwise, as the blade leaves

[1] 'Etude graphiqu edu coup d'aviron en canoë,' *Bulletin de l'Association technique maritime,* 1904.

the water the speed of the boat is still rising. It is interesting to note that in one experiment, when the sculler purposely sat still at his back-stop for some time and then suddenly rushed his slide forward for the next stroke, there is a sudden increase of speed as the slide rushes forward, and this in spite of the fact that the curve of pressure on the stretcher shows that the sculler had to exercise a marked pressure with his feet in order to steady himself as he approached the front-stop. The rising curve of speed of the boat is converted into an abrupt curve of descent at the beginning of the stroke, the check being due to the fact that the sculler had sprung back his body from the stretcher before his blades had fairly caught hold of the water. It is important to distinguish clearly between the two kinds of pressure on the stretcher. During the slide forward, when the body is either moving in the opposite direction to the boat or is stationary, pressure on the stretcher has no effect in retarding the speed of the hull. But when the feet are used to propel the body in the same direction as and faster than the boat is moving, the hull is visibly retarded.

In this country interest in the theory of rowing was greatly stimulated by the publication of Dr. Warre's *Grammar of Rowing*, a booklet giving the substance of three lectures delivered to the Oxford University Boat Club in 1907. The *Grammar* is a reaffirmation of the principles mainly of fixed-seat rowing as practised and taught by Dr. Warre himself. As an exposition of the practice of oarsmen of a bygone generation, and therefore of the traditional English style, it is admirable, but it cannot be said to have added anything to our knowledge of the theory of oarsmanship. Indeed, Dr. Warre disclaimed any intention of dealing with the higher problems of the art of rowing, and confined himself rather to elementary things that should be taught to beginners. But a diagram purporting to represent the path described by the oar during the stroke led directly to a prolonged controversy on the theory of the oar. This diagram represented the oar as doing things that are mechanically impossible, and in the appendix to the published edition of his lectures Dr. Warre yielded so far to criticism as to insert an amended diagram which does more or less accurately represent the facts. The story of these diagrams is instructive as showing how very little the theory of rowing was understood by oarsmen at a comparatively recent date. Dr. Warre was by common consent the leading authority on oarsmanship. It was he who had introduced and perfected the modern style of rowing suited to keelless boats in 1857. He had taught and trained generations of first-class oarsmen at Oxford and afterwards at Eton. He was regarded as a sort of high priest of rowing; the repository of the true faith and doctrine of oarsmanship. Yet his first diagram demonstrates that, in his matured opinion, the boat is propelled no less than 12 feet during the stroke; that is to say, he believed that the travel of the boat during the stroke is nearly as great as in the run between the strokes. His description of the amended diagram in the appendix shows that he was evidently puzzled by the discovery that by far the greater distance is travelled during the run. Without doubt, Dr. Warre was a master of the art of oarsmanship and had an unequalled genius for imparting the mysteries of the craft, and this story is only another illustration of the familiar fact that genius, if it be true genius, is independent of theoretical exactitude. But for the ordinary mortal, who is not a genius, it is as well to be secure about mechanical principles. The immediate and happy result of Dr. Warre's lectures was an awakening of interest in the theory of rowing evinced by numerous contributions to the *Field* newspaper. Much of what was published had been anticipated by Mr. Atkinson and by MM. Lefeuvre and Palliotte, and even by Euler himself, as the contributors would have discovered had they plunged into the literature of the eighteenth century.

Mr. A. Cruickshank of the Vesta Rowing Club gave in the *Field* a velocity curve for a complete stroke, illustrative of what should occur in accordance with Dr. Warre's theories. The curve shows acceleration of speed following immediately on the catch at the beginning of the stroke, and is no doubt true for the centre of gravity of the whole system of boat, men, and oars, but surely incorrect for the acceleration of the hull itself.

Mr. R. W. Blakeley, a practical oarsman and coach, after a criticism of Dr. Warre's diagrams of the action of the oar during the stroke, rediscovered Mr. Atkinson's turning-point, stating that 'somewhere between the tip of the blade and the button there is a neutral point which has no fore and aft slip and may be taken as the fulcrum'. This point Mr. Blakeley believed to be the neck of the blade, and gave a diagram of the movements of the oar which is fairly in accordance with fact, but curiously enough he does not seem to have noticed that his diagram demonstrates, what Mr. Atkinson had shown twelve years earlier, that the turning-point or fulcrum shifts its position during the stroke, travelling towards the button at the beginning and back towards the neck before the middle of the stroke is reached. Mr. Blakeley also called attention to the fact that 'during the recovery, the boat not only has the speed acquired from the stroke itself, but also an additional shoot due to the swinging of the crew's bodies towards the stretcher'. Conversely he showed, by reference to a simple experiment, 'that swinging away from the stretcher, unless the blade is in the water, actually pushes the boat back'. In this discovery he had been anticipated by MM. Lefeuvre and Palliotte, but altogether Mr. Blakeley's is a very thoughtful and well-reasoned letter and an important contribution to the theory of rowing. It is republished in Sir Theodore Cook's *Coaching for Young Crews.*

Following upon Mr. Blakeley's letter to the *Field* is one from Mr. A. Cruickshank, a curious mixture of sound statement of mechanical principles and failure to appreciate the import of the principles enunciated. He states: 'An oar acts simultaneously in a dual capacity: in propelling a boat as a lever of the second order and in producing slip (i. e. accelerating a mass of water in an opposite direction to the line of advance) as a lever of the first order. Slip cannot be eliminated in any form of propulsion, oar, paddle, or propeller.' Nothing can be more correct or more explicit. It should be noted that it is because the oar acts in a dual capacity that we get the ‘ turning-point ’, a fulcrum which shifts its position considerably in relation to the oar, but inconsiderably in relation to the line of advance of the boat. Mr. Cruickshank goes on to say : ‘ An oar in propelling a boat cannot have back pressure on the blade ’—that is very true, but what follows is more doubtful—‘ i. e. no part of the blade moves in the direction that the boat is advancing.’ Had he been acquainted with Mr. Atkinson’s work and had studied fig. 9 of Mr. Atkinson’s second paper, he would have seen that, if the stroke is rowed in a certain way, the turning-point, in the last third of the stroke, lies between the neck and the tip of the blade, and at the finish is very near the centre of effort of the blade. This implies that for a considerable part of the stroke a part, and an increasingly large part, of the proximal area of the blade is moving in the direction in which the boat is advancing. Yet as long as the pressure is kept up and the oar is being accelerated it does not back water, because there is an air cavity, and not water, on the convex or forward surface of the blade. From this principle, already shown to be erroneous, Mr. Cruickshank deduces the following proposition : ‘That the maximum travel of a boat when the blades are in the water (and this is irrespective of the pace) can only be the length of the oar from the thowl to the neck of the blade multiplied by the cosine of the angle of catch plus the same distance multiplied by the cosine of the angle of finish, minus at least one inch for the slip of the neck.’ From which he makes the further deduction that, with a twelve-foot oar, measuring 5·58 ft. from the button to the neck of the blade, the oarsman sliding up to within three inches of his work, the travel of the boat during the stroke must be 6·30 ft., the oar moving through an angular distance of 79° (45° at the beginning and 124° at the finish). Had Mr. Cruickshank been acquainted with Mr. Atkinson’s experiments he would have paused before committing himself to such a statement, for the latter’s fig. 6 in *Some More Rowing Experiments* shows that, in fact, an oarsman in a tub-pair moved his boat through a distance of about 7·15 ft. for an exactly equivalent angular movement of the oar. Mr. Atkinson's oarsman appears to have begun his stroke, i. e. to have fully immersed his blade at position 2 of his fig. 6, and to have finished at position 13, the angle of the oar at the beginning being 42° and at the finish 127°. With this angular movement of 85° the boat travelled, according to the scale of feet attached to the figure, almost exactly 8 feet. Assuming that the oar was extracted at position 12 the figures are as given above. To begin at an angle of 42° the oarsman must have slid up to his work, and this is an additional refutation of Mr. Cruickshank's corollaries set forth in his tables of Elements of Oars and Sculls and estimates of work useful and work wasted, &c., with different kinds of rig, for it is part of his thesis that the travel of the boat when the blade is in the water is greater when the oarsman is set back from his work than when he slides up to it. Yet here we have an oarsman who, sliding up to his work, moved his boat appreciably farther than the maximum allowed by Mr. Cruickshank with the most favourable rig. If he had rowed a really effective stroke, which from a study of Mr. Atkinson's figure I am convinced he did not, he would have moved his boat still farther. The flaw in Mr. Cruickshank's reasoning is that he takes no account of the movement of the turning-point, and of the further consideration that if the turning-point shifts its position, so also must the centre of effort of the blade. It further appears from a study of his diagrams of blade movement, that Mr. Cruickshank treats the oar chiefly as a lever of the first order, and by so doing ignores altogether the principle of the turning-point. So all his elaborate tables and calculations fall to the ground. It is not necessary to pursue this matter farther here, but I have dealt with it at some little length because, if his assumptions and deductions were correct, we should have to believe that a short stroke is more effective than a long one : a belief opposed to the overwhelming body of experience, but it had a vogue after the successes of the Belgian and later of the Sydney crew at Henley. Mr. Cruickshank's letter, tables, and diagrams are republished in Sir Theodore Cook's *Coaching for Young Crews*.

Passing over a letter from Mr. Ewing McGruer, another advocate of the short stroke, for he postulates that the angle moved through by the oar during the stroke should be not more than 70°, we come to a letter to the *Field* signed by 'Cox', which calls attention to a fundamental feature in the dynamics of rowing. Writing to the editor, he says : 'The point is that you failed to draw the distinction between the motions of the boat and of its centre of gravity, including the crew. The perfectly extraordinary jump in velocity at the end of the stroke may easily be observed by any casual spectator, but, in a sense, it is entirely fictitious. It is not the result of particularly good work, but of the fact that a very considerable mass of the cargo has suddenly transferred a large part of its momentum to the hull proper, i. e. the crew have "recovered" their bodies. The contrary effect at the beginning of the stroke is even more marked, a light boat with the crew well together stops almost dead every stroke as the work comes on ; but its centre of gravity has already commenced its next acceleration, before the *hull's* velocity has reached its minimum. Eight strong men simultaneously "springing off their stretchers" cannot fail to produce a reaction on the very light framework connecting those stretchers.' This, of course, is little more than a restatement of the conclusions of MM. Lefeuvre and Palliotte and Mr. Blakeley, but expressed in such emphatic form that it compelled attention, and several post-war oarsmen, whose mathematical and scientific competence is at least equal to their aquatic experience, adopted the view that the boat is necessarily stopped, and stopped almost dead, at the beginning of the stroke.

In 1922, Colonel A. G. Shortt wrote a long essay in the *Field*, working out in great detail the theories propounded by 'Cox', and I have before me a voluminous correspondence in which Colonel Shortt sustains his thesis with even more copious reference to figures and with a greater wealth of mathematical reasoning than in his published articles. Colonel Shortt was in his day an accomplished oarsman, a member of the Oxford Eight of 1884 and a winner of the Ladies'

Plate and Visitors' Cup at Henley. His opinions are entitled to great respect, yet I cannot accept his conclusion that the boat stops dead or nearly dead at the beginning of each stroke. A retardation of speed there certainly is, but that there is any necessity for its being as great as he makes it out to be, I take leave to doubt. Unquestionably there are crews—too many crews—who stop their boats so much that they seem to bring them almost to a standstill when the blades enter the water. But this is a result of bad rowing. The better a crew rows the less does it check the pace of its boat at the beginning of the stroke, and it is one of the tragedies of rowing that when a crew rows in the wrong way its efforts to do more work only result in greater retardation of the speed of the boat.

In November 1921, Mr. F. H. Alexander read a paper on the 'Theory of Rowing' before the University of Durham Philosophical Society, and it was published *in extenso* in vol. vi, part 3 of the Proceedings of the Society in 1922. The substance of this essay was afterwards communicated in a series of articles to the *Field*. Mr. Alexander's exposition of the theory of rowing is the most complete that has ever been published, and in most respects is in striking agreement with the practically contemporaneous articles of Colonel Shortt. It is pretty stiff reading, and I fear incomprehensible to any one who has not a sound elementary knowledge of mechanics.

The main criticism I have to make on Mr. Alexander's essay is that it is a pity that he is not himself an experienced oarsman. On the practical side of the question he had, I understand, the advice of a no less eminent oarsman than Mr. H. C. Bucknall, but in a matter of this sort external advice cannot supply the want of bodily experience. Hence it is that the essay, though impeccable in scientific form, fails to give a satisfactory solution of the many problems that confront practical oarsmen. Mr. Alexander, I imagine, has been led astray by the rigour of his logic and by the necessity of adopting certain mathematical artifices to satisfy his equations. For example, he states in more than one place that the arc swept through by the centre of effort of the blade of the oar is 12·24 feet in length. No oar ever swept through an arc of that length under normal conditions. As Mr. Cruickshank has recently pointed out, this method of reasoning is only applicable to an oarsman rowing in a tank, or when his boat is made fast to the bank, and does not give even an approximately truthful representation of what happens when the boat is under way and the oarsman's efforts are combined with those of his fellows. It is true that Mr. Alexander is in good mathematical company, for Euler makes use of the same device to simplify the problem, but it is apparent that however eminent he was as a mathematician, Euler's practical knowledge of the art of rowing was very small, and one may doubt whether Catharine the Great's navy derived any important advantages from his incursions into this unfamiliar field of research. Nevertheless, Euler did lay down several principles of fundamental importance, and Mr. Alexander, who follows his distinguished predecessor pretty closely, has done great service by reaffirming and amplifying those principles. It is in matters of the technique of oarsmanship that Mr. Alexander goes astray. He is unacquainted with the proper rhythm of the stroke. His ideal oarsman buckets forward sadly, misses his beginning, drags his stroke through the water and makes two pieces of it, lies back at an impossible angle at the finish, and is in mortal danger of catching a crab at the end of every stroke. The ideal crew which is to cover the Henley course in 6 min. 50 sec., at a rate of 33½ strokes per minute, without any opposing wind or current would, if it could complete the course, take 7 min. 2¾ sec. against a normal midsummer stream, but I doubt whether it would get to the top of the island without accident.

None the less, Mr. Alexander has made a most substantial addition to our knowledge of the theory of rowing, and if his premisses are wrong in certain particulars, the framework of his reasoning is so sound that when the necessary corrections are made the whole question stands in a much clearer light than ever it did before. I am indebted to him for most of the ideas contained in the following chapter.

I pass over the numerous books and articles written by Mr. E. D. Brickwood, Mr. R. C. Lehmann, Mr. D. H. McLean, Mr. Guy Nickalls, Mr. C. M. Pitman, and others, because, while they contain much sound, practical advice on the art of rowing, they are not and do not profess to be expositions of the theory of rowing. For that reason, perhaps, they are of the more interest and assistance to the practical oarsman. But, being incurably of the opinion that he who teaches or practises an art should be able to give sound reasons for what he teaches or practises, I propose, before dealing with rowing as an art, to make my own contribution to the theory of the subject.

CHAPTER II

THE THEORY OF ROWING

THE FIRST STROKE

THE first thing that must be clearly understood by any one who wishes to gain a clear idea of the theory of oarsmanship is that the 'crew', including hull, oars, coxswain, and oarsmen, is what is known in mechanics as a 'system', the component parts of which change their relative positions during the stroke and the swing forward. Thus, the outboard elements of the oars move in the opposite direction to the hull during the stroke: in the same direction as the hull during the swing forward. The oarsmen move in the same direction as the hull during the stroke: in the opposite direction during the swing forward. As the weight of the hull is at most 300 lb.; the weight of the oars about 72 lb.; the weight of the coxswain some 120 lb.; and the weight of the eight oarsmen anything from 1,120 to 1,420 lb., it is clear that the movements of the last named must be of considerable importance in shifting the centre of gravity of the whole system. For example: let us suppose that the crew is at rest and that oarsmen are sitting with their sliding-seats pressed against their back-stops. The hull of the boat settles itself in the water to a certain trim, depending, to some extent, on the distribution of the oarsmen's weights. The centre of gravity of the whole system will probably be near the fore [1] edge of No. 5's seat. If, now, the whole crew slides 16 inches

[1] As the oarsman sits facing the stern of the boat and is said to swing forward when he is moving towards the stern and to swing back when he is moving towards the bows, the terms commonly used by river oarsmen are apt to be misleading. Throughout this work I shall use the terms 'fore' and 'aft' to indicate positions and structures nearer to the bow or nearer to the stern respectively. None the less I shall adhere to the customary language in reference to the oarsman's movements, and must use such terms as 'front-stop' and 'back-stop' in the sense ordinarily given to them by oarsmen.

up to the front-stops, the centre of gravity of the system is moved aft and the trim of the boat is altered. The movement aft creates pressures on the immersed surface of the hull astern and diminishes pressures towards the bows, as a result of which the hull moves a certain distance forward and takes up a new trim. Conversely, when the crew slides back, pressures are increased towards the bows and diminished towards the stern, so the hull moves backwards. The same results follow from the fore and aft movements of the oarsmen when the boat is in motion. Hence, during the swing forward, the hull is slightly accelerated, and during the swing back it is slightly retarded, simply as a consequence of the movements of the oarsman's body and of the sliding-seat. The final result is that the movements counterbalance one another, but, as we shall see, during the stroke the retardation is more than compensated by the acceleration given to the boat by the oars, whereas during the swing forward, when the oars are out of the water, the acceleration of the hull due to the movement of bodies and slides has its full effect.

The movements of the hull due to the disturbance of the centre of gravity of the system must be clearly distinguished from the movements imparted to the whole system by the action of the oars. The movements of the component parts of a moving system within the system cannot make it move in any direction with regard to external objects. Thus, in the case just mentioned, when the oarsmen move aft the hull moves forward and vice versa ; but the system as a whole does not progress either backwards or forwards. The system can only be moved by applying force to something external to it. In rowing the muscular power of the oarsmen is applied by the oars to the water external to the system.

Let it be understood at the outset the motive power is the muscular strength of the crew. Oarsmen are told to use their weight, and it is very important that they should learn to do so with advantage. But weight, *per se*, is of no use ; it may be an encumbrance. What is required to propel the boat is power, and power is *mass* (or weight) *in motion*. In order to set his weight in motion the oarsman must use muscular force, and if his weight is great the muscular force required to move it at a given speed must be proportionately great. It is an error to suppose that a man's muscular power is proportional to his weight. In the physical measurements of undergraduates made in my laboratory at Oxford before the war the strength of pull of individuals was tested by a specially designed dynamometer. The results were tabulated according to age, and it would take too long to give a detailed account of them here. But they showed quite clearly that there is very little correlation between weight and strength of pull in any age-group from 18 to 23 years. The mean pull in all but one age-group was between 200 and 220 lb. The strongest pulls ranged from 320 to 360 lb., and are distributed pretty evenly among men whose weights range from 11 stones to 12½ stones. There are only two instances of men whose weights exceeded 13 stones who could pull more than 340 lb. Two men, whose weights were between 14 and 14½ stones, registered pulls below the mean of their age-groups. On the other hand, one individual in the 18 year old group, whose weight was only 8 st. 4 lb., pulled 256 lb., and in the 21 year old group two men, weighing between 10½ and 11 stones, registered pulls between 300 and 319 lb. Altogether some 1,500 individuals were tested, so the results may be taken as fairly applicable to the whole undergraduate population. These facts should make coaches chary of putting very heavy men into crews merely for the sake of their weight.

What is meant by using one's weight in rowing will be explained later on. For the present it is only necessary to keep in mind that the force exerted by the oarsman is primarily muscular force, and without further inquiry into the physiology of nerve and muscle it may be accepted as a fact that the muscular power of individuals varies within wide limits, and that heavy men are not necessarily strong men. Some are, but statistics show that men of medium weight are, on the average, stronger than heavy weights.

To return to the movements of the boat and oars. Although, as we have seen, the crew can cause movements of the hull by simply shifting their weights backwards and forwards, they cannot make the hull move by simply pushing or pulling against it. If, with their sliding-seats jammed against their back-stops and their oars resting idly on the surface of the water, the crew push as hard as they can against their stretchers with their feet, they do not move the hull in the slightest degree. They set up strains in the hull, but that is all. It is necessary to insist on this very elementary point because a careless reader of some of the authors quoted in the last chapter might gain the impression that any kind of pressure against the stretcher retards the forward movement of the boat. The authors in question are much too well acquainted with the principles of mechanics to suggest anything of the kind. To move the boat or to stop it when moving work must be done on something outside the boat. In the case mentioned above movement of the slides forwards or backwards, by shifting the centre of gravity of the system, depresses the stern or the bow, and thus work is done on the water, and the hull moves. But much the greater part of the oarsman's work is done by pulling on the oar when the blade is immersed in the water, and it simplifies matters if we deal with the propulsive action of the oar to the practical exclusion of other factors tending to accelerate or retard the hull. It must be remembered, however, that a very small margin of gain or loss per stroke will make all the difference between winning or losing a race, and every factor that helps to increase the run of the boat, be it only to the extent of two or three inches per stroke, will demand consideration in the proper place.

In rowing the oar is used as a lever, and there are two schools of thought about the action of the oar in this respect. Euler and, following him, Mr. Alexander and others deal with the oar as a lever of the first order, the power being applied at the handle; the resistance or weight to be moved at the centre of pressure of the blade; and the fulcrum at the thowl-pin of the rowlock. From this point of view attention is concentrated on the pressure obtained on the surface of the blade and on the area swept through by the blade during the stroke. Most of us are unconsciously thinking of the oar as a lever of the first order when we judge of an oarsman's capacity by his 'blade', that is, by the swirl made by his blade during and at the end of the stroke. On the other hand, Dr. Warre and Mr. R. Van der Waerden, the trainer of the winning Belgian crew of 1907, regard the oar as a lever of the second order, and references to the oar as an example of a lever of this order may be found *passim* in elementary text-books on mechanics. In this case the power, as before, is applied to the handle of the oar, but the weight to be moved is that of the boat, and is located at the thowl-pin; the fulcrum is at the centre of pressure of the blade. As the oarsman's object is to move his boat and not to shovel down a mass of water, it is preferable to think of the oar mainly as a lever of the second order, but the truth really is, as Mr. Cruickshank has pointed out, that the oar acts at once as a lever of both orders—as a lever of the first order in setting water in motion and thereby creating resistance at the blade: as a lever of the second order in utilizing this resistance as a fulcrum and so advancing the boat.

This dual action of the oar introduces complications into the stroke of which it is difficult to give an intelligible account, but it is as well to understand clearly at the outset that, in taking account of the forces acting on the oar, the numerical results are the same, whether we regard the oar as a lever of the first or the second order. For if we take an oar 12 ft. 4 in. long, with an inboard length of 3 ft. 9 in. and an outboard length of 8 ft. 7 in., the centre of pull P being halfway between the hands at a distance of 3 ft. 3 in. (= 3·25 ft.) from the button, and the centre of pressure on the blade B being 13 inches from the tip and therefore at a distance of 7·5 ft. from the button; [1]

[1] In placing the centre of pressure at 13 inches from its tip I follow most writers in taking the centre of gravity of the blade lamina as the centre of pressure. Mr. Alexander calculates the centre of pressure on the assumption that the pressures on the blade vary from neck to tip as $(Vt)^2$, Vt being the 'thrust-producing speed' of the oar.

and if we call the point where the oar presses against the thowl-pin T: when we treat of the oar as a lever of the first order, the power applied at P multiplied by the distance PT is equal to the resistance set up at B multiplied by the distance BT.

$$P \times PT = B \times BT.$$

And if we take P at 100 lb. and want to find the value of B

$$B = \frac{P \times PT}{BT} \text{ or } B = \frac{100 \times 3{\cdot}25}{7{\cdot}5} = 43{\cdot}333 \text{ lb.}$$

And the pressure on the thowl-pin is the sum of P and B:

$$100 + 43{\cdot}333 = 143{\cdot}333 \text{ lb.}$$

But if we treat the oar as a lever of the second order our equation becomes $P \times PB = T \times BT$, and if we want to find the pressure at T which is now the weight to be moved:

$$T = \frac{P \times PB}{BT} \text{ or } T = \frac{100 \times 10{\cdot}75}{7{\cdot}5} = 143{\cdot}333 \text{ lb.}$$

And the pressure at B, which is now regarded as the fulcrum, is the difference between T and P:

$$143{\cdot}333 - 100 = 43{\cdot}333 \text{ lb.}$$

Thus, whichever way we take it, there is no difference between the forces operating on the blade and at the thowl-pin for any given pull at the handle of the oar. But there is an important distinction between moving the boat past the point that the blade has taken hold of and

As he says, the value of Vt at the neck is obviously smaller than that at the tip. He gives the centre of pressure as situated at $8\frac{1}{2}$ inches from the tip. In dealing with statical pressures, the boat being stationary and the blade brought to bear on some unyielding object, the centre of pressure is the point of contact between the blade and that object, and for convenience of calculation I place it at 7·5 feet from the thowl-pin, or 13 inches from the tip of the blade in an oar of the dimensions given here. Similarly, though I do not consider that the dimensions of the oar given here are the best dimensions, I adopt them because they happen to be convenient for calculation when the centre of pressure is taken at 13 inches from the tip of the blade.

moving water past the boat with the blade. Upon this distinction depends the difference between good rowing and bad.

The principal forces acting on and through the oar have been fully considered by Mr. Alexander (loc. cit., pp. 161–3). They may be briefly stated as follows. The oarsman's pull, *H* in fig. 2 A, taken to be in a line with the keel of the boat, when the oar is at any angle

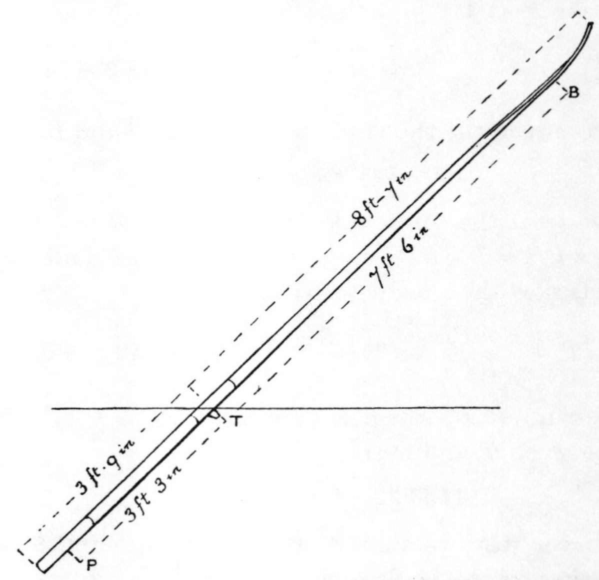

Fig. 1. The oar, showing proportions of inboard and outboard and centres of pull of hands and pressure on the blade.

less or more than a right angle with the side of the boat, may be resolved into two components: $P1$ normal to the axis of the oar, and O, acting along the axis of the oar and causing oblique outward thrust of the button against the thowl-pin. The pressure on the blade must be taken to be concentrated at the centre of pressure of the blade, and is represented by the line $P2$. If $r1$ and $r2$ represent the distances of $P1$ and $P2$ from the fulcrum at the thowl-pin, the pressure at $P2$ will be as much less than the pull at $P1$ as $r1$ is less than $r2$.

$P3$, the pressure normal to the axis of the oar on the thowl-pin, is the sum of $P1$ and $P2$.

Following Mr. Alexander we take $P1$ and that part of $P3$ which is equal to $P1$ as forming an inboard couple. As shown in fig. 2 B, that part of $P3$ which is equal to $P1$ may be resolved into components $H1$, which presses against the rowlock in the direction of the advance

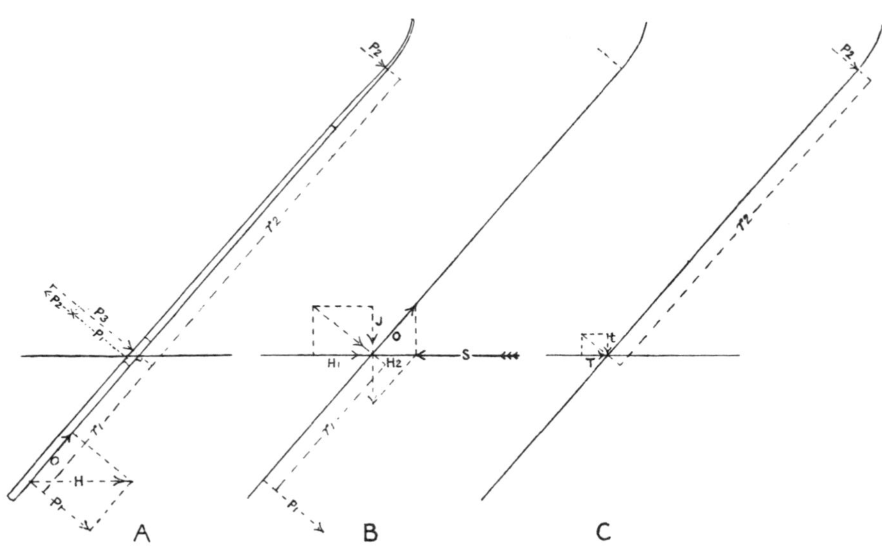

FIG. 2. A diagram showing the principal forces acting on and through the oar.

of the boat, and J, which presses inwards upon the thowl-pin and, as oarsmen say, 'pinches the boat'. But we also have to take into account the force O, a component of the fore and aft pull H, which as we have seen in fig. 2 B thrusts the button of the oar obliquely against the thowl-pin, and the farther the oarsman has 'reached forward', in other words the less the angle between the oar and the side of the boat, the greater is the forward thrust of O. The forces J and O, both acting on the thowl-pin, may be taken as the components of the resultant $H2$ acting in the direction of the advance of the boat.

If the reader will take the trouble to take the measurements from the diagrams figs. 2 A and B, he will find that the sum of $H1$ and $H2$ is exactly equal to the fore and aft pull H. So we find the whole of the oarsman's pull H transferred to the thowl-pin as a force acting in the direction of the advance of the boat. But we must feel inclined to say with Euler that the oarsman's task is *très pénible*, for none of this pull is directly available for propelling the boat. The reaction of the oarsman's feet on the stretcher, transmitted through the hull and rigging to the thowl-pin, is an equal and opposite force S acting against H, and as the thowl does not move in relation to the boat, the inboard couple seems to be wasted in setting up strains in the hull and rigging.[1] It is not really wasted, but before we consider how far any part of it is effective we must deal with the outboard couple. This (fig. 2 C) consists of the pressure on the blade $P2$ transferred to the thowl-pin as so much of $P3$ as is equal to $P2$. It may be resolved into components T and t. The latter, pressing inwards on the thowl, is added to J as part of the force which 'pinches the boat'. T, acting in the direction of the line of advance, remains as the force available for propelling the boat and, as the diagram shows, it is a small force relatively to H, the fore and aft pull of the oarsman.

So far I have followed Mr. Alexander, but have taken the liberty, in dealing with the inboard couple, to follow out the incidence of the forces operating at the thowl-pin in greater detail than he has. The end result is exactly the same, but it has seemed worth while to

[1] This statement that the thowl-pin does not move in relation to the boat reminds me that in 1880 Dr. Warre conceived the idea of utilizing the thrust of the oarsman's feet on the stretcher to impart movement to the thowl and so increase the power at the beginning of the stroke. He constructed an apparatus with a sliding-seat, a sliding-stretcher, and a sliding working thowl, the two last being joined by a connecting rod. I do not remember the details well enough to attempt an estimate of the amount and direction of the forces set in action. The practical effect was, that when he took his seat in the segment of a boat in which this fearsome apparatus was set up and took a strong pull on the oar against a counterpoising weight, Dr. Warre was shot backwards with great force and landed on the floor some three feet behind the machine. The experiment was not carried any farther.

demonstrate that a part of the forces which are usually reckoned as setting up stresses in the rigging, or ‘ pinching the boat ’, are really operative in exercising pressure on the thowl in the direction of the boat's line of advance. It is true that $H\,2$, as well as $H\,1$, is counterbalanced by the thrust of the oarsman's feet against the stretcher. But if $H\,2$ were non-existent, $H\,1$ would be less than H; and as S, the reaction on the stretcher, must be equal to H, the hull would be thrust backward if $H\,2$ were inoperative. It should be noted that the more acute the angle that the oar makes with the side of the boat the greater is $H\,2$ in comparison with $H\,1$. When the oar is at right angles to the boat $H\,2$ vanishes because its components J and O have vanished, and at this instant $H\,1$ is equal to H. When the oar has passed the right angle these forces reappear but act in opposite directions. J is now a pressure outwards, and helps to keep the button up to the thowl-pin, but O acting inwards along the axis of the oar tends to draw the button away from the thowl-pin.

So far the fore and aft pull of the oarsman represented by the line H has been taken to act in a line with the keel of the boat. But throughout the stroke the hands move on an arc, and if the oarsman conscientiously keeps hold with the fingers of his outside hand, as he should do, the outside shoulder also swings through an arc. Therefore the pull H is not in a line with the keel, and the corrections made for the obliquity of the pull when the oar is at any angle other than a right angle give rather interesting results. More especially when the oar is moving from 40° to 60°, O is diminished and $P\,1$ is increased by the same amount. As a result $H\,1$ and J are increased, and $H\,2$ is not only diminished in proportion to $H\,1$, but in consequence of the increase of one of its components J, and the decrease of its other component O, it no longer acts in the direction of the line of advance of the boat, but obliquely inwards as shown in fig. 3, $H\,2$. The sum of $H\,1$ and so much of $H\,2$ as is still acting in the direction of the boat's advance is no longer equal to S, and it would seem that this preponderance of the reaction of the oarsman's feet on the stretcher, small as it is, would tend to push the hull backwards. At all events remembering that the outboard couple gives us the force T available for propelling the boat, we might expect that T is diminished by the difference between $H1 + H2$ and S with a consequent loss of propulsive power. But the magnitude of the force T depends upon $P2$, and this in turn depends upon $P1$. As we have seen, the obliquity of the oarsman's pull increases $P1$, and therefore increases $P2$, and in turn increases T. So the loss at $H2$ is compensated by the increase of T; indeed it is just a little more than compensated, and there is no loss of propulsive force, but a trifling gain. So trifling that it might not be thought worth while to take it into account, but it must be remembered that in an eight-oared boat such trifling losses or gains on the part of individual oarsmen must be multiplied by eight, and this figure must be multiplied by the two hundred and more strokes rowed over the Henley course, or the five hundred and sixty or more strokes rowed over the Putney course. One cannot afford to neglect minutiae in rowing.

Many interesting results are obtained by plotting out the resolution of the forces operating at the thowl-pin for successive positions of the oar, say at every angle of 10° from 40° to 120°, during the stroke. It would take far too long to deal with these questions in detail, but one interesting result is that there is very little difference between the magnitude of the forces 'pinching the boat' when the oar is at 40° and when it is at 50°. As the oar swings from 50° to 70° these forces diminish rapidly; they become negligible when the oar is at 80° and vanish when it is at 90° to the side of the boat. But a careful investigation of the incidence of the forces at the thowl-pin affords no justification for those theorists who would have us place oarsmen some three to six inches away from their work, and would have us believe that a shortened reach forward with the oar gives a greater propulsive effect than a long reach.

It is also important to remember that there is no mechanical disadvantage attendant on the deviation from a straight fore and aft pull which is inseparable from a long reach forward. Whether there is any functional disadvantage is a question that must be dealt with in another place.

Thus far I have mainly followed Mr. Alexander, and so long as we think of the blade of the oar as being swept through the segment

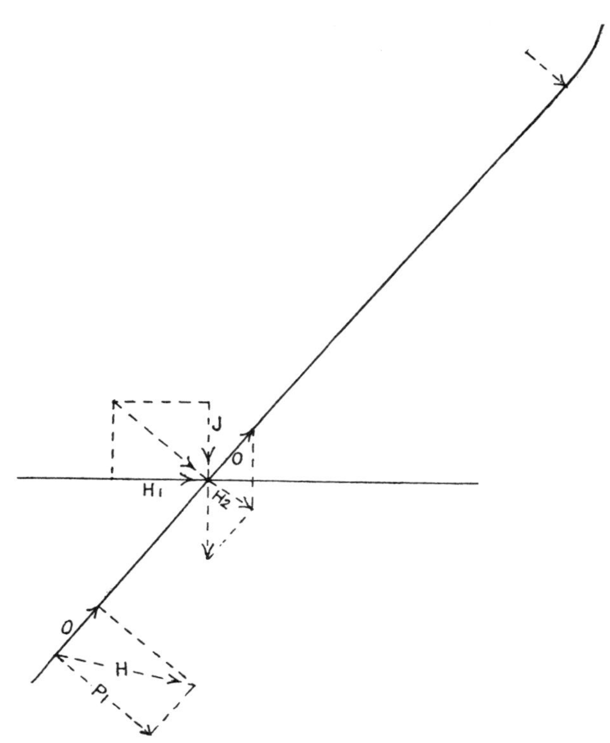

FIG. 3. A diagram showing the effect of the obliquity of the oarsman's pull.

of a circle, the pressure at $P\,2$ representing the resistance offered by the mass of water moved by the blade, in given time, through a given angle, his reasoning is unimpeachable. But in order that the blade may sweep through the segment of a circle the boat must be stationary, and if the boat is stationary we are not dealing with rowing properly so called, but with that baneful form of exercise obtained by the use of a rowing-machine, or a rowing-tank, or by lashing a boat to a raft and going through the motions of rowing with a reduced blade. Such exercises have about as much resemblance to rowing as an hour on the treadmill has to a free walk over a country down, and I venture to think that much of the deterioration in metropolitan oarsmanship that set in towards the end of last century was due to the detrimental effect of these supposed aids to the beginner. If a man wants to row let him go rowing; or if he cannot get a partner to row with him, let him go sculling; but let him beware of all kinds of substitutes for rowing. When in my Eton days we were rowing particularly badly, Dr. Warre used to tell us that we 'might as well sit on an island and try to row it along with a gridiron'; an apt description of the plight of a novice condemned to sit in an immovable section of a boat and shovel along water with a diminished blade. For it is of the essence of rowing that the boat is free to move, and if it be a light boat it is to a singular degree responsive to the efforts, well adjusted or maladjusted, of the oarsman.

This much is clear to begin with: that as soon as the blade of the oar encounters resistance at $P\,2$ and the boat moves forward through the water, the outboard part of the oar does not simply move through the segment of a circle, but is thrust outwards from the boat and pivots about a point which is not at the rowlock, but nearer to the neck of the blade than to the rowlock. This new instantaneous centre about which the oar pivots is the 'turning-point' first discovered by Mr. Atkinson. Mr. Blakeley, I think, was the first to suggest that the turning-point (which he called the neutral point) may at any instant be taken as the fulcrum. Whether it is legitimate to treat it as a fulcrum to the extent of taking moments about it at any instant, and calculating the variations in leverage that must ensue from the changing position of the turning-point, is a matter on which there may be differences of opinion. Some of my mathematical friends tell me that it is not legitimate. But this much seems to be certain:

that although the turning-point shifts its position to a considerable extent up and down the axis of the oar during the stroke, the locus in space of the turning-point is practically stationary in respect of the direction in which the boat is travelling. The turning-point, as shown in fig. 7, moves outwards from the boat in a curve convex towards the bows. At any instant the boat is being rowed past some point on this curve.

In order that we may study the problem of the turning-point more thoroughly let us imagine a condition of things exactly opposite to that which we have been considering. Instead of the boat being immovable, and the blade being rowed through yielding water, in which case the oar is acting all the time as a lever of the first order, let us suppose that the boat is free to move, and that the oarsman brings his blade to bear against some immovable solid object located at the centre of pressure of the blade. To simplify matters let us suppose that we are dealing with a pair-oar which is being started from standstill in still water; that the stroke- and bow-side oarsmen pull exactly together and with equal strength at every part of the stroke; and that they only reach forward so far that the oars make an angle of 50° with the side of the boat. The oar, *P* 1, *T*, *P* 2, in fig. 4, is now acting as a lever of the second order, the power *P* 1 being at the centre of pull of the hands, the fulcrum at *P* 2, where the centre of pressure of the blade encounters an unyielding object, and the weight to be moved is at the thowl-pin *T*. The oar is now working at a mechanical advantage because the distance from *P* 1 to *P* 2 must always be greater than the distance from *P* 2 to *T*, but the amount of the advantage varies at every instant during the stroke. *P* 1 *T* is a constant quantity, but *P* 2 *T* is greatest at the beginning of the stroke, when the oar is at 50° (or any less angle) to the side of the boat. It decreases until the oar is at 90°, then increases again up to 120°, or any greater angle through which the oar may be pulled. The shorter the distance from *P* 2 to *T*, the greater the pressure at *T* for any given strength of pull at *P* 1. But, conversely, the greater the measurement *P* 2 *T*, the greater is the distance through which the thowl-pin T is moved. This shows clearly in fig. 4, for the distances between T and $T\,1$, $T\,1$ and $T\,2$, &c. diminish as the oar approaches the right angle but increase again after the oar has passed the right angle. It seems paradoxical that the greater the pressure at the thowl-pin the less is the distance through which the thowl-pin, and therefore the boat, can be moved. But when the element of time is taken into consideration the paradox disappears; for if the acceleration is constant the unequal spaces are passed through in equal times (p. 48).

Let us now consider the movement of the oar in relation to the point $P\,2$. This is clearly the turning-point of the oar, and under the supposed conditions it is fixed in space but is not a fixed point upon the oar itself. For in the first part of the stroke the tip of the oar is being thrust outward, the out-thrust being greatest at the beginning of the stroke and diminishing until the oar is at 90° to the side of the boat. At this instant there is no out-thrust, but after 90° is passed the oar is pulled inwards and that to an increasing extent as it swings away from the thwartship plane. In consequence of this out-thrust and subsequent in-pull the turning-point $P\,2$, which at the beginning of the stroke was only thirteen inches from the tip of the blade, is 2·83 feet from the tip when the oar is at 90° and approaches the centre of pressure of the blade again in the last part of the stroke. The curve illustrating the excursions of the turning-point is shown as an inset in fig. 4. It is a continuous curve, and if the oar were carried back to an angle of 130° it would be perfectly symmetrical about the mean position of the oar at 90°.

The curve of the movement of the turning-point on the oar also affords a measure of the varying pressures on the thowl-pin during the stroke. For as $P\,2$ remains fixed in space the leverage of the oar is changing from instant to instant, and if we take $P\,1$ as 100 lb. and calculate the pressures on the thowl-pin for each position of the oar from 50° to 120° we get the successive values $143{\cdot}\dot{3}$, $149{\cdot}\dot{2}\dot{4}$, 153·27, 156·03, 157·01, 156·03, 153·27, $149{\cdot}\dot{2}\dot{4}$ lb. These, when plotted out on a similar scale, give the same curve as that of the turning-point on the oar.

It is furthermore clear from fig. 4 that, $P2$ being a fixed point, the

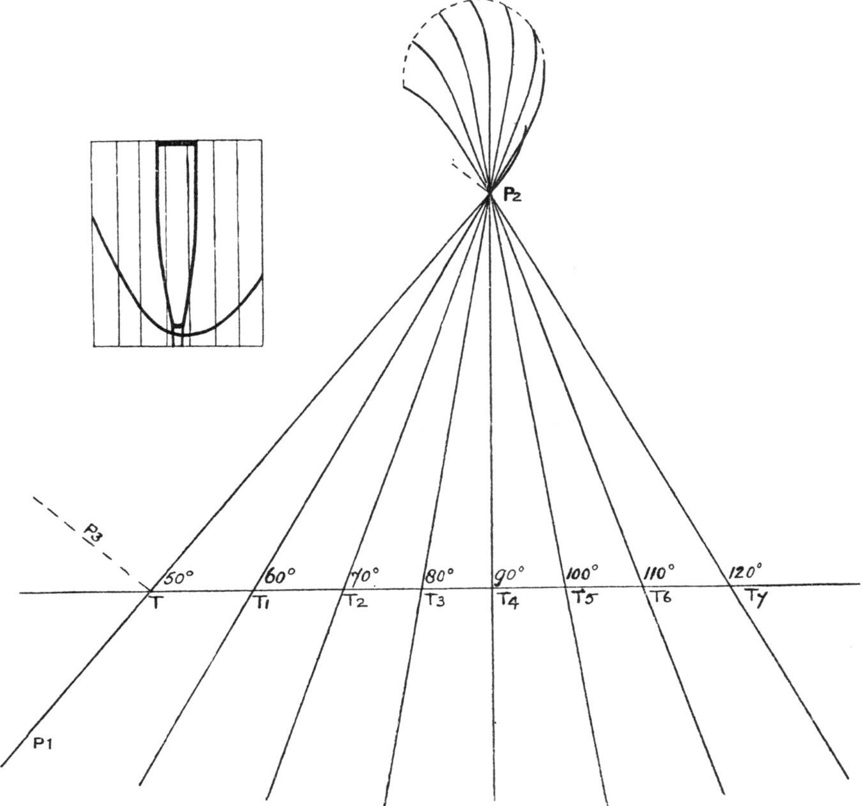

FIG. 4. A diagram illustrating the movement of the oar when the blade is brought to bear on a solid object.

oarsmen can only move the boat from T to $T7$ however hard they pull. By pulling harder they may make the boat traverse this distance in less time, but they cannot increase the distance. As the oarsmen's object is to cover a given distance in the shortest possible time this limitation has no practical inconvenience, and, as a matter of fact, the limit is only fixed when $P2$ is fixed and in actual rowing it is not.

To row with the blade against a fixed object is nearly as artificial and unlike the real thing as to row in an immovable boat. The distance through which the boat is moved in fig. 4 is 8·09 feet. It would take a strong pair more than two seconds to move their boat through this distance, and that is nearly twice as long as the time usually occupied in rowing the first stroke in a racing start.

This mention of the time taken to move the boat through a given distance raises the question of the force available to move the boat. Let us return to a racing eight. In a 12-stone crew the weight or mass to be moved by each oarsman is one-eighth of the weight of the crew plus one-eighth of the weight of the coxswain, plus one-eighth of the weight of the boat, plus one-eighth of the weight of the oars; in all about 226 lb. The object is to give the boat as much acceleration as possible in as short a time as possible. The limits are the strength of pull that each individual oarsman can exert, and the strength of the oars, for the latter may break under a sudden strain. The only reliable data that we possess about the strength of pull of oarsmen are contained in Mr. Atkinson's essays. We learn from his experiments that a certain oarsman (he weighed only 10 st. 10 lb., but that is not recorded in the published account) rowing at 22 strokes per minute in a tub-pair did nearly 500 foot-pounds work during the stroke, and that a short stroke. If, as is probable, the oarsman was rowing in fair rhythm and maintaining the usual ratio of 1 : 3 for oar in the water and oar out of the water (the entry and extraction being included in 'oar out', for we are dealing only with the period during which the oar is doing work), the time taken for each stroke was 2·72 sec., and the time during which the oar was actually doing work was 0·68 sec. Now 500 foot-pounds in 0·68 sec. is at the rate of 705·9 foot-pounds per second, which is 1·63 horse-power. Mr. Atkinson gives the horse-power for this stroke as 0·331, but that figure is obtained by dividing the work done by 2·72 sec., the time occupied by the whole cycle of stroke and feather, and is no measure of the effort made by the oarsman while the oar is in the water. From the fact that Mr. Atkinson's first indicator was unable to register the whole amount of the much stronger pull of two blues who were taking part in the experiment, and from other data, I conclude that a strong and skilful oarsman is able, for a single stroke, to do as much work as 880 foot-pounds for the period of one second, and that when racing he is pulling at something less than that strength though only for as much as half a second during any one stroke. As the whole weight of boat, crew, and oars is 1,800 lb., if the boat under the conditions represented in fig. 4 were moved through 8 feet in 2 seconds, each of the eight oarsmen, supposing them all to pull with exactly the same strength, would have to do $\frac{1{,}800 \times 8}{8 \times 2} = 900$ foot-pounds work. The speed of the boat at the end of the two seconds would be 8 feet per second. A very poor result, one might say, for so great an effort. But the truth is that the result is poor because the work is poor. For if we estimate the mean pull that each oarsman must exert to obtain the result we find that, as $f = \frac{vm}{g}$, the propulsive force required at each blade is $\frac{1{,}800 \times 4}{32{\cdot}2 \times 8} = 27{\cdot}95$ lb., and when we calculate the leverage of the oar this gives a pull of 64·5 lb. at the hands. A very weak pull, and in the supposed case it would be less because the outboard leverage is diminishing as the oar swings from 50° to 90°, and although it increases again up to 120°, it does not at that angle recover the same value that it had at the beginning of the stroke. I have dwelt upon this because it is important to remember that in every problem dealing with the strength of pull at the handle or with the number of foot-pounds work done by the oarsman in any stroke, the length of time taken to do the work must be taken into account. A weaker pull lasting for a longer time does not give as good results as a stronger pull lasting for a shorter time. Arithmetic may be invoked to prove the contrary, but this sort of arithmetic does not take into consideration the fact that in rowing it is very important not to cut any time to waste.

As I have said, the primary object in good rowing is to give the boat as high a speed as possible at the finish of the stroke in order that she may run as far as possible between the strokes, and this principle applies as much to the first as to all subsequent strokes.

Taking into account a number of data which it would be tedious to enumerate here, a crew may be said to be doing well, though not superlatively well, if in its first stroke in still water it moves its boat through 6 feet in 1·25 second. Then as a, the rate of acceleration (which we assume to be constant) $= \frac{2d}{t^2}, \frac{12}{1 \cdot 5625} = 7 \cdot 68$ f.p.s. At the end of one second the boat will have travelled 3·84 feet and will have a speed of 7·68 f.p.s., and at the end of 1·25 second it will have travelled 6 feet and will have a speed of 9·6 f.p.s. The mean pull of each oarsman necessary to obtain this result will be 123·795 lb., the pressure at each blade being $\frac{768 \times 1{,}800}{32 \cdot 2 \times 8} = 53 \cdot 644$ lb. Reference to Mr. Atkinson's records shows that this is a powerful pull, but within the capacity of a strong and skilled oarsman weighing 12 stones or thereabouts. The feeling of great effort experienced by an oarsman in overcoming the inertia of a boat during the first stroke consists in this : that he has to prolong his effort for 1·25 second, more or less, whereas when the boat is well under way his effort lasts for little more than half a second.

We can now consider the action of the oar during a first stroke in which the boat is moved through 6 feet in 1·25 second. To begin with, let us consider wherein the action of the oar, when pulled through yielding water, differs from what it is when the centre of pressure of the blade is brought to bear against an immovable object. At the same time we can conveniently take into account the combined action of the stroke- and bow-side oarsmen in propelling the boat.

In fig. 5 let the line AB represent the oar at an angle of 50° to the line of advance of the boat. If the blade were in contact with a solid object the united efforts of the bow- and stroke-side oarsmen

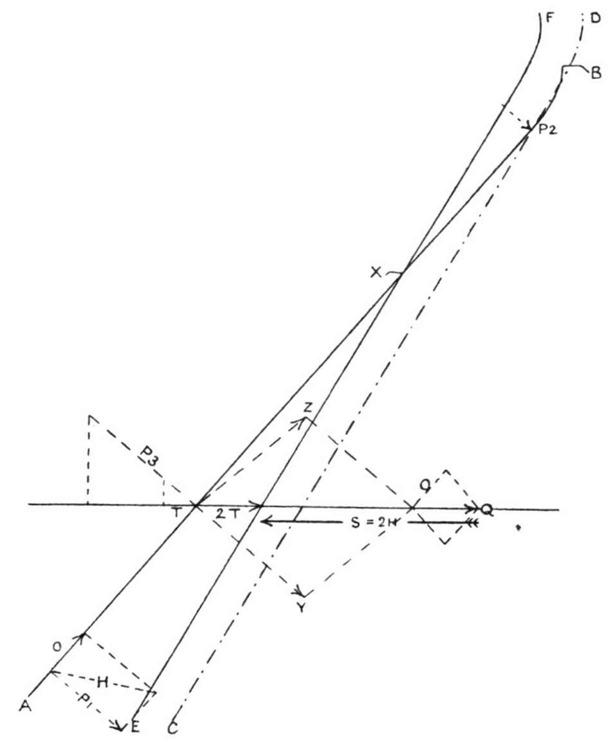

FIG. 5. A diagram showing how the action of the oar is modified by the simultaneous movement of the blade and of the boat.

would, when the oar has moved through an angle of 10°, bring the oar into the position represented by the broken line CD and the turning-point would be at $P2$. But when pulled through the water the blade is moving aft and the rowlock is moving forward: consequently, when it has turned through an angle of 10°, the oar will be in the position represented by the line *EF*, and *X*, the point of intersection of the lines *AB* and *EF*, will be the turning-point at that instant. It is because *X* is nearer to the rowlock than *P*2 that the boat is advanced through a less distance. It is because the blade has moved through the water the extra distance *D* to *F*, and the boat's advance has been diminished by exactly the same distance, that *X* is brought nearer to the rowlock. As *CD* is parallel to *EF*, it follows that the farther the blade is moved through the water, the greater will be the distance from *D* to *F*, the greater will be the diminution of the boat's advance, and the nearer *X* will be brought to the rowlock. But the greater the distance moved by the blade the greater is the mass of water displaced by it, and this involves a greater pull at the handle of the oar. The inevitable conclusion is that the harder the oarsman pulls the nearer he brings the turning-point of his oar to the rowlock, and the less the distance he advances his boat—a conclusion most disheartening to any one who cherishes the belief that he can make up for lack of skill by extra output of work. But he may derive some comfort from the reflection that, if he does move his boat through a less distance, he takes less time about it and so gets back on the swings what he loses on the roundabouts. Nevertheless, as we shall see more clearly farther on, an undisciplined and unskilful exhibition of mere strength does very little to increase the pace of the boat and involves a great waste of energy in imparting motion to the water.

Attention must be directed to the fact that, although the blade moves through a greater distance, the oar is not moved through a greater angle. The blade moves the greater distance because the boat is held back. In order to understand quite clearly how and why it is held back, we must again turn our attention to the forces acting on and through the oar. The pull *H* at the centre of effort of the hands is the measure of the force required to move the handle of the oar from *A* to *E*. *H* as before is resolved into the components *P* 1 and *O*. The measurement of *P* 1 determines the measurement of *P* 2 at the centre of pressure of the blade. The sum of *P* 1 and *P* 2 gives *P* 3 acting at 90° to the axis of the oar at the thowl-pin. It simplifies matters if we take $P3$ as a force tending to pull round the boat in the direction Y. And now we must take into account the equal force exerted by the oarsman on the other side of the boat tending to pull round the boat in the direction Z. The resultant of these two forces acts in the direction of the line of advance of the boat, but taken by itself is barely more than sufficient to balance the reaction of the two oarsmen's thrust on the stretcher. It is necessary to bring into the account, for both the stroke- and bow-side oarsmen, the force O acting along the axis of the oar and thrusting the button obliquely against the thowl-pin. The resultant of the two O components produces the force acting in the line of the advance of the boat to Q. The distance from Q to the point where the line EF cuts the line of advance of the rowlock is exactly equal to twice H and therefore to S, the reaction of the two oarsmen's feet on the stretcher. S is the force which holds back the boat. It may further be noted that if we measure along $P3$ a distance equal to $P2$ and drop a perpendicular on the line of advance of the rowlock we get T, which is just half the distance advanced by the rowlock. The other half is contributed by the oarsmen on the other side of the boat. This demonstrates that at the beginning of the stroke $P2$ is the only force directly available for propelling the boat. The only difficulty in this otherwise simple diagram is that the length of the line H is inversely proportional to the strength of pull at the hands. If it is desired to assign a numerical value to it and to the other measurements derived from it, it is necessary to calculate the strength of pull required to move the boat through the given distance.

The complete stroke of which fig. 5 is the first phase is shown diagrammatically in figs. 6 and 7. In order to give room for the scale of feet the inboard portion of the oar is not represented. This and the similar diagrams of which I shall make frequent use are founded on Mr. Atkinson's photographic record of a single stroke. They are very instructive when one has become thoroughly familiar with their meaning and method of construction. The base line represents the line of advance of the rowlock, and, as the boat is supposed to be moved through six feet in 1·25 second, we mark off six feet on a convenient scale along the base line and to the left of the figure draw a vertical line of the same length for the time scale. The most convenient time unit is one-tenth of a second. As the diagram represents a first stroke, the initial position of the oar is drawn at 50° to the side of the boat, as an oarsman does not reach forward to the full extent at the start. The final position is drawn at 120°, this being the angle at which the oar comes home most conveniently to the oarsman's body, as will be explained later on. A boat should be moved off smoothly and sweetly at the start, gathering way as it goes: this allows us to assume that the oarsmen give the boat uniform acceleration, and we can calculate the successive positions of the thowl-pin at intervals of, say, 0·25 second by the formula $s = \frac{a}{2} t^2$, in which s stands for the space passed through, a for the acceleration, and t for the time taken. At the end of each quarter of a second the distances moved through will be 0·24, 0·96, 2·16, 3·84, and finally, at the end of 1·25″, 6·0 feet. These distances are set off as points along the base line, and from them the lines representing the oar must be drawn at appropriate angles. In order to estimate these angles it is necessary to consider the curve of the turning-point of the oar. As Mr. Atkinson has shown, it is a continuous curve, convex in the direction of the boat's advance, and it must lie in the angle formed by the intersection of the lines representing the initial and final positions of the oar. The dimension of the curve will depend upon strength of the oarsman's pull at the beginning of the stroke. If he pulls very hard he will, as we have seen, bring the turning-point near the rowlock, will move much water aft with his blade, but will advance his boat a very little way. As he has the inertia of the boat to overcome, if his effort is very sudden and violent and he covers his blade at the moment that he makes his effort, he stands a good chance of breaking his oar at the button. If for lack of skill he and his fellow-oarsmen fail to cover their blades as they make the effort the reaction of their feet on the stretcher will push the boat backwards. In bumping races I have seen a crew, startled by the gunfire and making a wild effort to get its boat off the mark, travel backwards fully six inches and possibly more before the blades got fairly hold of the water. To avoid such mischances oarsmen are instructed to begin the first stroke firmly, but not too violently,

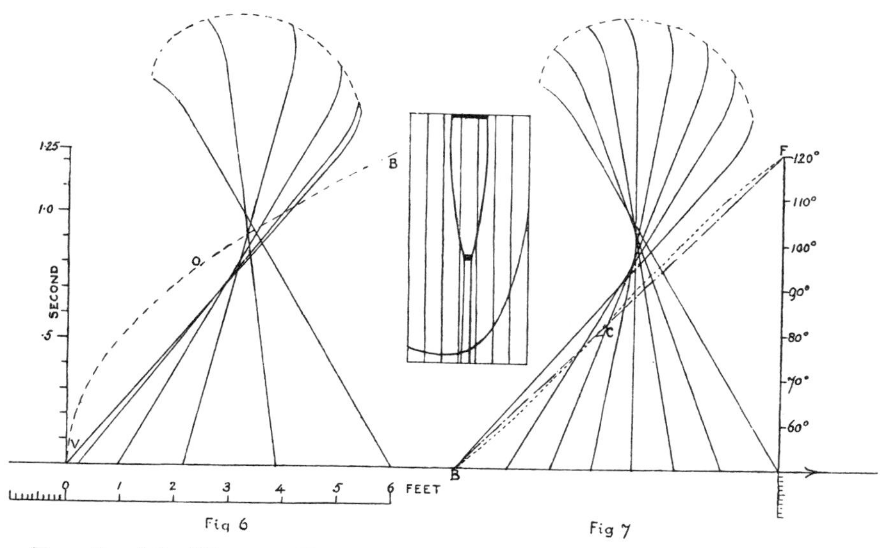

FIGS. 6 and 7. Diagrams illustrating the action of the oar during the first stroke.

and to maintain and increase the pull through the middle of the stroke and up to the finish. As the beginning is relatively gentle, the turning-point will not be brought too near the rowlock; but as the boat is stationary at the start and a strong reaction at the blade is necessary to set it in motion, the turning-point will be kept nearer inboard than in subsequent strokes when the boat is under way. To determine exactly where to place it for the second position of the oar in the diagram is largely a matter of trial and error; in fig. 6 it is placed 4·2 feet from the rowlock. Starting from this point and guided by

Mr. Atkinson's photographic record of a stroke, we draw in the turning-point curve and draw the remaining positions of the oar as tangents to the curve. We thus obtain fig. 6, which illustrates clearly enough the large sweep of the blade necessary to overcome the inertia of the boat in the first stroke and the slow initial speed rapidly increasing in the latter half of the stroke. By erecting ordinates from the points where the successive positions of the oar cut the base line and drawing abscissae at each quarter of a second's interval we get the acceleration curve *VOB* which is useful for checking the construction of the next diagram.

It is in many respects more instructive to make a diagram showing the positions assumed by the oar for every 10° angular movement. Having settled the dimensions of the turning-point curve in fig. 6, this is easily done by drawing lines at 60°, 70° . . . 110° tangential to the curve. We thus get fig. 7, which is of exactly the same dimensions as fig. 6, but shows eight positions of the oar and brings out many interesting features not readily ascertainable from the latter diagram. The correctness of the diagram may be tested by calculating the times taken by the rowlock to traverse the successive distances marked out by the positions of the oar along the base line. Drawing ordinates from these positions and abscissae from the calculated intervals along the time scale, the co-ordinates will be found to give exactly the same curve of acceleration as in fig. 6, so the two diagrams are in all essential respects similar. The best test of the value of these diagrams as representations of what should occur, even if it does not often occur, is the determination of the curve of the turning-point on the oar during the stroke. This is done by measuring the distances from the tip of the blade to the successive points of intersection along the turning-point curve of the lines representing the positions of the oar and then plotting out the curve as in the inset figs. 6 and 7. If this is a fair curve the stroke as represented by the diagram has been well and truly rowed. If it is an irregular curve the stroke has been rowed jerkily and the diagram represents a correspondingly clumsy performance. The curve of the turning-point on the oar, as we have seen, is a measure of the strength and character of the oarsman's pull. Mr. Atkinson's experiments show that there is a wide range of individuality in stroke form even among men who have rowed together and are presumed to row in the same style, so the diagram is susceptible of almost infinite variation to express individual peculiarities. As it is drawn it may not represent a perfect first stroke, but it does represent a very efficient stroke for the task to be accomplished, namely to move the boat 6 feet in 1·25 second.

An analysis of fig. 7 throws much light on the action of the oar during the stroke. The angular velocity of the oar must be proportional to the speed at which the hands move. As long as the arms are straight the speed of the hands is the same as the speed at which the body moves back, the speed of the body being in part due to the swing, in part to the movement of the slide. The arms should begin to bend as the oar approaches an angle of 90°, and in the latter part—rather less than half—of the stroke the hands are moving faster than the body, partly because the speed of the latter is diminishing. The angular movement of the oar is due partly to the passage of the blade through the water, partly to the advance of the boat. In this starting stroke the former factor counts for a large part, but not for as much as half, of the angular movement. Bearing these facts in mind we see that the boat travels unequal distances for every 10° of angular movement of the oar. If the boat travelled equal distances for every 10° angular movement of the oar, clearly the co-ordinates of vertical lines drawn at equal distances along the base line with abscissae drawn from the scale of angles on the right of the diagram would coincide with the diagonal drawn from B to F. But as the distances are unequal the co-ordinates give the line of double curvature about BF, from which we learn that for the first three-sevenths of the stroke the oar is swinging round rather slowly relatively to the speed of advance of the boat; but that for the remaining four-sevenths it is moving faster relatively to the advance of the boat, though in the last seventh it is again slowing down. This is due to the fact that as the oar swings from 50° to 70° it is being thrust outwards from the boat, more rapidly at first and more slowly afterwards; and as it swings from 110° to 120° it is being pulled with increasing rapidity in towards the boat; whereas between 70° and 110° the blade is moving more nearly parallel with (but in the opposite direction to) the line of advance of the boat and the oar is swinging through that part of its course in which it works at the best mechanical advantage.

The scale of angles on the right serves equally well for a time scale of sevenths of the whole time occupied by the stroke (in this case of equal periods of 0·1785 second), and from this we learn that, although the angular velocity of the oar varies in relation to the speed of advance of the boat, the unequal distances shown along the base line are traversed in equal periods of time. It follows that, although the oar does not move through equal angles in equal times, its angular velocity has the definite swing or rhythm indicated by the curve BCF.

Finally, invoking the principle of virtual velocities, which states that in any part of a machine that is moving slowly the pressure will be relatively great, and in any part of the machine that is moving rapidly the pressure will be relatively small, we may observe that at the end of the stroke the blade is moving relatively slowly and the handle of the oar is moving relatively fast. Therefore for any given pull at the hands the pressure on the blade will be great. As a matter of fact the strength of pull at the hands diminishes rapidly towards the finish whatever the character of the stroke, but, small as it may be, the pressure on the blade is not diminished in proportion. This pressure on the blade is of great use to the oarsman at the finish as it affords him the resistance necessary to slow up the movement of his body preparatory to the recovery. We shall have to take account of this in considering what is meant by an oarsman 'using his weight'.

A little reflection will convince the practised oarsman that all that precedes is conformable with his experience. At the beginning of the first stroke there is a sense of great effort due to the inertia of the boat. As the boat begins to yield to the effort the oarsman keeps up his pull and the sense of effort remains until half-way through the stroke, when the boat begins to gather way rapidly and the feeling of a steady tug against a big resistance gives way to the feeling that the effort is lightened but the speed of movement must be increased to keep up with the increasing pace of the boat.

I have taken a very long time to describe the first stroke and to get the boat off the mark. But for the sake of future brevity it has been necessary to describe the principles of the action of the oar thoroughly. As in rowing, so in the description of it, the first stroke takes a disproportionately long time in comparison with those that follow it.

CHAPTER III

THE THEORY OF ROWING

THE BOAT IN MOTION

We are now in a position to analyse the stroke when the boat—an eight-oar—is moving at high speed. For this purpose it is convenient to assume a sustained mean speed of 17 feet per second in dead water. A crew racing over the Henley course would be going faster than this in the early part and slower in the latter part of the course, but somewhere—I should judge between Remenham and Fawley—it will be travelling at this speed.

A mean speed of 17 f.p.s. sustained for 6,870 feet would bring a crew over the Henley course in 6 min. 44 sec. in dead water. This, in a midsummer stream running at the rate of 0·55 f.p.s.,[1] would give 6 min. $57\frac{1}{2}$ sec. in a dead calm. With a light following breeze the crew would get very near to the record time of 6 min. 51 sec.

The distance travelled per stroke in dead water at a racing stroke of 35·3 per minute, or one stroke in 1·7 second, would be 28·9 feet. For the crew would take 404·117 seconds to cover the course; and $\frac{404 \cdot 117}{1 \cdot 7} = 237 \cdot 71$ strokes rowed in the course; and $\frac{6{,}870}{237 \cdot 71} = 28 \cdot 9$. How much of this distance should be traversed during the stroke and how much during the run between strokes?

I have a slow-motion film of the Cambridge crew of 1923 taken at Ely at an early stage of practice.[2] The crew, I am told, was paddling at 22 strokes per minute. The camera seems to have been set to give

[1] In 1913, when the Leander crew did 6 min. 51 sec. in a heat, the current was estimated at this figure. I myself made several measurements of the rate of the current in that year and my observations tallied with the estimate.

[2] For the loan of this film I am indebted to the Hon. J. W. Fremantle.

about 50 exposures per second. There are 125 exposures for the whole cycle of stroke and feather. Therefore, if the crew was paddling at the rate of 21·8 strokes per minute (which is hardly distinguishable from 22 by the ordinary method of counting) each stroke would occupy 2·75 seconds, and the time taken for each exposure would be 0·022 second. On this reckoning I find that, when the entry and extraction of the oar are counted in the 'run', the ratio 'stroke' : 'run' is 1 : 3·1666; but when entry and extraction are included in the stroke the ratio is 1 : 2·37. It took 0·088 second to cover the blades as the oars entered the water, and 0·066 second to extract the blades from the water, altogether 0·154 second. This must be taken as a slow speed of movement at a slow stroke in early practice. I imagine that when a crew wound up to concert pitch is rowing at a fast stroke these figures are nearly halved, and that it is not far wrong to allow 0·044 second for entry and 0·036 second for extraction; in all 0·08 second.

In estimating the rhythm or ratio of stroke to run the onlooker (as also the oarsman) judges by ear rather than by sight, counting the audible 'smack' as the beginning and the rattle in the rowlocks when the oars turn on the feather as the finish of the stroke. The smack comes when the oar-blade is fully immersed; the rattle when it is extracted. Therefore, when oarsmen speak of a good rhythm being in the ratio 1 : 3, they are counting entry and extraction in the run and not in the stroke. For present purposes it is more convenient to count entry and extraction in the stroke, and adopting the figures suggested above for a racing stroke, we can make the duration of 'stroke' (entry and extraction included) 0·5 second, and of 'run' 1·2 second, giving a ratio of 1 : 2·4. Hence we get:

Time: stroke = 0·5″; run = 1·2″.

Distance: stroke = 8·5 feet; run = 20·4 feet.

Mean speed during stroke: $\frac{8{\cdot}5}{0{\cdot}5} = 17{\cdot}0$ f.p.s.

Mean speed during run: $\frac{20{\cdot}4}{1{\cdot}2} = 17{\cdot}0$ f.p.s.

Herein I differ altogether from Mr. Alexander, who makes the mean speed during the run considerably greater than the mean speed during the stroke. So I think it often is, in a crew that is rowing badly. But I have often observed, when watching the stem of a boat that is travelling really well, that it does not progress by a series of jumps, but seems to travel straight on, uniformly, without *visible* fluctuations of speed. In such case the mean speed during stroke and run must be the same, and there is little room for doubt that a good rhythm operates in producing the nearest possible approach to uniformity of speed during stroke and run.

We have now to consider to what speed the boat must be raised at the finish of the stroke to allow it to run 20·4 feet between strokes in 1·2 second.

The force retarding the boat during the run is almost wholly due to the friction of its immersed surface against the water. Wind pressure on a calm day does not count for much, as it is mainly against the oarsmen's bodies and they are moving aft. The immersed surface of an eight (I take a good boat built by Sims as an example) is 105 square feet, and at a speed of 10 f.p.s. the skin friction is 0·25 lb. per square foot. The total friction at this speed is therefore 26·25 lb. It has been ascertained that this frictional resistance varies, not exactly as the square of the speed, but as $v^{1 \cdot 83}$. But as there is also a residual resistance due to the kinetic energy expended by the boat in making waves, the total resistance may be taken as v^2, which when $v = 17$ f.p.s. is roughly 76 lb. In addition to this there is the windage and some small amount of additional resistance due to wave making. In the experiment with model boats that Sir John E. Thornycroft kindly made for me in his experimental tank at Bembridge, it was found that a pull of 0·021 lb. was required to give the model a speed of 351·75 feet per minute. The corresponding figures for a full-sized boat would be a pull of 84 lb. to maintain a speed of 17 feet per second, and this may be taken as the retarding force encountered when the blades leave the water. As the boat with crew, coxswain, and oars is taken to weigh 1,800 lb., if R is the retardation in feet per second,

$$R = \frac{84}{1800} g = \frac{84 \times 32{\cdot}2}{1800} = 1{\cdot}502\dot{6}.$$

Then if s be the distance travelled during the run, t the time taken to cover it, and v_0 the speed of the boat required at the end of the stroke,

$$s = v_0 t - \frac{1{\cdot}502\dot{6}}{2} t^2 \quad \text{or} \quad 20{\cdot}4 = 1{\cdot}2\, v_0 - 0{\cdot}751\dot{3} \times (1{\cdot}2)^2$$

$$\text{Therefore } v_0 = \frac{20{\cdot}4 + 1{\cdot}08}{1{\cdot}2} = 18{\cdot}08$$

on the assumption that R is constant during the run of the boat. Actually R diminishes as the speed of the boat decreases, but as the movement aft of the slides and bodies slightly increases the run of the boat, it will not be far out to take 18 f.p.s. as the speed required at the end of the stroke to allow the boat to run 20·4 feet in 1·2″, and to drop to a speed of 16·5 f.p.s. in doing so. But these figures fail to satisfy the conditions under which the boat is assumed to be travelling, as may be seen clearly if we consider that, if the initial speed during run is 18 f.p.s., and the final speed 16·5 f.p.s., the mean speed will be 17·25 f.p.s., which is too much. Moreover, they do not take into account the check given to the hull at the beginning of the stroke due to the crew ‘ getting on its feet ’. As this must be taken into account before we can get any farther, I must crave the reader's indulgence while I deal with the obscure but very important problem of the ‘ beginning ’ of the stroke.

As has been said, the film of the Cambridge crew of 1923 shows that it took 0·088″ to cover the blades at entry. During this period, occupying four separate pictures on the film, some of the blades are entering the water without making any splash whatever. In the next picture the work has begun, and there is a big splash sent up from the aft face of (oarsmen would generally say ‘ in front of ’) the blades. This must be distinguished from ‘ back-splash ’ which would be sent up from the forward or convex surface of the blades. During the 0·088″ that the blades were entering the water without making any splash whatever, they must have been travelling exactly as fast as the water was moving past them. For if they were travelling slower there would have been a big back-splash, and if they had been travelling faster there would have been a perceptible splash off their concave surfaces. At the rate of paddling the boat may be assumed to have been moving at a speed of about 13 f.p.s. at the end of the run, and that is the speed at which the water would be moving past the blades. To make the oar-blade travel at this speed the oarsmen, who were rowing correctly with perfectly straight arms, must have swung back their bodies at a rate of about 5·6 f.p.s., and to do this they must have exerted a considerable pressure on the stretcher. For that period of 0·088″ they were ‘ driving at their stretchers ’ and lifting back their bodies, yet their blades had not begun to do work in the water. The hull must have been pushed back in proportion to the movement of the bodies in the opposite direction, and this must have checked the speed of the boat materially. It would not stop it dead, or nearly dead, as some writers have suggested, for the momentum of 1,800 lb. moving at the rate of 13 f.p.s. is a bit more than eight oarsmen, however strong, could overcome in 0·088″. Now we come to the point : it is the check to the speed of the boat due to the reaction of the feet on the stretcher that gives the oarsman his ‘ beginning ’. He has started his body-swing at a rate sufficient to give the oar-blade a speed equal to the speed at which the water is moving past it : in doing so he reduces the speed of the boat, or what is the same thing, the speed at which water is moving past his blade. The moment comes when the speed of the oar-blade is greater than the speed of the water moving past it, and at that moment the blade meets with resistance and the ‘ beginning is caught ’. It is a fundamental principle, enunciated by Euler in the eighteenth century—but without a doubt acted upon from the time that an oar was first brought to bear upon a fixed thowl-pin—that in order to get resistance on the blade, in order to do work, the blade must be made to move faster than the water is moving past it. But from what precedes it is clear that the moment when the oar begins to move faster than the water may come earlier or later in the stroke. An oarsman may—and if he is not a first-class oarsman he generally does—move his body, and therefore his blade, at a speed exactly proportional to the speed of the boat for a period of one-tenth of a second or more. By just so long a period he has postponed the moment when the blade is moving faster than the water, and has failed to do any work. Yet all this time he must have moved back his body, and to move it back he must have exerted some pressure on the stretcher, and to that extent has retarded the boat. In an extreme case the oarsman may move back his body at a speed exactly proportional to the speed of the boat for the whole stroke, and then he will have done no work at all, except so much as is necessary to move back his body at the required speed. This happens in a well-trained crew when the coxswain calls 'Easy all' just before the blades enter the water. The oarsmen instantly shut off their work; the blades enter the water and the oarsmen swing and slide back with just sufficient speed to prevent any resistance being felt on the convex surfaces of the blades. They do no work towards propelling the boat, but they must put a certain amount of pressure on their stretchers, and to that extent check the speed of the boat. Incidentally, this is a good illustration of the capacity for nice adjustment of muscular movement developed in a well-trained crew. In an unskilful crew, if the coxswain calls 'Easy all' just before the blades enter the water, confusion and possibly disaster in the shape of crabs follows on the ill-judged word of command.

On the other hand, the oarsman may shorten the period during which his blade is moving at the same pace as the water moves past the boat. The more he shortens it the quicker he 'gets hold of the beginning' and the less does he retard the boat. In the theoretically perfect stroke the period would be infinitely small and the boat would be checked to an infinitely small extent. Often, in the attempt to get a very quick and hard beginning, a crew 'rows the blades in'; that is to say, it begins to swing back and accelerate the blades before they touch the water. The beginning, when it is caught, is caught very forcibly, but as long as the blades are being rowed through the air the boat is being pushed back by the reaction of the feet on the stretcher, and is visibly, as the expression goes, 'stopped' at the beginning of the stroke.

It is impossible, I think, even if it were desirable, to eliminate altogether the check at the beginning of the stroke, for this reason if for no other: that it takes time to cover the blade. How much time may be realized by considering the conditions as illustrated in fig. 8. When the oarsman's work is set at normal height, a 12 ft. 4 in. oar makes an angle of 8° with the surface of the water when the blade is fully immersed. The diagram shows that if the blade be brought down to as little as one inch above the surface of the water before entry it has to fall through nine inches before it is 'covered'. Oarsmen are often told not to try to put the blade in but to lighten their hands and let it drop in, because, it is said, it will drop in of its own weight faster than they can put it in. But is this correct? I am sure it is not, for if the blade were to drop freely under the action of gravity (which it does not, because its weight is partly counterpoised by the handle) it would take 0·2165 second to drop those nine inches; a quite inadmissible length of time when the stroke lasts only 0·5 second.

A spectator watching a good eight travelling end on towards him can see clearly enough that the blades enter the water at a much greater speed than this. After being turned off the feather the blades descend gradually until they are about two inches above the surface and then are suddenly speeded up, entering the water with a swift decisive movement not easily described in words. This movement, I submit, should not be vertical but curvilinear, the oar being started on its angular acceleration as the blades enter the water. In more familiar language, no time should be lost by first putting the blade in and then pulling, but the pull should come instantly as the blade is being put in. Then, as is indicated in fig. 8, at the first touch only the small area of the blade surface represented by the triangle $oA2$ meets with resistance, but as the blade sinks down the areas $oB4$ and $oC6$ rapidly take up the resistance, and finally the whole surface of the blade. The time taken is very small, not more than 0·05 second at a racing stroke, but in that short time the oarsman is relieved from an unduly sudden strain because the resistance does not come on all at once, but gradually though rapidly. And as the initial resistance is small the force available for propelling the boat (see fig. 2 C) is at first insufficient to balance the reaction of the feet on the stretcher, so the speed of the boat must be checked, but not to so great an extent as when either the first bit of the stroke is rowed in the air or the blade

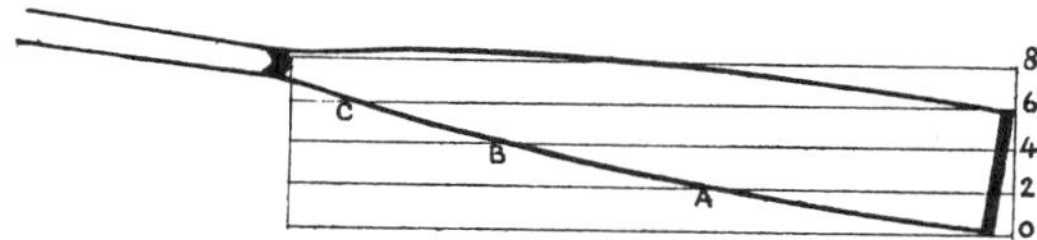

FIG. 8. A diagram illustrating the entry of the blade of the oar into the water.

is made to travel through the water without doing any work until it is covered. The slight check, however, is of material assistance to the oarsman in enabling him to 'get his beginning'. From a comparison of a number of photographs of good crews in action I opine that an oarsman is doing very well if he gets his work on when two inches of the lower corner of his blade are covered.

It is a belief very widely held among oarsmen that an eight-oar requires what they are pleased to call 'punch' at the beginning, but that a four-oar or a pair go better without punch. What they exactly mean by 'punch' I am not sure that they themselves understand, but from cross-questioning many of them I imagine that the sensation described by that name is obtained by delaying the angular acceleration of the oar until the blade is fully covered, thus materially checking the speed of the boat, and then getting a very solid feeling of resistance from the sudden thrust of the oar at lower speed of boat. The beginning is harder but not nearly so quick. Why this slower beginning should be supposed to be effective in a quicker moving eight-oar, but ineffective in a slower moving four-oar, I am at a loss to explain. Possibly because an eight-oar usually contains two or three slow-moving heavy-weights, and in order to obtain uniformity of work the speed of movement of the whole crew must be reduced to the capacity of the slowest of them. And because the mean speed of an eight-oar is considerably greater than that of a four-oar, greater quickness of movement at the beginning is demanded in the former than in the latter. But as far as I am able to judge, the cult of ' punch ' leads to a progressive deterioration in oarsmanship. The beginning becomes slower and slower, and the rate of stroke more and more funereal. Mr. C. M. Pitman, than whom I know no better judge of rowing, tells me that, watching crews on the Henley course from his post of observation at Remenham House, he becomes more and more disheartened as he sees and hears crew after crew go by, at slow speed and a dismally slow rate of stroke, their oars going ' plonk ' into the water. It is the *marche funèbre* held up to ridicule by Dr. Warre. It comes, I suggest, from radically unsound theory and teaching on the subject of the beginning. It is the almost universal opinion—I know hardly any one who would disown it—that in the ideal stroke the oar describes a rectangle. It goes vertically into the water as in the upper diagram of fig. 9; is rowed in a straight line through the water; is lifted vertically out of the water at the finish; and is carried back in a straight line on the feather. Now the limbs of living beings, and human beings are no exception, do not move in rigid straight lines but in curves, and the instruments that men manipulate, be they bats, guns, rackets, oars, or what not, partake of the curvilinear movements of the limbs. A rectangular motion of the oar is, I believe, impossible. If it were possible it would cramp the oarsman's movements to an inconceivable degree. Yet all young oarsmen are taught that the rectangular motion is the thing to aim at.

Now in my experience oarsmen, and especially young oarsmen, are perversely conscientious. They take the coach literally at his word, and the more they are secretly conscious that what he is telling them to do is unattainable, the more obstinate they are in making efforts to follow out his commands to the letter. The more obstinate they are the more stiff and cramped and hopelessly ineffective do their movements become, and their only and final consolation is that they gain the oarsman's crown of martyrdom, which consists in being always wrong when one is conscientiously striving to do what one is

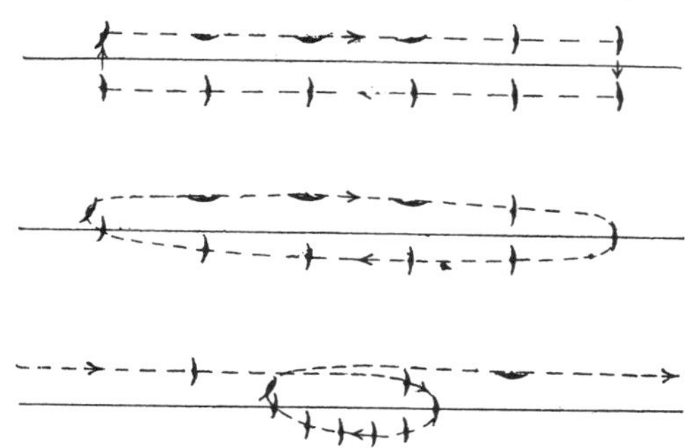

FIG. 9. Diagrams illustrating the movements of the blade of the oar during stroke and feather.

told is right. I verily believe that this anguish, this ascetic pleasure in always trying to do their duty and always failing to do it, is the only joy that seven-tenths of those who row in their College and other boats derive from rowing. But excepting that most teachers, by the use of formal precepts, try to make things as difficult as possible, I do not see why all oarsmen should not taste of the real and almost voluptuous joy of rowing. But if this addition to youthful pleasure is to be made, coaches must abandon the perverted ideals of the cubists for the more graceful outlines of Greek sculpture. There are no more rectangles in rowing than in the statue of the Apollo Belvedere.

I imagine that the correct representation of the path of the tip of the oar-blade, as it would be described in a stationary boat, should be something like an ellipse, the major axis of which is slightly inclined to the surface of the water, as in the middle diagram in fig. 9. But the actual path of the tip of the blade in space when the boat is under way would be something like the looped line shown in the lowest diagram. It will be objected that the blade is rowing light at the finish, but I answer no, it is not if the work is kept on to the finish, for in the latter half of the stroke the water is piled high against the blade, as may be seen in any good photograph. In conclusion, I appeal to coaches not to suggest to their pupils that the blades may be allowed to drop in, plonk ! by the action of gravity. They must be speeded up, and very actively speeded up, at the moment of entry.

To return from this long but necessary digression on the 'beginning' to where we left the analysis of the stroke on p. 53. After trial and error I find that the conditions with which we started can be satisfied approximately if the initial speed at entry is taken at 16·3 f.p.s.; the final speed at extraction at 17·6 f.p.s.; and if during entry the 'check' brings the initial speed down to 16·1 f.p.s., the time allowed for entry being 0·044″. On this scheme the boat is actually propelled by the stroke through $8{\cdot}5 - 0{\cdot}75 = 7{\cdot}75$ feet in $5 - 0{\cdot}044 = 0{\cdot}456''$, and as $\frac{7{\cdot}75}{0{\cdot}456} = 17{\cdot}0$ f.p.s., we get the required mean speed during the stroke.

But as the difference between 17·6 and 16·3 is less than 1·5 f.p.s. we do not seem to have sufficient speed at the finish of the stroke to allow the boat to run 20·4 feet in 1·2 second. Against this we must set the following considerations: The maximum speed of the hull is not at the finish of the stroke but about 0·15″ later, so the speed really rises to something like 17·7 f.p.s. after the blades leave the water. The movement aft of the oarsmen's weight during slide and swing adds a little to the speed of the hull during the run and prevents it dropping to 16·3 f.p.s. as soon as it would do if the oarsmen remained at their back-stops (see p. 23). We thus get the curve of speed of the hull represented in the upper diagram in fig. 10, and the mean speed of the hull during the run is 17·0 f.p.s., because the area above the mean speed line is equal to the area below it.

The hull continues to gain speed after the blades have left the water because, in a moving system, if any part of the mass is moving in the same direction at greater speed than the rest of the mass, the additional momentum of the former part, when it ultimately impinges on the latter part, will be transmitted to it. The oarsmen during the stroke are moving forward in the direction of the boat's advance faster than the hull is moving. In order to move faster they made a spring from their stretchers, and in so doing checked the speed of the boat. But in the latter half of the stroke that momentum of the bodies is given back to the boat—largely as work on the blades whilst the arms are bending and the movement of the bodies is gradually slowing up preparatory to the recovery. But if the oarsmen swing out their shoulders well at the finish and, having reserved four or five inches of slide to finish with, push out those remaining inches of slide hard with the legs, they will give an additional impetus to the boat as they arrive at their back-stops and cause the boat to shoot forward at the end of the stroke. This utilization of the momentum given to the bodies in the earlier part of the stroke to sustain the work on the blades and to carry the hull forward in the latter half of the stroke is what oarsmen mean when they speak of 'using one's weight'. To use the weights effectively is the mark of a first-class crew. It saves labour while increasing pace, and gives a crew a magnificent appearance of sweep and power very pleasant to watch. The fine Leander crew of 1913 stroked by Mr. Geoffrey Tower, which equalled the record over the Henley course in one of its preliminary heats, gave a good example of how a crew should use its weights. It had a splendid sweep out at the end of the stroke; shoulders, slides, and hands moving in perfect unison, and a trained eye could see the impetus given to the hull by the swing back of the bodies at the finish. The winning New College crew of 1897 was another fine example of the proper way to use the weights, and I do not think my memory plays me false when I bracket the Leander crews of 1891 and 1893 with these record makers. The Leander crew of 1891, it will be remembered, was the first to establish the record of 6 min. 51 sec. over the Henley course. More recently the Third Trinity (or Eton Vikings) four of 1922, 1923, and 1924 has given a fresh example of the value of using the weight properly, and the New College four of 1913 was hardly its inferior in this respect.

Plotting out the figures with which we started in accordance with the principles subsequently developed, we get the speed curve shown in the upper diagram of fig. 10. It shows the slight check at the beginning of the stroke followed almost instantly by a steady rise in speed due to the prompt and effective work of the blades. The swing out of the bodies carries the acceleration of the hull beyond the limit of the stroke but not with any sudden jerk. The fall in speed during the run is modified by the smooth and even movement of swing and slide aft, and the check in speed does not begin until the blades have entered the water and begun a new stroke. The curve is drawn carefully to scale, and the reader will readily perceive that a boat travelling with such slight fluctuations of speed would appear to a spectator to be moving at a uniform pace. By way of comparison I give in the lower diagram of fig. 10 a speed curve which represents, as nearly as I am able to draw it, the figures for his ideal eight given by Mr. Alexander on p. 172 of his essay on the theory of rowing. I hope I do not misrepresent Mr. Alexander, but after many attempts I have not been able to fit his figures into any other scheme. In one not unimportant respect I have been obliged to alter them. He makes his boat travel 10·35 feet in 0·7 second during the stroke and 19·7 feet in 1·09 second during the run. But a study of his fig. 16 shows me that he has included in the stroke, at both ends of it, periods and distances which I have included in the feather. Making the alterations necessary to bring his reckoning into conformity with mine, I find that his boat travels 8·75 feet in 0·52 second during the stroke and 21·30 feet in 1·27 second during the run. The initial speed at entry, that is,

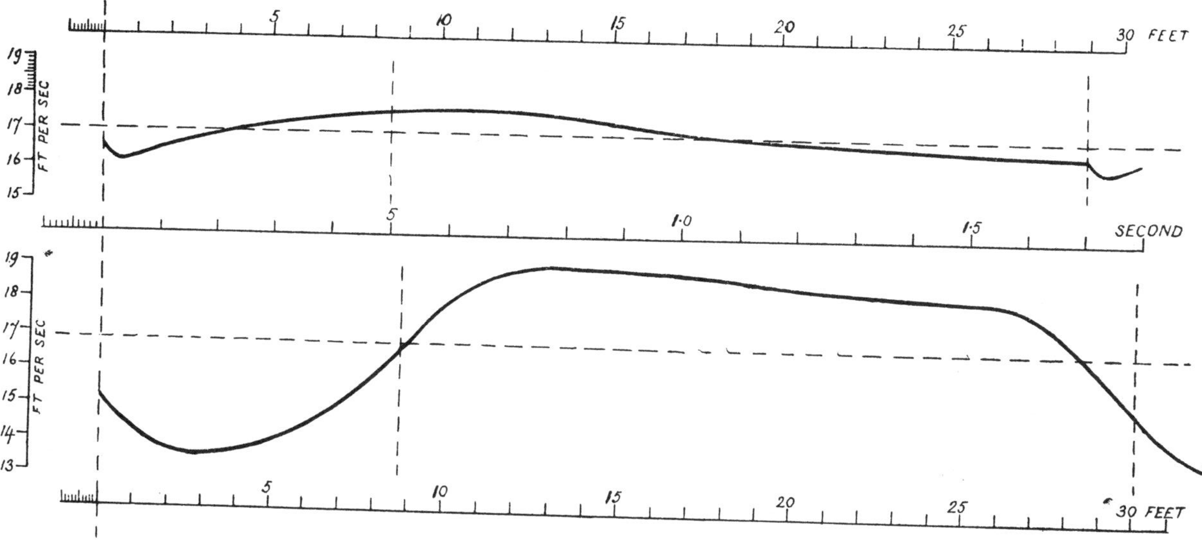

Fig. 10. Diagrams showing the speed curves of an eight-oar.

at the moment when the blade enters the water, is 15·2 f.p.s. and the final speed at extraction, that is, at the moment when the blade leaves the water, is 16·76 f.p.s. With these corrections the rhythm of Mr. Alexander's ideal crew becomes quite orthodox, but the whole character of the stroke is in no wise altered. The contrast between the two curves is very great; and it is obvious that in the lower curve there is a great and unnecessary waste of labour, due to the boat's speed being reduced to 13·6 f.p.s. in the early part of the stroke. I am inclined to think that Mr. Alexander has exaggerated the drop in speed at the beginning and has been too much influenced by MM. Lefeuvre and Palliotte's diagrams, which do show a very marked check as the blades entèr the water. Some such drop must occur if the oarsmen begin their swing or slide back before their blades have caught the water; and the drop in this case is exaggerated because, as clearly appears from a study of Mr. Alexander's fig. 16, the oarsmen are 'rowing in'; that is to say, they have begun the acceleration of their bodies while the oars are descending into and before they have entered the water. It is because of this abrupt drop of speed at the end of the run that the speed of the boat has to be raised to 18·96 f.p.s. at the recovery. I refrain from giving comparative figures of the work required to raise a boat's speed from 16·1 to 17·6 f.p.s. and from 13·6 to 18·96 f.p.s. because the data are too uncertain to allow any exactitude in numerical results, but it is obvious that the work required is very much greater in the latter case. It should be observed that nearly all that part of the oarsman's effort that checks the speed of his boat is spent in accelerating his body. As the extra speed of bodies is returned to the hull at the end of the stroke, the more the boat is checked at the beginning, the greater will be the rise of the hull's speed at the recovery. Contrariwise, the less the boat is checked at the beginning, the less will be the rise of speed of the hull at the recovery, because, when his blade meets with the resistance of the water, the oarsman cannot accelerate his body to the same extent as when rowing the first part of the stroke in the air. In the one case the oarsman speeds up his body before the resistance comes on the blade and literally throws his weight on the handle of the oar. In the other case the first part of the stroke is a hard muscular tug, and the body is moving at its fastest in the latter half of the stroke when the hull has shot forward in response to the tug at the beginning. The upshot of the whole matter is that at some part of the stroke the greater part of the work is done by the momentum of the body weight; in another part of the stroke the main work consists of a muscular pull against the resistance on the blade. At which part of the stroke the muscular pull or the momentum of the body comes chiefly into use depends on the style of the oarsman. But a consideration of the two curves in fig. 10 leaves no doubt as to which is the most effective style of rowing. The oarsman who checks his boat unduly at the beginning is wasting a valuable asset at every stroke, namely the speed given to the boat by the previous strokes. To repair this waste he must put forth a greater effort than the oarsman who has not wasted his assets. Although he may for a time go as fast as, and even faster than, his more economical opponent, after the lapse of two or three minutes the element of fatigue comes in and the spendthrift will succumb through sheer exhaustion. I say he may move as fast or even faster because, if he does not 'row in' quite so badly as Mr. Alexander's oarsman, he will not check the way of his boat so much just before entry. The boat will run farther between the strokes and the mean speed of the whole cycle of stroke and run will be raised. But it must be observed that the mean speed can only be raised on the condition that the boat is checked to a less degree, and the less it is checked the more will the speed curve approximate to the ideal of the upper curve of fig. 10. There is room for an almost infinite number of gradations between this and the exceedingly bad stroke rowed by Mr. Alexander's oarsman.

The question now arises, How is it that in spite of the considerable extra output of work Mr. Alexander's crew travels at a less mean speed than mine? Perhaps it is necessary to give some idea of the difference in the work done in each stroke by the two different crews, though I do not pretend that the figures are very accurate. Assuming that each crew is composed of men of the equal weight of 12 stones, each oarsman has, at each stroke, in addition to the 226 lb. accounted for on p. 38, to take his share in overcoming the resistance due to skin friction, which at a speed of 17 f.p.s. will be about 84 lb. The total weight to be moved by each oarsman is therefore about 236 lb. In calculating the work done it is not necessary, indeed it is very confusing, to deal with the hull and the oarsmen separately. We have only to consider the acceleration given to the whole system, and as the drop in speed of the hull at entry while the bodies are being accelerated is compensated by the rise in speed at recovery when the momentum of the bodies is restored to the hull, we can take the initial speed at entry and the maximum speed during the run as the points from which to measure the acceleration given to the whole system during the strokes. If this be the right method of reckoning, my oarsman picks up the boat at 16·3 f.p.s. and in a stroke of 0·5 second duration raises it to a speed of 17·7 f.p.s. : in other words, he gives it an acceleration of 2·8 f.p.s. Therefore the work done is $256 \times 0{\cdot}5 \times 2{\cdot}8 = 330{\cdot}4$ foot-pounds per stroke.

Mr. Alexander's oarsman (and here I take his original figures) picks up his boat at 16·0 f.p.s. and in a stroke of 0·52 second duration raises it to a speed of 18·96 f.p.s. That is an acceleration of 5·7 f.p.s. The work done is $236 \times 0{\cdot}52 \times 5{\cdot}7 = 599{\cdot}5$ foot-pounds per stroke.

Mr. Atkinson, as the result of the experiments with his rowing indicator, gives the mean work per stroke in foot-pounds as 396, the maximum measured being 571 and the minimum 267 foot-pounds. These values, it must be remembered, were registered in a tub-pair and for one out of a small number of strokes rowed. The work done by my ideal oarsman seems low, but as he has to row 238 strokes at the rate of 35·3 strokes per minute he is really undertaking a large amount of exertion and will be sufficiently fatigued at the end of the course. The work done by Mr. Alexander's ideal oarsman seems unreasonably high, but from the account given on p. 40 it does not appear to be beyond the capacity of a first-class oarsman. It is, however, more than doubtful whether any oarsman, however great his strength and staying power, could maintain such a high standard of work for seven consecutive minutes even at the relatively slow stroke of $33\frac{1}{2}$ strokes per minute. But even if he could, he is not getting sufficient pace out of his boat to win the race, and we come back to the question, How is this great excess of work to be accounted for if it does not give sufficient speed to the boat ? It is not spent in moving water in front of the blade, for my oarsman actually sweeps his blade through a slightly larger arc than Mr. Alexander's, and it is necessary that he should do so in order to get the blade reaction to maintain a slightly higher mean speed. The answer is that a boat travelling with such great and abrupt fluctuations of speed as are depicted in the lower curve of fig. 10 will bob up and down in the water and will create waves, not high enough to be very conspicuous, but of considerable amplitude. A hard-working but unskilful crew dissipates an amazing amount of energy in making waves. But all said and done on the subject of work in foot-pounds and other rather doubtful calculations, it is a familiar thing to see a good crew winning as it likes and pulling up quite fresh at the finish, while the beaten crew reaches the post in a pitiable state of exhaustion. *Vis consili expers !*

After this disquisition on the effect of the stroke in propelling the boat we may take into consideration the stroke itself. Fig. 11 is a diagram of the stroke rowed by my ideal oarsman. It is constructed on the same principle as fig. 6, the oar being represented in the successive positions it would occupy at intervals of 0·0625 second, not in the positions it would occupy for every 10° angular movement as in fig. 7. It is with fig. 6 rather than with fig. 7 that it should be compared, allowance being made for the fact that nine positions of the oar are shown instead of six, and that in fig. 11 the oarsman is reaching forward to his full extent, so the oar at entry makes an angle of 40° with the line of advance of the rowlock. The great and obvious difference between the two diagrams is due to this : that in fig. 6 the boat is starting from standstill and is being accelerated at the rate of 7·68 f.p.s. for a period of 1·25 second, whereas in fig. 11 the boat has an initial speed of 16·3 f.p.s., reduced by the check at entry to 16·1 f.p.s., and is being accelerated at the rate of only 2·8 f.p.s. for a period of only 0·5 second. The angular velocity of the oar, which is due partly to the speed of movement of the blade but chiefly to the speed at which the boat is travelling, is much greater in fig. 11 than in fig. 6, and the spaces traversed in equal periods of time are much more nearly uniform. They are not, of course, quite equal because the initial speed of the boat is checked at the beginning of the stroke, and this check, though it is so small as to be scarcely measurable in a small-scale diagram, is allowed for in the drawing. In the subsequent intervals there is a slight progressive increase due to the acceleration of the boat's speed, but again in a small-scale diagram the increments are hardly perceptible. If there were no acceleration, but the boat were moving through equal spaces in equal intervals of time, it is clear that the co-ordinates of the successive stations of the oar along the base line with the equal intervals of time shown along the scale of feet per second (or with the scale of angles) on the left of the diagram would all fall upon the diagonal *BF*. But as the spaces moved through in equal intervals of time are not equal, the co-ordinates give an acceleration curve as in fig. 6; but in this case the curve is so flat and rises so little above the diagonal that I have not drawn it. A moment's reflection will show why this curve is so flat. It is because the rate of acceleration of the boat is small proportionally to the initial speed at the beginning of the stroke. The initial speed is the asset referred to above which it is the oarsman's business to conserve and add something to during the stroke. The co-ordinates of the successive stations of the oar along the base line with the angles actually formed by the oar at each station give the line of double curvature *BCF* about the diagonal *BF*. It is similar in character to the curve *BCF* in fig. 7, but more pronounced, and it is worthy of remark that in both figures the point C, where the curve crosses the diagonal, coincides very nearly with the ordinate drawn from the base line when the oar is at an angle of 80°. The reasoning given in explanation of figs. 6 and 7 on p. 47 applies equally well to fig. 11 and need not be repeated here, but there are some special features in fig. 11 which require consideration. The turning-point curve, as determined by the intersections of the lines representing the successive positions of the oar, is here a wide and open

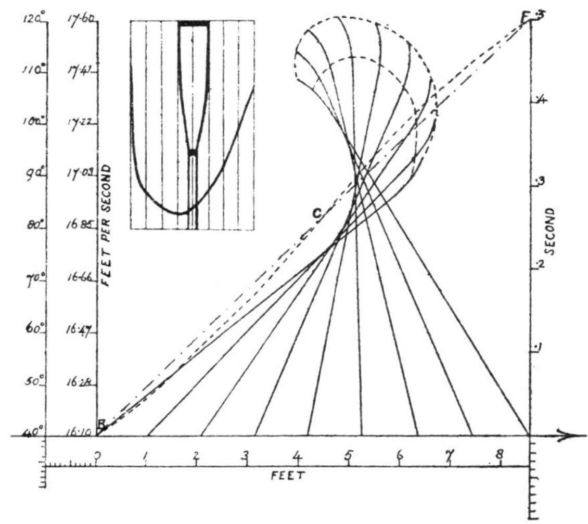

FIG. 11. The stroke diagram of a good oarsman.

curve. A little consideration and a comparison of figs. 7 and 11 shows that the farther the boat travels during the stroke the wider the turning-point curve will be. Contrariwise, the tighter the turning-point curve, the less distance will the boat travel between the strokes. It is clear that the width of the turning-point curve (as measured by the length of the chord drawn from the first to the last points of intersection) depends upon the movement of the turning-point along the oar as shown in the inset in fig. 11. From this we see that the turning-point (as in Mr. Atkinson's fig. 9) starts from a point near the centre of pressure of the blade, moves inwards along the loom of the oar while the latter is swinging from 40° to about 75°, then turns outwards and rather rapidly moves back towards the blade, ending at sixteen inches from the tip. It is instructive to compare the curve of the motion of the turning-point along the blade as shown in the inset figs. 6 and 7 with that in fig. 11. The greater the movement of the blade in proportion to the movement of the boat, the nearer does the turning-point approach the rowlock. The nearer the turning-point is brought to the rowlock, the less distance the boat will travel between the strokes. The speed of blade through the water depends on two factors. Firstly, the strength of pull of the oarsman, or to put it more explicitly, the distance through which the oarsman is able to move his body in given time. Secondly, on the speed at which the boat is moving, for in the extreme case of the boat being stationary any pull at the handle of the oar, however weak, will move the blade through the water. From which we may conclude that if the oarsman gets a very hard and quick beginning he will set water in motion at a corresponding speed from his blade and will bring his turning-point nearer to the rowlock. But the reaction of the blade work accelerates the boat, and as the speed of the boat increases the speed of blade becomes proportionally less than the speed of boat, so the turning-point begins to travel back again towards the tip of the blade. This seems to be in flat contradiction to what we learned from the curve BCF, that the angular velocity of the oar is slow relatively to the speed of the boat in the earlier part but relatively fast in the latter part of the stroke. There is, however, no contradiction, for the angular movement of the oar is not the same thing, nor can it be described in the same terms, as the path described by the blade and especially by the broad extremity of the blade during the stroke. This can readily be understood by a consideration of the curve described by the tip of the oar or preferably, if one wished to obtain numerical results, by the centre of pressure of the blade. It is clear from fig. 11 that in the first phase of the stroke the oar is moving but slowly in a direction parallel but opposite to the line of advance of the boat. That means that the angular velocity of the oar is low. On the other hand, in consequence of the initial speed at which the boat is travelling, the blade is thrust outwards at great speed from the boat, the out-thrust being greatest at the beginning and becoming less as the oar approaches the thwartship plane. As the oar is thrust out it is continually entering and setting in motion water previously undisturbed. In the first six-hundredth of a second the tip of the blade is thrust out nine inches, at the end of 0·125 second it has been thrust out seventeen inches, and by the time the oar reaches the thwartship plane the out-thrust is almost exactly equal to the whole length of the blade. As the blade is thus entering and attacking new water it is clear that a much larger mass of water is set in motion than is the case, for instance, in figs. 6 and 7, where the curvature of the line traced by the tip of the blade is much shallower. But, as has already been explained on p. 48, the out-thrust of the oar by itself does nothing to maintain, still less to increase, the speed of the boat. It rather retards it, and is a contributory cause to the check in speed at the beginning. The oar-blade is thrust out at a rate proportional to the speed at which the boat is travelling simply as a consequence of the initial speed of the boat at the beginning of the stroke, and *qua* out-thrust does no work at all towards propelling the boat. To be effective in propulsion the oar must be given angular acceleration while it is being thrust out, which is the same thing as saying that the pull must come on as the blade enters the water and must not be delayed until the blade is fully immersed. When the angular acceleration is combined with the out-thrust the blade makes a very powerful scoop in the water, a scoop of very much the same character as a fast swimmer makes with his hands. Any one can test for himself when swimming the difference between extending the arms straight in front of him and then swinging the straightened arms round and swinging the arms round while they are being extended. The power and pace gained is much greater in the latter method. As far as I am aware the mathematics of a scoop have not been fully worked out. At any rate several highly competent mathematicians to whom I have broached the subject have fought shy of it. As the oar-blade does make a scoop, and the scoop is more pronounced the better the boat is travelling, the subject seems to deserve further investigation. It is a really important point that the scooping action of the oar practically eliminates 'slip' in the early part of the stroke. Slip is a word used in a technical sense by marine engineers to indicate that part of the power expended by the propeller, be it screw, oar, or paddle, in imparting kinetic energy to the water. In each case so much water is moved aft in order that the ship may be moved forward. It is an unfortunate word because it suggests a loss, something that has slipped away and might conceivably have been husbanded and made use of. It should suggest the accomplishment of the end desired, namely the reaction obtained by setting a mass of water in motion, which reaction is the power available for propelling the ship. But if the instruments of propulsion are ill adapted to their purpose or if the power is applied in an unsuitable manner, the energy expended in setting water in motion may be disproportionate to the speed given to the ship. In such case slip involves an element of waste which it is the business of marine engineers to get rid of. In rowing the slip of the blade of the oar varies considerably according to the character of the stroke rowed, and it is the business of the coach to teach his pupils to row a stroke in which there is as little waste of energy as possible through slip. In such a diagram as fig. 11 the slip of the oar is measured by dropping verticals from the centre of pressure of the blade at the initial and final positions of the oar and measuring the distance between them along a line parallel with the line of advance of the boat. We are at once confronted with the question, Where is the centre of pressure of the blade, and is it the same at all parts of the stroke? As explained in the foot-note on p. 26, Mr. Alexander, for reasons that are clearly adequate, puts it at 8½ inches from the tip of the blade. But in such a stroke as that represented in fig. 11, in which the oarsman is assumed to give his oar angular acceleration when at the most two inches of the lower corner of his blade are immersed, the centre of pressure will be near the tip of the blade : I estimate about $2\frac{1}{2}$ inches from the tip. As the blade covers the centre of pressure will rapidly move up to $8\frac{1}{2}$ inches from the tip, and we may leave it at that until the finish. Then, as the turning-point is moving up the blade and in consequence the proximal part of the blade is moving in the same direction as the boat is advancing,[1] the centre of pressure must shift out again towards the tip, though to a less extent than it would do if the blade were not curved. The result is that the curve of the path of the centre of pressure does not conform to the curve of the path of the tip of the blade, but has the shape shown in fig. 11. The tip of the blade for a period of 0·06 second is being thrust out in the direction of the boat's advance. For nearly the whole of this period the blade is being covered and the boat's way is being checked. But the centre of effort is not thrust out to the same extent. It is moving nearly at right angles to the boat's line of advance, and as long as it is doing so there is no slip of the oar. In the diagram the slip begins when the oar is at an angle of 57° and increases rapidly until the oar is at 90°. Thereafter it diminishes ; very rapidly in the last phase of the stroke. As might be expected the slip—or shall we say the mass of water set in motion ?—is greatest during the period when the oar is acting at the greatest mechanical advantage. The total slip of the centre of pressure of the blade as shown in fig. 11 is 24 inches. Mr. Cruickshank gives the slip, presumably for the 1908 Leander Olympic crew, as $21\frac{5}{8}$ inches, but he takes the centre of pressure of the blade at fourteen inches from the tip. If it is taken at $8\frac{1}{2}$ inches the slip is increased to $26\frac{1}{2}$ inches, yet he only makes the boat travel 6·7 feet during the stroke. Clearly, in rowing, there are great possibilities of wastage through excessive slip. But, as I shall explain farther on, Mr. Cruickshank's oarsman rows in a style exactly opposite

[1] This part of the blade is not backing water, as Mr. Cruickshank supposes, because there is an air cavity behind the blade, clearly visible in a suitable photograph.

to that represented in fig. 11. That it is possible to row and to get some speed out of the boat in the style depicted by Mr. Cruickshank I do not deny, but I am certain that the Leander crew of 1908 did not row in that style. Without wearying the reader by going into further detail I wish to insist on the fact that, if he succeeds in rowing a stroke of the character depicted in fig. 11, the oarsman can and does get as near as circumstances allow to the ideal inculcated by his coach; namely, to stick his blade into a point as far back (really as far forward) as possible in the water and to row the boat past that point. To put it in other words, the desideratum at the ' beginning ' is not to hit at, but to *grip hold of*, the water. The combination of out-thrust with angular acceleration of the oar at the moment the blade enters the water gives that ' grip ' if the oarsman has reached out far enough. But if, through overreach or mere incapacity to move quickly enough, he fails to give the required amount of angular acceleration to his oar the water will not be gripped and he will have reached out in vain. Here it may be observed that if an oarsman is set back from his work so far that, however far he swings forward, his oar cannot make an angle of less than 50° or thereabouts with the lineof advance of the boat, his power of hitting at the water will be increased, but his power of gripping hold of the water will be *pro tanto* diminished. There are other disadvantages, for if he slides out full sixteen inches and swings back his shoulders properly at the finish, the oar at the end of the stroke will be at an angle of 130°. In this position not only is the mechanical advantage of the oar diminished but, as explained on p. 36, the oar is being pulled outwards from the rowlock. It is largely trailing behind the boat, and the extent to which an oar trails after it has passed the thwartship plane can hardly be realized unless one has experimented with a model boat and a model oar rowing in sand so that the track of the blade may be watched and preserved for study. I may say here that, with a little practice in the use of the model, a stroke in all essential respects similar to that of fig. 11 may be traced in sand with great precision. If the oar is started at 50° and pulled through to 130° the diminution in the distance through which the model boat travels is very perceptible.

Lastly, let us see how all this agrees with the experience of a first-class oarsman. I asked a very eminent oarsman, whose many successes obviously depended more on the extreme quickness with which he 'got hold of the beginning' than on gracefulness of body action, to describe to me as accurately as possible his sensations during the stroke. He said that he had a feeling of great effort, almost of a holdfast, in the early part of the stroke. But before the middle of the stroke was reached this sense of effort passed away, and for the whole of the latter part of the stroke he was occupied in moving back fast enough to keep pace with the boat. This accords with my own experience when rowing well, but not at all when rowing badly and 'missing the beginning'. If the reader will refer again to the curve BCF in figs. 11 and 12, he will see that it is entirely compatible with the oarsman's sensations. The angular velocity of the oar is a measure of the speed at which the oarsman moves his body; in the later part of the stroke his hands rather than his body. In the early part of the stroke the angular velocity of the oar is low: the oarsman is meeting with great resistance and is pulling hard to overcome it. Before the middle of the stroke is reached the great resistance is largely overcome. The oarsman can move back at greater speed, the angular velocity of the oar increases as the arms bend, and the handle of the oar comes home, but at the last slows up again before the hands touch the body.

Let us now consider some other types of stroke, and first of all the only direct evidence we have of a stroke actually rowed, to wit Mr. Atkinson's photographic record. Fig. 12 is founded on a very careful enlargement of part of fig. 6 of his essay *Some More Rowing Experiments*. The diagram has been reversed and the positions of the oar have been drawn at the end of every 10° angular movement by the method described on p. 46. From a study of his fig. 7 I am satisfied that Mr. Atkinson's oarsman (a real live oarsman in action, it must be remembered, and not an ideal or imaginary oarsman) began his stroke in the water when the oar was at an angle of 42·5° and finished it at an angle of about 122·5°. He was not a perfect oarsman by any means, for he seems to have reached out till his oar was at an angle of 37°, to have paused a moment, to have made a bit of a snatch at it, and finally to have got hold of the water at 42·5°. At the finish he seems to have swung back a bit after his blade left the water and therefore to have carried his oar back to 132° before bringing it forward on the feather, a habit to which many oarsmen are addicted. Omitting these initial and terminal lapses, fig. 12 is as nearly an accurate representation of the stroke as I am able to draw. The rate of stroke was 22 per minute. At a ratio of 1 : 2·4 for stroke and run the time occupied by the stroke would be 0·79 second and the boat, a tub-pair, was advanced 7·9 feet. On this reckoning the mean speed of the boat would be about 10·0 f.p.s. or 200 yards per minute, a respectable speed for a tub-pair. The dimensions of the stroke are modified by the slow speed and the extra resistance offered by a heavy wide-beamed clinker-built boat. The area swept through by the blade is large in comparison with the travel of the boat; in other words, the slip of the oar is large. But in all essential respects the stroke is of the same character as that depicted in fig. 11, and the curve *BCF* of the angular velocity of the oar and the curve of the turning-point on the oar shown in the inset are of the same type. Here it may be observed that a careful examination of Mr. Atkinson's fig. 7 shows clearly that the initial turning-point of the oar at the instant of entry is close to the centre of pressure of the blade. It starts there because at the beginning the blade is fixed in the water relatively to the advance of the boat, but as the oar is thrust out it must run very rapidly up the blade and is some nine inches up the loom by the time the oar has swung through an angle of 10°. Mr. Atkinson seems to have overlooked this feature when he estimated that the turning-point is some 37 inches from the tip of the blade at the beginning of the stroke. It is a great part of the oarsman's art to so instantly immobilize the blade by getting a firm grip of the water at the beginning as to start his turning-point at or near the centre of pressure of the blade. To do this is to get a good and true beginning. We shall see presently what very different results follow from a false beginning. I call the reader's special attention to the fact that Mr. Atkinson's photographic record is a complete justification of my ideal stroke rowed under very different conditions of boat and speed.

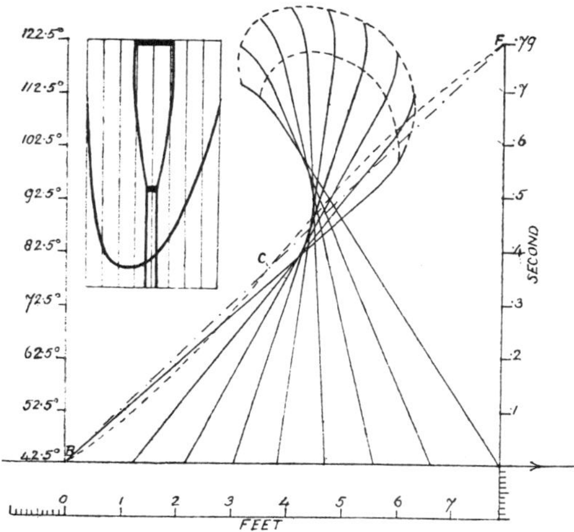

FIG. 12. Stroke diagram founded on Mr. Atkinson's photographic record.

Fig. 13 is an enlargement of so much of Mr. Alexander's fig. 16 of which it can be said with certainty that the blade is in the water and doing work. The drawing is reversed, but I have not in this case attempted to draw the oar in the positions it would occupy at the end of every 10° of angular movement but have simply followed Mr. Alexander's lines. I have, however, brought the stroke to an end when the oar is at 121° because I do not think it could possibly be prolonged much farther: certainly not to 131° as he indicates, but at that position the blade, as shown by the path of its tip in his drawing, is manifestly on the feather. The point, however, is of no great importance. The main features of the stroke have already been dealt with on pp. 62–65. The chief points to be observed in the diagram of the oar are the following. In consequence of the abrupt check given to the speed of the boat at the beginning the out-thrust of the tip of the blade is pronounced : indeed it is exaggerated and would probably tend to check the way of the boat still farther. However that may be, the blade of the oar is for the moment immobilized relatively to the advance of the boat and the oarsman has succeeded in getting a very firm grip of the water at the beginning. So far so good, and if we look at the turning-point curve, the graph of which is given separately at *ctpf*, we see that all goes well and the curve is fair until the oar arrives at the thwartship plane. Then the oarsman gives an extra dig with his oar : the turning-point moves abruptly back from *t* to *p*. Then the oarsman lets off his work again and the turning-point moves from *p* to *f*. All this is faithfully reflected in the curve of the movement of the turning-point on the oar as shown in the inset. The stroke is rowed in two pieces, and the reader will now understand why I have said that Mr. Alexander's imaginary oarsman is in mortal danger of catching a crab at the end of every stroke, and that it may be doubted whether he would get as far as Remenham without a catastrophe. The reader will also note the great prolongation of effort indicated by the curve *BCF*, suggestive of exhaustion at an early period in the race. The stroke, however, if it could be rowed, is economical in this sense : that the slip of the centre of effort of the blade is at most 21 inches. Though defective in several respects its type is the same as that of figs. 11 and 12.

In fig. 14 we have a wholly different type of stroke. The upper part of this oar diagram is simply a reproduction on a reduced scale of Mr. Cruickshank's representation of the movement of the oar-blades (fig. 9 on p. 20 of Sir Theodore Cook's *Coaching for Young Crews*). I have completed the figure by drawing in the loom of the oar as far as the line of advance of the rowlock. I might have reproduced a very complete but in all essential respects a similar diagram by Mr. Blakeley, published as fig. 4 on p. 16 of the same work. But I have chosen Mr. Cruickshank's figure because it represents his notion of the style of rowing of the Leander crew of 1908 over the latter half of the Henley Olympic course. He gives the rate of stroke as 36 per minute; the mean speed as 16·357 f.p.s., or 27·3 feet per stroke. He says that while the blades were in the water the boat moved 6·70 feet and ran 20·6 feet with the blades out of the water. The time occupied

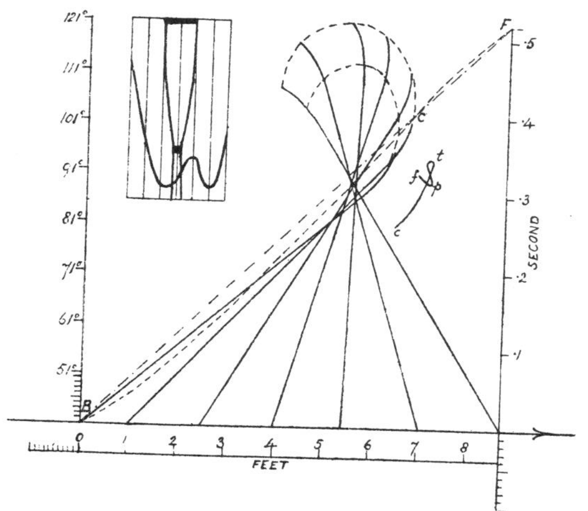

FIG. 13. Stroke diagram of Mr. Alexander's oarsman.

by 'stroke' was 0·407 second and by 'run' 1·258 second, a proportion of 1 to 3·08. I have long been puzzled by this exposition of the performance of the fine Leander crew which, by common consent, reproduced the best traditions of English oarsmanship. I venture to say that its oar action was very similar to my fig. 11, and in any case not in the least like Mr. Cruickshank's or Mr. Blakeley's figures. For an analysis of these diagrams shows that we have here a theory of oarsmanship fundamentally different from the University style in which that Leander crew rowed. I have little hesitation in saying that this theory is the basis of what has come to be known as the

Thames Rowing Club or Jesus College, Cambridge, style, about which there has been so much controversy in recent years. Let us examine it with the aid of fig. 14. The oarsman is sliding up to his work and reaching forward to the full, for his oar makes an angle of 40° at the beginning. But his finish is short, for at the last position the oar is only at an angle of 112°. At this angle the shoulders would hardly be carried back past the perpendicular. The stroke savours of winter practice in a tank, for at the beginning the turning-point is brought very near to the rowlock, and in a stationary boat the turning-point is, of course, at the rowlock. Necessarily the boat's speed has been seriously checked at the beginning, the extent of the check being indicated by the short distance it travels during the first 10° angular movement of the oar. The distance travelled by the boat increases, and the area swept through by the blade correspondingly diminishes, till the oar is at 90°. After this the angular velocity of the oar increases relatively to the advance of the boat, a feature which is somewhat obscured in the diagram by the fact that the last position of the oar is drawn at 112° instead of 110°. From the law of virtual velocities we perceive that the pressure on the thowl-pin is greatest at the beginning and least in the middle of the stroke. Conversely the pressure on the blade is greatest in the middle of the stroke and least at the two ends. Comparison with figs. 11 and 12 shows that this is exactly the opposite to what happens in the more orthodox University type of stroke, and that in the latter the pressures both on blade and thowl-pin are more uniform throughout. In fig. 14 the curve BCF, representing the angular velocity of the oar in terms of the distance travelled by the boat, is of entirely different character to the same curve in figs. 11 and 12. The turning-point curve, represented separately at ctp, makes a long sweep convex in the direction of the boat's advance, but when the oar is at 90° it turns round and commences a descending sweep which, if it were continued, would be concave in the direction of the boat's advance. This reversal of the turning-point will, if the blade is fully covered, put the oarsman in danger of catching a crab, and as I write I read in the current number of the *Field* of an epidemic of crab-catching at the Kingston Amateur Regatta, in crews whom I suspect of rowing on the principles set forth in Mr. Cruickshank's diagram. Lastly, the curve of the turning-point on the oar, as shown in the inset of fig. 14, is the reverse of that in figs. 11 and 12. It descends towards the blade and after the middle of the stroke turns and travels up the loom again. In Mr. Blakeley's diagram the turning-

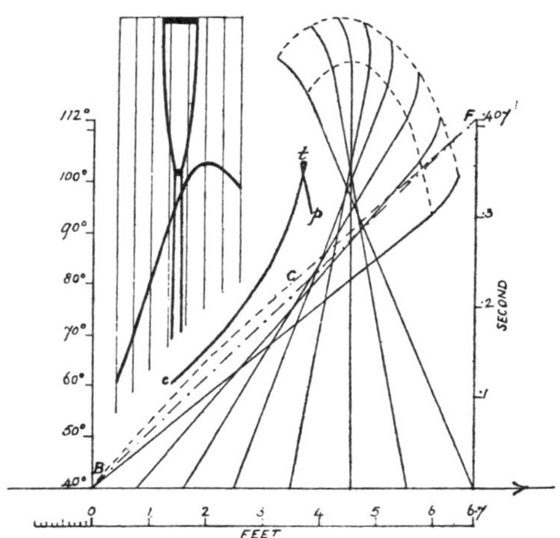

FIG. 14. Stroke diagram after Mr. Cruickshank.

point curve is similar, but, as he makes his oarsman begin with the oar at an angle of 45° and finish at 120°, it begins somewhat nearer the neck of the blade and moves farther up the loom at the end of the stroke. He also gives the travel of the boat during the stroke as 6·916 feet (6 ft. 11 in.), some $2\frac{3}{4}$ inches farther than Mr. Cruickshank's estimate, and that with a 12-foot oar, which should give a shorter stride than the 12 ft. 4 in. oar wielded by Mr. Cruickshank's oarsman. Even with this advantage in hand, Mr. Blakeley argues that the 45° angle of attack is back-breaking, and that the proper angle would be 60° on a fixed seat. Mr. McGruer (*Coaching for Young Crews*, p. 21) would make the angle of attack 55°, and the angle of finish 125°. Passing over the fact that after 120° the handle of the oar comes inconveniently far inboard at the finish, this stroke of Mr. McGruer's would be short, for the oar is only swung through 70° instead of 80°, as in figs. 11 and 12. This brings us to the point : the type of stroke depicted in fig. 14 (and presumably taught by Messrs. Cruickshank, Blakeley, and other advocates of the less acute angle of attack) necessitates a short stroke. For it is obvious from a close inspection of fig. 14 that if the oarsman slides up to his work and reaches forward far enough to ' attack ' at an angle of 40° he has a task wellnigh impossible to perform. His boat is stopped nearly dead, and he has to row the centre of effort of his blade through more than one foot in less than 0·05 second. I doubt whether the strongest oarsman could do it : if he could he would require an unusually strong oar. Mr. Cruickshank, I suspect, was aware of this difficulty, but as he was giving his rendering of the stroke rowed by the 1908 Leander crew, and knew that crew reached out very far forward, he has put the angle of attack at 40° and has camouflaged his diagram by putting in an additional position of the oar at 45°. I have omitted this extra position in fig. 14, and by so doing have exposed the practical impossibility of the oarsman's task. Be it observed in passing that the oarsman in fig. 11 has no such impossible task. He only has to move the centre of effort of his blade through 0·45 foot (something less than 5½ inches) in 0·06 second. He is thrusting out his oar at greater speed, but that is another matter : the momentum of the whole system enables him to do that and so to get his ' grip ' at the beginning. But if Mr. Cruickshank's oarsman begins his work at 50°, still better at the angle of 55° recommended by Mr. McGruer, his task is comparatively easy, and oarsmen who row in this style do not reach out much beyond 50°, for the very good reason that if they do they have set themselves a task they cannot perform.

It is evident that to pull such a stroke as that of fig. 14 (supposing him to begin at an angle of 50° or thereabouts) an oarsman must row in a very different style from him who rows such a stroke as that of figs. 11 or 12. Let us try to picture the style. The stroke is short; therefore it must be very powerful while it lasts. The impact of the blade at entry must be sharp and forcible, for in this method of rowing it is essential that the mass of water encountered by the blade should be moved aft with as much speed as the force available allows. Therefore the oar is given angular acceleration before it enters the water, and I gather from conversation with Mr. S. Fairbairn that this is the cardinal principle of the style of rowing he advocates: that the blade must strike the water at the first touch, much as the paddle-boards of a paddle-wheel strike the water. This involves acceleration of the body before the blades enter the water, and this in turn involves retardation of the speed of the hull through the reaction of the oarsmen's feet on the stretcher. This retardation is minimized by curtailing the length of swing forward and driving back the slide as sharply as possible without swinging the body up to the perpendicular. For by this means the centre of gravity of the greatest part of the mass of the moving system, namely the body weights, is moved through a less distance in given time in the direction of the boat's advance than it would be if the slide's action were delayed and the body swung back at once to the perpendicular. Consequently, the reaction on the hull is less. This question will have to be considered in detail farther on when dealing with muscular action in rowing: for the moment it need only be said that the instantaneous drive back of the slide transfers a large part of the work from the muscles of the buttocks and loins to the extensor muscles of the legs. As the oar moves athwartship, the resistance to the movement of the blade increases and the motion of the hull is increased in a corresponding degree. The net result is that the angular velocity of the oar is greatest at about 70°, and thereafter decreases gradually until the end of the stroke, as is shown by the curve *BCF* in fig. 14. The hands come steadily and smoothly home to the body and the recovery of the oar with the wrists is facilitated. But as the slip increases after the oar has passed 90°, the finish of the stroke is not so strong as in figs. 11 and 12, in which the slip of the blade diminishes towards the end of its course.

The stroke in fig. 14 being of short duration, the time given to the run must be prolonged if the boat is to move 20·6 feet in 1·258 second between the strokes, as it should do on Mr. Cruickshank's reckoning. Therefore the slides and bodies must come forward with almost exaggerated steadiness and smoothness. The extra fraction of time given to the run is permissible because of the large blade reaction during the stroke. The slip of the centre of pressure measured from the position of the oar at 50° is 24 inches, and as this indicates the same amount of water moved aft in shorter time, the swirl off the oarsmen's blades will be greater than in the orthodox University style.

This analysis of Messrs. Cruickshank's and Blakeley's diagrams is descriptive of the methods adopted by the Thames Rowing Club and by Jesus College, Cambridge, in recent years, and followed by several Metropolitan and up-river clubs. They are largely characteristic of Colonial and American oarsmanship and of some Continental crews that have visited England. The resulting characteristic style might well be called the mechanical style, for it is just that which an engineer or mathematician, starting from *a priori* principles and founding his reasoning upon the action of machines (such as the paddle-wheel) with which he is familiar,[1] would necessarily evolve and recommend. Unless I am very much mistaken it is the style dictated by Euler's mathematical reasoning, but whether or no it has the sanction of such high scientific authority, the style has something to say for itself. Demanding a lower order of skill, it is more easily and quickly taught to the average oarsman. As its principles are few, simple, and consistent with mechanical doctrines, it is possible to obtain a much

[1] Thus Mr. Sydney Barnaby: 'There are four different kinds of propellers apart from sails—the oar, the paddle-wheel, the screw and the water-jet. The first and oldest of them—the oar—may be used in two ways. The action may be intermittent as in rowing . . . or it may be continuous as in sculling.' [Sea-sculling with a single oar astern is here referred to.] 'When used as in rowing it is exactly analogous to a paddle-wheel, while the action of a scull closely resembles that of a screw.'

greater degree of uniformity in the course of a limited period of practice than in a crew which is striving to execute the more difficult bodily movements required by the University style. In eight-oared rowing, uniformity counts for a great deal, and the successes of the best exponents of the mechanical style—for example, the Sydney New South Wales crew of 1912—have been due to the almost uncanny mechanical precision with which they rowed. They were inhuman in their exactitude, and more suggestive of 'Robots' than of flesh and blood. Judged by the final test of speed maintained over a course not much exceeding a mile in length, the style can claim a no inconsiderable meed of success: an almost unbroken success as long as it is confronted by something short of excellence in what must be called in contrast the orthodox style. But the mechanical style has its limits both of speed and endurance. It has never beaten a really good sample of the orthodox style, and has nothing to its credit over the four-mile Putney course. The Cambridge crews stroked by Mr. D. C. R. Stuart incorporated elements of the mechanical style, and were successful as long as they had very inferior Oxford crews to compete against. But this hybrid style received a severe overthrow in 1909 and has not since been heard of. Nor had it much prospect of permanence, for a reference to figs. 12 and 14 must satisfy any one that these two styles are unmarriageable. They are incompatible at every point, and an oarsman habituated to the one method can find no place in a crew rowing in the other. The one stroke is, in comparison with the other, totally roundabout.

It must not be supposed that the Belgian crews that won the Grand Challenge Cup in 1906, 1907, and 1909 rowed in what has been described above as the mechanical style. M. R. Van der Waerden's letter to Mr. W. B. Close, published in the *Field* for 9 October 1909, is sufficient proof of this. It is true that M. Van der Waerden advocates a slight swing back of the bodies before the blades touch the water, and, as the Belgian bodies were not swung so far forward as ours, this would introduce some little modification into the first part of fig. 11. But the turning-point curve and the action of the oar in the middle and at the finish of the stroke would be similar. A great deal of nonsense was talked about the Belgian style, and various misinterpretations of it led to a sad deterioration in the rowing of various English clubs who thought to copy it. To my mind, allowance being made for differences due to the use of broad blades and swivel rowlocks, it most nearly resembled the style of the Leander crew of 1880 that made the record at Henley over the old course round Poplar Point. The fact is that the Belgians had a stroke of uncommon merit in M. R. Poma, and in M. O. de Somville a no. 7 whom one would have been glad to include in any English crew. It was a treat to watch M. de Somville lift back his weight from the stretcher at the beginning of the stroke. With these two to give the lead in the stern it is not wonderful that the Belgians were able to defeat the rather poor crews that we were able to pit against them in those years. But in 1908 they were no match for the fine Leander crew carefully trained in the best English style for the Olympic Regatta.

Enough, perhaps more than enough, has been said about the action of the oar in rowing. It is now necessary to put in that very important factor, the man, who has hitherto received very little attention. Fig. 15 shows four positions of the oarsman as seen from above during the stroke. These drawings are not imaginary. The outlines are traced from photographs of a model who sat for the four positions, and in each was pulling hard at the oar, so that his muscles are shown at the tension proper to that part of the stroke. The oar action is not quite the same as in fig. 11, for it is calculated for a speed of only 16 feet per second in dead water, which would be nearly 7 min. 25 sec. over the Henley course. To obtain exactly the same results as in fig. 11 the positions of the oar, and therefore of the man, would have to be spaced out a trifle farther and the time scale would have to be altered accordingly. But the general character of the drawing is not affected by the fact that the oarsman is not represented as rowing at full strength. It should be noted that in the position of the beginning

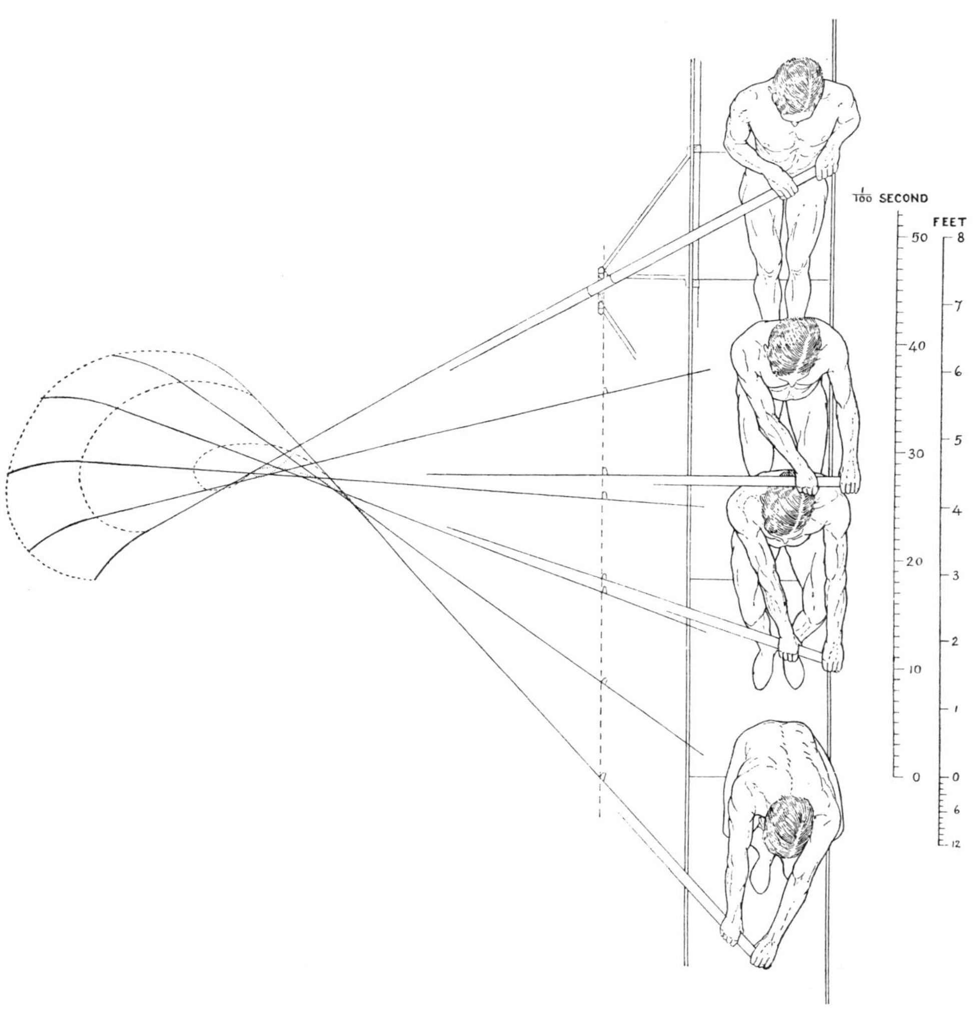

Fig. 15. A drawing showing the movements of the oarsman and oar in space during the stroke.

the oarsman has already begun to lift his body back and his slide has moved back an inch or so. Therefore he is not reached forward to the fullest extent and the oar is at an angle of 42°. In the second position the body is swung back to the perpendicular and the slide has been moved back about 5½ inches. The oar is at an angle of 72°. In the third position the arms have begun to bend, the body is swung back a trifle past the perpendicular, and the slide has been moved back a little more than 12 inches. The oar is now at 90°. In the final position the hands have come home to the body but are not yet dropped, the elbows are drawn back, the body and shoulders are swung back well past the perpendicular, and the slide is driven out to its full extent of 16 inches. The oar is now at 120°, and it should be noticed that at this angle the hands come in to the body in a position convenient for the recovery. At a greater angle the outside forearm and wrist would come too far across the body and the elbow would be stuck out. It will be observed that both at the beginning and the finish the oarsman is not swinging quite straight, but is leaning a trifle away from his oar. This is because what is miscalled 'the leverage', i. e. the distance from the centre of the seat to the thowl, is 31 inches, and the oar is 3 ft. 9 in. inboard. With an oar of this length inboard the spread of the outrigger should be 32 inches. The oarsman might have reserved rather more than 3½ inches of slide to finish out with, otherwise the drawing shows the correct positions of the body and slide in relation to the movement of the oar. The drawing also gives a clear idea of the distance in space through which an oarsman moves in the course of the stroke and of the relative speeds at which the body and hands are moving in the successive phases of the stroke. Finally, the drawing shows that the motion of the oar as worked out theoretically in this chapter is consistent with the most approved manner of combining the actions of body, slide, and arms.

CHAPTER IV

THE ART OF ROWING

THE RECOVERY AND SWING FORWARD

εἰδήσεις δὲ καὶ αὐτὸς ἐνὶ φρεσὶν ὅσσον ἄρισται
νῆες ἐμαὶ καὶ κοῦροι ἀναρρίπτειν ἅλα πηδῷ.

It is a hackneyed quotation, but worth repeating if only to remind my readers that rowing is one of the oldest arts in the world. The Phaeacians were masters of the oar and prided themselves on their style as well as on their boats. The theory of rowing relates mostly to the instruments and the maximum efficiency that can be got out of them. The art relates almost wholly to the man who supplies the motive power which sets the instruments in motion. The art of rowing, like all other arts, is founded upon rules, the outcome of long experience. The rules existed long before any theory was formulated, but if they are good rules, they must conform to true theory. My excursion into the realm of theory assures me that the rules accepted by the best English oarsmen are good, and that there is a certain shape and sequence of bodily movement that is to be preferred above all others. So this chapter is dogmatic. Its main purpose is to insist, and to go on insisting, on the necessity of obeying the rules.

When he has taken his seat in the boat and before he is called upon to come forward, the oarsman should make sure that he is sitting comfortably in the correct position. Cricketers and golfers pay great attention to their 'stance', that is to say to the position they assume preparatory to entering into action. The oarsman should be no less attentive to his position, but, as he is not standing but sitting, one must speak of his seat rather than of his stance. There is, however, this much in common between oarsmen, cricketers, and golfers: that in each case the arms seem to be the primary agents in the effort they are about to make, but in reality the effectiveness of their effort will depend upon the use of their feet.

The oarsman should be squarely seated on his buttocks, not on his tail. The body, even when he is at the easy, should be comfortably upright, but not stiffened or strained in any way: its weight well balanced on the seat. The straps should be fairly tight round the insteps; the heels close together; the toes turned out as far as the straps will allow: that will be at an angle of about 45°. The heels and soles of the feet should be pressed flat against the stretcher, and the oarsman, by slightly swinging his body and moving his slide backwards and forwards, should test his position and make sure he can readily bring his balance on his feet. The shoulders should be square, but entirely without constraint. The back of the blade should rest lightly on the surface of the water. The handle of the oar should be held lightly in the fingers; the outer hand close to the end of the oar; the inner hand about four inches from the outer; the wrists below the level of the knuckles, as the oar is in the position of the feather. The oarsman should make sure that his hands are right before starting to row. The knuckles of both hands should be parallel with the long axis of the oar; the oar held lightly between the thumb and first two fingers of each hand, but not grasped in the palm. When the oar is at right angles to the boat the wrists should be bent very slightly outwards from the middle line. On no account should the grasp of the oar be taken with the little and ring fingers of either hand. The head should be naturally poised on the neck: the chin up, and neither head nor neck poked forward. When the oarsman is comfortably seated in the easy position an imaginary vertical plane passing between his heels and fork should divide his body and head into equal halves. That is what is meant by 'sitting square to one's work'.

When the oarsman is sitting easy as above described and the boat is at rest, it should never be allowed to go off an even keel. Though the hands are inactive they still control the balance of the boat and must maintain just so much pressure as to prevent any lopsidedness or lurch. A crew that allows its boat to lie over to one side or to roll about when easied, has already stamped itself as third-rate before ever it sets about rowing. Finally, when at the easy, every member of a crew should be alert to obey instantly every instruction of the coxswain. In a strong stream or a high wind, failure to do instantly what the coxswain requires may get the boat into difficulties, with the risk of breaking an oar against the bank or getting in the way of another passing crew.

If I seem to lay unnecessary stress on all this, it is because inexperienced oarsmen are apt to be very slovenly in a boat, and they lose more than they know by being so. One of the best oarsmen that I have known, the late Mr. L. R. West, used to make a point of sitting upright in a correct position whenever the boat was easied, and he attached great importance to it. I have always found that to settle myself comfortably and correctly on my seat, and to get the feel of myself, and of the balance of the boat when easied, was of great assistance in starting me on the right course of action when called on to paddle or to row. The posture of the body and limbs can be adjusted when they are still. Once the oarsman has started upon the continuous movement of the stroke he is never in the same posture for two moments together. Therefore the rule is, look to your position when easied ; to your movements when actually engaged in rowing.

In starting a boat the coxswain's normal words of command are : 'Get ready : come forward : are you ready ? Paddle' (or 'Row', as the case may be).

On the command, 'Get ready', the oarsman, who may have been sitting very much at ease, should promptly assume the position described in the preceding paragraphs, and if he is a novice, should consciously correct the positions of his hands, feet, and body. It is only after long experience that he will have learnt to assume the correct positions instinctively.

On the word, 'Come forward', he should bend the body forward from the thigh-joints; straighten out the arms without boring forward his shoulders; bring the slide up to the front-stop, and be braced up, ready and alert, but not in any way stiff or constrained. Normally the back of the blade of the oar should rest lightly on the surface of the water: always when starting against the stream. It is only when starting from a stake boat on a down-stream course that the blades are squared in the water to take the resistance of the current at the word, 'Are you ready?' Experienced oarsmen know this, but I have seen College crews turn their blades half over and lift them off the water at the word, 'Are you ready?' It is impossible to keep the boat steady under these conditions, and steadiness and accuracy at the start are all-important. On the word, 'Paddle' (or 'Row'), the oarsman should promptly and neatly engage the oar in the water by raising the inside wrist and forearm, and without a moment's hesitation should bring both feet to bear on the stretcher and lift back the body from the loins. Too much importance cannot be attached to starting the first effort from the feet. If a man begins from his feet he will probably stay on his feet for the rest of the row. If he starts by pulling with his arms and shoulders, the chances are that he will go on pulling with arms and shoulders till ordered to easy.

A discussion of the art of starting and getting a boat under way may be deferred to another chapter. We will suppose that the boat has been started and is settled down to a normal rate of paddling, and will attempt to describe and analyse the various movements of the stroke.

In the year 1875, Dr. Warre printed for private circulation at Eton his famous *Notes on the Stroke*. Second and third editions, emended and corrected to include the use of increasing lengths of slide, appeared in 1880 and 1898. For vigour, clearness, and brevity, these notes cannot be surpassed, and I had intended to repeat and utilize them as the basis of a more elaborate analysis of the movements of rowing, but have found it necessary to abandon my original intention and to substitute my own epitome of the stroke. Dr. Warre was never familiar with the use of long slides, and probably, to the end of his days, looked upon them with disapproval. Hence his notes, admirable as they are, represent the application of the principles of fixed-seat rowing to short sliding-seats, rather than the accumulated experience of the last forty years in the use of long slides. Other treatises have appeared dealing in detail with the principles of sliding-seat rowing, and with most of these I am more or less in agreement, but they suffer, in comparison with Dr. Warre's notes, in being too diffuse for the purpose of the practical oarsman. I have therefore attempted, with how much success my readers must judge, to follow Dr. Warre's example by writing an epitome of the stroke ; so concise that it can be committed to memory and utilized in broad outline by coach and oarsman alike, without undue emphasis on detail, which is apt to confuse both instructor and instructed if too frequently and too lengthily insisted upon.

The epitome is followed by an analysis in which the details of movement and position are treated with as much length as seems necessary to explain fully the reasons for the methods that are recommended, and to establish a theory of modern oarsmanship in the English style on a sound basis of physical fact and common sense. I have endeavoured to supply that practical insight into the nature and order of succession of the twenty-seven (or more) distinct points or *articuli* of the stroke without which, Dr. Warre insisted, no one should attempt to coach any crew, or indeed any individual, however rudimentary that individual's knowledge of rowing may be.

My epitome further differs from Dr. Warre's in that I recognize three phases in the stroke : the stroke in the water, the recovery, and the swing forward. On a fixed seat the swing forward cannot be dissociated from the recovery. It is the movement of the slide that introduces a third phase. But in all that follows it must be borne in mind that the body should never stop still. The movements of the oarsman are continuous, and one phase passes into another without any break of continuity.

It is convenient to begin the description of the stroke with the recovery. It is assumed that the oar has come home with the hands and body in the correct positions : the lower part of the body firm and upright ; the shoulders drawn back ; the elbows bent and carried well back past the sides ; the fingers of both hands well hooked round the handle of the oar and pulling on it as long as the blade remains in the water ; the inside wrist well arched ; the outside wrist somewhat flatter. The knees are assumed to have been well flattened down and the heels of both feet driven firmly into the stretcher to support the body and drive out the last part of the stroke. Starting from this point the epitome of the stroke is as follows :

The moment the thumbs touch the body drop the hands smartly straight down, but not more than is sufficient to bring the blade clear out of the water ; then turn the oar on the feather by sharply flattening the wrists, and at once straighten the elbows so as to carry forward the hands in a straight line to the front ; simultaneously, by an elastic movement of the hips, incline the body forwards from the thigh-joints, allowing the knees to relax a little, but not so much as to bring forward the slide. As soon as the oar and the body have been recovered in this way, without any break in the continuity of the movement, carry on the forward swing of the body from the thigh-joints and allow the knees to bend steadily upwards so as to bring forward the slide, taking care that the body is always travelling in advance of the slide. Let the stomach and chest come well forward, the lower part of the body pressed towards the thighs, the back bending down in one piece from the seat and kept as nearly straight as it can be without constraint ; the head held up, the eyes fixed on the outside shoulder of the man in front. The elbows should be straight, the arms allowed to swing freely upwards from the shoulder-joints to compensate the downward movement of the body during the swing ; the

oar held lightly between the fingers and thumbs and not pressed upon, the weight of the arms alone being sufficient to maintain the blade in its proper straight line as it goes back ; the button of the oar lightly pressed against the sill of the rowlock ; the wrists depressed a little below the level of the knuckles. The shoulders, though slightly braced back, should not be stiffened and should partake of the free swing forward of the loins. As the slide comes forward the knees should open out evenly from the middle line, just sufficiently to make room for the stomach but not so far as to shift the position of the feet on the stretcher, the forward movement of the body and slide being regulated by the uniform bending movements of the knees and ankles and by the pressure of the feet on the stretcher. As the hands pass forward over the feet the oar should be turned neatly off the feather by raising the inside wrist and forearm, allowing the handle to come into the grasp of the inner side of the palm of the hand but without shifting the position of the fingers ; keep the outside wrist flat and the fingers of the outside hand securely hooked round the handle of the oar. As the body and slide come forward to their full extent the soles and heels of both feet should be pressed against the stretcher, the shins nearly vertical, the knees close below the armpits, the thigh-joints bent to their fullest extent, the flanks and ribs pressed close against the thighs. Both body and slide should slow up till they come to the momentary full stop necessary for the reversal of the forward movement. At this instant the weight of the hands and arms on the handle of the oar is released ; there is a prompt, decisive uplift of the hands, during which, without the loss of a thousandth part of a second, the action of the body and slide must be reversed by springing back from the stretcher. The initial impulse should come from the feet, the heels being

driven well home, and the weight of the body must be lifted back from the thighs by a swift and strong action of the loins so that the trunk springs back to the perpendicular during the first four or five inches of the backward travel of the slide. During this action the fingers of both hands should be firmly hooked round the handle of the oar, but all tightening of the grasp must be avoided ; the arms are straight, being pulled taut by the resistance of the water to the blade of the oar, and the shoulders must be kept firm but not stiff. The blade having gripped hold of the water and the beginning of the stroke having been effected as described, the stroke must be continued by forcibly pressing down the knees, so as to drive back the slide and maintain the backward swing of the body in conjunction with it, the loins and back being held firm, so that the oar is driven through the water with a force unwavering and uniform. As the wrists pass over the knees, the shoulders should be drawn back; the upper arms carried well past the sides; the elbows allowed to bend and drop to the rear; the wrists allowed to arch to compensate for the bending of the elbows. While the arms are bending home, maintain the pressure on the blade of the oar to the last moment by flattening down the knees and swinging the body back a little, but not far, past the perpendicular. At the finish of the stroke, the shoulders should be drawn well back; the chest should be displayed to the front but not stiffened or puffed out; the lower part of the body held firm and upright but not artificially strained; the roots of the thumbs, not the knuckles, touching the body a little below the breast-bone. From this position the movements of recovery are promptly recommenced.

I fear that my epitome falls far short of Dr. Warre's in the virtue of brevity and in that respect is inferior to his, for it is not so easily committed to memory. But I do not think that I have put in anything that can conveniently be left out. The twenty-seven distinct points or *articuli* of the stroke distinguished by Dr. Warre have been increased to forty-five, and nearly all the additions relate to the use of the slide. The matter being so complicated I trust that I may be exonerated from the charge of want of conciseness.

Passing to the detailed analysis of the movements, I should explain, in the first place, that although the treatment of muscular action in rowing has been relegated to a special chapter, it is not possible to analyse, or to give reasons for, the various movements of the oarsman, without some reference to human anatomy. But it is not to be expected that all coaches, still less all oarsmen, should have an expert knowledge of anatomy, and I have therefore endeavoured to exclude technical terms and considerations as far as possible from the following pages. Where necessary, reference is made to the anatomical figures and explanations contained in the 12th and 13th chapters. The reader who wishes to obtain a real insight into the theory of oarsmanship is recommended to study these chapters closely, for it is not possible for any one ignorant of the elements of the structure and functions of the human body to superintend and direct a complicated sequence of muscular movements. Let it be understood, however, that the acquisition of a limited range of anatomical knowledge is only for the purpose of understanding the why and the wherefore of the rules of the art of oarsmanship. A coach who should attempt to instruct his pupils by telling them to use this or that group of muscles at particular parts of the strokes would justly incur the resentment of his crew and would court the failure that attaches to pedantry.

Beginning with the movements of the recovery, there are two distinct sets of movements : the recovery of the oar, and the recovery of the body. Under the heading of the recovery of the oar we include : the extraction of the blade from the water ; the turn on the feather ; and the start of the blade on its course backward. All this is accomplished by the use of the wrists and elbows ; the shoulders should take no share in the recovery of the oar. As a preliminary to the correct movements of the wrists, it is necessary that the oar should not be grasped tight in the fists as it approaches the body, and that the wrists should be arched, so that the roots of the thumbs and not the knuckles touch the body when the oar comes home. When the movements of the recovery begin it is important that the proper sequence should be observed. *First,* the hands are dropped smartly straight down ; *then* the wrists are turned ; *lastly* the hands are shot out in a straight line to the front. The thing, if well done, is done in a moment, but the proper sequence must not be sacrificed to rapidity of execution.

The object of the drop of the hands is to lift the blade of the oar square and clean out of the water and to lift it at once to the full height of the feather that is to follow. It is not necessary to feather high, except in very rough water. As the oar is more than twice as long outboard as it is inboard, a small movement at the end of the handle produces a considerable movement of the blade. Therefore the drop should not be exaggerated. It should be distinct, sharp and precise, but it need not be large. It is customary to use the word 'drop' to describe the action of the wrists in the recovery, and I have followed the usual practice, but am not sure that the word is not misleading. It is no passive fall of the weight of the hands that we are dealing with, but a smart and vigorous tap downwards, sufficient to overcome the excess of some four and a half pounds of weight of the oar outboard. The tap should be delivered chiefly with the palm of the outside hand because, not only has it the greater advantage in leverage, but in consequence of their position at the finish the two hands are unequally adapted to the movements of the recovery, and there is a natural and appropriate division of labour between them. The inside wrist, being fully arched, is in a disadvantageous position for tapping the handle of the oar downwards, but in a highly advantageous position for turning the oar. The outside wrist, being flatter, is in an appropriate position for dropping, but not for turning. To effect the drop, as soon as the thumbs touch the body, the fingers of the outside hand release their hold and the handle of the oar is instantly struck sharply downwards by the palm of the same hand, the centre of effort being the fleshy pads at the bases of the fingers. During the action the wrist should be kept firm and the forearm, wrist, and hand should move down from the elbow as from a hinge. It is a common fault to depress the forearm but to allow the wrist to go slack as the fingers release their pull on the oar, the result being that the wrist is lowered and the blade of the oar turned before it is lifted out of the water. Hence a feather under water or, at the best, a ' dirty finish '. The whole of this movement—a very small one—is done from the elbow. On no account should the upper arm and shoulder take any share in it.

The moment the oar is tapped down by the outside hand the inside wrist, which has followed the downward motion of the handle of the oar, is smartly flattened, the necessary turning movement of the handle being ensured by a momentary pinch or grip between the thumb and first two fingers of the inside hand. The outside hand takes but little share in turning the oar on the feather, but the wrists of both hands must act in unison : therefore the outside wrist is flattened down at the same time as the inside, but not so much, as it has never been arched to the same extent. If the movements of the drop and turn are performed correctly and in the right sequence the blade of the oar will be lifted square out of the water and turned so sharply on the feather that the last drops clinging to it will be flicked clean over the blade in the direction in which the boat is travelling. To sum up, the outside hand is mainly the dropper, the inside hand the turner ; but both hands should act together in extracting the blade and turning it on the feather. That this is the right principle I have no doubt : it was taught at Eton in my days and had the sanction of such eminent authorities as Dr. Warre and Mr. T. C. Edwards-Moss. It may be observed, in passing, that in the seventies and early eighties of last century we got our hands away much quicker than oarsmen ever do nowadays. We were expected to and did row a fast stroke. To be able to spurt at 48 without throwing up water was considered to be the acme of good oarsmanship, and we achieved it, largely because we were able to recover the oar with lightning-like speed, and so gain time for a controlled swing forward. But in this connexion a word of warning is necessary. Precision and accuracy are prerequisite to quickness of movement. The beginner must learn to drop first and turn afterwards, using the wrists correctly, and distributing the work between the two hands. As he learns correctness of action, he will acquire command of the oar, and can increase the speed. But he must not be encouraged to put the cart before the horse, and to practise speed in the hope that correct action will follow. Of a certainty it will not.

The beginner should also be taught to realize that the drop and turn of the hands are the essential things in the recovery of the oar ; the shoot away of the hands, though important, is a secondary matter. The blade must be extracted in the least possible fraction of time, with perfect precision and certainty, or there is the ever-recurring danger of catching a crab, especially in an eddy or in rough water. When the oarsman has lifted his blade clear of the water and turned it on the feather he is in no danger of any such accident, and the subconscious knowledge that he has the skill to clear his blade will react favourably on his movements at the finish of the stroke.

The shoot out of the hands to the front is accomplished, in the simplest possible manner, by smartly straightening the elbows. The action, when performed properly, is effected by the rapid contraction of the triceps muscles of the upper arms (see p. 314). The shoulders should take no part in it save that, as the elbows straighten, the upper arms should be allowed to swing freely up to a nearly horizontal position from the shoulder-joints. On no account should the shoulders be thrust forward after the arms. I must repeat, the shoot away of the hands is of secondary importance. The novice should not try to shoot away his hands quickly until he has mastered the correct sequence of the drop and turn and can perform these very important actions with promptitude and precision. In due time, when he is called upon to row a fast stroke, he must learn to make a quick shoot away of the hands follow on the drop and turn, and when he is quite proficient, the three movements will follow so rapidly on one another that they seem to be blended into one. But let him beware of trying to run before he has learned to walk. If he sets himself prematurely to shoot away his hands at a great pace he will, for a certainty, contract faults which no amount of subsequent coaching will be able to eradicate.

It is further to be remarked that there is a certain proportion between the pace at which the hands are shot away and the rate of the stroke. The lightning-like action necessary to clear the hands at forty strokes a minute and more is an exaggeration when paddling at twenty-six. Some famous oarsmen—I recall Col. W. A. L. Fletcher as an example—have been very deliberate in the recovery. But he was always scrupulously accurate in the sequence of the movements and could quicken his action to any required extent when called upon to row a fast stroke.

I venture to say that there is no movement in the stroke that is so commonly made a mess of as the recovery of the oar. Nearly all the errors committed, and they are many, may be traced to three cardinal faults, namely : grasping the oar too tight in the fists during the drop and turn ; exaggerating the scope of the movements ; trying to push away the oar by a forward thrust of the shoulders. These in turn may be traced back to a subconscious and quite mistaken conviction on the part of the oarsman that an oar is a cumbrous instrument requiring much force to set it in motion. Probably enough a pardonable mistake, founded on his experience of clumsily made and ill-balanced oars served out to him in the first few weeks of his apprenticeship. The captain of a well-organized boat club should take care that the veriest novice is supplied with a properly balanced oar. At rowing schools, young boys who are far from having acquired their full muscular development should be supplied with light oars, carefully balanced to relieve their wrists and arms of any undue exertion. Early experience leads to fixed mental habits, and it will be difficult to persuade a man, whose first attempts were a struggle with clumsy weapons, to rid himself of the notion that a big effort is required for the recovery. From the earliest stages the novice should be taught to realize that his grasp of the oar should be secure, yet so light as to afford the utmost freedom of play to the wrists. The requisite combination of firmness and delicacy of grasp may be conveniently illustrated by a fencer's grasp of his foil. It must be so firm as to prevent its being struck out of his hand, yet so delicate as to admit of lightning-like play of the wrist. An oar is a larger and heavier instrument than a foil, and in rowing both hands are brought into use, but the quickness of wrist required is scarcely less in rowing than in fencing. The oarsman can easily convince himself of the pernicious effect of grasping the oar tight in the fists by simply doing it, and then trying to go through the motions of the recovery. He will find that, in proportion to the intensity of his grip, the wrists lose their mobility : they are cramped by the muscular effort of the forearm and can only be moved so slowly and awkwardly that the upper arm and shoulder are perforce brought into action to thrust the oar-handle away from the body. It is important that the novice, when receiving instruction in the tub-pair, should have all this explained and practically illustrated to him. He should be made to realize how little effort of the arms is required to perform the movements of the recovery; how greatly the quickness and neatness of those movements are dependent on economy of effort. Exaggeration of the scope of the movements, leading to an unduly high feather and extra pressure on the rowlock, with accompanying unsteadiness of the boat, is only another instance of want of economy of effort. It has already been shown that the fault of forcing the oar away with the shoulders is the almost inevitable result of an unduly tight grasp of the oar, so we come to the conclusion that practically all errors of movement in the recovery are traceable to the habit of clinging on to the oar-handle as if for dear life. Finally the novice must be convinced, by precept and illustration, that if he forcibly thrusts forward his shoulders during the recovery he will give an impetus to the top of his body which he will afterwards be powerless to check. In short, he will have started that hurried and uncontrolled swing forward which is familiarly known as ‘ bucket ’.

It cannot be too strongly insisted on that the impetus for the recovery of the body is not obtained by the shoot away of the hands. The effort involved in thrusting the oar forward must tend to push back the body in the opposite direction. In fact, if the shoot away is properly performed, it has a certain steadying effect on the forward movement of the trunk and shoulders. The recovery of the body is effected simultaneously with the shoot away of the hands, and is a function of the hips, not of the shoulders. It is most difficult to make the oarsman realize that the forward movements of the hands and the body, though simultaneous, are quite independent of one another : that the shoulders and upper part of the trunk are not carried forward by the motion of the oar-handle, but by the muscular action of the loins. The correct method of recovering the body from the thigh-joints is rendered more difficult to explain because the muscles upon which the action depends are hidden deep in the body, behind and below the intestines, and their very existence is unknown to all but fairly expert anatomists. I have given detailed drawings and descriptions of these muscles and their attachments to the back-bone, hip-bones, and thigh-bones in Chapter XIII, p. 320, and the coach who would gain a practical insight into the movements of the body during the recovery and swing forward should study these pages with some care. It is sufficient to say, in the present place, that a correct recovery and swing forward depend upon the movement of the massive hip-bones known to anatomists as the pelvis.

To make himself aware of the position of his pelvis and of his power of moving it, the oarsman, when sitting in a tub-pair, should insert his thumbs into the upper part of the pockets of his shorts the fingers turned backwards and downwards and grasping his flanks. Pressing with his thumbs he will feel on either side a large bone, and moving his thumbs backward and a little upward, he will discover on either side the curved upper edge, the iliac crest, of the large iliac bone which forms the largest part of the pelvis. Maintaining his grasp of the iliac crests, let him bend forward the upper part of his body from the waist by contracting the superficial muscles of the front of the abdomen. He will find that the iliac crests have been hardly, if at all, moved forward ; that his back is rounded, his stomach hollowed, and the upper part of the trunk with the shoulders is doubled forward towards his knees. This, it need hardly be said, is the wrong method of bringing the body forward, but nevertheless the method adopted by ninety-nine men out of a hundred when they first begin to row, and by far too large a proportion of oarsmen who consider themselves proficient.

Now let the oarsman, maintaining the grasp of his flanks as before, make a conscious effort to push forward towards his thighs the iliac crests which he is grasping. He will find that the small of his back follows the forward movement of the iliac crests, carrying with it the upper part of the trunk, so that the whole body is brought forward in one piece : the stomach protruded and pressed against the thighs, the chest well to the front, the back more or less flat, the tail (or coccygeal bone) lifted a little off the seat, the shoulders unconstrained and capable of being braced back a little as the body comes forward. In short, he will discover that by pushing the iliac crests forward he can swing down the body in the position demanded by his coach. Furthermore, he will find that he can make this movement without any aid from his toe-straps, and that in making it he pitches the balance of his body on his feet. Having made this discovery, and directed his attention to that part of his anatomy which must be moved in order to get the correct action, the oarsman should follow it up and assiduously practise the movement ; a thing which he can conveniently do in the privacy of his room, sitting on a low seat with his feet on the fender or some other support in lieu of a stretcher. There is nothing forced or unnatural about this action of the pelvis. It takes place, quite unconsciously, whenever one is seated in a low easy chair and leans forward preparatory to getting up. The difference is that, in rising from a chair, one first of all draws back the feet and bends the knees. In rowing the legs remain extended at full length during the recovery of the body, and it is this difference in the attitude of the legs which makes the action of pushing forward the iliac bones seem unfamiliar and difficult. Practice soon habituates the oarsman to performing it correctly and easily under new conditions. It is not out of place to explain here that the muscles which pull the iliac crests and the small of the back (that is the lower part of the vertebral column) forward are attached to the lowermost vertebrae of the backbone and to the iliac crests and pass down along the inner or concave sides of the iliac bones to their insertions on the upper ends of the thigh-bones. Their action is to draw the pelvis towards the thighs when the latter are fixed or, conversely, to raise the thighs towards the pelvis when the latter is fixed. Hence it is necessary to fix the thighs ; in other words, to keep the knees down during the recovery of the body. I have been at pains to give as clear and simple an account as possible of this group of muscles, known as the ilio-psoas group, in Chapter XII, and recommend coaches and oarsmen alike to take the trouble to master the somewhat difficult details of their arrangement.

I have said that it is necessary to keep the knees down during the recovery of the body. This apparently simple statement requires some qualification. At the finish of the stroke the knees should be pressed down quite flat, and should remain flat while the hands are being dropped and turned. But as soon as the hands shoot away and the body is simultaneously started on its recovery, the knees should be allowed to relax a little. Not sufficiently to start the slide forward, but just so much as to allow free play to the thigh-joints, which are the pivots on which the pelvis rotates. This point requires emphasis, for it is not very long since that sundry coaches of great reputation insisted on the knees being kept flat and pressed down during the recovery of the body. They were asking their pupils to achieve the impossible, and the consequences were deplorable, the more so because they insisted on the knees being kept quite flat whilst the body was being swung forward through a very considerable angle. This is an action which cannot be performed, because, in the act of straightening the legs and pressing the knees flat down, a number of accessory muscles are brought into use, whose united action is to fix and steady the thigh-bones in their sockets in the pelvis. Whilst they remain in action the hinge of the thigh-joints is, as it were, locked, and the lock must be released before the hinge can work. This can be demonstrated practically by any one who seats himself some 8 inches above the ground, with his legs extended straight in front of him, and tries to bring his hips forward. He will at once be aware of a feeling of constraint in his legs, and will find himself unable to move his hips forward to any extent. But, on raising his knees ever so little, the feeling of constraint vanishes, and the hips can be inclined forward from the thigh-joints in a perfectly easy and natural manner. We have here an example of false and perverse doctrine, based partly upon ignorance of anatomical fact, partly upon misapplication of a perfectly sound principle. It is quite right that the knees should be pressed down and the slide jammed against the back-stop until the blade is clear of the water. Therefore, it was argued, it is a good thing to keep the knees pressed down still longer to prevent the slide from slipping forward during the recovery of the body. But the argument took no account of the fact that, by the act of recovering his body, the oarsman passes into a reversed phase of movement incompatible with the muscular contractions necessary to keep the knees flat and exert a pressure in the direction opposite to that in which the body is now required to travel.

To sum up: *after* the blade is extracted from the water and turned on the feather and *while* the hands are shooting out to the front, the body must be recovered by a free and elastic action of the hips, the knees being allowed to relax and bend a little, but not so much as to start forward the slide. The ideal is that, as the body swings up to and some little distance beyond the perpendicular, the slide should cease to press against the back-stop, but should remain in contact with it.

The recovery is now completed and the oarsman's movements pass into the phase of the swing forward. I shall suggest (p. 165) that at the end of the recovery there should be a slight check—a steadying point—from which the forward swing of the body and the movement of the slide take their start. This suggestion must not be taken too literally. In early stages of practice, usually in the tub-pair, but also occasionally in the eight (or four), it will be found useful to make the oarsmen come to a dead stop at the end of the recovery, and then, after a short pause, set out on the swing and slide forward. This, however, is a species of drill or discipline, the purpose of which is to give the oarsman control over his movements and to check the ever-present tendency to rush forward after his arms. It has the same value as the goose-step, or going through the motions by numbers, in military drill. It teaches balance and control, and gives the recruit time to fix his attention on the movements he is performing. Too long a persistence in it induces stiffness and artificiality, and it should be discontinued as soon as the oarsman has learned to recover his body into balance without hurrying up his slide or diving forward his shoulders after his hands. But I maintain that every oarsman ought to be able to bring himself to a standstill at the end of the recovery when told to do so. If he cannot he has not acquired such control over his movements as will prevent him from bucketing forward when called upon to row or paddle at anything more than a lugubriously slow rate of stroke. In actual practice there should be no check or pause whatever at this or any other part of the stroke, but there should be an imaginary steadying point, a sort of mental check, at the end of the recovery which can be translated into an actual check on the word of command.

As the recovery passes into the swing forward the oarsman should strive to attain length of reach, not by stretching out his arms and shoulders, but keeping up the initial action of the hips at the recovery. He should continue to press forward his stomach and flanks towards his thighs, and as his body swings it should by its impetus start the slide on its travel forward. As the slide comes up the knees bend steadily, and gradually open out from the middle line, to a degree sufficient to make room for the stomach. All the way forward swing and slide should go in combination ; for every bit of swing a corresponding bit of slide and vice versa. It is all-important that the swing, which was started before the slide began to move, should be kept in advance of the slide throughout the movement.

It is a difficult matter to inculcate and even to describe a correct swing forward. It should be at once free and bold, smooth and balanced. It is the period of rest for the oarsman during which he is gathering energy for the next stroke. Therefore every unnecessary exhibition of energy should be avoided. The muscles of the back and shoulders should be relaxed, yet not so much as to produce limpness. The oarsman should understand that in ordinary life, whether standing or sitting in a natural upright easy posture, there is a certain muscular effort required to maintain the upright attitude. Physiologists speak of a *tonic* contraction of the muscles, an effort of which we are unconscious, but of which we nevertheless recognize the existence when the nerve centres which originate and regulate the muscular contractions are by any means put out of action. For example, when fainting a man falls limp and lifeless to the ground, even from a sitting position. This muscular tone must be preserved, and in early stages of practice must be almost consciously preserved, throughout the swing forward. The difficulty is that so many oarsmen will rush into extremes. Told to relax the muscles of the back, they obey instructions so literally that they nearly inhibit the tonic contraction necessary to maintain an upright posture. Their backs bend, the shoulders become flaccid and fall forward, the head drops down; in short, they are 'all of a heap'. Conversely, when told to sit up, they forcibly contract the muscles of both the back and front of the body; assume a rigidity of attitude that prevents any freedom of swing, and waste much valuable energy in setting opposing groups of muscles into action. They exhaust themselves by doing work upon their own bodies, but this work has no effect on the propulsion of the boat.

It is difficult to deal with men who insist upon exaggerating the instructions of their coach. Some seem to be wilfully perverse in this matter, but all but the most obstinate can generally be set right when they are made to realize that all that is required is consonant with common sense and common experience. During the swing forward the body and shoulders must be so far braced up to their work that the back is not limp, the shoulders and head not allowed to drop forward. But there must be no muscular effort in the sense of straining the muscles of the back and shoulders against their opponents on the other side of the body. In short, throughout the swing forward the body and shoulders must be in an easy, natural, unconstrained position, but none the less elastic and alert.

The proper combination of swing and slide forward presents many difficulties. It is a besetting sin, even with experienced oarsmen, to pull up the slide by dragging at the straps with their toes. The moment they begin to pull on the straps they check the swing of the body: the slide arrives prematurely at the front-stop and there is still a considerable angle for the body to be swung through. But as the knees are now raised to their fullest extent it is extremely difficult, if not impossible, to continue forward the swing of the hips and lower part of the trunk, so the oarsman makes the best of a bad situation by doubling his shoulders over his knees; then he is both 'short' and 'overreached'. Often enough, to avoid overreach, he omits the unfinished part of the swing altogether. In order to cure this it was the practice, in the first decade of the present century, to teach men to swing their bodies to the fullest possible extent forward before bringing up the slide. This was rushing to the opposite extreme, and the results were not happy. For, having swung down his body as far as possible, the oarsman, when he began to slide forward, found that the room required for his rising thighs was already occupied by his body. As it is impossible for two such solid objects as thighs and body to occupy the same locus in space at one and the same time, the difficulty had to be surmounted somehow, and different individuals adopted different methods of surmounting it. Frequently they did not utilize the whole length of the slide forward. But whatever the compromise adopted, the last part of the slide forward was a cramped action : undue strain was thrown upon the legs, the hips were commonly pushed back a little as the thighs rose, and the position of the body and limbs at the full reach forward was unfavourable for springing back sharply from the stretcher. Much of the laborious action and ineffective effort that disfigured English amateur rowing at this period, and led to a succession of defeats at the hands of foreign crews at Henley, is to be attributed to this mistaken idea that the body should be swung to its fullest extent before the slide is started forward.

In general, if the body has been properly recovered by an elastic movement of the hips as prescribed above, the prognosis for a good slide and swing forward is favourable. But some oarsmen *will* stop the swing after the recovery and pull forward the slide by use of the toe-straps. Commonly enough they use one strap more than the other, and add a crooked swing to the vice of hurrying up the slide. The only remedy I know of is assiduous practice in a tub-pair with shortened slides and without straps. If the fault is obstinate recourse must be had to a fixed seat. In point of fact every beginner should learn to row on a fixed seat without straps, and should only be permitted the use of these aids (for they are not indispensable) when called on to row a moderately fast stroke. It must be admitted that, for those who have unfortunately learned to rely on them, rowing without straps is a severe form of discipline. But the coach should be inexorable and turn a deaf ear to protests that it is impossible to dispense with them. *Experto crede.* I myself when a boy had to row without straps under Dr. Warre, and when past middle age have rowed many miles without them, on full-length slides, in company with my son. We soon came to regard them as superfluities, at all events at a slow stroke. The lessons to be learned are: that a firm finish of the blade in the water is essential to proper balance of the body at the recovery; that the hips can readily be recovered and swung forward without the aid of the straps; but that efforts to dive forward the shoulders and swing the top to the exclusion of the lower part of the body end in disaster.

The impetus of the forward movement of the hips is quite sufficient, indeed it is more than sufficient, to bring up the slide. The slide's motion has to be steadied, and the only agents that can steady it are the legs. They are bedded on the stretcher, the one firm and fixed support that the oarsman has to rely upon. His action during the swing forward is in many respects comparable to that of a man stooping down to make a standing jump off the ground. In both actions the body is flexed on the thigh-joints; the buttocks are approximated to the heels; the knees and ankles are bent steadily, and, as they bend, they support and control the downward movement of the body. The end result in both cases is a rapid uplift of the weight of the body followed by a vigorous extension of the legs; in a word, a jump. In the swing forward the oarsman will do well to imitate the movements preparatory to a standing jump. Let him observe that, when stooping down to jump, he does not arch up his back nor thrust forward his shoulders. To do so would put him at a great disadvantage when the moment comes to spring up, so he naturally and unconsciously keeps his back flat and braces his shoulders as he should do when rowing. Let him further study, and make himself conscious of, the feeling of support and control afforded by his legs as the body stoops down to jump. The same sense of support and control should be felt in the legs as the slide and swing come forward in rowing. For the oarsman the stretcher is the solid ground from which he is to spring, and his legs are the masters and controllers of his slide and swing down. They, and they alone, can regulate the pace. The most experienced oarsman will find it necessary to study the steadiness and smooth action of his legs during the swing forward and through them to acquire mastery over the slide. Unskilful oarsmen play all sorts of tricks with their legs as they slide up. Some keep the knees close together, leaving no room for the stomach to come forward. This causes them to double the top part of the body over the knees and to assume an attitude inimical to a sharp spring back. Others spread out the knees too far, flattering themselves that by so doing they make more room for the body to come forward. But the structure of the thigh-joints and the attachments of the muscles to the hips and thigh-bones are such that, when the knees are turned out beyond a certain limit, the free action of the joints is impeded. The swing is actually shortened and the muscles used in springing back are at a disadvantage. Moreover, when the knees are spread out too far, only the outer and weaker sides of the feet can keep contact with the stretcher: thus the firm support on the solid ground is impaired. Individuals differ so much in width of hips and in length and proportion of limbs that it is not possible to lay down a hard and fast rule about the angle at which the knees should be turned out. But every oarsman can judge it for himself by again having recourse to the analogy of a standing jump. The position of his legs when fully stooped down for a jump is that which they should assume when he is full forward in a boat.

The common fault of turning out the knees at different angles is invariably due to pulling more with one foot than with the other on the straps. It should be corrected by teaching the oarsman not to rely on his straps. An unequal pull on the straps invariably produces a crooked swing of the body, but it does not necessarily follow that every form of crooked swing is the result of pulling unequally at the straps. The handle of the oar, in its movement forward, describes the segment of a circle, and there is always a tendency for the body to follow the oar and to swing down against the inside leg, even when the knees are turned out quite evenly from the middle line. This tendency is exhibited, in a more or less marked degree, even by first-class oarsmen, as may be seen by an examination of a number of instantaneous photographs. In the old days of fixed-seat rowing, and in the days of short slides that succeeded them, great importance was attached to swinging the trunk forward in a straight line and to keeping the shoulders square.

Dr. Warre in his *Grammar of Rowing* lays stress on the imaginary median plane which divides the oarsman's body into two equal halves and passes between his feet. In this plane the oarsman should keep his nose throughout the movements of the stroke. It is as important on a long as on a short slide, and as important on a short slide as on a fixed seat, to swing down the trunk in this median plane and not to twist round the loins in the direction in which the handle of the oar is travelling. If the body has been recovered and its farther swing forward maintained by drawing forward the hip-bones by the use of the ilio-psoas group of muscles, as explained above and in more detail in Chapter XIII, p. 320, and if the stomach and chest have been brought well forward and the knees turned out evenly from the middle line, there is little danger of screwing the body forward. By 'screwing' I mean twisting round the backbone in the region of the lower ribs. The proper position of the shoulders as the oarsman reaches out to his fullest extent is another matter. They should be braced and kept as square as possible. But, owing to the circular movement of the handle of the oar, they cannot be kept quite square, and the coach should be careful lest, by too much insistence on the ideal, he encourages his pupils to adopt rigid and artificial positions destructive of all freedom of movement.

Fig. 16 is copied from a photograph of an oarsman stretched out to nearly, but not quite, the full extent of the reach forward. The camera was fixed vertically above the model, and gives a view which under normal conditions is only possible for an observer stationed on a bridge and watching a crew passing beneath him.

The photograph shows the oar at an angle of 43·5° to the side of the boat, its extremity falling just within the mesial line drawn through the centre of the oarsman's body and between his heels. The inside arm is nearly parallel to the side of the boat, the inside wrist raised, and the inside shoulder a little drawn back. The outside hand is considerably in advance of the inside, and is stretched across to the inside of the centre of the body. In this position the raising of the inside wrist is insufficient to compensate for the greater reach demanded from the outside arm, so the outside shoulder has perforce been extended farther forward than the inside. If it were not, either the outside fingers must quit their hold of the oar, or the oar-handle must be brought much nearer to the body, reducing the reach forward. It should be observed that the photograph represents, not the full reach forward, but the beginning of the stroke, so the body has already been lifted back a little from the thighs and the shoulders drawn back. At the moment when the oar enters the water the angle of the oar to the boat would be more acute, the hands farther across the boat, and the outside shoulder necessarily more advanced than it is in the picture. In fine, it is impossible to reach out full forward on a sixteen-inch slide, and to maintain the grasp of the oar with the outside fingers, without extending the outside shoulder to some extent. The shoulders cannot be kept quite square, and it is contrary to reason that they should be; for the shoulder-joint is not supported by a rigid framework, nor immovably attached to the thorax, but is placed at the end of a lever formed by the collar-bone in front and the shoulder-blade behind, and is intended by nature to be thrust forward and drawn back with the movements of the arms. To keep the shoulders square to the thorax when the arms are extended as in rowing involves contraction of the opposing muscles of the back and the breast, and whilst the shoulders should be braced by a tonic contraction of these muscles, such as has been referred to above, any conscious contraction with the view of preserving squareness of the shoulders will nearly certainly be excessive and lead to rigidity, both of the shoulder-joints and of the thorax, which will be inimical to the free play of the arms and to the respiratory movements of the chest.

This is a matter in which the wise coach will exercise discretion, neither allowing his pupils to flop forward with limp shoulders, nor being so rigorous about exact squareness as to curtail freedom of action and prevent the assumption of an easy and natural position at the full reach forward. He should take notice that, if the shoulders are kept rigorously square, the oarsman cannot follow the forward movement of the oar, unless (1) he lets go the grasp of the fingers of the outside hand, or (2) unless he pulls the button of the oar away from the rowlock, or (3) unless he twists round his backbone so as to bring his shoulders and thorax facing half right (or half left as the case may be), with the shoulders parallel to the handle of the oar. In each case a fault involving loss of precision and power at the beginning of the stroke will have been induced by sacrificing the natural physiological action of the shoulders to a false ideal of symmetry. A fixed-seat oarsman, seated some 10 to 12 inches away from his work, cannot cause his oar to make a very acute angle with the side of the boat, and can therefore square his shoulders much more than an oarsman using a long slide. But even a fixed-seat oarsman must bring forward the outside shoulder to some extent, and for the

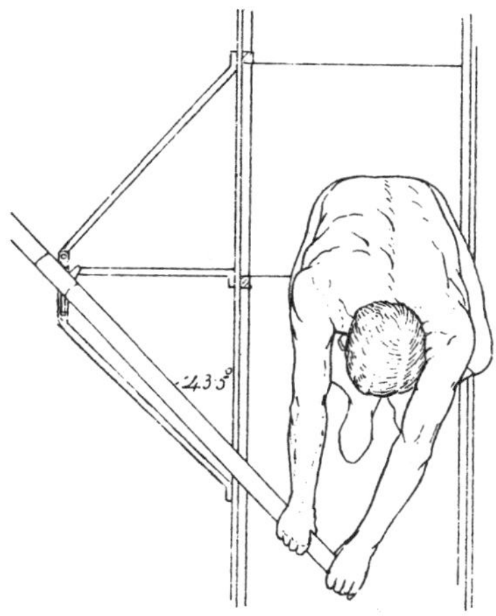

FIG. 16. A life study of an oarsman at the beginning of a stroke, as seen from a position vertically above his seat.

rest, the rules of fixed-seat rowing cannot be applied too rigorously to sliding-seats. The conditions are different. A moderate advancement of the outside shoulder does not involve an 'overreach'. An overreach is a conscious effort to add to the length of the stroke by thrusting forward both arms from the shoulders and bending the upper part of the trunk over the knees. Some very effective oarsmen, particularly in the decade preceding the war, exhibited a pronounced

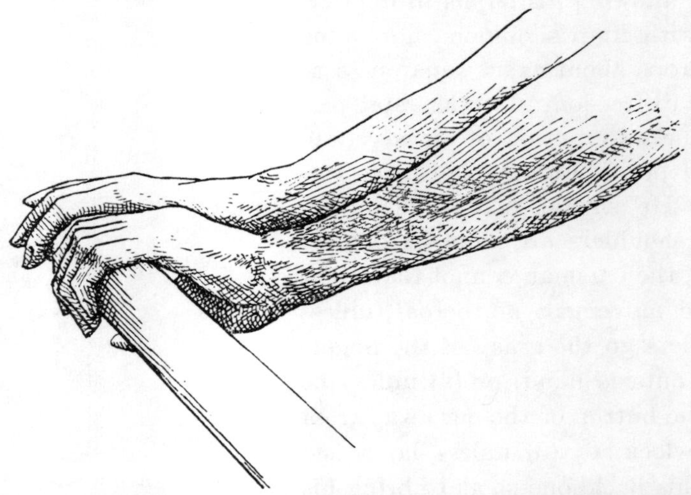

FIG. 17. The correct position of the hands and wrists during the feather.

overreach. They rowed a very long stroke and achieved great things. But it may be said, without fear of contradiction, that they lost as much as, or more than, they gained by the extra inches of reach forward, and some of the best of them suffered defeat from the New South Wales crew of 1912, which was conspicuous for its short forward reach.

In this connexion it must not be forgotten that, as the body swings down, the shoulders descend to a lower level, and that it is necessary, for the maintenance of an even feather, that the arms should swing upward as much as the shoulders descend. By no other means can the hands be maintained in their proper straight line as they go forward. To allow of this sympathetic upward swing of the arms they must have perfectly free play in the shoulder-joints, and this is hampered if the shoulders are either set rigid with the object of keeping them square, or strained forward in the attempt to get extra length of reach. The upward swing of the arms, compensating the downward swing of the body, is an important factor too often overlooked. Throughout the feather the button of the oar should be pressed pretty firmly against the sill of the rowlock. This is a useful aid to steadiness and

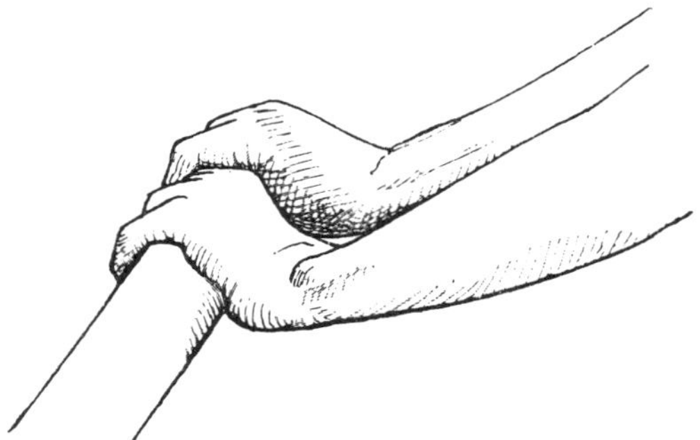

Fig. 18. Wrong position of the hands during the feather. The grasp is too tight and the wrists are depressed too much.

straightness of the swing forward of the body, and is of assistance in maintaining the feel of the boat as it runs between the strokes. In an eight-oar the coxswain should keep a sharp look-out on the buttons, and correct any oarsman who draws his away from the sill. It is a fault which can hardly be recognized by a coach on the bank.

As long as the blade is on the feather the wrists should be depressed below the level of the knuckles, as shown in fig. 17, and the oar should not be grasped in the palms of the hands as in fig. 18, but held lightly yet securely between the fingers and thumbs ; particularly between the first two fingers and thumb of each hand. The knuckles should be parallel to the long axis of the oar, and any grip with the little and ring fingers, tending to bring the knuckles obliquely across the oar, should be carefully avoided. The importance of holding the oar in the fingers and not in the fists has been emphasized again and again by Mr. W. B. Woodgate, and one cannot well be too emphatic on the subject. Both elbows should be straight—it is a very common fault to crook the inside elbow—and just so much pressure should be brought to bear on the handle of the oar as is necessary to maintain the blade in its proper straight line as it goes back. Any excess of pressure means a skied feather and an unsteady boat. When the novice takes his seat in an eight-oar he should be taught to realize he holds the balance of the boat in his hands as he swings forward. As long as eight pairs of hands are moving smoothly forward in the same horizontal plane, and eight oar-blades are sweeping evenly back at the same level above the water, the boat cannot roll from side to side. An old hand, even if his form is deficient in other respects, will have learned that every movement of the boat is communicated, through the handle of the oar, to his sense of touch. It should be the aim of the novice to cultivate this sense of touch, and to be responsive to any unevenness that he becomes aware of in the movement of the boat. It is the sensitiveness of touch of the hands that constitutes good watermanship. It is lost if the oar is gripped as might be the throat of an enemy.

Throughout the swing keep the eyes up and fixed on the outside shoulder of the man in front. Stroke should not make a study of the coxswain's feet, but should keep his eyes on some object well in rear of and to the off-side of the boat. If the eyes look down the head inevitably follows the line of sight. The shoulders follow the droop of the head, and very soon the oarsman is unconsciously bearing down on the handle of the oar and skying his feather. It may be taken as an axiom that eyes down mean heavy hands.

In my experience one of the most serious of the minor difficulties that confront the oarsman is to turn the blade neatly off the feather at the proper time. With the fixed rowlocks generally used in England it ought not to present any difficulty, for the button is cut to a shape which, provided that it is pressed well up to the sill of the rowlock, turns the oar to the required extent, and at the right time, without guidance from the hands. The coach should demonstrate this in the tub-pair by placing the palm of one hand flat against the end of the oar-handle and pressing the button against the sill. The pressure causes the oar to turn off the feather of its own accord.

In the actual movement of rowing all that the hands need to do is to follow the natural movement of the oar, the inside wrist and fore-arm being lifted above the level of the knuckles, and the oar allowed to come more into the inner or thumb side of the palm of the hand as it turns over. Take care that the knuckles are not forced down below the level of the wrist as the oar comes off the feather. It is important that the position of the fingers should not be shifted nor the grasp of the fingers tightened as the oar turns off the feather. When the action of the inside wrist is correct the distal joints of the fingers remain in exactly the same place as they were during the feather, and the oar, as it turns, seems to roll over into the angle between the thumb and first finger as the wrist is raised. The grasp is rather more secure, yet the pressure of the hand is if anything lightened. At the same time the outside wrist is raised just sufficiently to bring the wrist level with the knuckles, and the two first fingers of the outside hand should be well hooked round the oar, but the palm of the hand should not share in the grasp.

I have laid great stress on holding the oar lightly during the feather and in turning off the feather, but must guard against misinterpretation by insisting equally strongly that the wrists must not be limp nor the grasp nerveless. Many oarsmen think that they are carrying out instructions by shifting about the fingers. Often they will finger the oar-handle as if it were the keyboard of a piano, and that in a timid and hesitating matter, as though lightness of touch were synonymous with feebleness. The oar must be manipulated with the same firmness yet flexibility of hand as a cricket bat, a racket, or a golf club. The point is that it must not be gripped as though in a vice, but the grasp must be firm enough to maintain full control. The oar should turn off the feather pretty quickly, but without a jerk. Some authors have recommended that it should be turned off slowly and gradually. But this is surely wrong, for the shape of the button is such that, when it is pressed up to the sill, the oar turns quickly at the appropriate moment, and any attempt to counteract its natural movement is a piece of bungling interference. Moreover, it is essential that, when the blade is turned square, the button should engage in the working thowl of the rowlock. If the oar is turned gradually off the feather its loom remains close against the stopping thowl, and has to travel back to the working thowl as the blade enters the water. In this way a minute but valuable fraction of time is lost at the beginning of the stroke and, insignificant as it may seem, it involves an appreciable loss of firmness where firmness is most needed.

When reached out to the full extent forward on a sixteen-inch slide, the oarsman is doubled up in a very remarkable manner (figs. 20 and 34), and it requires long practice and training to enable him to assume the correct position without constraint. The soles of the feet and the heels should be firmly bedded on the stretcher ; the leg from knee to ankle should be nearly or quite vertical ; the thighs turned out just so far as to allow the knees to come up to the armpits. The flanks and ribs should be pressed as close as possible against the thighs. The head should be held up, but not strained or thrown back. The arms should be straight but not rigid, the inside wrist raised and the outside wrist flat ; the outside shoulder drawn a little forward, the inside shoulder kept a little back. The muscles of the body and limbs should be braced up and alert, ready for the effort that is to come, but opposing groups of muscles should on no account be set in action against one another. In brief, the oarsman should feel that he is gathered up and supported upon his feet, ready to spring.

In the matter of length of reach forward a coach should be exacting up to a certain limit, but should be careful that this limit is not over-

Fig. 19. THE OXFORD UNIVERSITY FOUR, 1869

stepped. The proper limit is a natural one, determined by the position of the thighs when the slide is brought up to the front-stop. Then the whole side of the body, the ribs and flanks from the armpit down to the hip-joint, should be squeezed as tight as possible against the thighs ; the knees being opened out just sufficiently to let the chest and stomach come well forward between the thighs. Farther than this the lower part of the body cannot go, and any attempt to transgress this natural limit must result in an overreach. For the extra length that many oarsmen seek to gain can only be attained by arching the dorsal region of the back and pushing forward the head, neck, and shoulders in the effort to carry the upper part of the body a bit farther beyond the knees (see fig. 34 'full forward'). An overreach is detrimental to precision of movement at the beginning of the stroke, and induces lack of uniformity of action in the crew as a whole, some men having to struggle much more than others to gain the extra bit of swing forward. The struggle is inimical to a good beginning and the want of uniformity is not compensated by any slight additional length of stroke attained. The reader is invited to compare figs. 19 and 20. The first shows the great length of forward reach attained by the best exponents of fixed-seat rowing as exemplified by the celebrated Oxford University Four of 1869. The bodies are inclined forward at an angle of nearly 47° from the vertical, and when in movement probably were swung still farther forward, the position of the knees on a fixed seat offering no obstacle to an even greater flexion of the hip-joints than could be attained when sitting in position for the photographer. Fig. 20 is taken from a snapshot of a celebrated oarsman of the period immediately preceding the war. The length of reach forward is phenomenal, the body being inclined at an angle of 51° from the vertical. The energy of action is apparent, but the

FIG. 20. An exaggerated reach forward.

overreach is pronounced. One would say that the oarsman could not avoid shooting his slide, but, as a matter of fact, this particular individual never shot his slide, though ninety-nine out of a hundred who might succeed in getting into such a position could hardly avoid doing so. Fig. 21 is a sketch from life to illustrate what I conceive to be the useful limit of the swing forward on a long slide. Here the body is inclined forward at an angle of 40° to the perpendicular and is pressed close against the thighs ; the head and neck are held up and the shoulders are not unduly stretched forward. The oarsman is clearly in a good position for springing back from the stretcher, and as he may swing back 25° past the vertical at the finish, he will have moved his body through an angle of 65°, a length of swing which will be found ample if every bit of it is co-ordinated with the movement of the slide. As a rough rule an oarsman may be told to put a knee into each armpit, but I do not think it necessary or desirable that his knees should go behind his armpits.

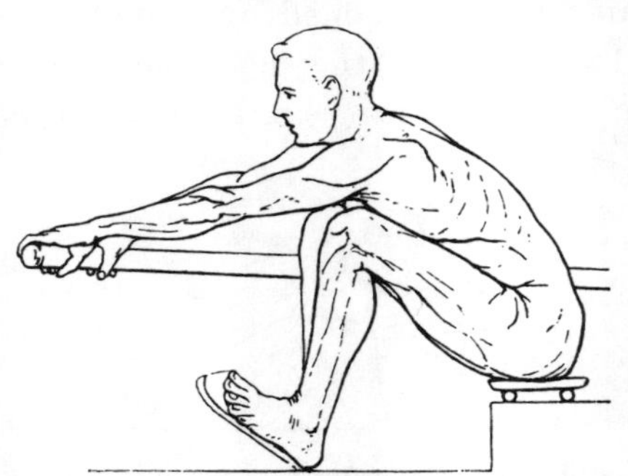

Fig. 21. The reach forward without overreach. In the absence of the gunwale the swing forward looks shorter than it really is.

In conjunction with all this it must be remembered that position is not everything. The most irreproachable position will be of no effect unless there exists along with it a high degree of alertness of mind. The oarsman must be mentally as well as physically ready to spring, and must be confident that he can and will make his effort promptly, at the right moment.

Nearly all beginners and not a few seasoned oarsmen find it difficult to bend their ankles sufficiently to keep their heels on the stretcher when full forward. They must not be allowed to plead incapacity, but must be made to persevere in the attempt to bend the ankles and keep the heels up. It is wonderful how much flexibility can be acquired by practice. In obstinate cases of stiff ankles recourse must be had to bending movements outside the boat. The lunging actions in fencing or sword exercise are valuable correctives of stiff ankles. Similarly, most oarsmen find great difficulty in bending forward the hips to the required extent. The old military exercise of bending down to touch the toes, while keeping the knees straight, is a specific for giving flexibility to the hips. But, as a general rule, exercises which simulate the movements of rowing are harmful. An oarsman's movements are conditioned by, and must harmonize with, the movement of the boat. Extraneous exercises and gymnastics can never reproduce the motion of a boat and, in my experience, invariably lead to disharmony between the man and the craft he is propelling. They also tend to piling up unwanted muscle in the wrong places, and as a result one may see a man with the arms and torso of a Hercules, yet lamentably incompetent to move as quickly as the pace of the boat demands.

Finally, it cannot be too strongly insisted upon that all the complex movements of the recovery and swing forward that have been analysed and considered in detail, must be blended together into one harmonious whole. The proper sequence must be observed, but there must be no fragmentation or syncopation. In a good crew the swing forward is a balanced and rhythmical, but a bold and continuous movement : arms, body, and legs all working together. Further, the swing should resemble that of the upstroke of a pendulum in so far that its velocity should diminish as it approaches its full limit.

CHAPTER V

THE ART OF ROWING

THE STROKE

Nearly all the actions hitherto described are but the preliminary to the all-important exhibition of energy that propels the boat through the water. The oarsman should have a clear conception of what is required of him when he makes his effort. He should understand, and be quite sure that he does understand, that he is not so much required to set water in motion and shovel it along past the side of the boat, as to stick the blade of his oar as firmly as he can into a given spot in the water and to lift the boat as far and as quickly as possible past that spot. His attention must be concentrated on moving the boat, not on stirring up the water.

The ways in which a boat may be propelled in one direction by using the oar to set a mass of water in motion in the opposite direction have been discussed at sufficient length in Chapter III. There we learned that, in order to obtain the nearest approach to the ideal of fixing the blade in the water, the boat's way must not be checked unduly, and the blade of the oar at entry must at one and the same time be thrust out from the boat and given angular acceleration. The simultaneity of the two movements, causing the blade to travel in a slight curve, convex in the direction of the advance of the boat and nearly at right angles to it (see figs. 11 and 12), is what constitutes the 'catch at the beginning'. To make sure of obtaining this firm catch hold of the water is the most difficult part of the oarsman's art. It demands great quickness and precision, together with the nicest possible adjustment of the movements of hands and body, lest the one should be an instant too soon or too late in relation to the other. It is only on this matter of how the beginning is caught that I am at variance with Dr. Warre's *Notes on the Stroke*. He wrote: 'As the body and arms come forward to their full extent, the wrists having been quickly turned, the hands must be raised sharply, and the blade of the oar brought to its full depth at once. At that moment, without the loss of a thousandth part of a second, the whole weight of the body must be thrown on the oar and on the stretcher, by the body springing back. . . .' It is my experience that a coach may repeat and vary the phrasing of these instructions *ad infinitum*, yet somehow, in ninety-nine cases out of a hundred, the required result is not produced.

Evidently there are two factors to take into consideration: the entry of the blade into the water, and the spring back from the stretcher. The great difficulty is to make the effort of the body correspond exactly in time with the entry of the blade.

The entry is effected by raising the hands sharply. Without a doubt they must be raised sharply, for if they are not the blade will not enter the water with the necessary speed. Yet, on any afternoon at Oxford, one may see crew after crew go by, the members of which are obviously and conscientiously 'raising their hands sharply' but failing by a long way to 'catch the beginning'. Something is wrong, and it is often hard to detect what that something is. Most usually close observation will show that the defaulting oarsman tightens his grasp on the oar at the moment when the blade should descend into the water. The extra grip depresses the oar-handle ever so little, or at all events prevents it from rising. The blade is either flicked up a little, or remains stationary above the surface of the water, and that at the moment when it should be descending and in the twinkling of an eye immersed and thrusting against the water. Consciously or subconsciously the oarsman is aware of this and with his tightened grip forces the arms upwards by an effort of the shoulders. The blade of the oar descends into the water with a splash, with a considerable amount of vertical but no horizontal impetus. For a moment it is actually retarding the boat and the back-splash is the accusing sign.

Another oarsman, when reached full forward, is unprepared for the spring back. He must pause for a moment to poise himself on the stretcher and adjust his shoulders before raising his hands and springing back. When he does raise his hands, he gets his weight on well enough, but is ' half a blade late '. The boat has moved on while he waits and his oar does not begin its work until it is approaching an angle of 50°. The opportunity of getting a firm grip by quasi-immobilization of the blade has been lost and cannot be overtaken.

A third oarsman springs back without having raised his hands. The blade travels obliquely down to the water and hits it hard when it enters it. But the first part of the stroke has been rowed in the air with all the attendant disadvantages described in Chapter III.

A fourth oarsman covers his blade quickly and neatly enough, but does not spring back with sufficient speed. He ' feels for the water ', and, as explained on p. 54, this means that for an appreciable period of time—it may be for as long as 0·088 second—he is making his blade travel no faster than the water is moving past it. He is reducing the speed of the boat in order to get his thrust, and when he does get it up goes a fine splash from the aft face of his blade, which often gives the impression of hard work done. A heavy slow-moving crew that feels for its work punishes itself severely in the effort to get back the speed of boat destroyed at the beginning of the stroke. A slow-moving individual in a quicker-moving crew punishes his fellow-oarsmen and is the most common variety of the gentleman whom I have described as a ' stopper '.

To get a firm and true hold of the water at the beginning of the stroke, the oarsman must have raised his inside wrist when turning off the feather, and have brought the lower corner of the squared blade as near to the surface of the water as can safely be done without making contact. The actual height above the water will vary a little in rough or calm weather. The subsequent rise of the hands which brings about the immersion of the blade is a knack, most readily acquired by keeping steadfastly in mind the fact that the oar is both longer and heavier outboard than inboard, and that a slight movement at the handle produces a large movement at the tip of the blade. By measurement I find that, when going through the motions of rowing, when fully reached forward I instinctively raise my hands from three to three and a half inches upwards. The middle finger of the inside hand being 9 inches from the end of the handle, this uplift will give 10 inches vertical drop to the tip of the blade, sufficient to cover it to the full. As the oar is heavier outboard than inboard, the blade begins to drop by the action of gravity as soon as the weight of the hands and arms is taken off the handle. As explained on p. 56, the action of gravity is much too slow to cover the blade at the required speed, but as the blade falls downwards a very light uplift given to the handle by *outstretched* thumbs speeds up the downward movement of the blade. If the oar is gripped the thumbs are closed on the handle in opposition to the fingers and the quick uplift is hindered, if not made impossible. Therefore, at the required instant, the oarsman must not only remove all pressure of his hands from the handle, but must also give it a quick and distinct lift upwards. His instinct is to take a firm grip of the oar preparatory to pulling it towards his body, but this instinct is entirely wrong and must be replaced by the acquired habit of giving it a lift up with his thumbs without contracting the flexor muscles of the fingers in the slightest degree. There must be no opposition between the thumbs and the fingers: the sensation should be that the latter, while remaining bent, let go their grasp. Whilst this uplift of the handle is in progress the oarsman must, by an instantaneous contraction of the muscles of the loins and buttocks, reinforced, or rather initiated by, a simultaneous springing action of the knees and feet, lift back the whole weight of his body. The fingers, which have remained hooked round the oar while the grasp is let go, instantly take the whole strain of the resistance of the water to the blade and the beginning of the stroke is accomplished.

It requires no small effort of mind on the part of the oarsman to relinquish the grasp of his oar at the moment that he is going to do work with it, and to retain what seems to him a most precarious attachment to it by hooked fingers. It is the business of the coach to convince him by precept, and frequently by example in the tub-pair, that any clenching of the hands on the oar ; any additional grip between the fingers and thumbs ; any seizure with the intent to do extra work with the hands and arms, will assuredly spoil the beginning. At the moment that work is to begin the hands and arms should be conceived of as things buoyant in the air ; as floating upwards with a distinct lifting power and carrying with them the handle of the oar. Equally the coach must convince his pupil that it is the combination of uplift of hands with spring back from the stretcher that gives the beginning. They must go together. If they do not, either the beginning is missed or there is a false beginning—a hit at the water like that given by the blade of a paddle-wheel.

At the same time the beginner should be cautioned against letting go with the fingers of the outside hand. This is a fault commonly associated with a too fierce grip of the inside hand. In such a case, at the beginning of the stroke, the oar is pulled back by the inside arm and the fingers of the outside hand, previously extended, are only bent round the handle after it has been pulled back some two or three inches. The first two fingers of the outside hand should always be hooked round the oar and should seem to take the whole strain of the beginning. When the oarsman thinks that he is throwing the whole strain on the fingers of his outside hand, the probability is that he is distributing the work pretty evenly between his two hands, so great is the tendency to use the inside to the exclusion of the outside hand. It should be pointed out in this connexion that the outside hand has a considerable advantage in leverage.

Fig. 22 shows the correct position of the wrists and hands at the beginning of the stroke. The points to be noted are : that the elbows of both arms are quite straight ; that in the inside arm the wrist is raised above the level of the knuckles but not excessively arched ; the knuckles are parallel with the long axis of the oar ; all four fingers share in the pull, but the oar is held in the fingers, not in the palm of the hand. In the outside arm the wrist is quite flat ; the two terminal joints of the first two fingers, and in large measure those of the third finger also, are firmly hooked round the handle and are clearly taking a large share of the pull, but the little finger, being much shorter than the others, cannot conveniently be bent round the oar and may be allowed to be straight on it, as in the drawing. The thumbs of both hands are beneath the oar, but are not used for grasping during the

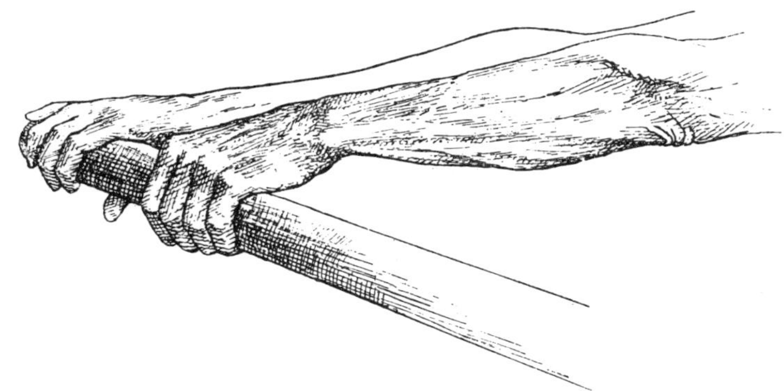

FIG. 22. The oar held correctly in the fingers at the beginning of the stroke. The inside wrist is sufficiently arched ; it has been slightly flattened by the strain of the pull on the oar.

pull and, in fact, are wanted only when the oar is turned on and off the feather. When teaching a beginner to row, a coach should be as rigorous about the positions of wrists and fingers as is a drill-sergeant when teaching a recruit to handle his rifle. The correct positions can be learned in early stages without great difficulty, but bad habits when once acquired are extraordinarily difficult to eradicate. Fig. 23 illustrates an indifferent, and fig. 24 a thoroughly bad, position of the hands and wrists at the beginning of the stroke. In both the oar is too tightly clutched in the palm of the hand.

At the moment the blade is immersed to its full depth in the water the whole weight of the body must be thrown on to the oar and the stretcher by the body springing back. It is easy enough to write this, or to tell the oarsman to do it: it is quite another thing to get it done. No amount of exhortation or verbal explanation is sufficient. The coach must take the oar himself in a tub-pair to show how it is done, and he must be sure that the way he shows is the right way.

It is before all things necessary that the beginner should have a clear notion of what is expected of him. If he can be persuaded to give his mind to it, he can begin best by again referring to the analogy

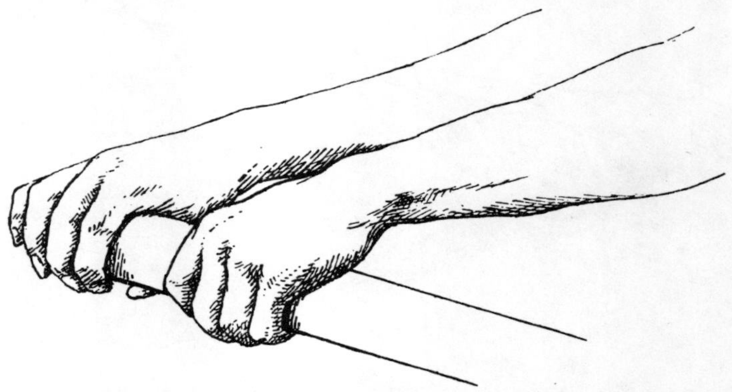

Fig. 23. The oar grasped too much in the palm of the inside hand at the beginning of the stroke. The inside wrist is too flat.

of a standing jump. Let him stoop down as before and take a jump, directing his attention to the natural sequence of his bodily movements. He will find that, having stooped down with bent knees and with the trunk bent on the thigh-joints, the first thing that he must do, in order to make any sort of a spring up from the ground, is to set the weight of his body in motion by lifting up his trunk from his thighs. Further, that in making this movement he must keep his back and shoulders braced up, the back nearly flat, and the whole body moved in one piece from the thigh-joints. If, during the lift, the back is allowed to bend in the region of the waist and the shoulders are allowed to droop forward it is impossible to make an effective jump. During the lift up of the body, he will find that he has brought his weight to bear on the fore part of his feet and that his legs are acting like springs, the ankle- and knee-joints co-operating with the hip-joints to set the body in motion. As soon as the mass of the body has acquired a certain upward impetus, the legs are forcibly extended to accelerate the movement of the body and a final spring off the toes lifts body and legs together from the ground. The oarsman drives down his heels and does not spring off his toes, otherwise the correspondence with

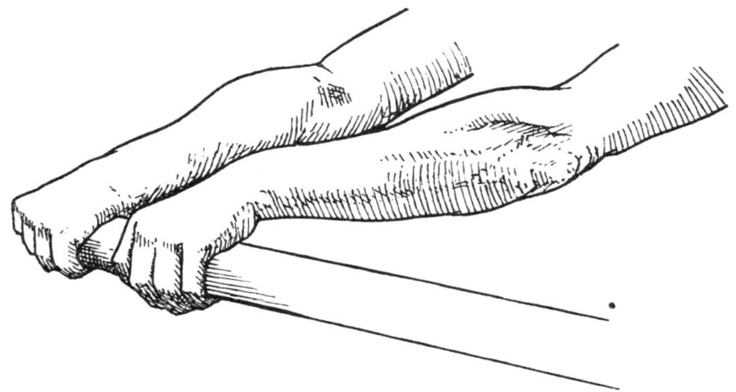

Fig. 24. A clumsy and unduly tight grip of the oar in the middle of the stroke.

the movements of sliding-seat rowing is nearly exact. In rowing, it is equally necessary to start the whole movement from the feet; the mass of the body must be set in motion before the legs are extended; when it is set in motion the legs act as powerful accelerators of the movement of the body; the muscles of the back and shoulders must be braced up and the trunk must be kept in one piece and lifted up from the thigh-joints; no yielding of the backbone is permissible. In both cases the action is carried out by a combined effort of the legs and body, the first effect of which is to set the weight of the body moving as quickly as possible. Having repeated the natural movements of the standing jump a sufficient number of times to realize, and make himself conscious of, the sequence of the combined actions of body and legs, the oarsman should compare the results of, firstly, lifting up his body from the stooping position without making any spring from the feet; secondly, of forcibly extending the legs without having first lifted up the body from the thighs. In both attempts he will find that his action is incomplete, and that he cannot lift himself more than a few inches from the ground. More especially, if he directs his attention to it, he will miss a certain sensation of springiness in the knees which is a *sine qua non* for an effective jump. After this practice let the oarsman take his seat in a gig-pair, and without embarrassing himself with an oar, let him try to spring back from the stretcher as he sprang from the ground. As soon as he has satisfied himself that he can repeat the initial movement of a standing jump by making the spring from his feet and knees lift back his body swiftly from his thighs, let him take an oar and try to apply these actions to the movements of rowing. He may not succeed at the first attempt, because the object to be achieved in rowing is very different from that of jumping, and he must therefore bring his weight to bear on his heels instead of on his toes; but after a few trials he will begin to realize that in proportion as he succeeds in lifting back the weight of his body by taking a spring from his feet, he will succeed in driving forward the boat with a minimum of effort to himself. I do not know a better way of making the would-be oarsman realize what is meant by the expressions, 'Be quick with your feet'; 'Spring back from the stretcher'; 'Get your body on', and others hurled at him from the tow-path or from the stern of a boat: unless, indeed, he is fortunate enough to get a seat behind some master of the art and to feel, as well as see, how the thing is done in the course of a fairly protracted journey on the river. But the Gods seldom descend from Olympus to lend their aid to struggling mortals. Their divinity is hedged about by fear lest, when their active days are past, they may fail to reproduce the form upon which their reputations were built. Those still in the full exercise of their powers are generally too much occupied to spare time and strength in setting the stroke to inefficients.

To return to the analysis of the beginning. A good oarsman will so couple up the actions of the body and legs that they aid and reinforce one another at every point of the stroke. A moderate oarsman may have a good body lift, or a good leg-thrust, or may exhibit the one and the other at different parts of the stroke, but fails to couple the actions together. That is the root of the whole matter ; the leg-work and body swing must be coupled together. But what do we mean when we speak of ‘ coupling them together ’ ?

We mean that three powerful groups of muscles situated in the back, in the buttocks, and in the thighs must be brought into action simultaneously at the beginning of the stroke, and must remain in action throughout the stroke, mutually aiding and reinforcing one another. Let us, with the aid of some simple diagrams, consider the relations of the body and legs in the full forward position and their possible subsequent movements during the stroke. Fig. 25 shows the oarsman fully reached out. The ankle-, knee-, and hip-joints are bent as much as is possible. The foot is bent at an angle of about 55° to the leg ; the leg at an angle of 60° to the thigh ; the angle between thigh and body is reduced to nearly 20°. At the end of the stroke (fig. 26) the knee is straightened out ; the angle between foot and leg is opened out from 55° to nearly 130° ; the angle between thigh and body has been opened out from 20° to about 125°. The reader should distinguish between the angle through which the body moves with reference to the thigh and the angle through which it moves with reference to the horizontal. The latter is only 60°, but it may be more in the case of an oarsman who overreaches a little and swings very far back. A little consideration shows that the angles through which the thigh and leg, taken together, move are much greater than the angle through which the body moves, and it is not surprising that an oarsman, when first set to work on a sliding-seat, instinctively makes use of the great freedom of action permitted to his limbs and ' shoots his slide '. That is to say, he tries to get on his work by thrusting back the slide with his legs, making very little use of the muscles of his hips and back. Some use of his buttock and back muscles he must make, for if he did not, when his legs are straightened out at the end of the stroke his body would be in the position indicated in fig. 27. The worst slide-shooter never finishes in quite as bad a position as that, but will have drawn back his hips and shoulders sufficiently to bring him into the position illustrated in fig. 28, an attitude familiar enough in second-class rowing. But,

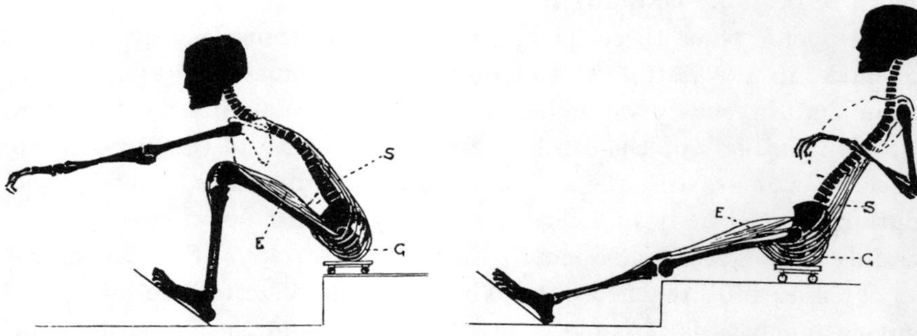

FIG. 25. A diagram illustrating the full forward position.

FIG. 26. A diagram illustrating the correct position at the finish of the stroke.

though used to this extent, the action of the buttock and back muscles has been entirely subordinated to the action of the leg muscles, and the trunk never acquires an effective momentum. A crew rowing in good time and thrusting in this manner with the legs may kick their boat along at a considerable speed, but, powerful though it may be, the single group of muscles which has to bear nearly all the burden soon tires : the stroke becomes shorter and less efficient, and under sustained pressure the crew presently breaks up. This evil was recognized at the Universities soon after the introduction of sliding-seats, and a remedy was sought by teaching oarsmen to fix their knees at the beginning of the stroke and to lift their bodies up to and even past the perpendicular, as if on a fixed seat. After the beginning of the stroke had been effected in this way, the knees were forcibly flattened down and the slide brought into use. This was a great improvement on slide-shooting methods, and possibly to this day there are some who will maintain that this is the proper method of using the slide. I myself am inclined to the opinion that it is the best method when the travel of the slide is less than 12 inches and the men are seated 4 to 6 inches away from their work. Some crews, notably the Leander crew of 1880, rowing in this style, attained a speed that has seldom been surpassed. But when the knees are raised as high as they

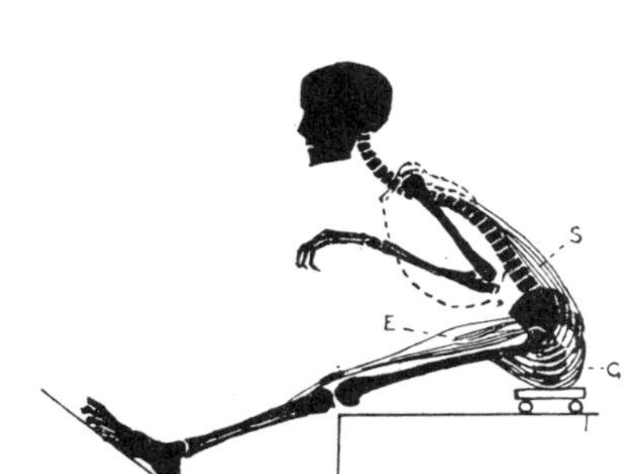

Fig. 27. The slide driven back without lifting up the body.

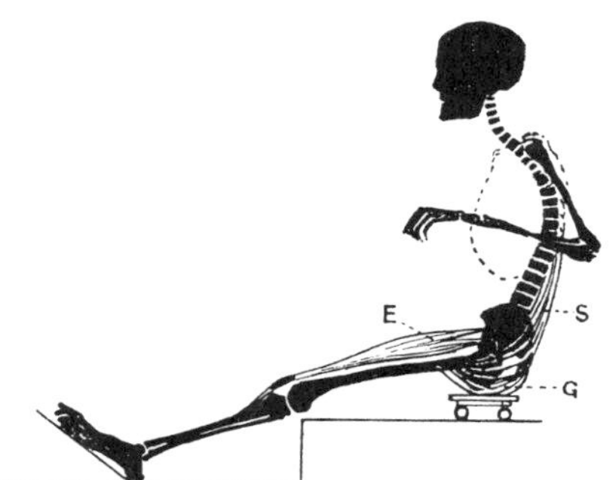

Fig. 28. A sloppy finish.

must be on a 16-inch slide, the effort required to fix them at the beginning of the stroke is so considerable, and throws so much strain on the limbs in consequence of the opposition set up between the flexor and extensor muscles, that the oarsman loses too much of his power of springing back from the stretcher. His legs are largely out of action during the first part of the stroke and his ‘ beginning ’ loses force proportionally. Moreover, in this style of rowing, whether on long or short slides, there is the disadvantage that the whole work is thrown first upon one set of muscles, then upon another, instead of being equally distributed between them. It is as if, when there are two men to move a heavy weight, one should carry it for half the required distance and the other for the remainder of the distance. It is a much greater economy of effort when both combine to move it for the whole distance.

The most effective and therefore the most correct way of using a long slide was introduced into this country by the Canadian professional sculler Edward Hanlan. Though well built and muscular he was what would nowadays be considered a light weight, scaling a pound or two under eleven stones, but on and after his arrival in England in 1879 he astonished everybody by the ease with which he romped away from much more powerful opponents in a succession of contests for the Championship of England and the Championship of the World. The tideway amateur clubs, then in the heyday of their power, were not slow to profit by his example. Some years later the Universities, Cambridge first under the influence of Mr. Muttlebury, followed suit. Oxford, taught by a succession of defeats, learned the lesson from Cambridge and in the early nineties of last century produced a succession of great oarsmen, of whom Col. W. A. L. Fletcher was *primus inter pares*. This was to my mind the Augustan age of English rowing. In those years there was no doubt as to what was the right thing to do.

'*Start swing and slide together, but swing back so sharp at the beginning that the body is upright before the slide has had time to travel more than 4 or 5 inches. For the remainder of the stroke keep slide and swing together : the slide should arrive at the back-stop as the hands touch the chest.*'

That is the statement of the true faith ; of the way in which the thing ought to be done. The question is, how to set about to get it done ? Let us return to the use of diagrams. In figs. 25–8 the principal muscles concerned in lifting back the body and thrusting with the legs are indicated in a very diagrammatic manner. The leg-thrust is effected by a group of muscles on the front and sides of the thigh known to anatomists as the *quadriceps extensor femoris* (see fig. 54 and p. 345). They are much more extensive and complicated than the single muscle marked *E* shown in the diagrams, but this one is sufficient to illustrate their action. This muscle is shown as attached above to the hip-bone: below it passes into a strong tendon which is firmly united to the knee-cap and continued beyond it as a very strong tendon running down a little beyond the knee-joint, to be firmly attached to the front of the upper part of the shin-bone. As the knee-cap works freely like a pulley in a deep groove at the lower end of the thigh-bone, the muscle *E*, when it contracts, pulls on the tendon and the knee-cap, at one and the same time flattening the knee, and, when the leg is bent, exerting a strong downward pressure on the knee-joint, which thrusts the foot against the stretcher. By themselves the extensor group of muscles give thrust but not spring, and if they are not used in conjunction with the other muscles about to be described, the oarsman simply pushes away his slide to the back-stop.

As has been explained by the analogy of a standing jump a spring involves the active lift up of the weight of the body at the same moment that the extensor muscles of the thigh begin their work. This lift back of the body from the thighs is primarily a rapid opening out of the thigh-joint, which, in the act of swinging forward, has been bent up as much as nature allows. A prolonged study of the muscular action involved has convinced me that this lift back is a much less simple affair than is generally supposed, and I have been at pains to give as full and intelligible an account of it as possible in the anatomical chapter of this book, to which the reader is referred for details (pp. 343 et seq.). In the present place I will do my best to make the main principles clear in simple language, and with the aid of diagrams. Partly for simplicity's sake, partly because every beginner should be thoroughly grounded in the art of lifting back his body correctly on a short slide, I begin by explaining how the thing was done by old-fashioned oarsmen rowing on slides with a travel of only 6 or 8 inches. It must be understood that on a short slide the oarsman was seated so as to finish 14 inches away from his work, that is, 14 inches away from a line drawn athwartship from the working thowl of the rowlock.

With a slide movement of only 6 inches, he could only come up to within 8 inches of his work, and it is clear that the few inches of slide available for his use were just those which correspond to the last 6 inches of a 14-inch slide. If used up too soon they would have brought the oarsman, in the middle of his stroke, to a position relative to his rowlock which properly belonged to the finish. Therefore it was necessary for him to 'hold his slide' at the beginning and to reserve the use of it for the last half of the stroke. He did not begin to flatten down his knees and drive his slide back until he had lifted his body up to, perhaps even a trifle past, the perpendicular. How is it possible for a man to use his legs to spring off the stretcher at the beginning of the stroke and yet avoid thrusting back his slide ? I will try to explain how it is done. The first thing that both coach and oarsman must be clear about is the fact that the thigh-joints, about which the hip-bones and the whole body swing as on a pivot, are not flush with the seat, but are situated some 3 inches above it. The pair of bones on which we sit (anatomists call them the ischia) project that much below the sockets of the hip-bone into which the heads of the thigh-bones fit, and their lower surfaces are shaped something like the rockers of a rocking-chair, presenting curved surfaces on which the hip-bones, and with them the whole body, can be rocked to and fro. When the oarsman is reached out to his fullest extent forward the hip-bones are nearly vertical, or at the most inclined a trifle forward from the vertical. At the end of the stroke they are inclined to a considerable degree backwards. It is on the power of rapidly rotating the hip-bones backwards through a sufficient angle that the spring back of the body at the beginning of the stroke depends. The reader should examine carefully the four successive positions of the hip-bones illustrated in figs. 65 A to 68 A. Two sets of muscles are brought into use : the hamstrings and the buttock muscles. Their exact relations and actions are explained in detail in the anatomical chapter of this book. For the present it is sufficient to say that the hamstrings, a powerful set of muscles situated at the back of the thigh, are attached by one end to the most prominent part of the ischia or rocker-bones of the hip, by the other end to the lower leg just below the knee, as is indicated, very diagrammatically, in fig. 29. From inspection of this figure it is obvious that, if the hip-bones are held immovable, contraction of the muscle *H* will pull back the leg and bend the knee. But if, on the contrary, the knee is fixed and the hip-bones are allowed full liberty of movement, contraction of the hamstrings must pull the rocker-bones towards the knee and thus cause the whole hip-bone

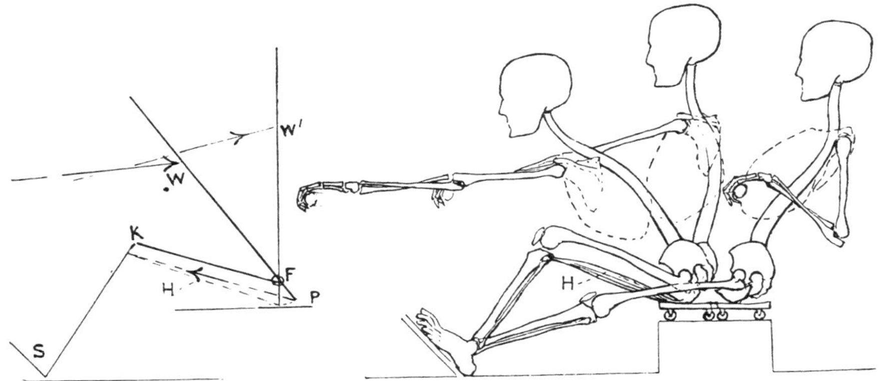

FIG. 29. A diagram illustrating the old-fashioned method of 'holding the slide' on a short sliding-seat.

to rotate backwards about the thigh-joint as a pivot. At the beginning of the stroke the knee is held fast, partly by certain muscles in front of the shin whose action will be explained in Chapter XIII, partly by the contraction of the extensor muscles in front of the thigh. To a certain extent, then, we have muscles acting in opposition to one another, for the hamstrings tend to bend the knee, the extensors to straighten it. But it must be understood that, in every case where a joint has to be temporarily fixed in order that another joint related to it may be set in movement, the muscles which actuate the former joint must always act in opposition to one another in order to fix it. In this case the two sets of muscles acting together do what is needful: the extensors fix the knee and the hamstrings lift back the hips.

In the case of an oarsman who has learned to keep the muscles of his back taut as he springs back at the beginning of the stroke we may regard the trunk and hip-bones as a lever of which the thigh-joint is the fulcrum F in fig. 29, the ischia are the short arm FP, and the rest of the hip-bones and the vertebral column are the long arm FW. It is an elementary proposition in mechanics that a small movement at P in the direction PK produces a large movement at W in the direction W^1. In other words, the action of the hamstrings results in a sharp lift back of the upper part of the body, provided always that the back is kept firm and in one piece by the simultaneous and co-operating action of the appropriate muscles. It is the joint use of the hamstrings and extensor muscles which gives that feeling of spring from the knees and feet of which the oarsman can readily make himself aware if he directs his attention to it.

The body is also lifted back from the thighs by the action of the powerful muscles of the buttocks, known to anatomists as the glutaei. They are attached behind and above to the hip and tail-bones near the middle line and pass obliquely outwards and downwards on either side to be inserted, partly on the outer side of the upper part of the thigh-bones, partly on a long flat band of tendon which covers the outer side of the thigh and is inserted on the lower leg just below the knee-joint. The position and action of the glutaei are indicated sufficiently for present purposes by the muscle marked G in figs. 25 to 28. The buttock muscles, when they contract, extend the thigh-joint. This means that at one and the same time they pull down the thigh-bone (thus reinforcing the action of the extensor muscles of the thigh) and pull back the hip-bone. In other words, they open out the angle between hip and thigh.

The lower end of the backbone is firmly attached to the hips, and if it were rigid would be lifted back by them when the hamstrings and glutaei contract. But it is so far from being rigid that, straight as the oarsman's back may be, the backbone is to some extent bent forward during the swing (fig. 25). When thus bent it is pulled back again by the powerful group of erector spinae muscles (*S* in figs. 25 to 28), often referred to by oarsmen as the 'rabbit muscles' because they are strongly developed in and form nearly the whole of the edible part of the rabbit's back. These, though they are perhaps of even more importance in the latter half than at the beginning of the stroke, must from the very first be forcibly contracted, both to straighten the backbone and to keep the whole column of the back firm and cause it to move in one piece with the upstroke of the hips.

All four groups of muscles must be brought into action the moment the blade of the oar enters the water. The 'spring from the stretcher', the 'quickness on the feet', are ensured by the prompt and vigorous use of the extensor muscles of the thigh. The sharp lift back of the hips is effected by the forcible and instantaneous contraction of the hamstrings and buttock muscles, which, at the moment of the beginning, should undertake a good deal more than a third share of the work. The firm and unyielding back, without which the efforts of legs and hips would be of no avail, is the outcome of a strong and prolonged contraction of the 'rabbit muscles', which are responsible for connecting the lift of the hips with the top part of the body.

It must not be supposed, however, that any practical result can be obtained by the coach enjoining the use of, and the oarsman attempting to put into action, such and such a set of muscles at this or any other given part of the stroke. We learn to perform complex and co-ordinated muscular movements by forming a general concept of what is required to be done, and how it ought to be done, and then setting about to try and do it. There are many trials and many failures, until at last we learn to do the thing correctly. The important thing is that we should start with a correct general concept of the most appropriate method of performing the desired action. Here it is desired to move back the whole body and shoulders as quickly as possible from the full forward position to the vertical. Only too often the coach adopts the direct but wholly erroneous method and tells his pupil to throw back his shoulders. Sometimes he will even commit the absurdity of encouraging him to throw back his head. The pupil's attention is directed towards the thing to be moved, but not towards the seat of the motive power. He makes great muscular efforts with the upper part of his body, sometimes also with his neck, but the muscles upon which the effective performance of the required movement depends are left unexercised because his attention is directed elsewhere. To obtain the desired result the coach should tell him to keep his knees firm, to keep his back in one firm piece, and to try to lift back as sharply as possible that part of his posterior anatomy which is touched by the upper margin of his shorts. He may use other methods of exhortation and explanation, but, whatever they may be, he should never lose sight of the importance of directing his pupil's attention to the fact that the motive power resides in the lower and not in the upper part of his body.

Before continuing we must put our oarsman back on a long slide. The difference between the use of legs and body on a short and a long slide is simply this : that on the latter the oarsman slides up to his work, 8 inches in advance of the hypothetical old-fashioned oarsman who began the stroke at 8 inches and finished it at 14 inches from his work. As these extra inches forward clearly belong to the beginning and early middle part of the stroke, to make effective use of them the thrusting action of the legs must be brought into use at the outset. The extensor muscles of the thighs are used, not only to fix, but also to flatten the knees at the beginning of the stroke. This need not, and should not be allowed to, diminish the use of the hamstrings and buttock muscles in lifting back the body from the thighs. Their action is precisely the same as on the short slide.

An oarsman may often be seen to thrust with his legs and contract his buttock muscles with no much better result than to push out the small of his back. This, because he has not brought his 'rabbit muscles' into action. His back yields to the strain of the oar : the top part of his body and the shoulders are not lifted back and his leg-thrust is consequently ineffective. Another oarsman may be seen to straighten up his spinal column and to throw back his shoulders with great energy by the violent contraction of the rabbit muscles, at the same time thrusting hard with his legs. He makes a great display of force and often passes for a very hard worker, but there is something wanting. A trained eye will detect a lack of connexion between the actions of his shoulders and his legs. He is not ‘ coupled up ’ because he has not made proper use of his buttock muscles. Of all the faults committed in rowing I think I dislike most this failure to couple up, for, in committing it, the oarsman is not only doing laboriously work that may be done with far greater precision and ease, but is deceiving himself, and too often his coach also, by the obviousness of his labour. I dislike it the more, because such an oarsman is so conscious of his effort, and so self-satisfied with his consciousness of it, that it is hard to make him believe that he is in error and that he could put forth just as much and more useful driving force at far less expense to himself. He is spending his substance in riotous effort, and, as is the habit of spendthrifts, he rejoices in his own extravagance.

At the risk of wearisome reiteration I repeat that, for the perfect accomplishment of the beginning, there are four groups of muscles to be used simultaneously, and of these four the most important are the hamstrings and the buttock muscles, for, if they are left out, the others are unconnected. Moreover the use of the hamstrings and buttocks is essential to a real spring from the stretcher. Without them a man may thrust with his legs, but his thrust is of the nature of a poke, without any elasticity in it. To return again to the analogy of a standing jump. In a jump the initial lift up of the body weight, upon which the efficiency of the spring depends, is effected by the hamstrings and buttock muscles. So it should be in rowing. But although in ordinary life these muscles are in constant use, and therefore in good condition, and capable of much endurance, their use does not come naturally to an oarsman. Probably because, under ordinary circumstances, they are concerned with lifting the body up to and maintaining it in an erect posture on the legs, and as the sitting posture is adhered to throughout the action of rowing, the oarsman's nerve centres are satisfied by the sense of balance and support afforded by the seat and do not unconsciously send out the impulses necessary to set the muscles in question in vigorous contraction. However this may be, the habit of using them does not come naturally to the oarsman and has to be acquired by conscious practice. It is worth any amount of trouble to convince the beginner that his motive power is largely situate in his posterior anatomy.

During the first part of the stroke, when legs, loins, and back are doing all the work, the arms should be perfectly straight except for the raised position of the inside wrist (fig. 22). Indeed, if the beginning has been well caught, the strain on the arms is such that they are pulled taut, as is a hawser bringing a ship to her moorings. Even the arch of the inside wrist is flattened by the strain. But the beginner should not be told to keep his arms *rigid* lest, to satisfy his idea of rigidity, he should clench his hands on the oar. This would infallibly depress the handle and cause the blade to row light in the water. To prevent the shoulders from being pulled forward the muscles at the back of the shoulder-blades must contract, but as yet not sufficiently to draw back the arms. If the beginning has been well caught the oarsman will have arrived at the position illustrated in fig. 30. We see from the drawing, a copy of a photograph from the life, that the stroke has been started, but that much remains to be done. The wrists are still well in front of the knees, and the oar is still at an angle of some 65° to the side of the boat and is approaching, but has not yet reached, the point of its maximum mechanical efficiency. The body is so upright that a plumb-line through the shoulder-joint would pass through the hip-joint. There are 11 or 12 inches of slide still to go, and the knees are still largely bent. The drawing shows, better than words can describe, the contracted state of the muscles of the thigh and the tension of the muscles at the back of the shoulder, and the outside shoulder has already been drawn back from its advanced position at the beginning of the stroke. The pace of the boat has been accelerated by the work already done, but this acceleration is as yet far from having reached its maximum. To make the boat shoot forward as far as possible the oarsman has to sustain the pressure of the blade in the water with undiminished energy. He must sustain

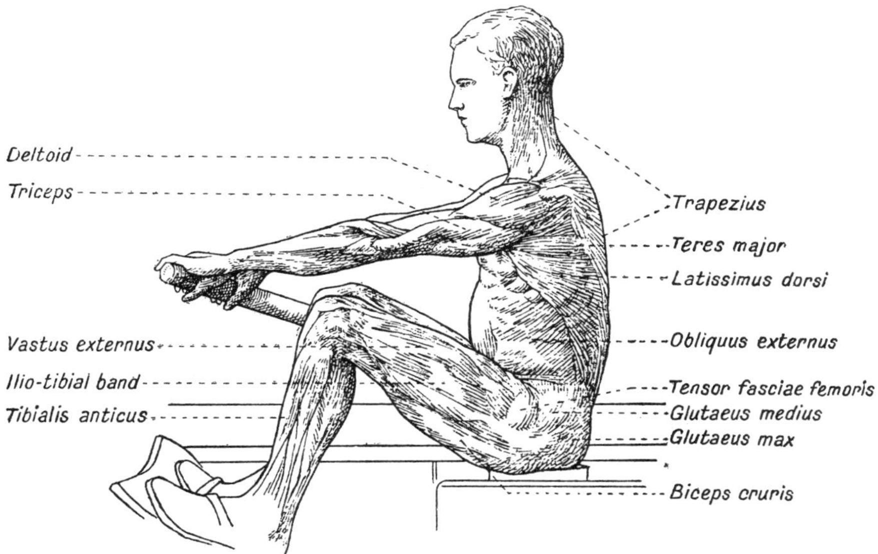

FIG. 30. The early middle of the stroke. The trunk is upright and the muscles of the thighs are contracting forcibly to drive back the slide. Observe the position of the left shoulder as compared with Fig. 65.

it by forcibly flattening down his knees and driving his heels into the stretcher. By so doing he transfers to his legs a large part of the work hitherto borne by the glutaei and erector spinae muscles, but these latter must still be kept in vigorous action to maintain the vertical position of the body. If they were to relax their effort while the legs are being straightened out the hips would be pushed back without carrying the upper part of the body with them, and the swing would come to an end. Therefore, for every fraction of slide back there must be a corresponding fraction of swing to maintain the shoulders vertically above the seat.

Up to now the arms have been quite straight, but as the oar comes to lie at right angles to the boat and the wrists pass over the knees, the arms begin to bend home and the stroke enters into its last phase, the finish.

To obtain full value for his exertions, the oarsman must maintain the pressure of his blade against the water with as little diminution as possible, until the oar has come home to his body and the moment comes for him to drop his hands and lift the blade out of the water. By the time the oar is at right angles to it the acceleration of the boat has been sensibly increased, and at the same time the oar has arrived at the position of maximum mechanical efficiency, an advantage not to be lightly thrown away.

When teaching his crew to finish out, the coach should be explicit on this point, that the boat is moving faster than at the beginning of the stroke, and that the movements of body and limbs must increase their pace in proportion. The oarsman must go with his boat and never let it slip away past his control. On the other hand, he will botch and bungle the business if he should try to outstrip the pace of the boat and tear out the oar with a violent effort of the arms. This sense of carrying on the work in harmony with the movement of the boat is nowhere more important than at the finish of the stroke. It is most important that in this phase there should be no break in the continuity of the work. The effort must not be transferred suddenly from one group of muscles to another. The temptation, when once the arms begin to bend, is to dispense with the use of the body and legs and to throw the last part of the work on the arms and shoulders. None but the best oarsmen are exempt from it. If the two first phases of the stroke, the beginning and the middle, have been executed properly, the oarsman will have four or five inches of slide left to push out with whilst his arms are bending and coming home to his body. At the moment that his arms begin to bend his body should be vertical; when the stroke is finished it should have swung back past the vertical, but not too far. Therefore he should have an appreciable reserve of slide and swing to utilize in the last third of the stroke. He must learn to prolong the action of the thigh and buttock muscles, flattening down his knees till the legs are quite straight, and swinging back the hips all the time. As he swings out the erector spinae muscles must not only maintain but may with advantage increase their effort. To sit up and swing out the upper part of the trunk and the shoulders while the legs are driving out the last four inches of the slide is not mere posing for the gratification of spectators, but a very real factor in increasing the pace of the boat. So great is the temptation to let the weight of the body settle down on the seat, and to allow the blade of the oar to wash out as the boat travels past it, that even the most experienced oarsman must constantly remind himself of the necessity of using his legs and loins at the finish, and every oarsman should make himself conscious that the action of bringing the oar home is referable to an effort in the region of the broad of his back, not to an effort of the arms and shoulders. The broad of the back, because there lie the great latissimus dorsi muscles whose action is to pull back the upper arm and to draw the elbows past the sides. The latissimus dorsi is, on either side of the body, a large triangular sheet of muscle, its base attached to the backbone from just below the level of the armpits downward to the tail; its lower angle also attached to the posterior part of the iliac crest. The angle subtending the base is a thick muscular mass forming the posterior wall of the armpit, and is produced into a flat tendon inserted on the upper arm-bone, about three inches below the shoulder-joint (see Chapter XIII, p. 330). From the very beginning of the stroke the latissimus dorsi, in conjunction with other muscles at the back of the shoulder-blade, has been in a state of tension, acting as one of the holdfasts of the upper arm and shoulder-joint: now it takes a more active share in the work and contracts forcibly yet steadily. A coach should illustrate the action of the latissimus dorsi by showing the beginner that, if the arm is extended at right angles to the body, as in rowing, and the shoulder and upper arm are then drawn back, the elbow necessarily bends and is carried past the side in the correct position with very little assistance from the biceps and other flexor muscles of the arm. It was largely by the correct use of the latissimus dorsi muscles that Col. W. A. L. Fletcher obtained the sustained and powerful finish that characterized his rowing, and as a coach he was wont to lay great stress upon their importance. Among more recent oarsmen, Mr. A. S. Garton was perhaps the best exponent of the action of these essential rowing muscles. The use, and misuse, of the other muscles of the shoulder is best relegated to the anatomical chapter of this book.

As the elbows bend and are drawn back past the sides the relation of the forearm to the hand is altered, and the wrist, more particularly the inside wrist, must be allowed to arch freely in order to accommodate the movement of the arm to that of the oar. In this connexion the importance of using the fingers as hooks, and of avoiding all temptation to clutch the handle of the oar in a tightened grasp, must be reiterated and insisted on. A tight grip of the oar inhibits the freedom of action of the wrist, and leads, among other things, to a feather under water or to washing out at the finish. If the movements detailed above are performed correctly, great freedom of play being allowed to the shoulder-, elbow-, and wrist-joints, while the muscles of the legs, buttocks, and back are doing all the work of the finish, the blade will be kept square at its full depth in the water and will be accelerating the pace of the boat up to the last. The finish is perhaps the weakest feature in latter-day oarsmanship. One may see in College and even in University crews every variety of incorrect wasteful action.

The most obvious errors at the finish of the stroke are lying back; tearing at the oar with a violent action of the arms and shoulders; squaring the elbows. These faults may be coexistent, or they may be committed separately. Of recent years the most prevalent has been that of lying back.[1] The attendant evils are threefold. The balance of the body is thrown so far back that the oarsman must perforce rely on his toe-straps to prevent himself from falling backwards, and is nearly certain to use his toe-straps before he has lifted his blade out of the water. He cannot at one and the same time pull in one and push in the opposite direction from his stretcher, so his finish, if prolonged, must also be weak. Undue strain is thrown upon the superficial muscles of the abdomen, and the oarsman is encouraged to rely on them instead of on the ilio-psoas group (see p. 320) for the recovery of his body, thereby incurring the risk of a strained stomach. The hands cannot be dropped straight down at the recovery, but must be slid forward along the inclined plane of the stomach in such wise that a feather under water or, alternatively, a washed-out blade are nearly inevitable. As lying back is the outcome of excess of zeal, of attaching undue importance to length of body-swing *per se*, a coach must insist on the fact that in rowing all exaggeration is harmful: not least in swinging back at the end of the stroke. After taking into account the tendency to exaggeration, lying back may generally be traced to want of combination of swing and leg-work in the earlier part of the stroke, in consequence of which the oarsman arrives at his back-stop before his arms have begun to bend home. To avoid finishing short he jams his slide against the back-stop and continues to swing back till his hands come in to his chest. Often, in the earlier stages of practice, a crew which is trying to cultivate a good length will lie back because it has not yet learned to slide properly and to get a firm hold of the water at the beginning. In such a case the coach may be fairly confident that the lie back will disappear as the beginning improves, provided that it improves as the result of a sharp lift back of the body, not as the result of kicking away the slide. A man who has four or five inches of slide to push out whilst his arms are bending home will have very little temptation to lie too far back.

[1] Written in 1922. In the last two years oarsmen have tended towards the other extreme, of not swinging their shoulders far enough back at the finish [G.C.B. 1925].

In other cases the fault is traceable to gripping the oar too tightly, stiffening the arms and shoulders, and failing to bend and carry back the elbows past the sides. Some oarsmen act as if there were a repulsion between the handle of the oar and the body, and will go on swinging back to an extreme degree rather than let them come into contact. This variant of lying back can be corrected by teaching them the proper use of the latissimus dorsi muscles.

Tearing with the arms and shoulders at the finish is often associated with an excessive swing back, but equally often with the opposite fault of 'meeting the oar', that is to say, pulling the body towards the oar at the finish by the use of the arms. In the latter case the legs, loins, and back cease to do their work, and the whole effort is transferred to the biceps and other flexor muscles of the arms. The shoulders are simultaneously pulled forwards and inwards by contraction of the pectoral muscles, and the elbows protruded from the sides. It is not of much use to tell such a one not to use his arms. The only cure is to transfer his attention to those more powerful regions of his body which should properly perform the work. Hoisting in the oar with the shoulders is not necessarily accompanied by excessive use of the biceps muscles. It is a fault common in somewhat bull-necked powerful men who prefer to use the upper fibres of the trapezius and deltoid muscles (see Chapter XIII, p. 328) and lift their shoulders towards their ears, rather than draw back the upper arm by the action of the latissimus dorsi. I recall an erstwhile famous oarsman who used to lift his shoulders in this way, and at the recovery dropped them with a crash which seemed to send a shiver through the whole boat. It was a superfluous display of muscular energy, and the worst of all such displays is, that they invariably detract from the less obtrusive efforts of legs, buttocks, and back, which are far more effective in propelling the boat. The ugly habit of sticking out the elbows at the finish is a result of not using the latissimus dorsi muscles. If they are in action the elbows must come past the sides. It should be stated in this connexion that, though the elbows should be carried well back to the rear, they must not be scraped close past the body. Elbows held too close to the sides cannot go far enough back: the shoulders are elevated, the elbows and wrists excessively bent, and the whole finish is peculiarly weak. I remember a period when excessive importance was attached to keeping the elbows close to the sides, and at the finish of the stroke many a crew looked like a line of poodles sitting up on their haunches and begging for biscuits.

To sum up, the oarsman will finish best and hardest who has a good bit of slide left to finish with; who sits up and is conscious that he is pulling with the whole of his back as his legs drive out the slide; who carries his elbows and the points of his shoulders well back, and leaves his wrists as much freedom of play as possible. The exact angle through which he should swing his body back may be open to argument. In my opinion he should swing as far back as the figure shown in fig. 26; that is, 25° beyond the vertical. It is just about the swing back of the New College crew which, rowing at a slower stroke than its more powerful Leander opponents, won the Grand Challenge Cup in equal to record time in 1897, and owed its victory to a remarkably hard and well-sustained finish, following on a correct use of slide and swing at the beginning and through the middle of the stroke. A photograph of this crew, taken a few yards below the winning post, will be found in Mr. C. M. Pitman's volume on Rowing in the Badminton series. The photograph is not very sharp, but considering that it was taken at the end of a very hard race—Leander led by nearly a length at Fawley, and New College only won by two feet—the vigour of the swing out and the uniformity of the bodies were remarkable.

I have seen it stated by a sufficiently prominent authority on rowing that a long finish is not worth the trouble bestowed on it. I can only say, to oarsmen and coaches alike, do not be deceived. No crew can realize its full potentiality for speed unless a firm beginning is prolonged into a hard and clean finish. That eminent oarsman, Mr. F. S. Gulston, in the latter days of fixed seats led the London

Rowing Club to victory, not by discarding the beginning, but by adding to it a long and powerful finish, and when sliding-seats were introduced demonstrated that they gave an additional advantage to the latter half of the stroke. Mr. Harcourt Gold, as fine a stroke as ever led a succession of crews to victory, owed much of his success to the manner in which he prolonged the work of his blade in the water. His methods were not strictly orthodox, but I have been greatly interested in watching him setting the stroke to crews of old blues in the last two or three years. The way in which his blade carries on the work beyond the usual limit must be seen to be appreciated. I have seen nothing like it for many years past. But let nobody forget that a good beginning and a firm middle are the indispensable prerequisites for a good finish.

We have now arrived at the end of the stroke. The hands are dropped and the round begins again. The analysis of the movements has proved to be long and full of minute detail. Much of it may be tedious, a good deal of it may seem unnecessary, but I would say this to every coach and to every oarsman who wishes to see his crew in the only place worth trying for—namely, in the first place—no detail is so small that it can safely be neglected. To ensure success your methods must be thorough, and thoroughness means attention to detail. We all know of crews which, by some lucky combination of qualities, have achieved unexpected success without showing even a respectable mastery over detail. But such successes are short lived ; the lucky combination does not recur, and defeat soon follows. On the other hand, a club which consistently maintains a high standard, which never is slovenly about detail, will always be in the position of a possible winner. It will have its ups and downs, but its traditions will always enable it to make the best of the material that it possesses, and its members will be inspired with the faith that their way is the more excellent way, and by that faith they will surmount all difficulties.

In conclusion, get a full grasp of detail but use it with understanding. The task is not easy, but it must not be made too difficult. It takes longer to learn than is generally supposed, and must be learned slowly, bit by bit. One thing may be learned this week, another next week, and by degrees the different bits can be pieced together. The novice is easily bewildered, and the enthusiasm even of seasoned oarsmen may be quenched by a too copious outpouring of detail. In this, as in other things, exaggeration is the bane of oarsmanship.

This chapter may fittingly conclude with a comparison of the actual with the ideal. Oarsmen row in such various shapes that only a few examples can be given of actual performance at different parts of the stroke. The examples have been selected from instantaneous photographs or from cinematograph films, and have been enlarged under a low power of the microscope with the aid of a camera lucida. They all are representations of University oarsmen in action. There is nothing to be learned from photographs of men posed in the different attitudes they are presumed to exhibit at different phases of the stroke.

Fig. 31, A, B, C, shows three positions occupied by a distinguished contemporary oarsman in one and the same stroke. In A he is on the swing forward. The position is good. The body is swung forward well in advance of the slide and is being brought forward from the hip-joints. The head and neck are well poised, and the shoulders are neither unduly elevated nor thrust forward. The knees are rising to bring the slide forward. The oar is held lightly in the fingers of the outside hand, but the outside elbow might be straighter. In B the oarsman has just got hold of the water at the beginning of the stroke. The position is faulty to this extent : that too much reliance is placed on a backward fling of the head in order to lift back the body from the thighs. The result of starting the effort from the upper instead of from the lower part of the body is shown in C. The head is thrown too far back ; the oarsman is thrusting with his legs and pulling with his shoulders, but the loins are not sufficiently firm to make a satisfactory connexion between his upper and lower extremities. The position is not bad, but not wholly satisfactory. Fig. 31 D should be compared with the drawing immediately above it. It represents a very tall powerful oarsman in the same phase of the recovery as A. The position is faulty. The hips have not been brought forward; the stomach is hollowed; the back is arched; the shoulders are elevated and unduly thrust forward; the oar is too tightly grasped in the fists. The slide, however, is being kept under control.

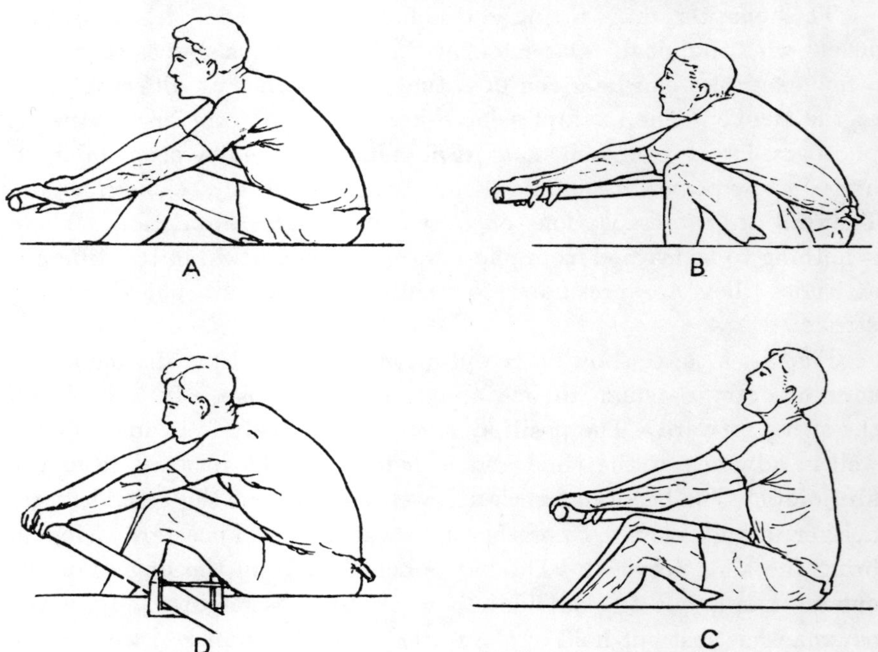

Fig. 31. Some rowing positions, the oarsmen paddling. For description see text.

Fig. 32 represents four oarsmen at the same point of the stroke. The drawings are made from a single picture on the film, and the diminishing size of the figures is due to perspective. The wrists are just passing over the knees and the arms are beginning to bend. The drawings afford a good illustration of the familiar fact that an oarsman always looks better from the off than from the near side. The fault in all four figures is that the slide is too far back, and the knees pressed farther down than they should be at this point in the stroke. All four oarsmen will arrive at their back-stops some time before the oar

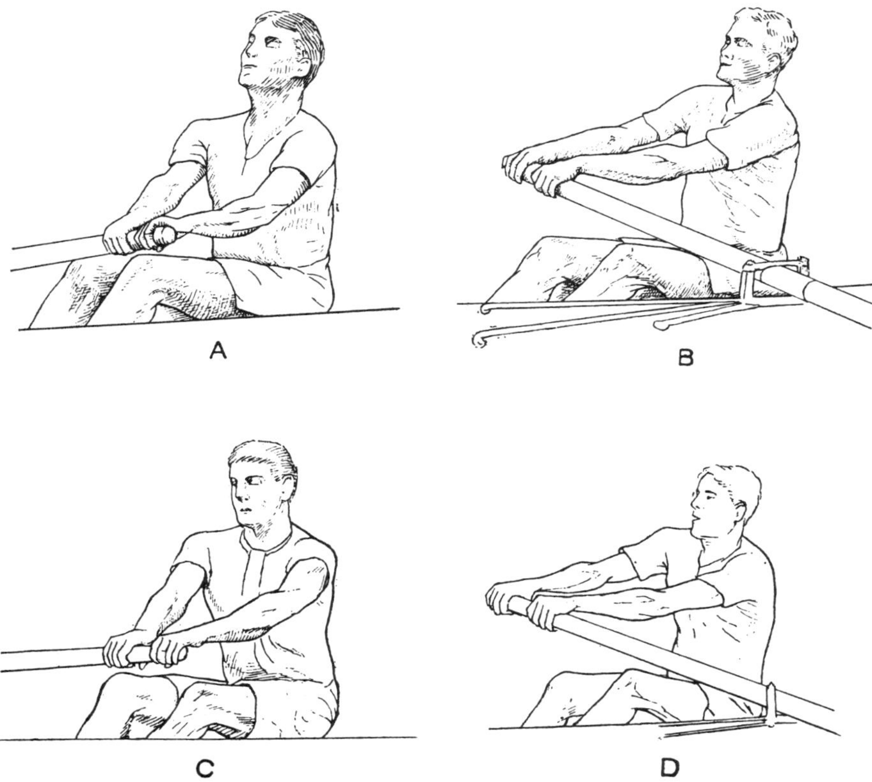

Fig. 32. Four oarsmen at the same phase of the stroke. For description see text.

comes home to the chest. The idiosyncrasies of the several oarsmen are obvious enough. A and B have lifted their bodies well up to or past the perpendicular, but both are relying too much on a toss back of the head. C is in a very easy unconstrained position, but has not lifted his body far enough back: he is obviously relying too much on his leg-thrust and has 'shot his slide'. D is a good example of a rough, hard-working oarsman. His body is firm and he has got a strong pull on his oar. But he is using his legs unequally; the position of the shoulders is awkward; the inside wrist is too flat. The attitude suggests a forthcoming hoist with the arms and shoulders to finish the stroke. The succeeding pictures on the film show that this expectation was realized. It is a trivial but interesting detail that the eyes of all four oarsmen are nearly closed. Most oarsmen open the eyes wide during the swing forward, and close or nearly close them during the effort of the stroke.

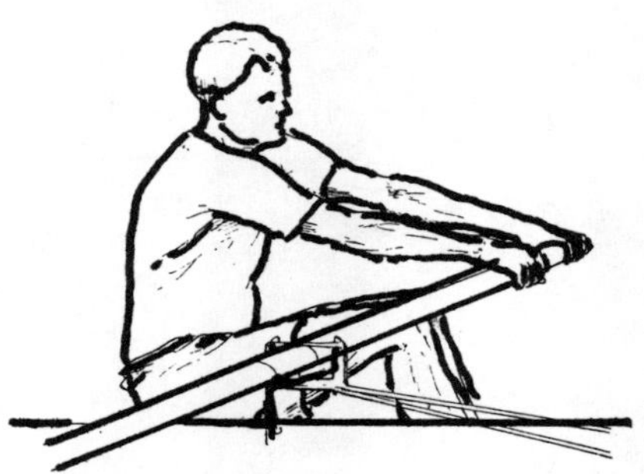

FIG. 33. An oarsman rowing at 40 strokes per minute in the middle of a hard race.

All the drawings in figs. 31 and 32 are taken from photographs of crews paddling at a slow rate of stroke. Fig. 33 depicts a noted pre-war oarsman rowing at the rate of 40 strokes per minute at a critical point in a race which, incidentally, he won in record time. The photographer has caught him at almost exactly the same point in the stroke as in fig. 32: the arms are just beginning to bend. The drawing is introduced to show how greatly an oarsman's appearance is spoiled by comparatively venial faults. The body is leaning towards the rowlock (this is no great fault) and the head is lolled over in the same direction. The shoulders are pulled so far forward by the strain of the oar that the arms look unnaturally long. These things catch the eye and mar the style. But cover up the top part of the figure and it will be seen that most of the essentials of the stroke have been well executed. The lower part of the body is firm and upright, and there is every evidence of full co-operation between legs and loins. The knees are still well raised, showing that the oarsman has reserved a sufficient length of slide to ensure a powerful drive with the legs at the finish. The main fault is that the draw back of the shoulders has been postponed to too late a period in the stroke. This will involve a large and ungainly movement of the shoulders, as the arms bend and the elbows are drawn back past the sides.

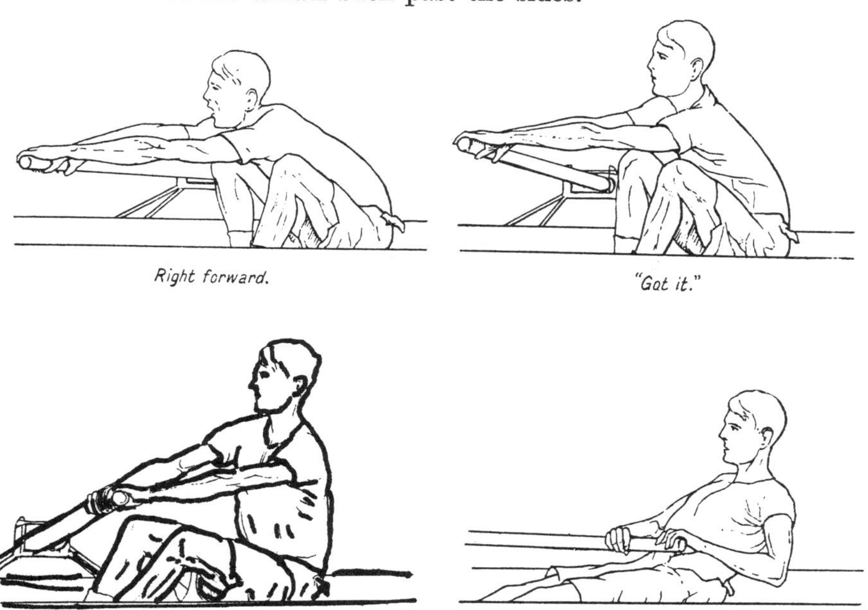
Right forward.
"Got it."
The middle of the stroke.
The finish : hands dropped.

Fig. 34. Four positions of an oarsman during a single stroke, as shown on a cinematograph film.

In fig. 34 are represented four positions of an oarsman who, in my opinion, is not only the best exponent of rowing at the present time, but the most polished and graceful of all long-slide oarsmen whom I have ever seen. The one fault is in the position 'full forward'. Here he is overreached, a fault which he shared with every other member of the crew in which he was rowing. To obtain an abnormal and unnecessary length of reach forward he has bent the lumbar region of the back to the fullest possible extent. The strain of the position and his almost tortured anxiety to make sure of the beginning are evidenced in the oarsman's facial expression. It is instructive to compare this drawing with fig. 20. The angle to which the body is swung forward is about the same. In fig. 20 the oarsman has allowed his head to drop forward so far that his shoulders are nearly on a level with his ears. But his position is in this respect the better of the two: that the extreme length of reach forward is obtained by drawing forward the hip-bones, not by bending the back in the lumbar region. It is evident to the anatomist that the oarsman of fig. 34 can only lift back his body by a very rapid and powerful use of the erector spinae muscles. The next position, labelled 'Got it', shows this group of muscles in operation at the beginning of the stroke. It is an admirable position, for it illustrates, far better than words can describe, the proper way to get the pull with the lower part of the body, in combination with the legs, at the moment when the blade of the oar enters the water. Observe the strongly contracted state of the hamstring muscles on the lower side of the thigh. This position should be compared with fig. 31 B.

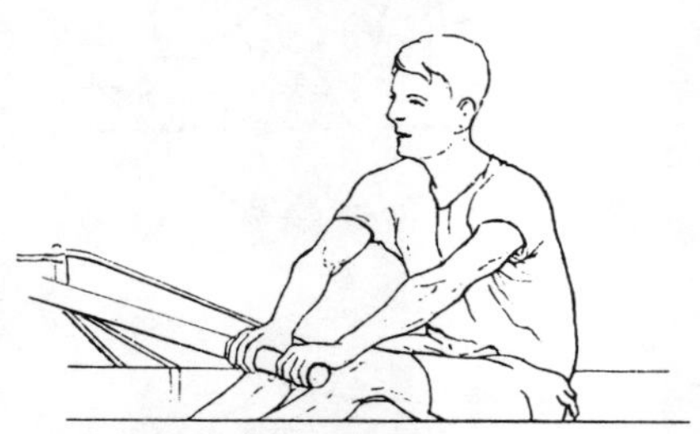

Fig. 35. The swing forward. Arms and body recovered: knees beginning to rise.

The position labelled 'mid-stroke' in fig. 34 shows the back fully straightened by the action of the erector spinae muscles. It is an ideal position. The head is held up and naturally poised on the neck. The trunk firm and upright, but not constrained in any way. The arms are still straight, but the outside shoulder is being drawn back in exactly the right way, at exactly the right time, by the use of the latissimus dorsi muscle. (Compare the position of the shoulders and head in fig. 33.) The knees are still raised, leaving an ample length of slide for the thrust of the legs at the finish of the stroke. The last drawing in fig. 34 shows the body swung back to the fullest extent and the hands dropped to recover the oar. Again the position is admirable. The head and neck are nicely poised. The shoulders are drawn well back and kept down. The elbows are carried well past the sides to the rear. The chest and stomach are well exposed to the front. The knees are straight and pressed down. There is nothing that is not correct, yet the attitude is easy and free from all constraint. Clearly nothing has been done by way of supererogation, for the sake of show. *O si sic omnes!* It should be noted that the two lower figures, taken from a different part of the film, come out on a slightly smaller scale than the two upper.

Fig. 35 shows the same oarsman on the swing forward. The arms are straight; the body recovered well past the perpendicular; the knees just beginning to rise. Again the whole posture is easy, natural, and correct.

My outlines do scant justice to the grace and attractiveness of the original. The pictures on the film are not very sharp, and I have found it difficult to trace finer details under the microscope. But, such as they are, the drawings are sufficiently accurate to enable the reader to visualize the action of a very polished and very efficient oarsman at various phases of the stroke. Nothing is so helpful as a clear mental picture of the successive positions which are the outcome of correct and well-balanced action.

CHAPTER VI

ON RHYTHM

It cannot be too strongly impressed upon a beginner that rowing is continuous movement and not a series of postures. If the movements are correctly performed and follow naturally and easily on one another, the cinematograph will give a series of postures upon the film, each of which will be graceful and satisfactory to the critical eye. For in rowing the camera does not disclose a series of unfamiliar and apparently grotesque positions as it does in the case of a galloping horse. Every part of a good oarsman's action, when instantaneously fixed, is satisfying to the aesthetic sense. But it must be confessed that there are very few oarsmen whose style is so perfect as to stand the ordeal of the critical analysis of the film.

In one respect, at least, rowing is analogous to a round dance, such as the valse: its movements go through a certain round which is repeated at regular intervals. In other words, it is rhythmical, and being rhythmical, it has its accents and its balanced periods.

There is no part of rowing on which opinions differ so much as on what constitutes good rhythm. Nor is this wonderful when one considers that rhythms are infinitely variable. The rhythm of a valse differs greatly from that of a polka; both are very different from the rhythm of the two-step or fox-trot, yet each of these dances is in its own way rhythmical. The valse has its own distinctive rhythm, yet there are endless sub-varieties of the valse, each with its own slight variation of rhythm. In rowing the rhythm of the fixed seat differs from that of the sliding-seat; a crew on 12-inch slides will row with a rhythm different from that of a crew on 16-inch slides. A light nimble crew, such as a good school crew, rows with a rhythm different from that of a less nimble crew of heavy weights. There are also rhythms appropriate to an eight-oar, a four-oar, a pair-oar, and a sculler. One cannot lay down a rule for rhythm, but one may safely say that a coach should be careful to inculcate a rhythm appropriate to the crew he is dealing with. He will court failure if he tries to apply a fixed-seat rhythm to sliding-seats or a heavy-weight rhythm to light weights or vice versa. In each case the rhythm at high speed is very different from that of the paddle.

Nevertheless it is possible to lay down certain principles about rhythm in rowing which must be observed, though variation is permissible within well-understood limits. In every stroke there are two accents, a greater and a lesser accent. The greater accent, which may be compared with the tap of the big drum in a military march, should be laid on the beginning of the stroke. The lesser accent should be laid on the recovery. It is necessary to emphasize this because many coaches, probably all coaches who have not rowed in really first-class crews, lay the greater emphasis on the recovery. 'Get your hands away sharp'; 'Listen to the rattle of the oars in the rowlocks', are the exhortations which one hears with the greatest frequency if one strolls down the banks of the Isis or Cam when practice for Torpids or Summer Eights, Lents or Mays, is in full progress. As a consequence nine crews out of ten are wasting their strength in exaggerated movements at the finish and in the recovery of the stroke, and are putting out their efforts at the wrong time—at the recovery, when all that is required is to disengage the oar neatly from the water and to bring the body back into balance, instead of at the beginning, when all the force available is required for the propulsion of the boat. It is, of course, desirable—for first-rate oarsmanship it is absolutely necessary—that the hands should come away quickly from the chest at the recovery; but it is not necessary, indeed it is altogether undesirable, that the oars should bang and rattle in the rowlocks. With a well-greased button pressed firmly up to the sill and working thowl of the rowlock, the oarsman whose wrists are supple and quick—they cannot be quick if they are not supple—who expends just the required amount of energy to lift his oar out of the water, turn it, and start it on its motion forward; who does all this with his wrists and does not indulge in superfluous efforts of his shoulders, such an oarsman will make no rattle at all in the rowlocks. This is a point on which the late Mr. R. S. de Havilland used to insist in his Eton crews, and it used to puzzle the boys until they realized exactly what he meant. But, it will be objected, the rattle of the oars is necessary to mark the time and give the crew a rallying-point from which to start the movement forward to the next stroke. The answer is, that the oarsman should concentrate his attention on the time at the all-important beginning of the stroke: that is where his foot should come to the ground with the tap of the big drum. And if he gets his beginning, he will soon become aware of a much better sound to serve as a rallying-point at the recovery. It is the 'swash' of the water as it leaves the oar-blade: quite a characteristic sound and not very easily expressed in a syllable. To my own ear it sounds more like 'chŭf' than anything else. It should be a clean crisp sound. If it is too much of a swash it means that the blade has rowed light towards the end of the stroke. I do not mean to say that the rattle of the oars in the rowlocks is not useful in the earlier stages of practice, when the wrists are still awkward in their action and the 'beginning' not yet firmly established. But it is not a mark of excellence but of immaturity: it should be minimized and got rid of with all convenient speed.[1]

The major accent of the stroke, the sound made by the blade entering the water, should also be crisp and clean. If it is a squashy

[1] My son, whose power of picking up a crew for a sudden effort has possibly never been surpassed, tells me that a smooth noiseless recovery carries with it an important addition to the resources of a stroke. For he was wont, when about to make a spurt, to signal his intention to his crew by a sudden and forcible rattle of the oar in the rowlock at the recovery, thus introducing an abrupt variation in the rhythm, to which the crew never failed to respond. Obviously the effectiveness of such a signal depends upon the absence of a rattle in the rowlocks under normal conditions. He further assures me that the impossibility of making an audible rattle in a swivel rowlock is a grave disadvantage to a stroke when he wishes to rally his crew.

sound the beginning has been missed. Dr. Warre used to illustrate it by throwing a pebble very hard vertically into the water as we lay in Windsor Lock. It can be imitated by clapping the hands together with the palms hollowed. To my own ear it is best represented by the syllable 'fŭtt', given very sharply and decisively, but perhaps 'clo͝op' represents it best for most ears. It certainly is not a 'crunch', as some writers have suggested, nor is it exactly a 'whack', but rather a very firm and forcible 'pop'. Any one who has heard and felt it in a first-class crew will not readily forget it. The trouble is that it never is heard but in a first-class crew, and first-class crews are rare. It is, however, a thing to aim at, and can only be attained by getting the oarsman to concentrate his attention on the principal accent at the beginning of the stroke.

There is a short period between the accent at the beginning and the accent at the recovery of the stroke, and a long smooth period occupied by the swing and slide forward for the next stroke. It is important that this latter period should have a sense of swing and sweep in it. It is a period of lively yet balanced and measured action, and should not on any account resemble a creep or a crawl. The older school of oarsmen inveighs, with much justice, against the slow rate of stroke adopted in practice by modern crews, not only by sliding-seat crews but also by those rowing on fixed seats, as in Torpids at Oxford, or the Lents at Cambridge. The *marche funèbre*, Dr. Warre called it in his *Grammar of Rowing*. It is largely attributable to a false sense of rhythm and undue constraint in the swing and slide forward.

The whole rhythm of the stroke, then, may be represented by a sound formula, somewhat of this kind:

Fŭtt—Chŭf , Stēăd-ĭ-lў,

the syllables of the word 'steadily' being pronounced distinctly and separately but with a certain run in them as befits a dactyl. I do not pretend that this is quite right, but it is nearer the mark than any formula I know of and will be found useful by coach and oarsman alike.

In connexion with rhythm, it should be borne in mind that the stroke has three phases : the stroke through the water, the recovery, and the swing forward. Commonly it is thought of as consisting of two phases only, the swing forward and the swing back ; but this is apt to lead to 'bucket '. The recovery is a very distinct phase in the stroke and should be suitably stressed, but not exaggerated.

It is very important that the finish of the stroke should not be confused with the recovery. During the finish the blade of the oar is covered and doing work in the water. The knees should be well flattened down, the lower part of the body firm and upright, the shoulders and elbows drawing back, the oar drawn towards the body by hooked fingers. The recovery lifts the oar out of the water, turns it on the feather, starts its backward horizontal sweep on the feather, and, by an elastic reaction of the hips, of which more anon, brings the whole body up to, and a trifle beyond, the perpendicular. The recovery completed, the swing of the body starts the next phase of the stroke, and the slide is allowed to come forward.

One of the commonest faults in rowing, leading to thoroughly bad oarsmanship, is the tendency to muddle up the finish and the recovery. The unskilful oarsman, as the handle of his oar approaches him, seems to have no confidence in his power to lift his blade out of the water. He is flurried ; prematurely lets go the pressure of his feet on the stretcher ; hooks his toes into the straps ; grasps the oar tightly in his fists ; by a hoist of the shoulders drags his hands upwards towards his chest ; and then, with a wrench, extracts his blade from the water and pushes forward his shoulders, leaving himself in a position in which control of the slide and swing forward is wellnigh impossible.

Equally common is the fault of hurrying through the recovery into the swing. In this case the oarsman flings forward his arms from the shoulders after the manner of a man diving into the water, giving an impetus to the upper part of his body which he is powerless to check. The body hurtles forward after the arms, carrying the slide with it, and the rest of the movement forward is either an uncontrolled rush or, as is frequently the case, the oarsman, in obedience to the exhortations of his coach to be steady forward, tries to put the drag on by stiffening the muscles of his back and shoulders as he approaches his front-stop. In either case the true rhythm of the stroke is destroyed and a firm and well-timed ' beginning ' is impossible. It was an old and useful notion at Eton, but it seems to have long since fallen into desuetude, that the stroke ended and a new stroke was begun, not when the hands touched the chest, but after the wrists had been shot away and the oar recovered. At that point there was a slight check, a steadying point, from which the swing forward of the new stroke started. Interpreted as the transition from one phase of the stroke—the recovery—to another phase—the swing forward—it is a very useful notion and may be used freely in the endeavour to correct the common fault of bucketing forward.

The rhythm of the stroke is the mental measure of the rate and times at which the various parts of the stroke must be performed. It is largely the means by which the mind co-ordinates the various actions of the body and limbs. It is as important in rowing as the rhythm of the music is in a dance, and a crew should strive to attain to the correct measure from the earliest stages of practice. But it must be borne in mind that it is an auxiliary, and does not comprehend the whole art of rowing. Before leaving the subject I must reiterate that the rhythm should be *lively* ; it should not be dreamy, and above all things it must not be grave and funereal. It should be a spirited quickstep, not a slow march. It is permissible, in crews which have attained to a high degree of excellence, to paddle at a very slow rate of stroke with the least possible exertion. This used to be called ' slumming ', and when it is well done the movements of the crew seem to vanish into the rhythm ; the whole motion becomes almost a dream. But ' slumming ' is one of the finer arts of oarsmanship and is not to be recommended until the later stages of practice, when the crew is securely welded together. The Third Trinity crews of the early years of the century used to exhibit the art in great perfection, but the Jesus College crews of succeeding years were, I think, in error in using it as a means of obtaining uniformity and cohesion instead of relegating it to its proper place as an exhibition of perfect cohesion already attained. Their rowing, good as it was in many ways, always had an air of dreaminess about it, and their apparent lack of vigour became actual when they were pushed hard by crews whose pace was as good as their own.

CHAPTER VII

ON OARS

If there is one thing more than another that oarsmen are faddy about, it is their oars. No crew enters upon its training for a race of any importance but the question arises, What length of oar shall we row with? When the length overall is decided on, the further questions arise: What shall be the length inboard? and what shall be the width of the blade? Too often the question is decided without any clear understanding of the principles of the lever upon which the efficiency of the oar depends. Yet these principles are very simple, and the problems that arise, beyond those which can be solved by simple arithmetic, relate chiefly to the convenience of the oarsman.

It has been explained at ample length in Chapter II that an oar functions, at one and the same time, in two capacities: as a lever of the first order in setting water in motion, and thereby creating the resistance without which it could not function at all; as a lever of the second order, in moving the boat past the area swept through by the blade. Sufficient emphasis has been laid on the fact that the primary object of the oarsman is to move his boat as far as possible whilst the blade is in the water. If the oar is relatively long inboard the oarsman gains in leverage in this sense: that the power he applies at the handle will overcome a greater resistance at the blade. But he loses leverage in the sense that he moves his blade through a shorter arc. Conversely, if the oar is relatively short inboard, the oarsman loses in leverage in the sense that the same power applied at the handle can overcome only a lessened resistance at the blade. But he gains in the sense that his blade describes a longer arc. This elementary fact is illustrated in the diagram on p. 169, fig. 36, in which *HR* represents the handle and *RB* the outboard length of an oar 12 ft. 6 in.

long, with an inboard length of 4 feet. The proportions are exaggerated purposely, to make the principle clear in a small-scale diagram. *HRB* shows the oar at the beginning, inclined at an angle of 40° to the side of the boat, and *H′RB′* shows it at the finish after it has turned through an angle of 80°. An oar of exactly the same length overall, and making exactly the same angles with the side of the boat at the beginning and at the finish, but with an inboard length of only 3 ft., is represented by *hrb* and *h′rb′*. It is manifest that the arc *hh′*, which is the distance through which the oarsman has to pull his hands, is much shorter than the arc *HH′*, but when we look at the arc described by the tip of the blade *bb′* is longer than *BB′* by just the same amount as *hh′* is shorter than *HH′*. Such a diagram as this does not take into account the position and movements of the oarsman, but it is sufficiently obvious that the shorter oar inboard demands a shorter outrigger. A little reflection shows that the man with the shorter oar inboard must be seated well back from his work and is practically limited to a fixed seat ; whereas the man wielding the oar with the greater length inboard must slide up to his work, and with that great length of handle, must slide back as far as the length of his legs will allow. Postponing the question as to which of the two oars entails the greater exertion on the part of the oarsman, we see at the outset that variations in the inboard length of the oar involve alterations in the length of the outrigger, or what amounts to the same thing, the distance athwartship that the oarsman is seated from his rowlock ; in the distance that he is seated away from his work ; and in the length of his slide, if sliding-seats are in question.

I must point out here that oarsmen introduce a needless source of error by calling the distance from the centre of the seat to the rowlock the ‘ leverage ’. Many are misled by the term into imagining that a longer outrigger gives a greater leverage. But, the inboard length of the oar remaining the same, it does nothing of the sort. It only alters the position of the oar-handle relatively to the oarsman’s body at all parts of the stroke. It would save much confused thinking if oarsmen would make use of a good nautical term and call the measurement in question the thwartship distance from the rowlock. For brevity's sake it may be referred to as T. D.

Mr. W. B. Woodgate, whose knowledge of all questions relating to fixed-seat rowing was unrivalled, has told us that, long before he had learned to row, experience had shown that the best proportion of

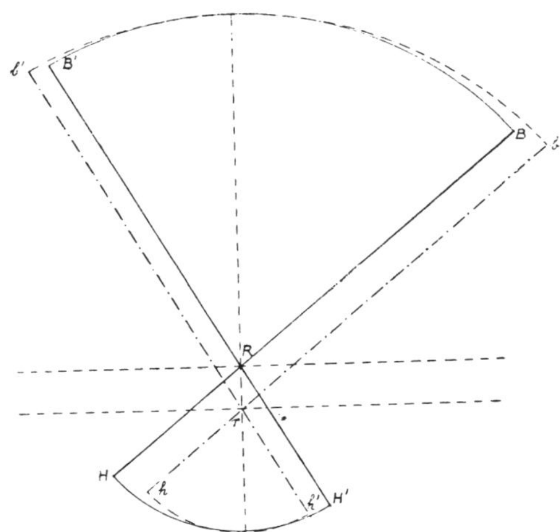

Fig. 36. A diagram illustrating the effect of altering the inboard length of the oar.

inboard to outboard length was, if the oar is divided into twenty-five parts, seven parts inboard and eighteen parts outboard. Whatever the length of the oars overall, these proportions were carefully observed. This must have been after the introduction of outriggers, for in the mighty sweeps 15 feet long and upwards wielded by our forefathers the inboard length was of somewhat shorter proportion. With the advent of outriggers, the long body-swing, and the catch at the beginning, the standard length of oars seems to have been fixed at 12 ft. 6 in. ; partly, I surmise, for this reason, that 25 goes exactly six times into

150 inches. Hence the standard inboard length was $6 \times 7 = 42$ inches. For oars of less length overall, the inboard length was cut down in proportion.

As fixed-seat oarsmen usually sat 11 or 12 inches away from their work, the position of the handle of the oar in relation to their shoulders at the finish was very different from what it is in the case of a man sliding up to his work and using a 16-inch slide. The thwartship distance of the seat from the rowlock must have been shorter than the 31 inches now customary. How much shorter it was in racing eights I do not know, but in the Eton *Monarch*, of which I have a very accurate plan made for Sir John E. Thornycroft, the measurement is 30 inches. In point of fact, fixed-seat oarsmen did not bother themselves overmuch about this detail, because, as I remember well, on taking one's seat in a fixed-seat boat, one was always told by the coach to shift one's seat a little to one side or the other to bring the body 'square with the work'. This expression really referred to the position of the hands at the end of the stroke. It will be found that, with this thwartship measurement, a man sitting 12 inches away from his work, using an oar 3 ft. 6 in. inboard, brings his hands home to his chest in the proper position: the point on the oar midway between the two hands opposite to the breastbone.

With the short measurement inboard, fixed-seat oarsmen used longer and narrower blades than have been seen for some fifty years. Mr. S. H. Woodhouse tells me that the oar with which he won the Grand Challenge Cup at Henley, in the record time for fixed seats, measures 12 feet overall, with an inboard of 3 ft. 5 in., the blade being 3 ft. 3 in. long and 5 inches wide. This oar, he says, is some inches shorter than was usual. The length of blade to some extent eases the oarsman, as it brings the centre of pressure farther inboard, but, as Mr. Ewing McGruer has pointed out,[1] the long narrow blade is wasteful, for more work is absorbed in pivoting it about its centre of pressure. The modern blade is 2 ft. 8 in. or 2 ft. 9 in. in length;

[1] *Coaching for Young Crews*, by an Old Blue, 1921, p. 21.

as a rule, 6 inches in width, and more curved towards its tip than the old blade. The change in the shape and dimensions of blades seems to have come in with the use of sliding-seats, though I have not been able to ascertain the exact date at which the change took place. As early as 1876 I rowed in Lower Boy Pulling at Eton with the modern type of blade, though our boats were old-fashioned in-rigged wherries, known to Etonians of those days as ' cedars '. I remember to have seen a few of the old-fashioned narrow-bladed oars in use, but they were regarded as obsolete.

Though the blades changed, the inboard measurements of the oar did not, at any rate for some seven or eight years after the introduction of sliding-seats. *Argonaut* (the late Mr. E. D. Brickwood) gave the average dimensions of oars, for use with 16-inch slides, as 12 ft. 6 in. overall, with 3 ft. 6 in. inboard. The following table of measurements shows that oars of these proportions were in common use at the time he wrote:

	Length Overall.	*Length Inboard.*	*Width of Blade.*
	ft. in.	ft. in.	inches.
Oxford, 1877 (' dead heat ')	12 2	3 6	6
Leander, 1880 (record time for Henley old course) .	12 4½	3 6½	6
Eton, 1878	12 0	3 5	5¾
Eton, 1879	12 4	3 5	6
Eton, 1880	12 0	3 5	6⅛
Eton, 1881	12 6	3 6	6

But when I arrived at Oxford in 1882 I found that the established length of oar was 12 ft. 6 in. overall, with a 6-inch blade and an inboard of 3 ft. 8½ in. My experience is that these proportions can hardly be bettered, though there is a good deal to be said for cutting down the width of the blade to 5¾ inches in a 12 ft. 6 in. oar. But of this question of long versus short oars more anon. The present question is, What is the proper inboard length of an oar ?

For fixed-seat oars, the answer is that the dimensions should be those given by Mr. Woodgate, but some little allowance may be made in connexion with the distance that the oarsman is seated from his work alongships.

Since I began writing this chapter I have been studying this question at Eton in conjunction with Mr. E. W. Powell and Mr. C. A. Gladstone. Up to last year (1924) the work in all fixed-seat boats had been placed 12 inches away from the seat, regardless of the size of the boys. The oars were of the same dimensions as those used in sliding-seat boats. The conditions were so obviously unsatisfactory that Mr. Powell and Mr. Gladstone decided to put the work at 10 inches in all the classes of boats used by the smaller boys. When this was done, the oars formerly in use proved quite unsuitable. On their asking my opinion on the subject I told them that the oars I had rowed with at Eton were only 3 ft. 5 in. inboard, and that this was the standard measure for oars in fixed-seat days. As a result of our correspondence we made a fairly exhaustive investigation. A number of oars were made ready by adjusting buttons to different inboard lengths, and some old oars were cut down to a length of 11 ft. 8 in. overall, with an inboard length of 3 ft. 3¾ in., that is to say, to very nearly the proportions recommended by Mr. Woodgate. The different oars were tested in four-oars and pair-oars by boys of different ages and sizes, and we rowed with them ourselves. At the conclusion of the experiments opinion was practically unanimous.

When the oarsman is seated 10 inches away from his work and the thwartship measurement from the rowlock is 30 inches, the proper length inboard of an oar measuring 12 feet overall is 3 ft. 5 in. This brings the hands into the right position relative to the body at the end of the stroke. An inboard measurement of 3 ft. 6 in. is clearly too long, and if it is increased to 3 ft. 7 in. or 3 ft. 8 in. the inside hand is brought right across the body at the finish, the outside elbow is protruded, and the oarsman screws out of the boat. Even when the oarsman is seated 12 inches away from his work, the inboard measurement of 3 ft. 5 in. is sufficient, but it may, in this case, be increased to 3 ft. 5½ in. or even to 3 ft. 6 in. for broad-shouldered boys or for men. With the

11 ft. 8 in. oar buttoned at 3 ft. 3¾ in., the thwartship distance from the rowlock should be reduced to 29¾ inches. These shortened oars are intended for the use of boys weighing 8½ stone and under. They are not a whit too small. We found that we could do sound, hard work with them, and they were very handy at a fast stroke. We concluded that, for small boys, the width of the blade should not be more than 5¾ inches. Experiments were also made with sculls, in whiffs in which the sculler was seated 10 inches from his work. Here we found that with sculls of the normal length inboard, allowing a reasonable overlap of the hands in the middle of the stroke, the finish was very awkward. It was clear that, on a fixed seat, a sculler must be seated at least 12 inches away from his work, and it was decided not to interfere with the measurements established by long use. In the course of these experiments we tested the balance of the oars by shifting strips of lead up and down the loom, both inboard and outboard. We found that an 11 ft. 8 in. oar comes most sweetly to hand when the centre of gravity of the whole oar is 1 ft. 9 in. outside the button. In a 12 ft. 6 in. oar, buttoned at 3 ft. 5 in., the C. G. should be about 1 ft. 9¾ in. outside the button. It is to the highest degree important that an oar should be properly balanced. In my rowing days old Edward Ayling was a past master in the art of making well-balanced oars. Of late years balance has been too much neglected, and oar-makers have concentrated their attention on devising double-girder, tubular, box-loom, and other patent oars of very doubtful value, the balance of which is often extremely faulty. I shall refer again to this very important question of balance.

The reader will have observed that, in making experiments with different inboard lengths of oar, the crucial question was not one of ideal proportions for leverage, but to fit the oar to the man at the finish of the stroke. That is the root of the whole matter. Whether on a fixed seat or on a sliding-seat, the inboard length of the oar must be such that, at the finish of the stroke, the hands, held 4 inches apart on the oar, are equidistant from the median line of the body. If the oar is too long inboard the inside forearm is pressed against the front of the body ; the inside wrist is too much flexed laterally and its freedom of action is cramped. If the oar is too short inboard the outside forearm is brought across the body and the oarsman can hardly avoid letting go the grasp of the outside fingers at the finish. In either case a correct action of the wrists at the recovery is difficult, if not impossible. It need hardly be said that the inboard length of the oar is related to the T. D. An oar which is too long inboard with a T. D. of 30 inches will be about right if the latter is increased to 31 inches. Hence there is a certain amount of liberty for selecting the most advantageous proportions of inboard and outboard length of oar, limited on the one hand by the considerations dealt with above ; on the other hand, by the fact that the outrigger must not be made so long that it is weak.

It is obvious that the conditions are quite different for fixed and sliding-seats. A fixed-seat oarsman rarely sits and finishes more than 12 inches away from his work. At that distance the inboard length of the oar should be relatively short. It should not exceed 3 ft. 7 in. when the T. D. is 31 inches, and the best measurements are those recommended by the long experience of oarsmen of a past generation : length inboard, 3 ft. 6 in. ; thwartship distance, 30 inches. An immense amount of injury is done to oarsmanship, at the Universities and elsewhere, by setting young oarsmen to row on fixed seats with oars of an inboard length designed for sliding-seats.

On a sliding-seat of the normal length, an oarsman, if he slides up to his work, finishes 16 inches away from it. If he is set back from his work, he finishes just so many inches farther from it: as much, it may be, as 19 or 20 inches. In any case he requires a greater inboard length than a fixed-seat oarsman, but if he is set back from his work the inboard length must be increased still farther. To maintain a proper proportion between the two arms of the lever the outboard should also be increased. There is a good deal to be said for setting back the work 3 inches and increasing the length of the oar both inboard and outboard. But I have never heard of its being done. There is nothing to be said for setting back the work and shortening the length of the oar, but that is exactly what has been done on more than one occasion. I can recall a crew which, with work set 3 inches away from the thowl alongships and 31 inches athwartships, used oars 11 ft. 10 in. long, buttoned at 3 ft. 7 in. with $6\frac{1}{2}$-inch blades. The result was that the rowing was very short, and at the finish the handle of the oar came nearly under the inside armpit. By dint of rowing a very fast stroke with amazing energy and determination this crew was very successful, but it had no very strong opponents to overcome. Its success was attributable to the exceptional vigour of the oarsmen and not to the rig that they adopted. In less worthy hands the rig, and the style of rowing engendered by it, proved an utter failure. From a mechanical point of view there was this much to be said in favour of it : the inboard length of the oars was not too great in proportion to the outboard.

I have before me the record of observations and experiments, extending over many years, for many different crews, made by the late Colonel W. A. L. Fletcher. As he does not give numerical results the record is hardly worth publishing here, but in general his conclusions tally very nearly with mine. He found that oars 12 ft. 6 in. overall, buttoned at 3 ft. $8\frac{1}{2}$ in. or 3 ft. 9 in., with a narrow blade of $5\frac{1}{2}$ inches or less, are much faster than any shorter oar, provided that the crew is strong enough to use them. Second to these he placed oars 11 ft. 10 in. long overall, buttoned at 3 ft. 7 in., with $6\frac{1}{2}$-inch blades. Oars 12 feet overall, with 3 ft. 8 in. inboard and 6-inch or $6\frac{1}{2}$-inch blades, did not give as good results as 11 ft. 10 in. oars. All intermediate lengths of oar with from 3 ft. $8\frac{1}{2}$ in. to 3 ft. 7 in. inboard, and blades varying from $5\frac{1}{2}$ to $6\frac{1}{8}$ inches in width, Colonel Fletcher described as 'slow'. My experience is almost exactly in agreement with his, but, for the shorter type of oar, I prefer 12 feet overall, with 3 ft. 7 in. inboard and a 6-inch blade, when the T. D. is 31 inches.

One of Colonel Fletcher's experiments is of special interest. Using a 12 ft. 1 in. oar, 3 ft. 7 in. inboard, and a 6-inch blade, he found the crew fast when the T. D. was 31 inches ; slow when it was 29½ inches. As there is so much confusion of thought about leverages, it is necessary to emphasize the fact that, in both trials, the leverage of the oar was exactly the same. A pull of 100 lb. at the centre of effort of the hands gave a pressure of 39·5 lb. at the centre of pressure of the blade. The only alteration was in the thwartship measurement, miscalled the 'leverage'. What was the effect of altering the thwartship measurement ? In the first place, supposing the oarsman to have reached forward and swung back exactly the same distance in both trials, it affected the length of the arc described by the centre of pressure of the blade. In the second place, it altered the position of the handle of the oar relatively to the body of the oarsman, at all parts of the stroke. This is illustrated by fig. 37, in which the skeleton of the shoulder-girdle is indicated for three positions of the oarsman (these positions are carefully measured from photographs) ; the oar at a T. D. of 31 inches is drawn in continuous lines and at 29½ inches in broken lines. With a T. D. of 31 inches the oar is represented as forming an angle of 40° with the line of advance at the boat at the beginning of the stroke, and it is moved through 80°, finishing at 120°. This is the normal for full reach forward and swing back, when the oarsman is sliding up to his work. The arc AB described by the centre of pressure of the blade measures 10·8333 feet (10 ft. 10 in.). With the T. D. at 29½ inches, the oarsman reaching out and swinging back to exactly the same amount as before, the angle at the beginning of the stroke is 38½° ; at the finish, 121°. Therefore the oar is moved through an angle of 82½°, and the arc $A'B'$ (necessarily nearer in towards the boat than in the previous case) measures 11·0833 feet (11 ft. 1 in.). Thus we learn that, the length of swing of the body being the same, the shorter the thwartship measurement from the centre of the seat to the thowl, the greater is the area swept through by the blade. This seems advantageous, but it is punishing to the oarsman because, in beginning with his oar at an angle of 38½°, he has transgressed what I hold to be the limit (40°) to which the oar ought to be carried forward at the beginning of the stroke. He is wasting power in ‘ pinching the boat ’. The extra bit of length at the finish seems to be a gain. Furthermore it must be remembered that, if the stroke is rowed through in the same period of time, the longer sweep of the oar outboard entails greater effort. If longer time is allowed

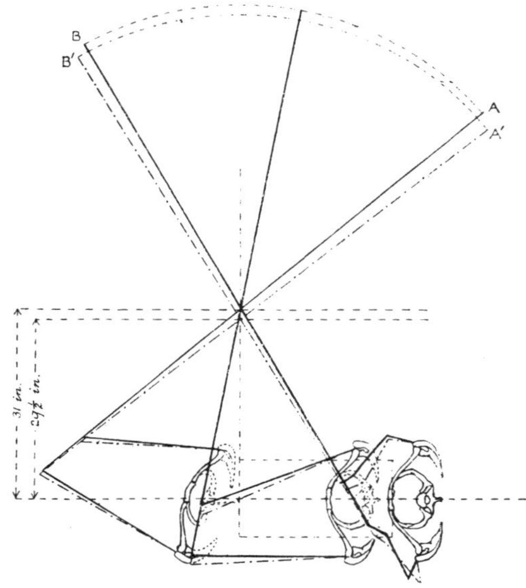

Fig. 37. A diagram illustrating the effect of altering the thwartship distance of rowlock from centre of seat. To save space the outboard of the oar has been reduced by half.

for the longer stroke in the water, the rate of stroke must fall. There is no obvious mechanical advantage in reducing the T. D., nor is there any serious disadvantage. Indeed, if the oarsmen were placed an inch or two farther away from their work alongships, one would expect to obtain a distinct advantage. Yet with this rig the crew, *teste* Colonel Fletcher, was much slower. To find the explanation of this we must look at the effect of altering the length of the outrigger on the oarsman's movements. In fig. 37 the arms are represented by straight lines drawn from the middle of the shoulder-joint to the knuckle of the middle finger of each hand. The lines are continuous when T. D. = 31 inches ; broken when T. D. = 29½ inches. As lengthening T. D. has the same effect as shortening the oar inboard, the oarsman's arms have to follow the handle of the oar rather farther across the boat when T. D. = 31 inches than when T. D. = 29½ inches, but there is no great advantage or disadvantage, one way or the other, at the beginning of the stroke. Towards the middle of the stroke, when the oar is approaching an angle of 80° and the shoulders are square to the work : if T. D. = 31 inches, the handle of the oar does not project so far beyond the outer shoulder as to make the pull of the outside arm fall inconveniently far outside a line drawn parallel to the axis of the boat, which latter is the true line of the fore and aft swing of the body as well as of the travel of the slide. But the diagram shows that when T. D. = 29½ inches the pull of the outside arm is inconveniently askew to the true line of the swing and slide. To test this point, let the reader stand opposite a railing of convenient height and, grasping the top bar as if it were an oar with both hands, pull backwards as in rowing. He will instinctively place himself opposite the point half-way between his two hands in order to get the greatest strength of pull. Now let him shift himself only a few inches to one side, keeping his shoulders parallel with the bar. The relative weakness of the pull, when the hands are no longer opposite to the body and the arms are askew, is manifest. The most effective part of the stroke is the middle part, when the oar is moving from some 15° in front of, to a like distance behind, a line drawn athwartships through the working thowl-pin of the rowlock. That is the period in which it is acting at the greatest mechanical advantage. To make the best use of it the work should be set so that during this period the pull should be as nearly in a straight line as possible. With a T. D. of 30 inches and an inboard length of oar of 3 ft. 5 in., the pull of the outside arm is as nearly as possible parallel to the true fore and aft line of the swing of the body, and this is doubtless the reason why fixed-seat oarsmen adopted these as their standard measurements. An inboard of this length, however, is not suitable for use on a 16-inch slide, for reasons already stated and to be dealt with in more detail in the next paragraph. It is necessary to increase the inboard length on a sliding-seat. As a consequence the sliding-seat oarsman is at a disadvantage compared to the properly rigged fixed-seat oarsman in the middle of the stroke. Surely, it is folly to increase this disadvantage by making the inboard of the oar unnecessarily long.

A too great length inboard has its attendant disadvantages at the finish of the stroke. Fig. 37 shows that, with an inboard length of 3 ft. 7 in., when T. D. = 31 inches, each hand is nearly equidistant from the median line of the body at the finish, and the inside wrist and forearm are in the best position for dropping and turning at the recovery. If the oar were shorter inboard, or if the oarsman finished farther away from his work, the outside hand would be brought so near the middle line of the body that it could hardly retain its hold of the oar and would be nearly useless for the recovery. When T. D. = 29½ inches, the inside hand is nearly opposite the middle line of the body, and the position of the forearm is such that the oarsman must either shift the grasp to the little and ring fingers, in which case he loses power and control at the recovery: or he must bend his wrist so much laterally, in order to retain the grasp of the first and second fingers, that it is cramped and incapable of any freedom of action. The position of the oar relatively to the body at the finish of the stroke is better illustrated by fig. 38, but in this case the oar was 3 ft. 9 in. inboard and T. D. = 32 inches. The thumb of the inside (right) hand comes very near the middle line of the body. The outside hand is below the nipple of the left breast. This drawing is a correction of a photograph taken from a position vertically above the oarsman. In the original T. D. was only 31 inches: with this measurement the oar was too long inboard, and the oarsman was screwing out of the boat.

We may conclude that Colonel Fletcher's crew was slow with a T. D. of $29\frac{1}{2}$ inches, because the pull became weak just at the point where it should have remained strong, and because the hands were in a disadvantageous position for the recovery. The same results follow when, with a T. D. of 31 inches, the oar is too long inboard. This discussion emphasizes a fact which cannot be insisted upon too strongly. *The man is much more important than the oar.* The position in which the oarsman can use his weight and muscular power to the greatest advantage counts for much more than the trifling and often illusory advantages sought for by making alterations in the leverage of the oar.

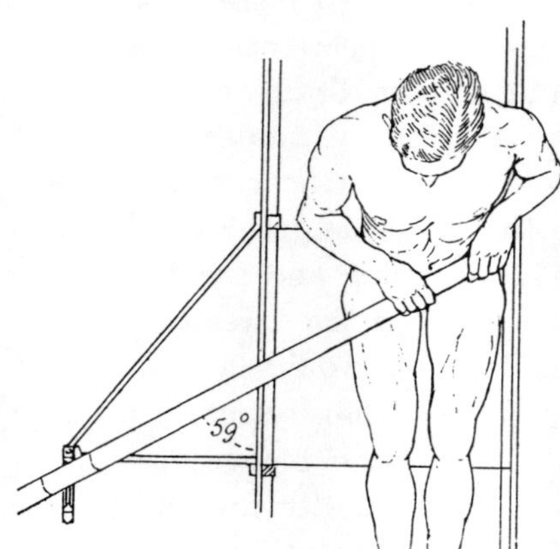

Fig. 38. The proper position of the hands at the finish of the stroke: from a photograph taken from a position vertically above the oarsman's seat.

About the year 1890 there was a craze for increasing the length of the oar inboard. The Oxford crew of 1891 was composed, from bow to stroke, of oarsmen of exceptional merit. It should have been able to row right away from a very uniform and spirited, but physically much inferior, Cambridge crew. It only succeeded in winning by a short half length, after a tremendous tussle, in which Mr. G. Elin, the Cambridge stroke, covered himself with glory. Mr. C. W. Kent tells me he has no doubt that the relative failure of his crew was due to its rowing with oars with the absurd inboard length of 3 ft. 10 in., increased in some individual cases to 3 ft. 11 in.

The craze for such abnormal measurements soon died out, but to this day oarsmen have a predilection for an excessive length inboard. As a consequence there is hardly a modern oarsman who does not swing away from his oar in the middle of the stroke and finish in a lop-sided position. This crooked swing means unequal use of the muscles on the two sides of the body, with a corresponding loss of power. The pull is far stronger when both sides are used equally.

In the matter of length overall of oars I am, and always have been, obstinately δολιχήρετμος. The longer oar gives the greater stride. It has been proved by experience, as witness Colonel W. A. L. Fletcher's experiments and many New College crews who have over-

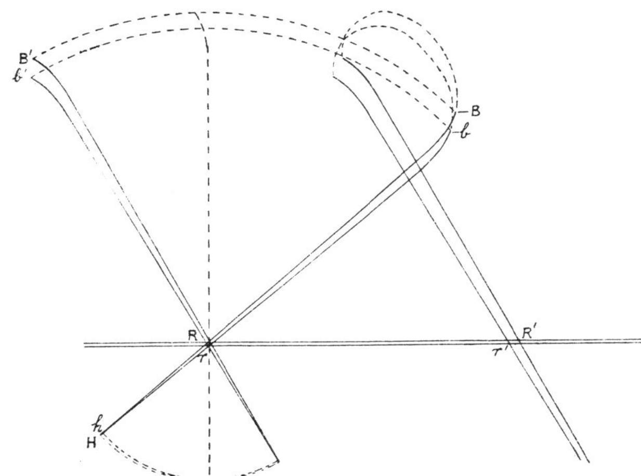

FIG. 39. A diagram illustrating the advantage of the long oar. For description see text.

come opponents of greater physical strength and of at least equal skill to themselves. Mr. W. B. Woodgate was a consistent advocate of the long oar, and has given an ingenious diagram proving its theoretical advantage. I reproduce it in fig. 39 with certain modifications to make it more nearly consistent with what actually happens.

HB represents an oar 12 ft. 6 in. long, with an inboard of 3 ft. 8¾ in. It is buttoned at *R*, which is placed 32 inches, thwartship measure, from the centre of the seat. *hb* represents an oar 12 feet long, with an inboard of 3 ft. 7 in. It is buttoned at *r*, 31 inches from the centre of the seat. R, R' is the line of advance of the rowlock for the long oar; r, r', the line of advance for the short oar. The oarsman is supposed to reach forward exactly the same distance to H or h. With this reach forward the short oar makes an angle of 40° with the side of the boat. The long oar, with a longer T. D., makes an angle of 41·5°. There is an initial advantage in that the long oar tends to pinch the boat less than the short oar. Whichever oar is in use the oarsman is supposed to swing back exactly the same distance. The short oar makes an angle of 120°, the long oar an angle of 119° at the finish of the stroke. Therefore the short oar moves through an angle of 80°, the long oar through an angle of only 77·5°. One might think that the short oar gives the longer stroke in the water, but, if the boat were stationary, the arc BB' described by the tip of the longer oar would be longer than the arc bb' described by the tip of the shorter oar, because the radius RB is greater than the radius rb. When the boat is in motion, the distance RR', through which it is moved by the longer oar, is greater by 2½ inches than the distance rr', through which it is moved by the shorter oar. This extra bit of acceleration during the stroke will cause the boat with the longer oar to travel a like distance farther during the run, so the total gain per stroke due to the use of the long oar may be taken as 5 inches. Observing that the effective leverages of the two oars are practically identical (a pull of 100 lb. at the centre of effort of the hands giving, in each case, a pressure of 40 lb. at the centre of pressure of the blade) we may express the difference between the two sizes of oar as follows: If two crews of equal skill and weight, equally boated, were to row stroke for stroke, at a rate of 35 per minute, over the Henley course, the crew using the longer oars would, at the end of seven minutes' rowing, be 102 ft. 1 in., or about a length and three quarters, ahead of the crew using the shorter oars. But there is no magic in this. The gain in speed involves an extra effort on the part of the oarsmen, for more work is required to move the boat through the longer distance in the same time at every stroke. One cannot get ninepence for fourpence any easier in the rowing than in the economical world. But there is this distinct advantage, that with the T. D. at 32 inches, the longer oar makes a less acute angle with the side of the boat at the beginning of the stroke, and therefore less work is wasted in 'pinching the boat'. There can be no doubt that the long oar is the faster, and much faster than a 12-foot oar of which the outboard length has been curtailed by making the inboard more than 3 ft. 7 in. But if the T. D. is 31 inches, the long oar has all the disadvantages of too great length inboard. The angle moved through by the oar for the same reach forward will be the same as with a 12-foot oar, and the same waste of work will result from pinching the boat at the beginning. The angle through which the oar is moved being greater, the work required will be greater, and the oarsmen will soon feel the strain. This is alleviated by cutting down the width of the blade to 5½ or even to 5¼ inches, which involves a loss of blade reaction. There is no advantage in balancing a gain in one direction by a loss in another. With a T. D. of proper length there is no reason why the blade of a 12 ft. 6 in. oar should not be 6 inches wide, or at the least 5¾ inches. Looking at the very heavy crews of the present day, I can only agree with Mr. Woodgate in expressing my wonder that they should profess themselves unable to wield oars of the dimensions in common use forty years ago. It should not be forgotten that thirty-eight years ago, in a year when the river was not abnormally low, the Grand Challenge Cup was won in 6 min. 53½ sec. by a narrow margin, in days when 12 ft. 6 in. oars were in general use. In truth, modern oarsmen are quite able to use long oars if they have a mind to, and with very good effect, as was proved by the New College crew of 1911.

On the subject of broad blades I have only this to say: I have tried them again and again, but have always had to cut them down to 6 inches before the end of practice. A blade over 6 inches in width is too much for a crew which is trying to keep a decent length of swing. Of these two things I am more certain than of anything else pertaining to rowing: that a blade over 6 inches in width involves a shorter length of swing ; and that, *ceteris paribus*, a long swing—I do not mean an overreach—will always overcome a short swing.

As for the shape of blades, I can only say that Mr. Ewing McGruer is clearly right. The correct blade is that which has its area concentrated near the tip. Barrel-shaped and coffin-shaped blades are wrong in principle and have nothing to recommend them.

I do not wish to suggest that all crews should be fitted with the same length of oar and the same rig. Much depends on the strength, the experience, and the temper of the crew : on the character of the race to be rowed and on the tactics it is proposed to adopt. Generally speaking, a light, lively crew will be better suited with shorter oars, a heavy powerful crew with long oars. If rushing tactics at a fast rate of stroke are to be adopted, short oars are the best for the purpose. If it is proposed to row a waiting race, long oars should be chosen. If a crew which has been rowing with long oars becomes stale before the end of practice, a change to shorter oars is often beneficial. But it is fatal to give long oars to a crew which has been practising for a long time with short oars. It must be borne in mind that a long oar is something like the bow of Odysseus : only a hero can bend it.

The following table may be found useful by coaches and captains :

Length Overall.	*Length Inboard.*	*Length Outboard.*	*Distance from Work Athwartships.*	*Length of Blade.*	*Width of Blade.*
ft. in.	ft. in.	ft. in.	inches.	ft. in.	inches.
12 6	3 8¾	8 9¼	32	2 9	5¾
12 3	3 8	8 7	31	2 9	6 to 5¾
12 0	3 7	8 5	31	2 8	6
11 10	3 6½	8 3½	30¾	2 8	6

The effective leverage is a trifle greater in the 11 ft. 10 in. oar than in the others. In the first three oars it is to all intents and purposes the same.

Whatever the length of the oar its balance is of the utmost importance. Nothing is more stimulating to good oarsmanship than an oar which seems to take hold of the water of its own accord at the beginning of the stroke and swings back on the feather with the ease and precision of a well-hung pendulum. The balance of an oar is not simply a matter of its gross weight nor of the excess of weight outboard relatively to the weight inboard, though it may be remarked in passing that modern oars are commonly too light outboard and at the same time too heavy as a whole. The two things that are of real importance are: (1) the moment of inertia of the oar about the button; (2) the distance of the centre of impact of the blade from its tip. In practice, it would seem, the two things go together: if one is right the other will also be right.

In 1910, being thoroughly dissatisfied with the balance of the different kinds of new-fangled oars supplied by the various oar-makers, I took up this question with the assistance of Mr. R. T. Edge of New College. We began our inquiry empirically, by making trial of a large number of oars, including my own oars of 1882 and 1883, and selecting for further trial and experiment those which were clearly the best balanced and the most easy to manipulate. Having ascertained the centre of gravity of each of the selected oars (which were of different dimensions), we altered the balance by shifting bands of lead up and down the loom, both inboard and outboard of the button. After making notes of the effect of altering the balance (which by the method adopted involved the increase of the total weight of the oar) Mr. Edge carried off the selected oars to the engineering laboratory and made them the subject of more exact experiment. The result of these experiments was that the oars designed by him for the New College eight of the same year were, in my opinion, the best that had ever been turned out by any maker. They were solid oars made by E. Norris of Putney, and their dimensions were the same as my Oxford oar of 1883, viz. 12 ft. 6 in. overall, with an inboard length of 3 ft. 8½ in. With these oars a crew of which I had no great expectations developed into one of the fastest that has ever rowed at Oxford. It had a magnificent length of swing and could row at the rate of 46 strokes a minute for two consecutive minutes without losing its length or showing any sign of being unduly hustled. Of the fiasco which deprived this crew of its chance of winning the Grand Challenge Cup at Henley I need say nothing here. It is sufficient to say that the crew set up a new series of records over the Oxford course, and that its merits were so generally recognized that New College had the honour, unique among College crews, of being invited to be one of the representatives of England at the Olympic Regatta at Stockholm in 1912. I am convinced that the phenomenal improvement made by the New College crew of 1911 during practice and the great speed it showed in racing were largely due to the scientific construction of its oars. Similar oars were ordered for the Oxford crew of 1912 and for the New College crew for the Olympic Regatta of the same year. But we never again got a set of such superlative excellence as that of 1911. Mr. Edge was unable to supervise personally the making of the later sets.

Towards the end of last year (1924) I again took up this question of the balance of oars with Mr. Edge's assistance. Acting under his instruction and advice, Messrs. Ayling & Son have taken the utmost possible trouble to produce a set of oars of the required character, and at the time of writing the Oxford crew of 1925 is using a new set which are certainly a great improvement on anything that has been made since the war.

The basic principle of Mr. Edge's design is to make the centre of percussion of the oar (or scull) about the button correspond as nearly as possible with the centre of impact of the blade in the water at the beginning of the stroke. The centre of impact was found empirically in 1911 to be 5½ inches from the tip of the blade in a well-balanced oar, but in oars departing more or less widely from what may be called a ' perfect ' balance it may vary from 3 inches to as much as 15¼ inches from the tip. After giving an extended trial to a set of oars in which the centre of impact varied within the above limits I can say that, as a matter of experience, the farther the centre of impact is from the optimum position of 5½ inches from the tip of the blade the more unwieldy is the oar irrespective of its gross weight. In testing these oars we made the unexpected discovery that, if the centre of impact is 12 or more inches from the tip of the blade, the oar feels too long inboard and causes the oarsman to screw out of the boat at the end of the stroke, though its dimensions are exactly the same as regards the proportion of inboard to outboard length as oars which feel, if anything, a trifle too short inboard. Coaches who are confronted with an obstinate case of screwing out of the boat should ascertain the centre of impact of the oar used by the delinquent. It may well be the cause of the trouble.

It might be supposed that, when once the proper dimensions are settled, it is an easy matter to turn out a set of oars of the required pattern, but in practice it is not. The proper balance depends upon the distribution of the weight along the whole length of the oar, and this can only be tested by hanging the unfinished oar by the end of the handle and ascertaining the time taken for a complete swing when it is set in motion like a pendulum.

The principle on which Mr. Edge worked out the problem may be expressed as follows:

Let l_1 feet be the length from the working face of the button to the end of the handle.

Let l_2 feet be the length from the working face of the button to the end of the blade.

Let r_1 feet be the length from the working face of the button to the centre of impact.

Let r_2 feet be the length from the working face of the button to the centre of gravity.

Then the centre of impact is given by the following formula:

$$r_1 = \frac{k_1^2}{r_2} = \frac{k_2^2 + r_2^2}{r_2}$$

k_1^2 being the square of the radius of gyration about the button and k_2^2 the square of the radius of gyration about the centre of gravity of the oar.

If T is the time in seconds of one complete swing of the oar when suspended by the handle, k_2^2 can be obtained by the formula :

$$k_2^2 = (l_1 + r_2)\left\{\frac{T^2}{4\pi^2} \times g - (l_1 + r_2)\right\}$$

Combining the two formulae we get

$$r_1 = \frac{(l_1 + r_2)}{r_2}\left\{\frac{T^2}{4\pi^2} \times g - (l_1 + r_2)\right\} + r_2$$

Or we have a value for T

$$T = \frac{2\pi}{\sqrt{g}}\sqrt{\frac{(l_1 + r_2)^2 + r_1 r_2 - r_2^2}{(l_1 + r_2)}}$$

or

$$T = 1{\cdot}10726\sqrt{\frac{(l_1 + 2r_2) \times l_1 + r_1 r_2}{(l_1 + r_2)}}\,.$$

Hence if we fix the proportions l_1 and l_2 of the oar and ascertain r_2, we can find T corresponding to a length r_1, which latter measurement is fixed by assuming the distance $(l_2 - r_1)$ at which the centre of impact is from the end of the blade. To make an oar on this principle all that is necessary is to calculate T, to suspend the oar by the end of the handle, and to find out what is the time of a complete swing. The oar must have its weights adjusted until the time of a complete swing is the same as the calculated T.

The weak point about this method is that it does not enable one to calculate the measurements r_2 and r_1 for an oar of any given dimensions, and I have not yet found a mathematician who can give a formula for calculating the ideal lengths of r_2 and r_1. It might be thought that, when the proportion of inboard length (l_1) to outboard length (l_2) is fixed, there must be a distance r_2 from the button to the centre of gravity of the whole oar which, when ascertained, will give an invariable length for r_1. This, however, is not the case. In the original experiments in 1911 Mr. Edge found that *in solid oars* of good balance r_2 was 1 ft. 10½ in. from the button, and that in the best-balanced and handiest oars the centre of impact $(l_2 - r_1)$ was 5½ inches, more or less, from the end of the blade; the oars being 12 ft. 6 in. overall, with an inboard of 3 ft. 8½ in. Taking these values for r_1 and r_2 he was able to produce the superexcellent oars used by the New College crew of 1911.

But what should these values be for oars of somewhat different dimensions? After testing a number of oars of various dimensions and finding that r_2 and r_1 were very variable, I tried to solve the question by making a model oar on a $\frac{1}{6}$ scale corresponding to the following full-sized dimensions: Length overall 12 ft. 3 in.; length inboard 3 ft. 8¼ in.; length outboard 8 ft. 6¾ in. Following the experience gained in 1911 I made r_2 of a length corresponding to 1 ft. 10½ in. By carefully paring away the wood both inboard and outboard of the button I was able, without much difficulty, to make a shapely pair of model oars in which T was 1·252 second, giving a corresponding value of 5½ inches for $(l_2 - r_1)$ in a full-sized oar. I seemed to have solved the problem, and thought that if an oar were made of normal thickness at the neck of the blade and handle, and if the thickest part of the oar were made some 10 inches inboard of the button, and the loom were made to taper evenly from this point towards the neck of the blade and towards the handle, as is the usual practice in making an oar, the proper length of r_1 would be assured if r_2 were 1 ft. 10½ in. So I think it might be in a solid oar made of evenly grained wood. But in a set partly of tubular, partly of double-lined tubular oars made by Messrs. Ayling & Son and referred to above, $(l_2 - r_1)$ varied from 15¼ to 4 inches, though r_2 varied only from 1 ft. 10½ in. to 1 ft 11 in. Clearly r_1 is not determined by r_2. The result was disappointing, but it was clearly due to the fact that the makers had gone too fast and had assumed, as I myself was inclined to assume, that the proper balance of the oar could be obtained by simply making r_2 of a certain length. In a subsequent set of oars Messrs. Ayling & Son paid special attention to the distribution of the weight along the length of the oar, and the result was quite satisfactory. In this set r_2 varied from 1 ft. 8¾ in. to 1 ft. 9 in. and $(l_2 - r_1)$ from 5 to 6½ inches. I do not think it is possible, in the present state of our knowledge, to obtain more accurate results with tubular oars. As the balance of the finished oar depends on paring away the wood to the required extent either inboard or outboard of the button, it is obvious that a more accurate result can be obtained with a solid than with a built-up tubular oar, for the latter cannot be pared down to any considerable extent without weakening the wall of the tube. For my own part I think that solid oars of the single girder type are preferable to any of the patterns of tubular oar now in use, but Messrs. Ayling & Son assure me that it is no longer possible to obtain seasoned wood of the high quality necessary for the manufacture of reliable solid oars. I have no reason to doubt their word. In any case they have succeeded in making tubular oars which are every whit as handy and well balanced as the best solid oars of fifteen years ago, and are probably superior in the matter of stiffness. Moreover the heaviest of these oars weigh only a trifle more than 9½ lb., and this is a considerable improvement on recent practice. Some of the oars supplied to the University crews of 1924 weighed as much as 10½ lb., an altogether unnecessary weight even if we admit that the total weight of the oar is of relatively small importance as long as the balance is correct.

When making model oars I found that apparently trifling additions or subtractions of weight at the ends of the oar made a great difference to the moment of inertia. The copper band at the end of the blade is, as might be expected, influential in this respect. So is the brass plate under the leather and the button itself. Even a coat of paint on the blade upsets the balance of what was previously a perfectly balanced oar. Messrs. Ayling & Son tell me that they had the same experience when making the perfectly balanced set of oars which they ultimately turned out. It is not sufficient to test the oar in the rough and afterwards to affix the button and the copper band on the blade. All these things must be in place before the oar is tested. It follows that when oarsmen lengthen an oar inboard by nailing an inch or so of wood to the end of the handle, or when they cut down the blade from six to five and a half inches, they alter the balance of the oar, and this to a much greater extent than they think. Another fact that emerges from our experiments is that the balance of an oar cannot be adjusted satisfactorily by letting an ounce or more of lead into the handle or by fixing a strip of lead under the copper at the end of the blade. In any oar the blade must be of a certain size and strength ; the neck of the blade must be of sufficient girth and strength to withstand the strain without bending unduly ; the girth of the handle should be $6\frac{1}{16}$ inches. The greatest strain on an oar is at the button, and the weight of the material should diminish evenly from the button—or better from a point about ten inches inside the button—in both directions.

I have only been able to give an empirical rule for an oar of certain fixed dimensions. If it is desired to make a perfectly balanced oar of other dimensions the whole calculation must be made afresh with the aid of experiment. Let us suppose that a 12-ft. oar with an inboard length of 3 ft. $7\frac{1}{2}$ in. is required. From the experience already gained it is safe to fix (l_2-r_1) at $5\frac{1}{2}$ inches. Similarly, r_2 may be fixed conjecturally at 1 ft. $8\frac{1}{2}$ in. for a tubular oar with a button of modern dimensions (buttons are now made much larger than they were a few years ago). With these data T must be calculated and the oar, before it is finished off, must be suspended by the handle and pared down as required until its T corresponds to the calculated T. When a satisfactory pattern of the required dimensions is obtained it should not be difficult to make a complete set identical with it in every particular.

It must be confessed that all this involves a considerable amount of trouble and some laborious arithmetical work. Oar-makers, as a rule, are not capable of working out mathematical formulae and are apt to be impatient of carefully conducted experiments. But every Metropolitan or University boat club should be able to command the services of a member who has the requisite mechanical training and will devote the time necessary for making certain that the oars designed for the use of his club are fashioned according to plan. With increased experience capable mathematicians will no doubt be able to suggest further improvements and may be able to give a formula from which the balance of an oar of any required dimensions may be calculated. I have done little more than give a tentative discussion of the problem as far as it has been worked out by Mr. R. T. Edge. But in this matter of obtaining oars of the proper balance, I can assure my readers that it is well worth while to take trouble.

Enough has been written about oars. I will only add that, in my opinion, a short oar is more appropriate than a long oar to the shorter stride of a four-oared or a pair-oared boat.

CHAPTER VIII

ON BOATS

THE EVOLUTION OF THE EIGHT-OARED BOAT

THE history of eight-oared boats and of their evolution from the stoutly built, broad-beamed, seaworthy craft of the earlier decades of the nineteenth century to the long narrow fragile racing-boats of the present day has been so well told by Sir Theodore Cook[1] that it needs no recapitulation here. I imagine, however, that the history of eight-oared boats goes back much farther than he suggests, and cannot accept his view that the earliest boats in which Oxford and Cambridge oarsmen rowed their races were sea-boats, or that rowing only emerged from its associations with the sea at the beginning of the nineteenth century. When roads were few and so badly kept as to be almost impassable in the winter, the rivers were the natural highways of the country. It is known as an historical fact that for centuries the Thames was the great highway of London. It was by river that State prisoners were taken to the Tower and entered the fortress under the low and gloomy archway of Traitors' Gate. It was by river that Guy Fawkes conveyed his barrels of gunpowder to the Houses of Parliament. It was by river that the Archbishops of Canterbury passed to and from Lambeth Palace and the Bishops of London to Fulham Palace. The Sovereign travelled from Westminster to the City or to Hampton Court in his own state barge, and the City Companies maintained their own rowing barges, vying in the splendour of their furniture with the royal equipment. For convenience of locomotion the great noblemen preferred to build their houses on the river bank, and each house had its steps or landing-place near which its boats

[1] *Rowing at Henley*, by Sir Theodore A. Cook. Oxford University Press, 1919.

were moored. In addition to these were the numerous wherries, skiffs, and long-boats plying for hire and manned and owned by watermen who had passed their apprenticeship and earned the freedom of the river. The London watermen did a big trade before steam-boats came and swept them nearly out of existence. They were renowned for their skill in watercraft, and their accumulated experience evolved types of boat and oars quite independently of and different from the sea-going craft that plied their trade on the river below London Pool. Thus we find the fine lines of entry ; the sharp peaked prow ; the rowlocks permanently fitted on the gunwale ; the oars with buttons and curved blades ; features quite foreign to sea-oarsmanship. Roomy and seaworthy the old river-boats had to be ; for they had to carry their quota of passengers whose safety and convenience had to be studied, for the tideway is often rough and frail and heavily loaded craft are easily swamped. Boat-racing as we now know it originated in the natural rivalry among the Thames watermen and among the more splendid outfits of Royalty, the nobility, and the great City Companies.

Sir Theodore Cook says (op. cit., p. 77) that so far as can be discovered from the old records it was at Eton that the first type existed, in 1811, of those eight-oared racing-boats which first made their appearance at Oxford four years later. In that year the Eton fleet consisted of a ten-oared boat, the *Monarch*, three eight-oars, and two six-oars. But there were long-boats at Eton at least half a century before that date.

It is recorded in a manuscript entitled Nugae Etonenses dating from about 1760 and quoted in Maxwell Lyte's *History of Eton College* that in those days there were three long-boats called *Piper's Green*, *Snake*, and *My Guinea's Lion*, the first and third taking their names from 'Guinea' Piper, a celebrated waterman of the day. In 1798 we hear of a disturbance at Eton in consequence of many fifth form and some lower boys at Eton having rowed up to Maidenhead in defiance of the prohibition of the Head Master, and about this time we hear of fancy dresses being worn by the crews of the boats on the 4th of June and Election Saturday. The head boat, then as now, was a ten-oar called the *Monarch*, and on one occasion the crew appeared as galley-slaves fastened to their oars by gilded chains. Boating was a long-established form of amusement at Eton at the end of the eighteenth century, and in *Musae Etonenses* a nurse is supposed to warn her fondling against the perils awaiting him at school—

> 'In fragili cymba tua membra ignara natandi
> O noli Thamesis credere cautus aquis.'

It was a long time then before the fashion spread to the Universities.

The question that interests us is why the eight-oar came into favour in preference to the ten-oar or the handier and more easily manned six-oar. Six-oars were popular as racing craft a century ago. At Eton 'Upper Sixes' was the most important aquatic event of the year, and it appears that the race, while retaining the old name, was first rowed in eight-oars in 1848. The Westminster Water Ledger tells us that in the year 1813–14 the King's Scholars of that school rowed in a six-oared boat called the *Fly*, the crew including W. F. L. de Ros, afterwards Lord de Ros, who went up to Christ Church in 1816, and was an ardent supporter of rowing at Oxford. It was under his leadership that Christ Church went head of the river at Oxford in 1817, and maintained their place in the two following years, their stroke in 1818 and 1819 being Mayow Short, also an old Elizabethan. De Ros is mentioned by Sir Courtenay Knollys as the owner of one of the three four-oars to be seen on the river at Oxford between 1817 and 1820.

My grandfather, a schoolfellow and intimate friend of Lord de Ros, rowed many races with him at Christ Church, and was one of the crew of which it is recorded in the Eton Boating Book that in 1819 'Mr. de Ros came with three Christ Church men from Oxford in a light four-oared boat and challenged the Eton Eight. Their boat was steered by F. de Ros, then at Eton, and they were well beaten.' This defeat, however, was a sore subject, and I could never get an intelligible account of the race. I never succeeded in getting an account of the early and unrecorded days of Oxford rowing from my grandfather. He was a very old man, and had passed into his anecdotage before I began to be interested in the history of rowing. Many a time I led him up to the subject, but invariably, just as I thought I was going to get some information worth writing down, the name of de Ros, as captain of the Christ Church boat, came into the story. At this point my grandfather would say, 'Do you know the story of Lord de Ros?' and wandered off the subject to relate an episode in the subsequent career of that nobleman which had no connexion whatever with rowing. The only story he told me that had a definite beginning and end was that, after he had taken his degree but was still in residence as a Senior student of the House, he went down to Reading to witness a four-oared race between his College and a crew of the Household Brigade, stroked by de Ros, then a cornet in the 1st Life Guards. No. 3 in the Christ Church boat failed to put in an appearance, and after the Household Brigade had sat for some time in their boat waiting for their opponents the Christ Church captain (who I think was the redoubtable Mayow Short) said, 'Come, Bourne, step into the boat and row for us'. My grandfather took the vacant seat and, as he told me, they rowed right away from their opponents and won easily. Such was the fashion of boat-racing a hundred years ago. In those days it was the normal thing simply to take off one's coat for exercise and to undertake all kinds of exertion in a top-hat. A spectator suddenly called upon to take part in a race would not be in the least degree embarrassed for want of a suitable costume. I do not even know for certain whether my grandfather rowed in both or either of the Christ Church eights that were head of the river in 1818 and 1819, but I gathered from his conversation that he rowed in at least one of them. He evidently regarded the bumping races as of small importance and was much more interested in the four-oared events.

But eight-oars were now definitely establishing themselves as the boats *par excellence.* The first Westminster boat was launched in 1820, and it is recorded that in the following April she fairly beat the Eagle, one of the leading London Clubs then on the river, in a 'short' pull from Battersea Church to Putney Bridge, a distance of nearly two miles. We read further in the Westminster Water Ledger that on the 5th of February 1824 a new eight-oared cutter was launched and the name of the *Challenge* was given her. Also that 'this boat did beat every boat that it came alongside of, as also did the *Victory*'. She must, however, have been designed rather for safety in rough water down river than for speed, as the Westminster boys used to pull to Greenwich and back in her, and we learn that, on the occasion of the Eton and Westminster race of 1831, the Elizabethans on arriving at Maidenhead 'found the Eton boat-builders' men amusing themselves by putting their boat inside the *Challenge*, which was a regular man-of-war's gig'.

That boat-racing as a sport was introduced into the Universities of Oxford and Cambridge by Eton and Westminster men there is little room for doubt. We have seen that Eton led the way in the use of eight-oared boats, and boasted a ten-oar before the end of the eighteenth century. The ten-oar was a subtle compliment to Royalty, for the King's barge, which is still in commission, and has carried their present Majesties at the Henley Regatta, is fitted for ten oars, but only eight oars have been used since she was re-equipped for service by King Edward VII. Those who were at Henley in 1912 will not readily forget the splendid appearance of this vessel as she returned up the course from Greenlands after the luncheon hour, the sun breaking through a passing thunder-shower in a golden haze, and all the occupants of the pleasure boats behind the booms standing up with tossed oars and paddles. It was a truly regal spectacle, and the Eton boys must have been familiar with the appearance of the self-same boat when they enjoyed a special share of royal favour in the days of King George III. Small wonder that they fitted out their head boat in imitation of her. Mr. J. T. Phelps, one of the King's watermen, tells me that the royal barge, in spite of her breadth of beam, is built on good lines for speed, and that when she was taken down the river at the end of the war the crew rowed over the University course from Mortlake to Putney, on the ebb, in 28 minutes. The oars are 16 feet long, and about 3 ft. 10 in. inboard, with 6-inch blades. The thwarts are placed so close together that the oarsmen cannot reach out very far, and in their trial over the Putney course they had to row short strokes at the rate of nearly 40 per minute. It was evidently the prevailing practice to place the thwarts as near together as possible in the old type of river boat. In the Oxford boat of 1829, now returned to Oxford and on view in the University Boat-house, the thwarts are only 29 inches apart, and all the old pictures of eight-oared races show the hands of the oarsmen extended well over the thwarts of the men seated in front of them. The racing stroke must have been short and rapid until Fletcher Menzies introduced the long stroke with the catch at the beginning in 1841.

The royal barge is, as far as I know, the only survivor afloat of the state barges which plied on the Thames up to the end of the eighteenth century. But a little more than a year ago Sir John E. Thornycroft kindly sent me detailed plans of an eight-oared barge, the property of the Duke of Northumberland, which in all essential features is similar to the royal barge. It has lain neglected and almost forgotten at Syon House for many years past. Unfortunately so neglected that, when she was overhauled, her timbers were found to be rotten beyond repair; but the details of her construction have been faithfully preserved, and by the courtesy of the Duke and of Sir J. E. Thornycroft a sketch of her is reproduced here. She is 43 feet long with a beam of 6 feet; clinker-built with seven streaks of ½-inch oak planking. As in the royal barge there is a high poop with a seat for the coxswain, and in front of it a cockpit with seats on three sides to accommodate six, or with a squeeze eight persons. The thwarts for the rowers are 5½ inches wide and curiously irregularly spaced, the four stern oarsmen being farther apart than the four bow oarsmen. A gangboard, 11 inches wide, extends from bow's seat to the cockpit. The rowlocks project only three inches above the gunwale, and have more room between the thowl-pins than in the Oxford eight of 1829. The poop overhangs the rudder, projecting 17 inches beyond the stern transom, and terminates in a slanting taffrail 13 inches wide and 18 inches high. From the centre of the taffrail projects an upright, apparently with a hole in it for the reception of the flag-post, and on either side of this is a *U*-shaped piece of metal described in the plan as steering rowlocks, but they are more probably cleats for the flag halliards, or perhaps they may have served as elbow-rests for the

Fig. 40. The Duke of Northumberland's eight-oared state barge: built *circa* 1760.

coxswain, who, when the cockpit was covered by an awning, had to perch himself up on the taffrail with his feet on the seat at the back of the steering well in order to get a clear view over the top of the awning. The taffrail and the raised gunwale surrounding the cockpit and steering well are richly carved and decorated. This is the class of boat of which Shakespeare wrote:

> The barge she sat in, like a burnish'd throne,
> Burn'd on the water.

But the Syon House boat must be one of the last of the ducal barges, for she is believed to have been built in 1760. It is interesting to note that the stroke rowlock is on the port side of the boat, an anticipation of the modern practice, but unusual in those days.

It is clear that these state barges were *vaisseaux d'élite* in which the owners travelled from their riverside residences to Westminster and elsewhere. The eight-oared boat was the aquatic equivalent of the coach and six ; costly to maintain, splendid in its equipment, and appropriate only to great persons. Without doubt the owner of such a vessel took a pride in her, manned her with a picked crew dressed in his own livery, and was as jealous of her reputation for speed as is the owner of a Rolls-Royce car at the present day. Many a time a nobleman must have noted with satisfaction that his boat ' did beat every boat that it came alongside of ', and in days when men were ready to lay wagers on every event there must have been much rivalry, and considerable sums of money must have changed hands, as the result of trials of speed on homeward journeys. Westminster steps were the landing-place for the Houses of Parliament and for Court functions at the adjacent palaces of Whitehall and St. James. The informal contests starting from this point may well have suggested the long pull from Westminster to Putney as the proper course for the earliest inter-University races.

I have an old coloured print of Putney, drawn and engraved by W. Pickett and dated 1812, showing a four-oared passenger boat working its way up river. It has the high poop and taffrail characteristic of the King's and the Duke of Northumberland's barges. The coxswain is perched high up on the overhanging poop, his back resting against the taffrail, and apparently has the tiller between his knees. The object of the high poop is apparent. It is to enable the coxswain to have a clear view over the awning which shelters the passengers seated in the cockpit. In this boat the stroke is on the starboard side. Another old picture in my possession, drawn and etched by J. Whessell in 1824, portrays the confluence of the Cherwell and Isis, the Brasenose boat coming in. This must be the boat acquired by Brasenose in 1815, and therefore one of the earliest eight-oars used for racing in Oxford. The artist was evidently interested in the boat as he gives her dimensions : length, 41 ft. 8 in. ; width, 4 ft. 8 in. The high poop and cockpit have disappeared, but there are vestiges of the former in the shape of a high stern transom, and the rudder retains its old shape, the rudder-post being so high that the yoke for the attachment of the rudder-lines is on a level with the top of the coxswain's head. The oarsmen wear scarves slung diagonally over the shoulder as in the picture of the crew of the ' White Boat ' in the Exeter Barge, and some of them wear peaked caps such as are worn by the crew of the King's barge to this day. In this boat the stroke oar is on the port side. The Exeter White Boat was built at Plymouth in 1824, and shows no trace of derivation from the state river-barge. But the old type of eight-oared boat must have remained in use for many years after, for in Mr. W. E. Sherwood's admirable book on *Oxford Rowing* the picture of the Eights of 1833 (facing p. 13) shows the vestigial high poop with slanting stern-post and transom and long rudder-post identical with the Brasenose boat of 1824. There can be no doubt that these boats are the lineal descendants of the old state barges.

If I am right in suggesting that the eight-oared barge was the aquatic equivalent of the coach and six, a six-oar would have the rank of a coach and four, a four-oar of a carriage and pair, and lesser craft would represent the one-horsed carriages of humbler folk. The young bloods of Eton and Westminster were familiar from their childhood with the rivalry between the eight-oared galleys of their parents, and in their expeditions, processions, and contests would naturally attach to a ten-oar or eight-oar the prestige belonging to the splendid turn-outs of royalty and the nobility. As the young wet-bobs grew up and transferred their rivalries to the Universities, what more natural than that they should carry their school traditions with them and regard eight-oars as the noblest type of boat ? No doubt similar motives led to the cultivation of eight-oared rowing among the leading London clubs, such as the Eagle Club mentioned in the Westminster Water Ledger. Tradition lives long in the rowing world, and to tradition may be attributed the fact that to this day special κῦδος attaches to the winning of the Grand Challenge Cup at Henley. The fours, the pairs, and the sculls are by comparison minor events, yet, as an exhibition of personal prowess, surely the order ought to be reversed, and a winner of the Goblets should be more renowned than a winner of the Stewards' Cup, a winner of the Stewards' Cup more renowned than a winner of the G.C.C. It is true that a winner of the Diamond Sculls has a glory all his own, but in this case tradition is associated with professional boat-racing in which the individual skill and endurance of the watermen was always more highly thought of than combination in crews, as is evidenced by the establishment of Doggett's Coat and Badge in 1715.

The sketch on p. 199 is drawn carefully to scale, and the boat is represented as immersed to the load-water-line calculated by Sir John I. Thornycroft & Co.'s experts. Care has been taken to seat each oarsman correctly on his thwart. The large-scale measurements show that they were seated 12½ inches away from their work. The peaked caps and full-skirted livery coats are of the pattern worn by the King's watermen, and are, in fact, the pattern of livery worn in the eighteenth century. The details of the awning are taken partly from the King's barge, partly from Pickett's print of 1812. It is represented as extending beyond the cockpit to cover part of the steering well, the latter being so large that it was probably covered in and used to accommodate the Duke's lackeys and to hold such luggage as was wanted on the journey. Pickett's print is the authority for the position of the coxswain and the high flag-post on the taffrail. The King's barge flies the Royal Standard from a short mast placed far forward in the bows, but I do not think this was the usual practice. At Eton, where tradition is jealously preserved, the eights have always flown their flags astern on the 4th of June. The Oxford boats did the same as long as the procession of boats lasted, and flags are still flown astern by Cambridge crews after making a bump.

The King's barge was, I believe, built at one of the royal dockyards, and in the shape of its prow and in its buttock lines has many of the characteristics of a sea-boat. The Syon House boat is a typical river craft, and in every detail so closely resembles the pictures of the earliest eights at Oxford that one is tempted to believe that in 1815 Brasenose and Jesus Colleges simply acquired and adapted to their own purposes state barges, whose owners had no further use for them.

As boat-racing grew in popularity the clinker-built descendants of the eight-oared state barges gave way to carvel-built boats with a keel. The length was increased, the beam diminished, and flared gunwales soon gave way to iron outriggers. With outriggers the beam was still further diminished and the length still further increased until, in the years 1850–6, a length of 65 feet to 66 feet, with a beam of less than 2 feet, was the normal measurement for a racing eight. In such craft Oxford or Cambridge University crews used to win the Grand Challenge Cup at Henley. Four-oared boats of this type still survived at Eton in my school-days, but were to be found only at Goodman's lower-boy raft. Very good boats they were, and many a pull to Monkey Island and back did I have in them in the year 1876. They slipped along at a great pace when once one got the knack of propelling them, and were in every way superior to the clinker-built boats used for junior races at the present day.

The revolution in boat-building came in 1856, when the Royal Chester Rowing Club easily won the Grand Challenge Cup, rowing in a much shorter keelless boat built by Matt. Taylor, a ship's carpenter of Newcastle-on-Tyne, but largely designed, I believe, by Mr. J. B. Littledale, the stroke of the Royal Chester crew. At this time problems relating to the form and speed of vessels excited much interest. Steam propulsion had rendered obsolete the type of hull suitable to sailing vessels. Scott Russell's remarkable researches on the most economical speeds at which vessels could be towed in canals of given depth had given rise to much speculation, often of an extravagant kind, and his wave theory was being applied to ocean-going steamships. It is highly improbable that Matt. Taylor, a skilled craftsman, but ignorant of theoretical principles, should have designed a boat which, in its main features, embodied the highly technical, if also somewhat mystical, principles of Scott Russell. But to Mr. Littledale, who was related to the great Liverpool shipowners, such ideas were familiar, and a comparison of plans leads me to believe that the famous Royal Chester boat and its successors were an attempt to adapt the lines of the *Great Eastern* to a racing eight. However that may be, the characteristic feature of Matt. Taylor's boats was not so much that they were keelless (for, as Sir T. Cook has told us, the Claspers had introduced four-oared keelless boats some years before), as that they were shorter and broader than their predecessors. The Royal Chester boat was bought by Exeter College, Oxford, who rowed head of the river in her in 1857 and 1858. There is some uncertainty about her dimensions, but the boat built for Oxford by Matt. Taylor in 1857 was 55 feet long and 25 inches wide. With the change of boat came a considerable change in style. In 1857 Matt. Taylor himself steered the Oxford crew during training, to show them the proper way to send his boat along as quickly as possible. As the new boats were much quicker off-hand than the old the oarsmen had to concentrate their energy into a tremendous smite at the beginning of the stroke to get the best pace out of them. I have elsewhere (p. 275) given a description of the older style as I remember it, and need only say here that even to the half-instructed eyes of Etonians of the later seventies of last century the style of Dr. Warre was clearly different from that of Dr. Hornby. I remember clearly that Dr. Hornby's style was identical with that of his contemporaries, Sir Joseph Chitty and Mr. W. F. Short, while Dr. Warre's style was typical of that of many famous fixed-seat oarsmen who succeeded him. The one style was suited to the long, narrow, carvel-built, but keeled boats of the middle years of the nineteenth century; the other to the shorter, broader, keelless boats which came into use after 1856.

Although the introduction of sliding-seats in 1873, involving an increase of the rowing space allotted to each individual, should have led to some alteration in their dimensions, eight-oars did not much exceed 56 feet in length until the last decade of the century. But their beam was diminished, and this involved greater depth to obtain the displacement necessary to carry crews which year after year were composed of increasingly heavier oarsmen. It seems to have been a point of honour among boat-builders to reduce the depth also to the smallest possible amount, and in consequence, for a long period, which includes nearly the whole of my rowing career, crews were consistently under-boated.

A famous boat, the prow of which hangs on my wall, was built for Oxford by Swaddle & Winship of Newcastle-on-Tyne in 1878. She was used for five successive races at Putney, and only suffered defeat in 1879. Her dimensions as recorded by Mr. C. M. Pitman were: length, 57 feet; beam, 22 inches; depth forward, 7¾ inches; depth at stern, 6 inches; depth amidships, 8¾ inches. I am not sure that these are correct, for the depth of the stem at the point where it is scarfed on the kelson is really only 7½ inches, and a boat of the dimensions given must have been far too small for some of the crews she carried. Like all Swaddle & Winship boats she seemed a bit heavy off-hand, but kept her way wonderfully between the strokes. In 1883 the same boat was used till within a week of the race, when, as things were not going very well with the crew, she was discarded in favour of a new boat by J. Clasper, 58 feet in length, 22½ inches wide, 8 inches in depth forward, and 6½ inches depth at stern. She was therefore larger in every dimension than the 1878 boat, and as Oxford gained an easy and unexpected victory in her she has been quoted as an example of an exceptionally fast boat. To my mind she was no faster and certainly less comfortable to row in than the old Swaddle, but the extra displacement was no doubt an advantage to us in the rough weather that prevailed up to the day of the race. Here I may tell a hitherto untold story showing that the best judges may sometimes go wrong in their estimate of boats. The Cambridge crew of 1883 was, for those days, exceptionally heavy, averaging 12 st. 2¾ lb. J. Clasper had built for it a boat differing in every particular from the

Oxford boat, and considered (as he told me himself) that she was the best he had ever turned out. But Mr. Woodgate, who was coaching the Cambridge crew, would have nothing to do with her. She was, he said, weak, slow, and too small for the crew, though in the last particular she obviously was not. But the boat was condemned, thrown back on Clasper's hands, and left behind at Putney. In the following summer the London Rowing Club, looking for a boat to accommodate an exceptionally heavy crew, rowed a trial in the discarded Clasper, bought her, and won the Grand Challenge Cup in her in two successive years. She was, I believe, the fastest boat that Clasper ever turned out. Her dimensions are not on record, but I remember that she was not a long boat, but broad beamed, with an unusually flat floor for those days. Clasper had built a boat on somewhat similar lines for Oxford in 1882. She was so comfortable to row in that we called her 'The Arm-chair'. Trials showed that she was every bit as fast as the old Swaddle, but for some reason it was decided to use the latter for the race. J. Clasper was much chagrined by the rejection of his boats by one University and the other in two successive years, and thenceforward abandoned the broad-beamed, flat-bottomed type to which he was inclined, and evolved a series of boats of gradually increasing length until, in 1896, both Universities rowed in boats 62 feet long, but with a beam increased from 22½ inches to 23¼ inches. In the following years boats 63 feet in length and over were not uncommon. The boat-builders, ignoring the principles of Matt. Taylor's models, were returning to the dimensions of the old keeled boats of 1850–5. With the increase in length crept in a subtle change of style of oarsmanship. The beginning of the stroke, though inculcated, lost something of its sharpness. The finish was more prolonged and the recovery of the oar with the wrists became visibly slower. But the most marked change was a tendency to paddle at an abnormally slow rate of stroke. With this was associated an exaggerated overreach with the shoulders, and, in many crews, a lie back at the finish of the stroke. These tendencies were foreshadowed, though they had not actually materialized, in the fine Oxford crew of 1897. The Cambridge crews of 1899 and 1900, drilled to a high standard of proficiency by Col. W. A. L. Fletcher, were not wholly exempt from them. There was something stilted in their action, suggestive of an unknown factor working in opposition to the ideals which Col. Fletcher and the first-class oarsmen under his command were striving after. This factor, I now believe, was a type of boat not wholly responsive to the style of rowing aimed at.

In 1901 Dr. Warre created quite a sensation in the rowing world by designing for Oxford a short boat familiarly known as a 'Snubby'. Her dimensions will be dealt with farther on. Mr. C. M. Pitman wrote of her: 'On the whole the ship was a success. When the crew were off colour or not rowing up to their form she appeared to travel slower than an ordinary ship would have done under similar circumstances; but when they got well together, and caught the beginning sharply, she appeared to gain more than a proportionate amount of pace.' To this I may add that the boat was the making of the crew. For one reason and another I was in charge of that crew for an exceptionally long time. We had an excellent stroke in Mr. R. H. Culme-Seymour, and a good no. 6, but the rest of the material was not of superlative merit. It was, however, strong, and very conscientious. We practised for a long time in a 62-foot boat by F. Rough, but seemed to make little progress. Somehow things did not come off as they were expected to. On transference to the 'Snubby' a complete change came over the crew. Things that they were previously unable to achieve now seemed realizable. Though they had their ups and downs, as all crews have, from the day that they took their seats in Dr. Warre's boat the crew never looked back. They won a memorable race, and the popularity of the short type of boat might have been thought to have been assured. But in 1902 the same boat, carrying a heavier but less skilful crew, was badly beaten by Cambridge, and the boat-builders, and other critics who had a strong prejudice against Dr. Warre's design, took full opportunity of condemning it. Nothing more was heard of short boats for some years, although the Belgian crews that won the Grand Challenge Cup in 1906, 1907, and 1909 rowed in a boat only 58 feet long.

A study of the times of the winners of the Grand Challenge Cup supports the contention that the shorter boats were speedier than those which succeeded them. The new regatta course at Henley, starting a few yards below Temple Island and finishing at Poplar Point, was first laid out in 1886. In the same year long slides came into general use in the leading Colleges of Oxford and Cambridge. Longer boats began to come into use in 1893, and about the same time shorter oars became fashionable, though some clubs remained faithful to long oars. If we take the septennial averages of the times of the final heats of the Grand Challenge Cup from 1886 to 1913 we find that for the years 1886–92 the average time was 7 min. $5\frac{3}{7}$ sec.; for the years 1893–9, 7 min. $17\frac{4}{7}$ sec.; for the years 1900–6, 7 min. $9\frac{1}{7}$ sec.; for the years 1907–13, 7 min. $12\frac{3}{7}$ sec. It should be noted that the first septennial period includes 1892, the slowest year of the twenty-eight. The second period includes two unfavourable, but also one very favourable year. On the whole the weather conditions average out fairly equally for the four periods. The figures indicate a progressive deterioration in the speed of eight-oared boats. This is the more remarkable, because a similar comparison shows a progressive improvement in the average speed of the winners of the Diamond Sculls. And here we are confronted with the fact that, while eight-oars were getting longer, sculling-boats were getting shorter and wider. There is hardly an escape from the conclusion that, within certain limits, the shorter and wider type of racing-boat is the best for speed and, it may be added, for good oarsmanship, for whilst the skill of scullers was improving beyond all belief, that of oarsmen, by common consent, was deteriorating sadly.

CHAPTER IX

THE DIMENSIONS OF RACING EIGHTS

Unfortunately very few accurate measurements of racing eights have been preserved. The bald statements of length, beam, and depth forward, amidships, and aft, paraded from time to time in the sporting press, and copied uncritically into various books on rowing, do not and are not intended to give any definite information. Boat-builders are jealous of the secrets of their craft and are not disposed to betray them. What we want to know are: the lines of entry and run aft; the proportion of length to greatest beam; the length of the fore canvas and aft canvas; the exact space allotted to the oarsmen; the sectional curvatures and the immersed surface when the ship is fully loaded. All this can be shown only by a proper body-plan, and such plans are seldom forthcoming.

It is also unfortunate that such detailed measurements as exist are wanting in precision. When widths are given at the 'back' of the oarsmen's seats, we do not know whether the fore-edge or the aft edge of the seat is referred to—whether the term 'back' is descriptive of the seat in its relation to the man facing the stern of the boat, or the other way about. When widths are given one is at a loss to know whether they were measured across the gunwale or at the level of the thwarts or at the load-water-line. But with a little experience one can make pretty sure what the measurements do refer to. Of one thing one may be quite certain, that widths are never given at the level at which they are most important, viz. the load-water-line.

Necessarily, plans drawn from such carelessly defined measurements must be conjectural to a certain extent, nevertheless I give in fig. 41 plans of some boats of which the dimensions have been published with sufficient detail to admit of approximate accuracy.

In these plans the transverse scale is ten times that of the longitudinal scale. I had made drawings of these and several other boats in proper proportion, but the small scale imposed by the page of a book of this size makes them uninstructive. The great length of an eight-oar in comparison with its breadth misleads the eye and prevents a due appreciation of the really remarkable differences between various types of racing boats. The shortened deck-plans show that these differences are not trivial but fundamental.

The boat built by Sims & Sons for Cambridge in 1908 was used in the Inter-University Boatrace and at the Olympic Regatta of that year. She was purchased by the Christiania Roklub, and reappeared at Henley to win the Thames Cup in 1921. Being 61 feet in length, she is shorter than most of the boats built between 1895 and 1921, but I give a plan of her rather than of one of the 62- or 63-foot boats then in vogue, because I have very accurate drawings made for Sir John E. Thornycroft, into whose possession the boat eventually passed. Though differing slightly in detail from boats by other builders (for every boat-builder has his own secrets upon which he believes his reputation to depend), she may be taken as typical of the craft used by all the leading rowing clubs in England since the days when the firm of Swaddle & Winship ceased to exist—a period of more than a quarter of a century.

Looking first at her fore and aft lines: she is a long-waisted vessel, and it is not far from the truth to describe her as divisible into four parts longitudinally. The first quarter forms the fore-body, with a somewhat bluff entry and distinct traces of hollow lines at the bows. The second and third quarters form the long mid-body in which the oarsmen are seated. Amidships the sides of the mid-body are very nearly parallel, but they converge slightly fore and aft to join the lines of the fore-body and hind-body. The lines of the hind-body are somewhat fuller than those of the fore-body, making the run aft less fine by a good deal than the entry. As in all boats of this type the crew is seated far back, the bow canvas being 2 ft. 3 in. longer than the stern canvas. The greatest beam is at the fore-edge of no. 5's seat, 30 feet from the stem, but it is wider by only $\frac{1}{8}$ inch from the sections 5 feet in front and aft of it. A body-plan of this boat is shown in fig. 42. The sections are taken at intervals of 5 feet along the length

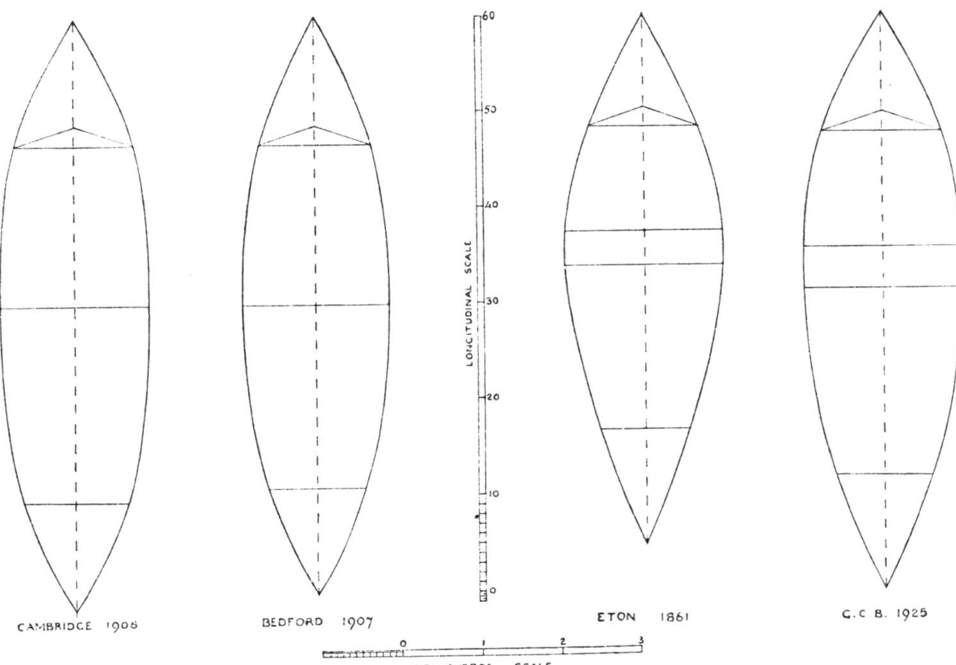

Fig. 41. Shortened deck-plans of four eight-oared racing-boats. The longitudinal scale is one-tenth of the transverse scale.

of the boat; those forward of the master section being shown on the right, and the aft sections on the left, in the conventional manner. A slight examination shows that hardly two sectional curves are the same, and that a template cut from the midship section could not be fitted along the sides of the boat. The fact that the aft sections are spaced differently from the forward sections has already found expression in the deck-plan, and it is further to be observed that the under-water lines are fuller in the hind than in the fore part of the ship. Different as the curves are they all fit some part of a set of 'ship's curves' such as can be bought from any mathematical instrument maker. Here the secrets of the boat-builder's art are disclosed. The 'ship's curves' are the outcome of long experience (fortified in later days by research) of the type of hull best suited to sailing vessels. Small variations of sectional plan were influential in giving 'stiffness' and therefore speed, when the main problem was to get the ship to stand upright under a large spread of canvas. It is an interesting example of the hold that tradition has on the mind of man that the secrets of the old ship-building yards are still handed down and cherished by those whose business it is to build boats depending on a motive power quite different from sails. There are also traces in this type of boat of the lines of the old state barges. The disposition of the load in the after part of the boat, and the enlargement of the lines to carry the load so disposed, are reminiscent of the cockpit with its quota of passengers necessitating an increase of carrying power in the stern.

The second plan in fig. 41 is of the boat designed by Cobb in 1907 for Bedford School. Her performances have been chronicled by Sir Theodore Cook (op. cit., p. 108), and are sufficiently remarkable, but it must be observed that she was never entered for a first-class race. Though departing somewhat boldly from the lines typified by the Cambridge 1908 boat she still retains traces of the traditions of the ship-builder's yard. Her entry is much longer and finer than in the Sims boat, and her midship lines sweep round with fuller contours towards the stern, so that she has practically no waist. The lines of the run aft are also long and fine, but are a trifle fuller than the lines of entry. This enlargement aft is necessitated by the distribution of the load, for the crew is seated even farther aft than in the Sims boat, the bow canvas being 13 ft. 4½ in., and the stern canvas only 10 ft. 8 in. long. The fore and aft lines are shapely and suggestive of speed. A body-plan of this boat would be of great interest, but the data are wanting. The depths of the sections, as recorded by Sir T. Cook, show that she was rather curiously cambered, apparently with the intention of bringing the centre of buoyancy well aft of the midship section. It is related that when this boat (affectionately nicknamed 'Granny' after many years of service) was worn out, an attempt to build a successor, on similar lines, but with a somewhat larger displacement, was a failure. One would like to know how it was proposed to obtain the larger displacement.

The third plan in fig. 41 is of the famous boat built by Matt. Taylor of Newcastle for Eton in 1861. Built on lines similar to those of the Royal Chester boat of 1856, this type of boat should be named after Mr. Littledale, who was indubitably the author of it. A glance at the plan shows that his innovations were not a matter of simply shortening the length, increasing the beam, and placing the master section rather farther forward. They betray a radically different conception of what a racing boat should be. All the time-honoured devices for giving the ship stiffness under sail, or for carrying a heavy load of passengers in the stern, are gone. The *idée mère* seems to be that of a steam paddle-wheel ship, the centre of gravity of the engines and boilers placed over the centre of buoyancy of the ship, and the paddle-wheels corresponding in position with that of the broadest beam. Paddle-wheels were still the dominant method of steam propulsion in 1856, and an inventive mind would naturally be struck by the analogy between propulsion by paddle-wheels and by oars. It is specially worthy of remark that Mr. Littledale seated his crew amidships. The stern canvas is almost exactly equal in length to the bow canvas, and although she was only 56 feet long, the stern canvas of the Eton boat was actually longer than that of modern boats of a length of 60 feet and upwards. It is clearly an object in the Littledale design to make the centre of gravity of the crew coincide as nearly as possible with the centre of buoyancy of the boat.

The Littledale type of boat, then, has a long fore-body with fine lines of entry; a somewhat longer hind-body with conspicuously long and fine lines of run aft; and a very short mid-body, the length of which corresponds exactly to the space between no. 4's and no. 5's thwarts. This mid-body would not be parallel-sided, for a slight curvature is necessary to make the fore-body lines run smoothly into those of the hind-body. Thus, the locus of the broadest beam is midway between no. 4's and no. 5's seats; 25 ft. 1½ in. from the stem. Yet it has been stated, and the statement has been copied in book after book, that Matt. Taylor placed the broadest beam of his boats far forward, at about the aft edge of no. 3's seat, and much wholly misplaced credit has been given to him for so daring an innovation. Simple inspection of the recorded measurements shows that he did nothing of the sort. He did place the broadest beam nearly 3 feet in front of the mid-thwartship section, but that is another thing.

The legend is, perhaps, due to the fact that Dr. Warre, who was a great admirer of the Matt. Taylor boats, did place the broadest beam of his more recent designs 21 feet from the stem in a 56-foot boat: that is, a little behind the aft edge of no. 3's seat. In this and in some other features he departed somewhat widely from the original Littledale plan, and without doubt intentionally, for the only reliable record of the dimensions of Matt. Taylor's boats is taken from his own notes.

The famous 'Snubby' in which Oxford rowed in 1901 and 1902 had a fore-body of 21 feet and a hind-body of 35 feet, her proportions in these dimensions being in a ratio of 3 : 5. Unlike the Matt. Taylor boats she had no mid-body, and the hind-body tapered uniformly aft from the master section. It was in consequence of this long tapering hind-body that Dr. Warre was obliged to give his boat a maximum beam of 27 inches, in order to obtain the required minimum width of 16 inches at the coxswain's seat. I should have liked to have given a shortened plan of this boat, but, as Mr. F. W. Warre informs me, the only transverse measurements that have been preserved are those at the master section and at bow's and cox's seats. These data are insufficient for the construction of a plan which shows up in exaggerated outline the fore and aft contours of a boat. Such a plan as I have been able to make from the dimensions kindly sent me by Mr. F. W. Warre shows a rather bluff entry and long fine lines of run aft. The centre of buoyancy must have been well forward of no. 5's seat. The floor is wide and nearly flat for the greater part of the length of the boat, and the camber is reduced to a minimum, being only one half-inch. The flatness of the floor results from the method of planning the sections on the 'twin-circle' principle as illustrated in fig. 42. Here I must digress for a moment to point out that Mr. Mark Barr's correction, quoted by Sir T. Cook (op. cit., p. 114), is based on a complete misunderstanding of what Dr. Warre wrote and of his method of construction. When he wrote, 'The projection of the line CF ($\frac{1}{4}$ in. more or less) to K facilitates the continuance of the curves Ad and Be to join in K and so form the bottom of the boat', Dr. Warre meant $\frac{1}{4}$ inch in the boat and not on his small-scale plan. The twin-circle boats were nearly flat-bottomed. I still possess a cupboard made from no. 7's segment of the boat in which I rowed at Eton in 1878, 1879, and 1880. A tracing made round the boat gives the sectional contour illustrated in fig. 42. The method of construction is obvious. The 'twin-circles' are small and do not meet in the median line of the boat even so far aft as at no. 7's seat. The projection of the line CF to K is exactly $\frac{1}{8}$ inch, as measured on the boat, and this amounts to exactly the thickness of her skin. The boat is to all intents and purposes flat-bottomed, and the section is that of a punt with the corners rounded off. I wish I had complete measurements of this boat. She was not a 'Snubby', but narrow, rather long-waisted and centre-seated. Photographs show that she was not more than 56 feet long. Built to carry a 10 st. 6 lb. crew in 1878, she had to carry 11 st. 8 lb. in 1880, and was able to do it because of the large carrying power afforded by the twin-circle section. She was undeniably fast in spite of, perhaps because of, her somewhat bizarre sectional form. In his later models, Dr. Warre made the diameter of each of his twin-circles half the width of the master section, thereby reducing the extent of nearly flat floor. The reader will perceive from fig. 42 that the line of the curved bottom of the floor of a twin-circle boat is such as would be made by a thread coiled in opposite directions round the two circles, and pulled nearly, but not quite, taut. It is a shallow catenary curve, and from its nature is quite accurately tangential to the two twin-circles. The ‘ snubby ’ type of boat was a later creation, and traces back its ancestry, not to the Matt. Taylor boats, which, as I have shown, were of paddle-boat form, but to the torpedo-boats and fast light cruisers built for the Royal Navy in the early eighties of last century. Dr. Warre was ever athirst for information about the forms of ships, and made the acquaintance of Scott Russell and Sir Nathaniel Barnaby. In 1880 he persuaded the last named, then Director of Naval Construction, to design a boat for the Eton crew. Sir Nathaniel gave us a stream-line boat ; very roomy forward, with a long and very fine run aft, so fine that there was scarcely room for stroke to sit in, and I had some trouble in finding a coxswain whose posterior dimensions were commensurable with the narrow space provided for him. To Dr. Warre's great chagrin the boat proved an utter failure, and was only used for a few days in practice. In 1881 I persuaded him to allow me to order a boat from Swaddle & Winship of Newcastle-on-Tyne, but he never liked her : she was not his child. He remained convinced that Sir Nathaniel Barnaby's design was right in principle, and in 1882 produced a new type combining those principles with some of the features of the Swaddle & Winship boat. The 1882 boat was a success, for she won the Ladies' Plate with great ease in that year, and again in 1884 and 1885. Undoubtedly she would have won in 1883 but for a broken stretcher in the final heat. That boat was the progenitor of the ‘ Snubbies ’ of later years. I write with some assurance on this matter, as I was present at a long after-dinner conversation between Dr. Warre and Sir Nathaniel Barnaby, when the latter laid down the law and enunciated the principles on which the ‘ Snubbies ’ were subsequently built.

It is regrettable that there is no record of the dimensions of the boats built by the firm of Swaddle & Winship beyond those given on p. 205. I think this firm adhered to some of the features of the Little-

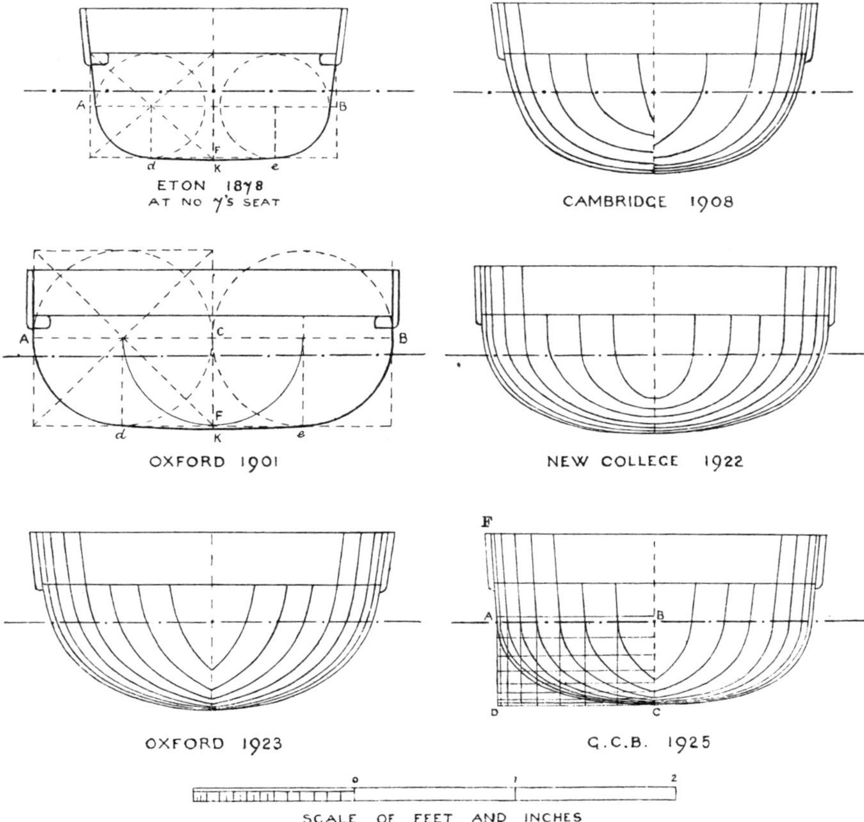

FIG. 42. Sections and body-plans of various eight-oared boats.

dale type, for in their boats the broadest beam was certainly farther forward than in the contemporary Clasper boats. About the year 1881, one Halford, who had been a foreman in Swaddle & Winship's yard, left that firm and set up business on his own account in Gloucester.

He produced a large number of boats at low prices, but they were flimsily built and soon went to pieces. While they lasted they were extraordinarily fast, and I believe that they embodied many of the features of the Littledale boats, for they were conspicuously of a different shape from the craft which we were in those days accustomed to. They had the features of the Swaddle & Winship boats, but much exaggerated, the beam being wider, the master section placed farther forward, and they were shallow with a flat floor. I believe that, in his attempt to undersell his competitors, Halford got into financial difficulties, and soon went out of business. There was a sale of his stock of boats at Oxford somewhere about the year 1884. With his disappearance and the demise of the firm of Swaddle & Winship some years later, the Clasper type of boat reigned supreme. F. Rough, who built many very good boats of this type, was the inheritor of his father-in-law's knowledge of design.

It was because I imprudently meddled with Rough's designs and got him to build a boat for New College in 1913, with the master section placed 2 feet farther forward than he was wont to place it, that I was led to take up the subject of boat design. This boat was a complete failure. The crew, row hard and fast as it might, could never get any real pace out of her. One should never meddle with other persons' designs. The failure of this boat led me to make a study of the shapes of fast-swimming fishes, selecting those which have the habit of swimming in shoals at or near the surface. For, I opined, Nature, in the course of long ages of evolution, must have arrived at a tolerably exact solution of the problem of the resistances of immersed or partially immersed bodies moving through the water. I soon found that, whatever their proportions, the lines of entry and run aft of fishes always give a curve of a certain character, which Professor H. H. Turner afterwards showed me to be a parabola. The study of fishes led me to make a number of models on a scale of $\frac{1}{12}$, in which the fore and aft lines were parabolic, but the master section was progressively shifted farther and farther aft towards the midship section. The models were duly tested on the Cherwell by towing them with a light silk line at the end of a light trout rod. The resistance could be pretty accurately gauged by the feel of the hand and by the bending of the top joint of the rod. The quality to which I attached the greatest importance, and which I still think is of most importance in a rowing-boat, was that of keeping way after the point of the rod had been lifted in such a manner as to let go the pull suddenly. Different models behaved very differently in this respect. I soon collected sufficient data to think myself justified in incurring the expense of a full-sized boat, which the New College crew of 1914 would not row in, largely, I think, because she was a gift horse, and they mistrusted her as such. In 1921 this boat was brought down from the shelf on which she had laid during the war. The New College crew of that year, though it contained no oarsmen of reputation, learned to row remarkably smoothly and well in her, and, contrary to all expectation, went head of the river. At the Henley Regatta they made a very creditable show in the final heat of the Grand Challenge Cup, and might have gone near winning if they could have rowed a fast enough stroke, but that they were unable to do. The boat seemed to do her best at the rate of 32 to the minute, and nothing more could be coaxed out of her. Suspecting that this was due to the great length of mid-body that I had given her, I made new models and experiments in the autumn of 1921, and in the following year produced a new boat, the body-plan of which is given in fig. 42. I will not weary the reader with details of her dimensions. Knowing that the eight fore-body sections were placed $33\frac{3}{4}$ inches apart, that there was a mid-body of 48 inches, and that the eight hind-body sections, similar in all respects to the fore-body sections, were placed 48 inches apart, any one who is sufficiently interested can reconstruct the boat from the body-plan. The bow canvas was 11 feet ; the rowing space 33 ft. 8 in. ; the cox-swain's room 2 ft. 6 in., and the stern canvas 11 ft. 4 in. in length. This boat proved very steady and comfortable to row in. She easily kept her place at the head of the river in 1922, and was largely used as a practice boat by the Oxford crews of 1923 and 1924. In the former year she made some new records over parts of the Nuneham course in good but not exceptional conditions. I am still puzzled by the behaviour of this boat. In the tank trials which I shall describe presently, a model of her gave poor results. But both in racing and in practice the boat itself has proved remarkably fast, provided that the crew is rowing long and well, with a good rhythm, a good beginning, and a well-sustained finish. Under these conditions, as shown in the photograph, fig. 43, she settles down a little at the stern, lifts her nose well out of the water, and seems to make no bow wave at all. But if the rowing is indifferent no amount of ill-executed hard work produces any response. She then buries her nose in the water, raises a conspicuous bow wave, and loses all her pace.

In August 1922 Sir John E. Thornycroft kindly invited me to test my models in his experimental tank at Bembridge, Isle of Wight. We were unable to reproduce the conditions of boat propulsion by oars. The models were towed, and a delicate and ingenious recording apparatus registered the speed corresponding to any given pull measured in fractions of a pound. By a well-known formula the speeds and resistances for a full-sized boat were calculated from the speeds and resistances registered by the models, and the necessary correction was made for skin friction. The results for the three most important models are given for speeds between 14 and 19 f.p.s. in fig. 44. The models represented: A, the New College boat of 1922, with a corresponding displacement of 1,780 lb., and a wetted surface of 105·3 square feet. B, a design which was afterwards utilized for the Oxford boat of 1923 and several others like her. The displacement corresponding to the model was 1,780 lb., and the wetted surface 109·2 square feet. C, a model of the boat built by Sims & Sons for Cambridge in 1908, her corresponding displacement being 1,792 lb., and her wetted surface 104·86 square feet.

Fig. 44 shows that model A gave remarkably even results for every 10 lb. increment of pull at all speeds within the capacity of

Fig. 43. THE NEW COLLEGE BOAT OF 1922

a racing eight. At low speeds up to and including a paddling speed of 15 f.p.s. B was slower than C, but at a speed of about 16 f.p.s. (about 7 min. 22 sec. over the Henley course) C lost its advantage, and for pulls of 70, 80, and 90 lb. was progressively slower than B. Indeed so much did the resistance created by C increase at higher speeds that with a pull of 120 lb. its performance was nearly exactly

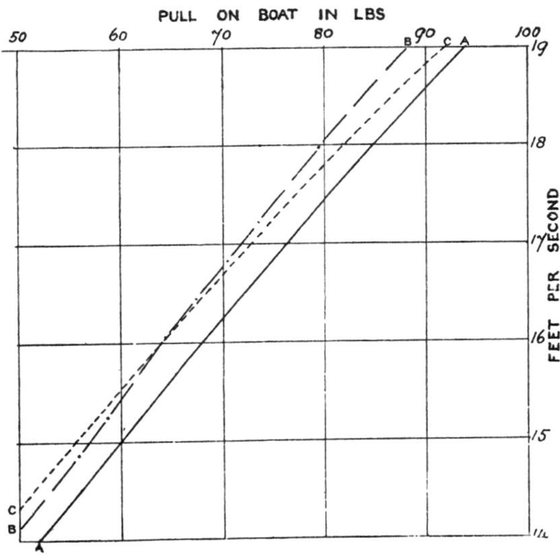

FIG. 44. Part of the graph of corresponding speed curves of models of: A, the New College boat of 1922; B, a design used for the Oxford boat 1923; C, the Cambridge boat 1908.

equal to A, both models giving a corresponding speed of 21·7 f.p.s. at this pull. Curiously enough at still higher speeds C again showed a superiority to A. But once it has passed 16 f.p.s. B shows a steadily increasing superiority over the other two models. Speeds much above 18 f.p.s. in dead water are, however, unattainable by racing eights. A first-rate crew may, in a short burst of a minute's duration, travel at something a little more than 18·5 f.p.s., but fatigue soon brings the speed down to 17 f.p.s. or less. Hence the behaviour of boats at higher or lower speeds than those shown in fig. 44 have no interest for us.

Examining the graphs more closely, the first thing that attracts attention is that A and C have nearly the same area of wetted surface, but B some 5 square feet more than A. If the resistance to be overcome were entirely or nearly entirely due to skin friction, both A and C would be faster than B. But after rising above a very low speed of 5 f.p.s. the pull required to give a given speed to A is always greater than that required by B and C, and at boat-racing speeds of 16–18 f.p.s. the pull required for a given speed is always greater for C than for B. The diagram indicates that the behaviour of model A is very consistent at all speeds. The resistance to her passage through the water increases very nearly, but not quite, as the square of the speed. At speeds between 15 and 21 f.p.s. the resistance over and above what is attributable to skin friction diminishes slightly. Models B and C are not so consistent in their behaviour, the former gaining and the latter losing proportional speed for pulls over 65 lb. For example, with a pull of 75 lb. B has a speed of 17·44, C of 17·28, and A of 16·86 f.p.s. If the resistance due to skin friction is taken at $V^{1\cdot 83}$, at a corresponding speed of 17 f.p.s. the skin friction resistance in the New College model would be 63·145 lb. The pull required to produce that speed was 76·25 lb. Therefore the residual resistance attributable to the wave-making features of her hull is 13·105 lb.—a high figure. On the same reckoning, in a boat corresponding to model B, the skin friction resistance is 65·244 lb., and the residual resistance 6·755 lb., a low figure indicating good lines for speed. In the Sims boat the skin friction resistance is 62·724 lb., and the residual resistance 10·276 lb.[1]

Summing it all up, the Sims boat, because of her smaller area of wetted surface, offers the least resistance at low speeds, but her lines

[1] The reader will understand that throughout the foregoing discussion the figures given do not refer to the models, but to full-sized boats whose dimensions and behaviour are calculated from the models.

are such that the resistance increases at racing speeds. The model which afterwards served as the basis for the Oxford boat of 1923, because of her relatively larger area of wetted surface, offers an undue amount of resistance at low speeds, but her lines more than compensate for this disadvantage at racing speeds. The New College boat, which is more 'snubbed' than the two others, has lines which involve a considerable resistance over and above the resistance due to skin friction at all speeds, but this extra resistance tends to diminish rather than to increase in proportion to the skin-friction resistance at racing speeds.

The outcome of these experiments was that model B, slightly altered with the view of increasing the displacement and minimizing the area of wetted surface, was adopted for the use of the Oxford crew of 1923. A body-plan of this boat is given in fig. 42. To reconstruct the boat the eight fore-body sections should be placed 3 ft. $0\frac{1}{4}$ in. apart, and the eight hind-body sections 4 ft. $5\frac{1}{4}$ in. apart. The mid-body is eliminated in deference to the theoretical principle that with its disappearance the resistance is reduced to a minimum. The curve of the master section is not a true ellipse but ellipsoidal, being struck from two centres by a method differing somewhat from that given by Mr. Mark Barr. A template cut from the master section fits all the other sections from stem to stern of the boat.

It would take far too long and, if done, it would not be profitable to describe the principles on which this boat was designed. It is sufficient to say here that they slowly evolved themselves out of an attempt to pursue to their logical conclusion Dr. Warre's visions of harmonic correspondence between the waves created by a boat in its progress through the water and the rhythm of the oarsmen's movements. This led to a sort of geometrical wild-goose chase, in the course of which I hit upon a number of curious relations of length to beam, beam to depth, and fore-body to hind-body, in which $\sqrt{\pi}$ constantly intruded itself. When it was all done the scheme seemed so fanciful that I did not venture to put it into practice, but I made a model embodying the dimensions arrived at, and it was the relative success of this model in the Bembridge tank experiments that finally emboldened me to launch the design as the Oxford boat of 1923. That the design is not altogether devoid of merit is evidenced by the fact that this boat won the Inter-University Boatrace in 1923, and the Grand Challenge Cup at Henley in 1924. Sister boats won the Grand Challenge Cup in 1923, and were head of the river at Oxford in 1923 and 1924. Mr. J. T. Phelps informs me that similar boats built by him have scored a number of wins in minor events.

All these are stream-line boats, and they have proved themselves to be undoubtedly fast, but have exhibited certain unexpected peculiarities. When the crew, or even any individual member of the crew, is not rowing with a rhythm suitable to the boat she rolls heavily : not with a continuous roll, but periodically, travelling steadily enough between the lurches. This suggests some want of correspondence between the wave-making features of the boat and the periodic acceleration given to her by the action of the oars. It must also be said that the sectional curve, though economical of wetted surface in relation to displacement, is not of a shape to promote stability. Though largely cambered fore and aft, these boats hold their straight way with remarkable persistency in calm weather, and are difficult to steer round such sharp corners as Grassy and Ditton on the Cambridge course. On the other hand, when the fin is placed in its customary position some six or seven feet in front of the stern-post, the boat's head pays off in a side wind. But this can be remedied by shifting the fin 3 or 4 feet farther forward.

For the rest these boats have all those qualities that are to be expected in craft in which the broadest beam is placed well in front of the midship section. They are extremely sensitive to good and bad oarsmanship, yielding a large profit to the former but something of the nature of a loss to the latter. They demand a sharp beginning, well-sustained leg-work at the finish, and most careful attention to the proper rhythm of the stroke. A conventional rhythm will not do :

it must be the particular tempo of the boat. Crews devoid of boat sense, whose notion of good oarsmanship is to whack their boat along by main force, get little encouragement from this type of craft. They get more profit from the long-waisted products of the ship-builder's art.

A grave disadvantage of these boats is that, until the crew has obtained a complete mastery over them, they do not inspire confidence. As a rule it takes weeks of practice for a crew to attune itself to its boat, and if during those weeks there is an increasing lack of confidence, due to an ever-present misunderstanding between the man and the boat, things will go from bad to worse, until the only course left open to a coach is a judicial separation. He must put his crew into another boat better suited to their capacities. Oarsmen are kittle cattle to drive, and it is only the very best of them who will endure present discomfort in the sure hope of better things to come. In this connexion it may be observed that a pair of oarsmen will endure a great deal of discomfort in their efforts to row together in perfect uniformity. Four oarsmen will endure a good deal. But when there are eight oarsmen it is a question of mass-psychology, which may take on a most unexpected character and bring a promising start to a disastrous conclusion.

For this reason wisdom must go hand in hand with science in the design of an eight-oared boat. Speed is necessary, but the comfort of the crew must be considered, or the conditions necessary for speed will hardly be attained. On the other hand, if comfort be too much considered and the conditions are made too easy, the crew will grow indolent. In the long run the boat which will satisfy the circumstances most likely to arise will be of the nature of a compromise. Let us consider what sort of a boat this will be, taking first the consideration of comfort. This depends, to no small degree, on the proper adjustment of a number of small details, such as the height of the seat above the heels, the height of the work, the proper rake of the stretchers, and so forth. These things depend, to a much greater degree than is generally realized, on good workmanship and the care which the boat-builder takes in every detail of construction. Whatever may be said about the shape of racing-boats, the workmanship put into them has improved out of all belief in the last thirty years. If one goes to the leading firms such as Messrs. Sims & Sons or Messrs. Bowers & Phelps, one may be sure of the most careful attention to every detail that affects the comfort of the oarsman, but it stands to the credit of the first named that they were the pioneers in the matter of excellence of workmanship. The second and more important factor in the comfort of the oarsman is stability. All racing-boats are ‘ crank ’, that is to say they are easily heeled over, because of the great proportionate weight of the oarsmen and the size of their bodies relatively to the weight and size of the hull. The centre of gravity of the loaded ship is high above the centre of buoyancy, and this must be accepted as a factor unalterable except within such narrow limits that they are of no practical importance. Width of beam makes for stability to a certain extent, but does not ensure it, as is evidenced by the fact that the Oxford boat of 1923 is broader in the beam than is usual in recent types of racing-boats. The form of the underwater section is influential. Round-bottomed boats approaching a semicircular section are unstable. The steadiest boats are those with a generous allowance of flat or only slightly curved floor, such as is afforded by the twin-circle form of section. The question that concerns us is whether steadiness is incompatible with speed. As about 85 per cent. of a boat's resistance is due to skin friction the sectional contour which gives the smallest area of wetted surface in proportion to the displacement would seem to be the most conducive to speed. This would be obtained by a semicircular section, but there are grave practical objections to this form. With a semicircular section the depth of the boat must be equal to half its beam. The beam at the master section cannot be reduced to less than 22 inches, for if it is, and if the boat is given reasonably fine lines of entry and run aft, the minimum width of 16½ inches required at bow's and stroke's seats cannot be obtained. With a beam of 22 inches and a semicircular section the depth amidships from the load-water-line would be $7\frac{3}{4}$ inches, making a total depth from the deck of $10\frac{3}{4}$ inches. Such a boat would not be unstable if the oarsmen could be seated at the customary height above the bottom of the boat. But the height of their seats has to be fixed in the first instance in relation to the top edge of the gunwale, otherwise they are not placed properly with regard to their work. So the crew would have to be seated unusually high up in the boat and that would make her very unsteady. A semicircular form of section leads inevitably to a very long, very narrow, long-waisted and deep boat, and it was just this type that was so decisively routed by the shorter, broader, and shallower Littledale boat in 1856. The ellipsoidal form of section adopted for the Oxford boat of 1923 avoids these difficulties and has greater carrying power for a less area of wetted surface than a true ellipse, but it certainly does not make for stability. A true semi-ellipse gives ample stability and is fairly economical in the matter of wetted surface, but does not lend itself readily to nice lines of entry and run aft. My experience leads me to the belief that elliptical bow sections create undue resistance at the entrance of the boat unless or until she lifts her nose out of the water as did the New College boat of 1922. The spiral involute recommended by the late Sir William Christie is economical of wetted surface, but has all the elements of instability. Dr. Warre's twin-circle form of section has great carrying power, admitting of a considerable reduction in the depth of the boat, which is in itself an advantage. It involves, however, some increase in the area of wetted surface, but as boats built on this principle have proved themselves fast, it seems that this disadvantage is compensated in other directions. Indeed, it is not necessary to worry overmuch about the question of skin friction because, whatever their shape may be, the dimensions of racing eights are so nearly similar that the area of immersed surface differs but little in boats of the same displacement. A boat built to carry a 12 st. 4 lb. crew has an immersed area of about 105 square feet. Suppose its form to be such that this area is increased by the large amount of 5 square feet: taking the frictional resistance as V^2, at a speed of 17 f.p.s. the increased resistance due to surface friction would amount to little more than 3½ lb. As the force effective in propelling the boat is almost exactly two-sevenths of the total force exerted by the oarsmen, this means that the extra 5 square feet of wetted surface would entail an extra pull of a little more than 1½ lb. for each of the eight oarsmen. Really it would be less, for the resistance varies as $V^{1 \cdot 83}$ and not as V^2. A good deal more than this can be gained by giving the oarsmen conditions under which they can lay out their strength to the greatest advantage. Therefore a small increase in skin friction may be neglected, provided that it really is compensated by other features.

The sectional plan involves the question of the run of the horizontal underwater lines fore and aft and the question of camber. Continuous lines of the same geometric curvature along the whole length of the ship are obtained when a template, cut from the master section, fits all along her sides. If the underwater lines are filled out, variations are necessarily introduced into the curves in various parts of the hull. A study of stream-line pressures leads me to the opinion that it is important that the fore and aft lines of curvature should be as true as possible, and this opinion has the sanction of such high mathematical authority as the late Sir William Christie. Dr. Warre's twin-circle method gives lines of perfectly continuous curvature with an inappreciable amount of camber until such time as the twin-circles, rolling past one another towards the median line, coincide in position and give a semicircular contour to that section of the boat (see fig. 42). From this point forward and aft the twin-circle method, carried to its logical conclusion, gives an appreciable but not an excessive amount of camber. As boat-builders say, the boat finds its own camber. I have always understood that Dr. Warre was opposed to any camber and built his later models with a perfectly straight floor. But Mr. F. W. Warre informs me that he varied his practice in this respect and sometimes allowed as much camber fore and aft as the twin-circle method imposed. Most frequently, however, he preferred a straight or nearly straight keel. The boats still used for trial eights at Oxford are 'Snubbies' built after Dr. Warre's designs, and in them the forward sections are brought down to the keel level by a line of reversed curvature, giving hollow lines of entry. But, as far as I can judge by an inspection of the boats, the aftermost sections are brought down to the required level (there is a small amount of camber aft) by drawing straight or slightly curved lines tangential to the diminishing segments of the twin-circles. The usual practice of boat-builders is to give camber to both ends of the boat, but much less forward than aft.

The question arises, What is the value, if any, of camber? Dr. Warre thought it had very little value, but his opinion, I think, was influenced by Sir Nathaniel Barnaby, for I remember his suggesting it and the latter's emphatic reply that it was all nonsense. Nonsense, no doubt, in sea-going vessels, in which depth at the forefoot and stern is necessary to keep them on their straight course in a sea-way. But even on the tideway, river-boats of 40 feet length and upwards do not encounter waves of such length and height as to deflect them from their proper course, and the artificial depth at bow and stern necessitated by a straight floor involves an appreciable increase of wetted surface without any compensating gain in displacement. If it has no other merit camber is a means of dispensing with unwanted wetted surface. Boat-builders imagine that it is a preventive against longitudinal oscillation, but I cannot see how it can be influential in this respect. Be the shape of the hull what it may, its trim must be altered by the transference of so very large a proportion of the weight fore and aft on the slides. The dip at bow or stern, however, is small, and it has been shown in Chapter II that the alteration in trim produced by the crew sliding aft is actually a source of gain to the speed of the boat. An excessive dip at the bows is prejudicial, but can be guarded against by keeping the centre of buoyancy sufficiently far forward. A considerable degree of camber undoubtedly diminishes the size of a boat's turning-circle and is useful where sharp corners have to be negotiated. In such broad-bottomed boats as that built for New College in 1922 I have departed from customary practice by introducing a large amount of bow camber, with the purpose of utilizing the pressure of the water on the inclined plane of the fore-body to give an upward lift to the bow. It has been objected that the speed at which an eight-oar travels is altogether insufficient to obtain any advantage from the principle of the hydroplane. But, on working out the figures, the objectors have been forced to admit that, even at the relatively slow speed of a racing eight, there must be some upward pressure. Colonel A. G. Shortt has estimated that it amounts to 10 lb. in the New College boat when travelling at full speed. That is not a negligible amount, and I leave my readers to judge from fig. 43 how far I was successful in the attempt to introduce the principle of the hydroplane.

Subsequent experience, however, has brought me so far into agreement with Dr. Warre that I think that camber ought to be reduced as far as possible. There can be no doubt that excessive camber makes a boat both unsteady and difficult to steer. It is a defect of Sir William Christie's spiral involute and of the ellipsoidal form of section used in the Oxford boat of 1923 that they both involve a large degree of camber.

After much trial and error I find the required conditions—which are not easily reconcilable—most nearly satisfied by the form of section shown in fig. 42, G. C. B. 1925. It has all the advantages of the twin-circle method and is free from some of its defects. It necessitates only a very moderate degree of camber, and has equal carrying power for a trifle less area of wetted surface. The principle on which the curve is constructed is shown on the left hand of the figure and may be described briefly as follows :

BC being the median vertical plane of the boat, make its length one inch more than the calculated depth of the boat below the load-water-line (the depth, of course, will depend upon the weight to be carried). Make *AB* equal to half the greatest beam of the boat on the load-water-line and complete the rectangle $ABCD$. Commencing at A, mark off along AB the successive half-widths of the number of equidistant sections into which the fore-body (or hind-body) is to be divided. As our measures are divided into eighths and sixteenths of an inch it is convenient to divide the fore-body (or hind-body) into eight equal parts. Adopting the parabolic form of entry and run aft the half-widths of successive sections from A to B are simply calculated by the formula $\left(\frac{x}{n}\right)^2 = y$. If $n = 8$ and y (otherwise AB) $= 12$ inches, the distances measured from A will be

$(\frac{1}{8})^2 \times 12$; $(\frac{2}{8})^2 \times 12 \ldots (\frac{8}{8})^2 \times 12$; viz. $\frac{3}{16}$, $\frac{3}{4}$, $1\frac{11}{16}$, 3, $4\frac{11}{16}$, $6\frac{3}{4}$, $9\frac{3}{16}$, and at the median line of the boat 12 inches. From each of the points thus ascertained drop a perpendicular to meet the line DC.

Divide the line AD into eight equal parts : using the same formula as above and commencing from D, mark off the successive points for a parabolic curve. The distances of these points from D will be $\frac{1}{8}$, $\frac{1}{2}$, $1\frac{1}{8}$, 2, $3\frac{1}{8}$, $4\frac{1}{2}$, $6\frac{1}{8}$, of the eight equal parts into which AD is divided. Through each of these points draw a line parallel to AB or DC, to meet BC. An even curve drawn through the intersections of the lines 1 and 7′, 2 and 6′, ... 7 and 1′ gives the required sectional contour. By this method we get a definite geometric relation between the sectional curve and the length and width of the boat, whatever the two last may be. Drawing the line AF tangential to the curve at the calculated load-water-line, we get the freeboard of the hull sloping outwards at a convenient angle. An eight should have three inches of freeboard, exclusive of the gunwale or sax-board, which is always $4\frac{1}{2}$ inches in depth.

A template taken from the master section and fitted successively to the points 1, 2, 3, ... 7 gives the remaining sections for both fore-body and hind-body.

We have now assembled the sections for the body-plan of the boat. Its transverse dimensions are settled, but we have to consider its longitudinal dimensions : what are to be the lengths of the fore-body and hind-body, and whether there is or is not to be a mid-body in which the width of the master section is carried for a greater or less distance down the boat. It should be observed that, whatever be the distances at which the sections are placed apart along the axis of the boat, so long as they are equal distances the lines of entry (or run-aft) will be parabolic at the load-water-line and at any horizontal level taken below the load-water-line.

By abstaining from making any variations of sectional plan below the load-water-line, we are committed in advance to a longitudinal plan designed, as far as may be, in accordance with the principles of the stream-line theory. As many oarsmen are shy of stream-line boats, it is necessary to be emphatic on this point : that, whatever the form of the hull, the stream-line forces are always operative and cannot be neglected without grave risk of failure. But the application of theory to practice in the design of an eight-oared boat is no simple matter. The crew must be given a certain amount of space, and its comfort and convenience must be provided for in a number of ways which interfere with an ideal design.

After considering the question from every point of view and giving due regard to the behaviour of the boats I have already designed, I have come to the conclusion that the proportions of Mr. Littledale's original model may safely be taken as a guide, but considerable modifications are necessary to adapt it for sliding-seats and for the heavy, long-limbed crews of the present day.

In fixed-seat days a minimum rowing space of 3 ft. 9 in. was required for each oarsman. With 16-inch slides the rowing space must not be less than 4 ft. 2½ in., and it is better to make it 4 ft. 3 in. Hence, if 56 feet was a suitable length for a fixed-seat crew, 60 feet, more or less, are required for a sliding-seat crew. This may be cut down to 58 ft. 6 in., but, unless the boat is given an unduly long mid-body, any reduction below that figure does not admit of sufficient width at bow's and stroke's seats. It is inexpedient to increase the beam beyond 24 inches on the load-water-line in order to obtain the necessary accommodation for the oarsmen at the two ends of the boat. Admiralty experiments have shown that an increase in the ratio $\frac{\text{beam}}{\text{draught}}$ has a definite effect in increasing the resistance, and I attribute the relatively unsatisfactory performance of the New College 1922 model in the tank trials largely to the fact that the corresponding beam of the full-sized boat is as much as 26 inches. During these tank trials Sir John E. Thornycroft made an interesting experiment with a model of the same fore and aft lines and the same displacement as the New College model, but in which proportions were altered to a length corresponding to 40 feet and a beam corresponding to 3 feet. This short and wide model, in spite of her having considerably less area of wetted surface than the other models against which she was pitted, offered more resistance than they at low speeds and at speeds corresponding to racing speeds, but came level with them at a corresponding speed of 21 f.p.s. and was much their superior at all higher speeds. The tank experiments at Bembridge indicate that the narrower the boat the less its resistance at low speeds, but this ceases to hold good when racing speeds are reached.

By making the length of the boat 60 feet and dividing this into a fore-body measuring 24 ft. 6 in., a mid-body measuring 4 ft. 2 in., and a hind-body measuring 31 ft. 4 in. in length, we get the proportions of the Eton boat of 1861, elongated to the extent necessary to give the crew a rowing space of 33 ft. 8 in. To construct such a boat from the body-plan the fore-body sections must be placed 3 ft. 0¾ in., and the hind-body sections 3 ft. 11 in. apart. By making the bow and stern canvas each 11 ft. 11 in. long the centre of buoyancy of the boat will coincide with the centre of gravity of the crew when half-way on the slide forward, thereby reducing the tendency to longitudinal oscillation to a minimum. The boat will have a displacement in fresh water of 1,866 lb.; that is to say, she will carry a crew of the average weight of 12 st. 5 lb., the weight of the coxswain being taken at 8½ stones, that of the boat at 290 lb., and that of the oars at 72 lb.

For a lighter crew it would be best to cut down the length of the hind-body by 18 inches and to shift the crew a proportional amount forward.

A shortened deck-plan of the boat is given in fig. 41. Although of the same beam and of the same fore and aft proportions as the Littledale boat she looks vastly different, and at a first glance seems rather to belong to the same category as the Bedford ' Granny '. In the one case the difference is due solely to the parabolic lines of entry and run aft, and it is obvious that these lines have the special advantage of giving plenty of beam for the whole length of the space occupied by the crew without any departure from the geometrical truth of the curve. The lines of the fore-body and hind-body would pass into one another without the intervention of the mid-body, which is inserted for the purpose of regulating the length of the waves made by the boat. The difference from the plan of the Bedford boat is fundamental. In our boat the greatest beam, and with it the centre of buoyancy, is forward of amidships, and the run aft is relatively long and fine. In the Bedford boat the lines of the run aft are filled out, the greatest beam is amidships, and the centre of buoyancy is aft of amidships. The purpose of the design is to seat the crew as far aft as possible.

Whether or no the builders of racing eights have consciously drawn their inferences from the behaviour of gigs and skiffs I cannot say. But it looks as if they have been influenced by the notorious advantage gained by placing the steerer as far back as possible in these craft, built as they are for the purpose of carrying two passengers in the stern. In up-river and provincial regattas in which mixed double-sculling races in gig-boats are popular events, those pairs who understand the game place their coxswain, who is generally a small boy, as far back as he can go. He sits on the stern transom holding the cross-head of the rudder in his hands. With this trim the boat, when under way, lifts her bows well out of the water and raises a big stern wave, the crest of which is some three feet astern of the rudder. The advantage in speed is enormous. A pair starting with its coxswain in the seat designed for his use has no chance against a pair whose coxswain sits on the taffrail. It is rather puzzling at first, for the big stern wave must mean a considerable increase of resistance. But watching a number of these races through a summer afternoon, I concluded that the advantage of perching the coxswain on the taffrail lies in the fact that the length, and therefore the area, of immersed surface of the boat is largely reduced, and that, at the relatively slow pace at which the boat is moving, the resistance due to the wave-making is of much less importance than the resistance due to skin friction. Clearly, however, the conditions in a gig-pair are quite different from those in an eight-oar.

Much may be written about the wave-making features of boats and the amount of 'residual' resistance that may be expected to be encountered when these features are well or ill adapted to the speeds which it is desired to attain. But it is time for me to bring this chapter to a close, and I will only deal with the subject in the briefest possible manner.

The laws of the resistance of ships are still imperfectly understood. The general principles are well known from the researches of Froude and others. A good summary of them may be found in the article 'Shipbuilding' in the *Encyclopaedia Britannica*. Stated in as few words as possible, the facts are these. A boat in its passage through the water makes two sets of waves. The one set, clearly recognizable at the bow and sides of an eight-oar, consists of diagonal waves, due to the diverging lines of the ship's 'entry'. These waves, once made, roll clear of the ship and produce no further effect on her resistance. But it must not be supposed, as I have seen stated, that they are of little or no importance. Energy must be expended in making them, and a boat with too bluff an entry forms large waves which run away with a corresponding amount of power. For this reason the resistance is materially increased in a boat which is too much 'snubbed', i. e. in one in which the fore-body is too short in proportion to the length of the boat.

The stream-line forces, for reasons too technical to be discussed here, cause an excess of pressure at the two ends of the boat, and a diminution of pressure along her sides. Hence two waves are formed, transverse to the line of advance of the boat, which accompany the boat in her motion, the one at the bow and the other at the stern. In a boat so long and of so shallow a draught as an eight-oar, these waves are very difficult to observe because, though they are of considerable length, their height is very small. But they can be distinguished in photographs taken broadside on, under suitable conditions of light, when the water is perfectly calm, and there are no disturbing influences due to the passage of other boats. Such photographs are not easy to obtain, but I have a certain number which show the transverse waves sufficiently well. It is necessary to make tracings and to multiply the vertical height of the waves three or four times in order to make them conspicuous.

The crest of the bow wave is not at, or even very near, the bows, but some distance aft of the cutwater. In boats of the same type its position is remarkably constant, some two feet in front of the triangular coaming in front of bow's seat. The mean of a number of measurements of photographs of boats built by F. Rough makes it 8 ft. 9 in. aft of the cutwater. This is about where one would expect it to be from the study of a stream-line diagram drawn round such a plan as that given in fig. 41, Cambridge 1908.

Aft of bow's seat there is a well-marked trough or depression, extending all along the midship part of the boat and nearly corresponding in length with the ' waist ' or mid-body of such a boat as is depicted in fig. 41, Cambridge 1908. The depression is deepest at no. 5's seat, and from this point ascends to the crest of the stern wave, which, when the crew is paddling, is a foot or so in front of the stern-post ; but when the crew is rowing hard, it seems to be shifted farther back and takes up a position just clear of the rudder. From the analogy of the bow wave, one would expect it to be much farther forward than this, but, for one thing, the full lines of the stern, whether intentionally or not, have the effect of throwing back the crest of the stern wave. For another thing there seems to be in all boats a considerable amount of 'lag', due to the mass of water adhering to the sides of the boat and carried along with it.

Following the usual notation we will call the distance between the crests of the bow and stern waves L', and from what precedes it is clear that the approximate value of L' is easily estimated when suitable photographs are available. In the 62-foot boats built by F. Rough it is from 52 to 55 feet. Unfortunately I have not got photographs showing with sufficient clearness the positions of the bow and stern waves in Dr. Warre's boats, in the Bedford 'Granny', or in any of the boats built by Messrs. Sims & Sons. From a consideration of their shapes, I can only hazard the opinion that in Messrs. Sims's boats the crest of the bow wave is probably farther forward than in Rough's boats and the crest of the stern wave at, or slightly abaft of, the stern-post. In the Bedford 'Granny' the fine entry must have brought the crest of the bow wave farther aft, and as the crest of the stern wave would be at or near the stern-post, the value of L' would be slightly diminished. In Dr. Warre's 'Snubbies' the crest of the bow wave was sufficiently conspicuous to attract attention, it must have been quite as far forward as in the Sims boats, but I opine that the crest of the stern wave was not more than two or three feet abaft of the coxswain's seat. If this were so the value of L' would be reduced to about 42 feet. It need hardly be said that there are no instantaneous photographs to show the positions of the bow and stern waves in the Littledale boats, but a comparison of the very sharp lines of entry and run aft of the Eton boat of 1861 with the bluffer extremities of more modern types suggests that in the former L' was reduced to as little as 35 feet.

However all this may be, and it is wholly conjectural, it is certain that the wave-making features of the New College boat of 1914 and 1922 are quite different from those of boats built by Rough or Sims at corresponding dates. In these, as in all the other boats that I have designed, I am able to calculate the position of the crest of the bow wave with some nicety. It is distant from the cutwater $3\frac{1}{8}$ (or possibly $3\frac{1}{7}$ or approximately π) of the eight parts into which the axis of the fore-body is divided in order to set out the parabolic curve. Very good photographs of both boats show the crest of the bow wave as nearly as possible in this calculated position, 8 ft. $9\frac{1}{2}$ in. from the cutwater, and therefore in practically the same position as in boats built by Rough. The difference is in the position of the crest of the stern wave, which is not far from the back of the coxswain's seat, about 7 ft. 8 in. from the stern-post. It is a marked feature in good photographs of these two boats, travelling at racing speed in perfectly calm water, that just aft of cox's seat, where the water rises to form the crest of the stern wave, its surface is broken up into little waves and eddies such as one sees in the wake of a boat. One may say that in these boats the wake begins 2 or 3 feet aft of cox's seat. No such phenomenon is to be seen in a photograph of any of the ordinary types of boat-builders' boats. In them the rising line of the stern wave is clear cut along the sides of the boat up to the stern-post and the wake begins at or abaft of the rudder. The stern rides rather high in the water and from two to three inches of freeboard are always clearly visible up to the stern-post. But in all the stream-line boats I have designed the stern seems to settle down a bit in the water, and so little freeboard is there astern that, when the boat is travelling fast, the stern canvas is often awash, even in calm water. This is regarded as a highly objectionable feature by boat-builders and they are at great pains to fill out the stern lines to avoid it. I will shortly give my reasons for believing that they are wrong. For the present we may confine our attention to the fact that, by giving fine lines of run aft and bringing the crest of the stern wave between 7 and 8 feet forward of the stern-post, the value of L′ is reduced to 42 feet in a 58 ft. 6 in. boat. It is about the same value as I estimate for Dr. Warre's 'Snubby'.

If Froude's experiments on ships and models of ships are applicable to racing eights (and I am not by any means sure that they are applicable), the conclusions to be drawn from this analysis of the wave-making features of different types of boat are as follows:

It has been ascertained that the speed in knots (V) of a ship is related to the length in feet (l) by the formula $V^2 = 1{\cdot}8l$. If L' be the distance apart of the component bow and stern waves (which is generally rather greater than the length of the ship), relatively small resistance occurs when V^2 = approximately $3{\cdot}6\ L'$, or any odd sub-multiple of $3{\cdot}6\ L'$. But when V^2 is not greatly different from $1{\cdot}8\ L'$ or any sub-multiple of $1{\cdot}8\ L'$, abnormal wave resistance is developed.

We may take 10·5 knots (which is about the speed at which a first-rate crew would travel to Fawley) as the desirable speed for an eight. Then V^2 will be 110·25.

When $L' = 53$ feet, its coefficient will be $\dfrac{110{\cdot}25}{53} = 2{\cdot}08$, which is not greatly different from 1·8, and the wave resistance is great. When $L' = 42$ ft, its coefficient is $\dfrac{110{\cdot}25}{42} = 2{\cdot}625$, which is farther from 1·8, but not sufficiently near to 3·6 to give really satisfactory conditions.

When $L' = 35$ feet its coefficient is 3·15, which is sufficiently approximate to 3·6 to account for the remarkable speed of the Littledale boats built by Matt. Taylor, if L' for these boats was really as little as 35 feet.

The most favourable value of L' for a speed of 10·5 knots is 30·625 feet, and this could only be obtained by cutting down the length of an eight-oar to about 43 feet. But even if this were practicable, it is far from certain that any advantage would be gained at the speeds at which a crew is able to propel one eight. The 40-foot model tested in Sir John E. Thornycroft's tank did show a marked superiority over the long models at high speeds, but fell short of them at speeds below 12·6 knots (21 f.p.s.). From this it may be inferred that, though they have some effect at 10 knots, the wave-making features of a boat are less influential than other factors at speeds below 12 knots.

Moreover it is doubtful whether the results of experiments made with models of which the length is only seven or eight times the beam are applicable to boats whose length is 30 times their beam. It seems clear that they are not applicable without some correction for the favourable coefficient of L', for in an ordinary ship L' is generally rather greater than the length of the ship, but in an eight it is always less, and may be considerably less, than the length of the boat. At the present time the data are insufficient for estimating the favourable coefficient of L' in racing-boats. But it is worth mention that in a 26-foot sculling-boat, with a best speed of 8·7 knots, L', on my method of reckoning, should be about 21 feet. At this value $V^2 = 3{\cdot}6\ L'$, almost exactly, and the fact cannot be overlooked that a sculler gets much more pace for the horse-power developed than any combination of oarsmen.

The evidence, as far as it goes, and it all points in one direction, is against increasing the length of racing-boats, be they eight-oars, four-oars, pairs, or sculling-boats.

There is another consideration arising out of R. E. Froude's experiments. The bow wave leaves a train of waves behind it, and if, as in a canal barge, the fore-body be very short and the mid-body very long, the crests of several such waves can be seen along the sides of the boat, their size diminishing the farther they are removed from the generating wave. If the fore-body be long and the mid-body short or absent, there will be only one such derivative of the bow wave in the boat's length, and its crest will be somewhere towards the stern, its exact position depending upon the lines of the vessel. If the crest of the derivative bow wave corresponds with the crest of the stern wave, the two reinforce one another and an abnormally large wave is produced astern, the maintenance of which involves the expenditure of a corresponding amount of energy. But if the trough of the bow wave corresponds with the crest of the stern wave, the resultant wave system is of reduced dimensions and there is a corresponding reduction in resistance. This being so, it is clearly of importance to make the features of the boat such that the trough of the bow wave shall correspond as nearly as possible with the crest of the stern wave. The stream-line theory indicates, and the indication is borne out by photographs, that if there is no mid-body, the trough of the component bow and stern waves will be at the master section. If the master section be placed amidships or nearly amidships, as is the practice of boat-builders, it follows that the bow and stern waves must be of approximately the same length, and that if the lines of the run aft are the same as those of the entry, a most undesirable coincidence of the crests of the derived bow wave and the component stern wave will result. It is to avoid this that the lines of the run aft are filled out in order to throw the crest of the stern wave so far back that the coincidence is obviated. It is obviated, but, as far as I am able to judge, to an insufficient amount. However one looks at it, it is impossible to make any approximation to a coincidence of the trough of the bow wave with the crest of the stern wave in a boat in which the master section is amidships and there is no considerable length of mid-body. How the case may be in such a long-waisted boat as the Cambridge eight of 1908 I am not certain. I am inclined to think that the relatively great length of nearly parallel-sided mid-body has the effect of shortening the length of both the bow and stern waves, and it is probable that the trough of the *second* derived bow wave corresponds with the crest of the component stern wave, thus giving favourable conditions. I am the more inclined to this opinion because this boat has proved to be fairly fast both in tank trials and in actual practice, and I am unable to account for her satisfactory performances on any other hypothesis.

If there is no mid-body, or only a very small length of parallel-sided mid-body, and the boat is ‘ snubbed ’ forward, i. e. if the fore-body is made shorter than the hind-body, as in Dr. Warre’s boats, in the Littledale boats, and in the boats I have recently designed, the bow wave must be shorter than the stern wave, for the trough of both will be at the master section.[1] It is not a difficult matter to so adjust the lengths of the fore- and hind-bodies that the most favourable coincidence of the trough of the bow wave with the crest of the stern wave is ensured. As we have seen, the effect of this coincidence is that the resultant wave system at the stern of the boat is reduced to such relatively small dimensions as to be comparatively unimportant. But the system of bow waves is not affected, and a survey of all the data at my disposal leads me to think that the length of the bow wave has an important though indirect effect on the speed of a boat propelled by oars.

We cannot neglect the fact that a rowing-boat is something quite different from a vessel propelled by sail, screw, or paddle-wheel. For at least two-thirds of any given period of time the oars are out of the water and the propulsive force is in abeyance. The somewhat paradoxical fact that the boat loses some of its speed when the oars enter the water, and gains somewhat in speed when the oars leave the water, has been sufficiently dealt with in Chapter III. Mathematicians frequently assure me that, if only we could so rig out and train a crew that one pair of oars was always at work, the boat would go much faster. An oarsman can only plead his experience in mitigation of his ignorance of mathematics, and say politely that he is quite sure it would not. A little reflection assures us that if the eight men worked in couples, one couple beginning when another was leaving off, the boat would always be having its way checked by the entry of a pair of oars, and all the advantage gained by the smooth transference of the weight of the crew towards the stern during the swing forward would be lost. In brief, a rowing-boat moves rhythmically, and her

[1] Experience shows that if, as a result of snubbing, the bow wave is much shorter than the stern wave, the boat is very uneasy. This defect can be remedied by the intercalation of a certain amount of nearly parallel-sided mid-body. If the mid-body is made long enough, the length of the stern wave can be made approximately equal to that of the bow wave, with the result that the boat is very steady and easy, but loses speed. The question of the interaction of the bow and stern waves in racing-boats is still very obscure.

progress is represented by an undulating, not by a straight line. In her progress she makes undulations in the water, and it is, I submit, part of the boat-builder's and part of the oarsman's art to bring about a harmonious relation between these two systems of inevitable undulations. I hold that the stern system of undulations, the train of waves generated by the stern wave and left behind the boat, has little relation to the movements of the oarsmen. But the bow system of undulations, involving at least two wave crests rising along the length of the boat, has an important relation to the action of the oars.

It is with some misgiving that I put forward my views on this subject, for they are not sufficiently well founded on fact to enable me to present them in logical or even moderately comprehensible form. Such as they are, I make the following suggestions in the hope that they may stimulate others, better qualified than myself to deal with such difficult matters, to make further investigations on the subject.

It appears to me to be something more than a fortuitous coincidence that, in boats which have proved fast in practice, the length of the bow wave, as calculated or as estimated from a study of photographs, is approximately the same as the distance travelled during the complete cycle of 'stroke' and 'run' by the boat when moving at her 'best speed'.

Every boat has a 'best speed'. It is the speed which a crew (I must postulate that it is an efficient crew) can maintain for a considerable period of time with the least proportional expenditure of effort; not, of course, with the least absolute expenditure of effort. When a crew is paddling as lightly as possible the boat moves so slowly that the only resistance to be overcome is that of skin friction, and under such conditions one boat is as nearly as possible equal to another. Nor is the 'best speed' the highest attainable speed. By dint of great exertions, at high rate of stroke, a crew can squeeze a good bit more than her best speed out of a boat. But the effort required is out of all proportion to the pace gained. To put the matter in a form familiar to oarsmen: in a race a crew goes off with a rush at the start. It commonly rows 22 strokes in the first half-minute and 40 strokes in the full minute. At this rate, which may be kept up for another half-minute, more or less, a good crew can achieve a dead-water speed of something over 18 f.p.s. But the pace cannot be kept up, and it is the mark of a good crew that it is able, at the end of the first rush, to settle down and, as oarsmen say, 'get into its stride'. This means that the rate of stroke drops to between 35 and 36 per minute, and the dead-water speed to about 16·8 f.p.s. This, or something near this, should be the best speed of the boat, and if it is the oarsmen experience a welcome sense of relief. The exertion required to produce the reduced rate of speed is diminished in such proportion that the crew is able to keep up a 'sustained mean dead-water speed' of some 16·8 f.p.s. for a mile or more. At Putney, where the rate of stroke drops to 32 or even to 30, a well-trained crew will keep up a sustained dead-water speed of 15·4 f.p.s.[1] (equivalent to 7 min. 42 sec. over the Henley course) for four miles.

At a rate of 35·3 strokes per minute, or one stroke in 1·7 second, at a speed of 16·8 f.p.s., a boat will travel 28·56 feet in the complete cycle of 'stroke' and 'run between strokes' in dead water. At a rate of 32 strokes per minute, at a speed of 15·4 f.p.s., a boat will travel 28·875 feet in the complete cycle of stroke and run. One may conclude that when a crew has 'settled down' for a good performance over a course of any length it should move its boat about 29 ft. per stroke. The 'best speed' of a boat, therefore, is not measured in terms of feet per second but in terms of distance covered per stroke. My thesis is that this distance should correspond as nearly as possible to the length of the bow wave, and that it should be half the length of the boat on the load-water-line, so that the crew may cover a full boat's length in two strokes. It follows that the proper length for

[1] The average speed of a good flood tide at Putney is taken at $2\frac{3}{4}$ miles per hour, or 4 f.p.s., so the actual speed at which the boat passes stationary objects would be 19·4 f.p.s. For actual speeds against the stream at Henley 0·55 is deducted from the dead-water speed.

a boat is 58 feet on the load-water-line. This was the length of the boat in which the Belgian crews won the Grand Challenge Cup in 1906, 1907, and 1909 and of the old boats up to about 1892, which, as I have shown, were speedier than the long boats which succeeded them.

My thesis depends upon a very complicated analysis of the ratio $\frac{\text{stroke}}{\text{run}}$ both in respect of time, when it involves the question of rhythm, and of distance travelled. I can only touch the fringe of the question here.

It has been shown in Chapter II that with an oar of given length outboard, properly rowed through an angle of 80°, the distance through which the boat is moved during the stroke must always be the same, whatever the rate of stroke and whatever the power applied at the handle. The time in which the boat is moved through that distance varies with the power. The acceleration given to the boat varies with the time taken to move it through the given distance. If the time is short the acceleration given to the boat is correspondingly great; if the time is long the acceleration of the boat is correspondingly diminished. The greater the acceleration the farther the boat will travel between the strokes in a given space of time, and vice versa; always supposing that the crew is sliding and swinging correctly. It has been shown (fig. 10) that to sustain the high mean speed of 17 f.p.s. during the stroke, a crew using 12 ft. 4 in. oars buttoned at 3 ft. 9 in. moves its boat through 8·5 feet in 0·5 second. The strongest crew has not the power to move it through that distance in less time for more than four or five hundred yards.

Take the not wholly imaginary case of a crew rowing at 40 strokes a minute and attaining a speed of 18 f.p.s. At this rate the boat will travel 27 feet per stroke, and if the crew is 'keeping its length' will travel 8·5 feet during stroke and 18·5 feet during the run, a ratio of 1 : 2·1763. Assuming that the work is so well executed that the mean speed during stroke and run is the same (see p. 60) the rhythm or time ratio will be the same, and the time taken for stroke will be 0·472 second. The power required to move some 1,850 lb. through 8·5 feet in this time is great, and the sense of effort to the crew will be increased by the fact that it is rowing out of tune with its boat. The distance travelled per stroke is shorter by some two feet than the length of the bow wave. It is possible, of course, to design a boat to make a bow wave 27 feet long; Dr. Warre's 'Snubby' must have made a wave of very nearly this length. But when the stroke is dropped to 36 per minute the appropriate speed for such a boat would only be 16·2 f.p.s. At this speed the time required for stroke would be 0·518 second. The oarsmen would not be working hard enough. But if they increased their work to the extent of rowing the stroke through in 0·5 second, they would give increased acceleration to the boat during the stroke; therefore the boat would travel at greater speed during the run, and would have travelled more than the distance appropriate to its wave length in 1·666 second, which is the time taken to complete the whole cycle of stroke and swing forward at the rate of 36 strokes per minute. To 'keep in tune with the boat' the stroke must be raised or, as generally happens, the crew must hurry forward to get in the next stroke at the moment when the boat has travelled the 27 feet appropriate to the wave length. It will begin to 'bucket forward' and will soon get short and scrappy.

From this we may infer that, in boats which are too much 'snubbed' forward, the crew will either have to keep up a high rate of stroke, or will tend to bucket forward, or will have to content itself with a lower rate of speed than will allow it to win a race against a good opponent.

Conversely, if the features of the boat are such that the bow wave is greatly increased in length the crew will tend towards a slow stroke. At first sight this may seem to be an advantage, for it would appear that the slower stroke is less exhausting to the crew. But a little reflection shows that the supposed advantage does not exist. On the contrary, an unduly slow rate of stroke is extremely exhausting. Let us suppose that the features of the boat are such that the length of the bow wave is 34 feet. It is, I believe, even longer in some boats in which the master section is 30 feet distant from the cutwater, but I prefer to make a moderate estimate. We have seen that the power required to move the boat 8·5 feet in 0·5 second gives it an acceleration which allows of a run of nearly 20·5 feet in the 1·2 second allowed for the swing forward. By that time the speed of the boat will have dropped to 16·6 f.p.s., the point at which a new stroke should begin, if the mean speed of 17 f.p.s. is to be sustained. But to allow the boat to travel a distance equal to a wave length of 34 feet it must be allowed to run on for another 5 feet, and this will occupy nearly 0·3 second of time. The length of time given to the swing forward must therefore be increased by this amount and the rhythm of the stroke must be altered from a ratio of 1 : 2·4 to 1 : 3·1. But at the beginning of the next stroke the boat's speed will be so much reduced that the oarsmen must make an extra effort to raise it again to a mean speed of 17 f.p.s. during the stroke. If they fail to make this effort the speed of the boat will fall. The greater effort gives the boat a greater acceleration in this sense, that it raises its speed from a lower figure at the beginning to the same figure as before at the end of the stroke. But as the speed at the end of the stroke remains the same the boat will travel no farther than before on the run, and the crew has to settle down to a laborious method of rowing, doing increased work at every stroke to gain the very doubtful advantage of swinging forward at a very slow pace for the next stroke. If any one should ask what becomes of the increased energy put into the stroke if it does not increase the pace of the boat, the answer is obvious. It is expended in sustaining a longer wave.

It is sufficiently obvious that this argument holds good for any lower speed that the crew may attain to at any lower rate of stroke. This is illustrated in the following table, in the preparation of which it is assumed that the crew maintains the same rhythm, viz. a ratio of stroke to run of $\frac{1}{2{\cdot}4}$ and the same length of stroke, at the various rates specified. On this assumption the boat would travel 28·9 feet during the cycle of stroke and run: 8·5 feet during the stroke and 20·4 feet during the run, whatever the rate of stroke, rowing or paddling.

Rate of Stroke per Minute.	*Time taken for Cycle of Stroke and Run in Seconds.*	*Time taken for Stroke. Seconds.*	*Time taken for Run. Seconds.*	*Mean Speed in f.p.s.*
35·3	1·7	0·5	1·2	17·0
32·0	1·875	0·551	1·324	15·4
30·0	2·0	0·588	1·412	14·45
24·0	2·5	0·735	1·765	11·56

The work done by the crew is sufficiently indicated by the third column, which, in the case of a 12 st. 4 lb. crew, shows the times taken to give such an acceleration to 1,850 lb. as will carry this mass on for a distance of 20·4 feet in the times given in the fourth column. The reader who may wish to make the laborious calculations necessary to ascertain the work done in foot-pounds per man at these speeds and rates of stroke is referred to on p. 66.

The figures show a definite relation between the work done, the rate of stroke, and the speed of the boat. This, I submit, is the ideal to be aimed at. When paddling the crew should economize its strength by doing just that amount of work which is required to maintain the rhythmic proportion between the stroke and the run, and the rate of stroke should be suitably low. When the crew is told to row, the rate of stroke should be increased in proportion to the extra work done. In the early stages of practice the crew cannot be expected to exhibit the fullness of power which will enable it to sustain a mean speed of 17 f.p.s. when fully trained. But the procedure is complicated and, as I think, vitiated by the blind cult of hard work which has too long held sway in the rowing world. At a quite early stage in practice a crew is ordered to row as hard as it possibly can at the rate of 26 or 28 strokes a minute. The result is a curtailment of the period of time that should be allowed for the stroke and an undue prolongation of the time that should be allowed for the run. The natural rhythm appropriate to the wave length of the boat is neglected, and it is simply a fluke if, in the final 'tuning up' for the race, the crew happens on the proper harmony between its own movements and those of the boat. It is an additional complication that boat-builders have met the school of brute force more than half-way, by designing boats which invite the laborious method of rowing described above. I am quite impervious to the sneer that I expect crews to win races without hard work. Nothing is more certain than that hard work is necessary for high speed. A glance at the figures in the third and last columns of the table proves it. All that I contend for is that the effective use of the full available power is a thing which an individual oarsman and a crew must learn gradually. An analogy will illustrate my meaning. A golfer will never learn to drive the ball far and truly if he begins by putting all his strength into the drive. He must first acquire mastery over his movements, adding strength to his stroke as he gains accuracy and control. When he has acquired complete mastery he can make a magnificent drive with such ease and grace of movement that he seems to have exerted no strength at all. But the effort is there, all the same : it is only masked by the skill of him who makes it.

I seem to have wandered from the subject of boat-design into a discussion of the art of oarsmanship, but that is only natural, for I am maintaining that the two are interdependent. Returning to the boat, I have the following suggestion to make in support of my theory that it is the length of the bow wave which is influential in respect of good speed and good rowing in racing-boats.

Let us take L' to stand for the length of the bow wave, instead of the distance between the crests of the component bow and stern waves. Then, on the formula $V^2 = 3{\cdot}6\,L'$, when $L' = 29$ feet, $V = \sqrt{29 \times 3{\cdot}6} = 10{\cdot}217$ knots, or 16·999 f.p.s. This reapplication of Froude's formula goes very far to confirm my view, arrived at on other evidence, that 29 feet is the appropriate length for the bow wave of an eight designed to sustain a mean speed of 17 f.p.s.

On the other hand, if $L' = 34$ feet, $V = 11{\cdot}063$ knots or 18·43 f.p.s.

The conditions seem very favourable for the highest speed attainable by an eight in a short spurt, but they are not so good as they look, for the rate of stroke would have to be as low as $32\frac{1}{2}$ per minute to obtain the desired correspondence between the distance travelled by the boat per stroke and the length of the bow wave. The power required to drive a boat at 18·4 f.p.s. at a stroke of $32\frac{1}{2}$ is superhuman.

In a very long-waisted, barge-shaped boat such as that delineated in fig. 42, the bow-wave system must be something like that depicted by Froude in his classical memoir on the resistance of ships. Not one, but two crests of derivatives of the component bow wave must appear along the sides of the boat. In such a boat the wave-making resistance is, as it were, accepted as a necessary evil and standardized. No attempt is made to recover any part of the energy expended in forming the bow wave. The designer's aim seems to be limited to reducing the area of wetted surface as far as possible and to obtaining the most favourable ratio of $\frac{\text{beam}}{\text{draught}}$. In these matters, it must be admitted, he is remarkably successful. But there is no question of bringing the performer into tune with his instrument, for the instrument has deliberately been made tuneless. It is as though a violinist were compelled to stretch his strings on a mere rectangular box as a resonator. No doubt a Paganini or a Joachim could extract music of more than average excellence from such an instrument, but who will deny that they could play incomparably better on a Stradivarius ? Very good oarsmen, trained by very good coaches, have done big things in boats of the type I am describing. But to my eye there has always been an obvious defect. The rhythm of the rowing has always seemed to me artificial and incommensurable with the movement of the boat. The better the crew the more I have been struck by a strange incongruity between the disciplined action of the oarsmen and the gait of the boat. Such crews give the same impression as a horseman who has a very firm and correct seat but is withal out of sympathy with his mount. I venture to say that if the Cambridge crew of 1900 had been 'sympathetically' boated it would have knocked at least twenty seconds off the time in which it actually won the race at Putney in that year.

I am entirely in agreement with Dr. Warre in attributing much of the decadence that followed hard on the heels of that classical exhibition of well-drilled oarsmanship to the type of boat that prevailed in the succeeding years. But I cannot follow his flights of imagination into the realms of music with the accompanying theories of harmonic curves, of boats seven octaves long, and so forth. I cannot, because I have tried to work these ideas for all they are worth and have found no profit in them. The analogy of music cannot be exact, for aqueous waves behave quite differently from aerial waves. Sound-waves, whatever their length, travel at approximately the same speed, and upon this fact the laws of musical harmony ultimately depend. In water the long wave travels the faster. Undoubtedly there is music in rowing. But it is the music of water, not of the air. Perhaps this is the reason why no musician has succeeded, though many have tried, in composing a song which truly fits the rhythm of rowing. The harmonics of water are unexplored. Indeed they are inappreciable to all but a very few persons. Those few are our great strokes. They may sin, as some of the greatest of them sinned, in matters of style. But they instinctively know the music of the water and have the power to compel their less appreciative fellow-oarsmen to obey the unknown laws of aqueous harmony. Probably those laws are very simple. Certainly the organs of perception to which we must ascribe the function of transmitting aquatic undulations to our nervous system are infinitely less complex than the elaborate apparatus by means of which we appreciate the infinite variety of sound. No doubt the aquatic sense (if I may so call it) is largely atrophied in ourselves. Comparative histology indicates that it is much more highly developed in fishes. One may hazard the speculation that in respect of this eighth sense a 'born stroke' is atavistic. His often uncanny faculty of perceiving rhythms, disturbances, undulations (call them what we will), inappreciable by other men derives, after aeons of intermission, from some remote aquatic ancestor.

CHAPTER X

ON COACHING

THE NOVICE ON FIXED SEATS

Of all matters connected with the art of rowing, coaching is the most difficult to write about. It is with great misgiving and reluctance that I undertake the task, the more so because nearly all that can usefully be said has been set forth in a pamphlet of less than twenty pages by Mr. Harcourt Gold.[1] It is a masterpiece of brevity, knowledge, and good sense, and should be read again and again by every one who proposes to undertake the training of any crew, however humble the race that it is entered for. But seeing how uncommon is that kind of sense which Mr. Gold calls common sense, I must take leave to doubt whether the most assiduous study of his pithy and shrewd advice will produce many coaches like himself. But surely his pamphlet, if read with understanding, should prevent much bad coaching. There is a point to which Mr. Gold attaches special importance, for he reiterates it, and I wish to add my testimony to his: 'Do not make rowing seem difficult.' Many a promising novice, not a few oarsmen who have got beyond their noviciate, and many a crew, have been spoilt by getting into the hands of a coach who imagined that he would get better work out of his pupils by magnifying the difficulty of the task before them.

Nevertheless, though it is the business of a coach to disguise the fact, rowing *is* difficult; that is to say first-rate rowing. Many try to attain to it, very few succeed. Can it be said that failure is altogether the fault of the coaches? In part, perhaps, because coaching is even

[1] *The Common Sense of Coaching*, by **Harcourt G. Gold, The Field Press, Ltd., Windsor House, Bream's Buildings, London, E. C. 4, 1920.**

more difficult than oarsmanship, and there are fewer good coaches than good oarsmen.

Of this, at any rate, I am convinced, that the theory that every man of good stamina and physique, sound in wind and limb, is potentially a good oarsman and can be made such by a proper course of coaching, is absurd and contrary to all experience. Doubtless there have been, and are, many oarsmen who might have been much better than they were, or are, if they had been consistently well coached throughout their careers. But that is another story. It is also very true, and it happens every year, that promising men and promising crews are spoiled by bad coaching. But that again is another story.

'Coaching' is nothing more than education in the particular art of rowing. The product of the education depends, not only on the teacher, but to a still greater degree upon the individual taught. It is not possible for even a superlatively good teacher to make a duffer into a first-class man. But it is possible, when preparing him for some special occasion, for an examination or a race, to make him a class better than he really is, and so to obtain results exceeding expectation. When one has coached all sorts of crews for a long number of years and at the same time has been engaged in the more serious work of education with its incessant preparation of batches of youth for examination, one comes to realize that nearly all the time it has been one's function to lift men out of the mire, to try to set their feet upon the rock, and to order their goings. Some there are who climb at once upon the rock and stay there, but, for the majority who pass through the hands of a College coach, the story is a recurrent one. Every year the men have to be lifted out of the mire, at the end of every season they slide back into it. The man who has been pushed up into a class better than he really is does not stay there, but reverts promptly to his true level. So in the next season one has to begin all over again, and the old hands are often more difficult to get into form than the new. Their faults are more deeply rooted, and the rank growth pushes its way first through the soil at the beginning of the season. But with a little diligence it can be pruned away, and one may reasonably expect that a College or Club oarsman will become a little more shapely, a little more effective in propelling the boat, in each succeeding year. Now and again an individual, who in two or three previous years has succeeded in keeping his place in the boat, but has nevertheless fallen far short of expectation, will in his last year of residence suddenly and unexpectedly develop qualities which, if they had manifested themselves earlier, would have gained him a place in Trial Eights or even in the University boat. I have known several who failed to secure this crown of an oarsman's ambition because they did not discover themselves until the opportunity had passed by. One or two of them had the compensation of winning the Grand Challenge Cup at Henley. Others had to be content with the knowledge that at the close of their careers they were the mainstays of their College boats. The moral of this is that it is never safe to discard an old stager, however disappointing his previous performances, without another trial. The difficulty is that, once he has taken his place in the crew, the old stager is difficult to get rid of. He may have deteriorated and is occupying a place that could be filled better by a younger oarsman, but his feelings and those of the crew have to be considered. The coach is oftentimes sorely puzzled as to the best course to be pursued. Sometimes the question has to be solved by reference to the doctor, who has been warned beforehand that an adverse verdict will be welcome. The truth is that in the great majority of boat clubs the number of active members is small; consequently the choice of material is limited and the coach is generally hard put to it to find eight men of sufficiently uniform training and capacity to make up a good eight-oared crew. Even when he has to select a 'Varsity crew he is often hampered for want of a sufficient number of suitable men to choose from. So it happens that, in ninety-nine cases out of a hundred, a coach has to content himself with making the best of such material as is at his disposal. The most successful coach is he who has the faculty of making something that will stand up out of almost any material that is supplied to him.

After this confession it may seem inconsistent to say that a coach must not make rowing seem difficult. Yet it is most true that he must not. In rowing, as in all matters where it is intended to secure a definite objective by combined effort, the first element of success is faith. Individually and collectively men must be led to have faith in themselves; faith in their colleagues; faith in their coach and his teaching; faith in the instruments, the boats and oars, which they use. It is by faith, believing that his is the more excellent way, that a man overcomes the technical difficulties of oarsmanship; by faith that he measures his own half-instructed efforts against veterans; by faith, when half-way through the contest he feels dead to the world, that he calls on himself for a fresh effort, and giving battle to giants, overcomes them.

Faith is not arrived at by making the end seem difficult and impossible of attainment. On the other hand, it will not be gained by pretending that there are no difficulties when there are many. The commonest mistake of an inexperienced coach is to bring too many difficulties into view at once. Knowing that the correct performance of one part of the stroke depends upon the correct performance of other parts, he is over-anxious to put all things right at once, and oblivious of the fact that his pupil can only attend to one thing at a time. Too much zeal on the part of the teacher quickly engenders despair on the part of the taught.

As rowing is continuous movement, and the action of the oarsman must always be correlated to the motion of the boat, the first question that arises is, How and where one should begin when teaching a novice? To this question I can give no definite answer. It is necessary to begin one way with one man and another way with another man; one way with this crew, and another way with that crew. There is no fixed and infallible method of coaching; no Montessori system whereby all pupils may be taught to master the elements and be brought in given time to a definite standard. My first advice to a coach is to rely as little as possible on method, as much as possible on the study of the temperaments and the physical capacities of the men he has to teach. It must always be remembered that no two individuals are the same and that no two crews are the same ; further, that individuals vary, sometimes to an extraordinary extent, under differing circumstances, and that crews vary quite as much as and often more than individuals.

It is therefore impossible to lay down any rules or to prescribe any special method of coaching. Any suggestions that are offered must be of the most general kind. The most important thing, in my opinion, is for a coach to recognize and maintain a due balance between individual and collective coaching. The principles to be observed were laid down long ago by Dr. Warre in his *Notes on Coaching*, but to this day, when preparing crews for a race, most coaches are too much addicted to individual coaching. Necessarily it comes first : a musical conductor cannot lead an orchestra until the members of it have learned to play their instruments correctly. The functions of a coach are in many respects analogous to those of a conductor, but in nearly all cases the same individual must first teach his men to use their instruments properly and afterwards bring them into harmony. The first step, the teaching men to use their instruments properly, is best carried out in a tub-pair, and this is the usual course at schools and the Universities. It has, however, this disadvantage : that rowing is most easily and quickly learned by imitation, and whenever it is possible, a novice should be placed behind at least a moderately proficient oarsman and encouraged to follow his actions as nearly as he can. It is obviously easier to do this in an eight- or a four-oar than in a tub-pair.

In any case, when dealing with a novice, the early lessons should be thorough, but as simple as possible. Many a beginner is disheartened by having too many things pressed on his attention at once. The first step with a beginner is to teach him to hold his oar properly, to dip the blade into the water and take it out of the water with some confidence and precision, and to perform accurately the movements of the wrists which turn the blade on and off the feather. In this matter good habits are everything and should be inculcated and insisted upon from the first. Bad habits are only too easily acquired, and when acquired are hard to get rid of. Quite a considerable number of lessons should be devoted to the handling of the oar; everything else being excluded, except that the novice must learn from the outset to sit and to maintain his feet and legs in the correct position. It really does not matter at this stage whether he gets any appreciable way on the boat, but in the interests of his future progress it does matter very much that he should learn, after he has put his blade into the water and got some little pull on it, to extricate it with ease and confidence.

When he has acquired some little skill in manipulating the oar, the beginner should be taught the rudiments of swing, care being taken that he brings his body forward from the thigh-joints and preserves his balance by the pressure of his feet against the stretcher. Here it is very necessary to remember that a novice, however robust and muscular he may seem to be, is weak and undeveloped with regard to the movements required in rowing. The muscles that he has to use are not in common use. He has to acquire the habit of using them, until in due time they become strengthened and developed by use. In the swing forward the novice brings into play muscles which in normal life are not much exercised. In the swing back he encounters the resistance of the water to his blade, and if he would row well this resistance has to be overcome by groups of muscles which normally are not used in the same sequence and combination, and many of them are not exercised to anything like the degree required in rowing. It follows that, in these early stages, the movements of the novice must be restricted, not only in respect of time and energy, but also in respect of amplitude. In other words, the novice must not be set to row for too long at a time; must not be encouraged to put out his full strength;

and must be allowed, even encouraged, to row short. The fundamental thing is that he should from the very first acquire the habit of using the right groups of muscles, in the right combination, at the right time. Length, hard work, endurance, are very necessary for complete oarsmanship, but they must be postponed until reasonably correct habits of position and movement have been acquired.

The crux of teaching a novice is ' work '. As soon as he has learned to dip his blade into the water and to pull his arms towards his body, he will encounter the resistance of the water to his blade. This resistance causes the boat to move, and for some little time the movement of the boat is a source of great embarrassment to the would-be oarsman. The resistance seems to be elusive : it slips away as soon as it is encountered, and in a moment the oar-blade is entangled in a swirl of water and it feels as if considerable force must be exerted to extricate it. When the beginner tries to put some swing into his stroke his oar-blade meets with greater resistance, the boat moves away faster, and his embarrassment is increased. But if his first lessons in handling the oar have been well learned he will soon get over it. At this juncture it is all-important to encourage him to keep up the feeling of resistance on the blade of the oar as his elbows bend past his sides and to have confidence in using his wrists to extricate the oar when the handle comes home to his body.

As soon as these preliminary lessons have been learned in a tub-pair the novice may be promoted to a roomy four-oar—an excellent type of boat, and, when judiciously used, a better vehicle for instruction than a tub-pair. The oarsman is now under new conditions. He is a member of a crew and has to learn to accommodate his newly acquired movements to those of his fellow-oarsmen. A number of new factors are introduced, mostly relating to time. To keep time when dipping the oar into the water ; to keep time when extracting the oar from the water ; to regulate the pace of the swing forward ; are matters of considerable difficulty to a novice, and his task is the less easy because the four-oar moves appreciably faster than the tub-pair, and he has to accommodate the pace of his movements to the pace of the boat. He will make no progress and will quickly forget what he has already learned unless he is given a good lead. Therefore a four-oar should never be manned by four novices ; the stroke should be at least moderately proficient, with a sufficient sense of rhythm to take his crew along at a uniform stroke regardless of the aberrations of the men behind him. At this stage of the oarsman's development imitation counts for a great deal, and the more experienced members of a boat-club should be ready and willing to help beginners over the most difficult part of their education by setting the stroke for them. The coach should not bicycle or run on the bank, but should stand up in the stern of the tub-four. From this point of vantage he can see more clearly movements of wrists, elbows, and shoulders ; can judge whether the men are seated in the proper position ; square to their work, with their feet pressed against the stretcher. Also, being closer to the men, he is saved from the necessity of shouting at them. Nobody likes being shouted at. Novices are generally over-anxious and nervous, and more often flustered than encouraged by a loud voice.

The early lessons in a tub-four are probably the most important in an oarsman's training. It is now that the foundations are laid of good or bad habits which will stick to him for the rest of his aquatic career. While making due allowance for inexperience, the coach should insist rigorously on correctness of position of body, legs, feet, hands, shoulders, and even of head and neck. Faults of position should be pointed out during an easy, and the oarsman should be made to correct them before starting for another spell of rowing. Faults of movement will be corrected best by a happy combination of individual and collective coaching. Success will most readily be achieved by taking all the four men together and concentrating their attention on one phase of the stroke at a time. They all have to do the same thing at the same time. Nothing encourages men more than the feeling that they are acquiring some uniformity of action. Nothing is more destructive of uniformity than coaching one individual for errors at one phase of the stroke ; another individual for errors at another phase. In my experience it is best to begin by getting the men to lift their oars out of the water together and to drop and get away the hands together, but at first not too quickly. A lot of time may profitably be spent on this without much regard to the propulsion of the boat. When some little proficiency has been acquired in clearing the blade at the finish and starting the feather on its backward course, the coach may turn the men's attention to the other end of the stroke and get them to dip the blades in together and to try to get a simultaneous feeling of resistance as the blades enter the water. He should at this stage discourage rather than encourage any attempt to pull hard, but should make sure that such pull as there is comes from the stretcher and that the weight is used in the pull. As soon as the men begin to learn to get a pull on the boat, and to feel the resistance offered by the water to their blades, the finish will again require attention, and the coach will have to explain that the oar should be pulled through evenly, the last part of the stroke not snatched at, but allowed to come through with the run of the boat ; the recovery marked by the prompt and simultaneous action of the wrists. After a spell of instruction on the finish and recovery it will be necessary to turn again to the entry of the oar and the pull ; and so on, always taking one thing at a time and getting the men to concentrate on the point under instruction and to try and do it all together.

About this time and as soon as the coach is satisfied that the preliminary lessons are taking effect, the novices should be given frequent opportunities for going out by themselves and practising what they have learned free from the constraint which the presence of a coach imposes on their efforts. After nearly half a century's experience there is one thing of which I am certain ; that is, that the only way to learn rowing is to row and to do plenty of it. Coaches are never plentiful, good coaches are very rare, and the man or boy who cannot trust himself on the water unless he is under supervision will never get as much practice as he requires. Nor will he learn what is essential to good oarsmanship—to keep a watch upon his own actions ; to acquire the habit of subconscious concentration on the task in hand, which, when acquired, will forbid him from ever rowing a careless stroke ; to learn to adapt himself, on his own initiative, to all the ever-varying moods of wind and water which in various degrees retard or favour the progress of the boat.

Latter-day oarsmen have become more and more dependent on coaching, and their dependence, both at schools and at the Universities, has increased to such a degree that they will hardly venture out in a boat unless there is some one on the bank to worry them. As they are always under instruction, always being checked for some real or fancied lapse of form ; as they are frequently taught one style by one coach and another style by another, they fail to gain confidence in their own powers and rowing becomes an irksome and apparently difficult task instead of a pleasure. The best way to assure oneself that rowing is not very difficult is to row often and for long distances. But for beginners it is a *sine qua non* that the stroke should be set by a competent oarsman, at any rate by one who is sufficiently proficient to set a tolerably correct example for the others to follow.

While novices may be allowed, and should be encouraged, to do a good deal of rowing on their own account, they should frequently subject themselves to lessons of twenty minutes or half an hour's duration. In these progress may be noted, faults that have developed themselves can be pointed out and remedied, and a fresh stock of aquatic experience gained for use in the next long journey without a coach. Under such a system men and boys will progress much more rapidly than if they have to spend two-thirds of their time waiting until their turn comes for an outing of some twenty or thirty minutes' duration ; very often less.

When he has four or more men to deal with a coach may make free use of his voice to encourage his men to move together, giving the cadence of the stroke by such words as ‘ Now ’, ‘ Drop ’, ‘ Steadily ’ ;

but he must be sure that he gives the right cadence. He should try to get his men, even in their early lessons, to appreciate the song of the stroke and to move their limbs and bodies rhythmically, as soldiers march to the tune of a band. But he should not always be calling the time, and for considerable periods should be silent, leaving the men to work it out for themselves. It is by trying to pull together in regular rhythm that individuals will make the most rapid improvement. If they can be persuaded to fix their attention on the rhythm, with due regard to the sequence of the movements that make up the rhythm, rather than on their own individual shortcomings, they will soon lose much of their awkwardness, provided always that they have been taught in their earliest lessons to handle the oar properly and to allow free play to the wrists. Too much individual coaching makes a man self-centred and self-conscious. Self-consciousness is almost synonymous with awkwardness, and a self-centred oarsman will never combine properly with the other members of a crew.

On no account should a coach prematurely incite his pupils to row hard. Until they have mastered the proper succession of the movements of body and limbs and have learned the connexion of those movements with the resistance offered by the water to the blade of a properly handled oar, any attempt to work hard will only result in mischievous misdirected efforts—screwing actions of the body; hoisting with the shoulders; wrenching with the arms at the finish; gripping the oar-handle tightly in the fists; and other evils. For the same reason no distinction should be made between 'paddling' and 'rowing' in the earlier stages of an oarsman's education. The distinction can only be made when proper habits have been acquired, the proper muscles strengthened by exercise, and the feeling of resistance of water to the blade of the oar acquired and appreciated. In these early days it is also quite beside the point to lecture men about the 'beginning'. A heavy tub-four moves relatively slowly, and the sharp 'beginning' which is of so much importance in lighter craft is a thing hardly to be achieved. There is probably nothing which mystifies and disheartens young oarsmen more than overmuch talk about the ‘ beginning ’. But it is of the utmost importance to teach them so to direct their efforts that they get a simultaneous feeling of resistance on their blades and their stretchers.

It is perhaps inevitable that novices should be set to race all too soon and before they have really learned good habits of rowing. Continuous practice in a heavy boat is monotonous, and it is supposed that the stimulus of competition is required to keep up interest. But much harm is done to nascent oarsmanship by Freshmen's races in the October Term and at schools by the tendency—a comparatively modern tendency—to multiply novice and junior races. The harm is greater when, as is the prevailing fashion, the races are rowed over a short course and take the form of bumping races. It would be far better, in my opinion, to harden novices by accustoming them to longer and longer journeys, and finally to test their capacities by setting them to do a long row within certain limits of time. At Oxford, for example, they might row to Nuneham Ferry and back, a prize being awarded to the crew that accomplishes the journey in the shortest time ; delay in locks being deducted from the whole time spent on the journey. I am told that something of this sort is done at Cambridge, where a much longer reach of river free from locks is available than at Oxford. If so it is highly commendable. If short races must be indulged in, coaches should impress on their crews that better results will be obtained by freedom and uniformity of action than by violent unco-ordinated effort.

When in due time the novice is promoted to a seat in an eight-oar he enters upon a new phase in his rowing career. The increased pace of the boat, its narrowness, its instability, the sense of hustle which every man experiences when he tries for the first time to row in unison with seven others, will retard individual progress, and in most cases lead to loss of a great deal of the form already gained. It is a time of difficulty and disenchantment, during which the coach is called upon to exercise large quantities of tact, forbearance, and leadership. Greatly as his most promising pupils seem to have deteriorated in form, he will be wise to ignore their backslidings for a day or two, and to confine himself to encouraging them to persevere and, whatever happens, to go on rowing and do their best to follow their stroke. Here let it be said that if it is important to have a tolerably experienced oarsman as stroke of a four-oar, it is doubly and trebly more important that the stroke thwart of a novice eight should be filled by some one who will row steadily and regularly, and if possible remain serenely indifferent to the vagaries of the men behind him. He need not be very lively nor yet possessed of those undefinable qualities which make a racing stroke, but he must be regular and fairly easy to follow. Given such a stroke the coach should not allow the shortcomings of individuals to distract his attention too much from the importance of getting the eight men to work as a whole. Until they have learned to combine to some extent no one of them can learn to row properly, and assuredly they will not combine if they are treated as so many disconnected units. As in the four, so in the eight, a coach standing up in the stern of the boat will have much more command over his crew, and will be able to give the cadence of the stroke much more effectively than by shouting across the river at them from a bicycle.

After two or three days, if they have rowed far enough each day and have not been unduly harassed by individual coaching, novices will begin to settle down to their work in an eight-oar, and the coach has to turn his attention to matters which have hitherto been allowed to remain in abeyance. Out of the whole number of men he has instructed he has to select a crew which will race, say, for the Torpids at Oxford or for the Lents at Cambridge. Up to date, making due allowance for differences in strength and build, progress will have been fairly uniform. One or two men may have shown exceptional capacity for oarsmanship. Some few will have proved so awkward or refractory, or will have disclosed such physical weakness, that it is not worth while persevering any longer with them. But the majority will be much of a muchness, and the readiness with which individuals respond to the higher demands made on them by an eight-oar requires to be carefully watched. Judgement must be suspended until the coach has been able to see how individuals shape in an eight after a considerable spell of practice. It will inevitably happen that some who seemed to learn quickly and easily up to a certain point will come to the end of their tether, and fall far short of their early promise. On the other hand, men who seemed stubborn and slow may keep on improving and give evidence of being made of better stuff than their more facile and eager companions. First impressions are bad guides in the final selection of oarsmen.

As the new hands begin to settle down, and to recover the confidence they acquired in a tub-four or tub-pair, the coach must begin to inculcate notions of length, work, and ' beginning '. It may be assumed that up to now the men will have been able to make little or no distinction between rowing and paddling. They should have learned to pull with some vigour, but are as yet too unpractised to lay out all the strength of which they are capable. They should have been taught to swing their bodies correctly, but will still fall short of the full limit of useful swing. They should know what it is to feel something of the weight of the boat on their blades, but will not hitherto have rowed under conditions that admit of a real ' beginning '. In the eight swing, work, and beginning soon claim the first places in importance. Perhaps the first thing that the coach should try to instil into the oarsman's mind at this stage is that work is swing and swing is work. To judge by results it would seem that many oarsmen have been taught to think that ' swing ' is the action of bringing their bodies forward ; ' work ', an unrelated effort to pull the blade through the water. They must be made to understand that swing enters into the whole stroke, and work is the result of it. The swing forward is nothing but the movement of the body into a position from which its momentum can effectively be brought into use to do work. In cricket, in golf, in the use of an axe or a sledge-hammer, the momentum of the swinging body is used to give power to the blow to be delivered.

But in these, as in nearly all actions but those of rowing, the body is lifted back in the preparatory movement and brought forward to do the required work. In rowing it is exactly the opposite, and this is probably the reason why a novice, when he is called upon to work, begins by putting a lot of energy into his swing forward and a wholly insufficient amount of energy into his swing back. The sense of insufficiency of power in the swing back is, in its turn, the reason why he grips his oar fiercely with his hands and tries to tug it home with his arms and shoulders. The coach must clearly and perseveringly impress on his pupils the idea that in the swing forward they are executing a movement analogous to that of a woodman when he lifts his axe, or a golfer when he lifts his club, to the point from which the blow is to be delivered. That the whole object of the swing forward is to get the body into a position from which the greatest power can be brought to bear, in the shortest time, at the appropriate moment, and that the arms are only the guides of the instrument (be it oar, axe, or club) and the transmitters of the power of the body to the handle of it. There are many different ways of illustrating the right principle, but not all will appeal with equal force to any given individual. The coach should never weary in finding new and apt illustrations and analogies to impress the right method on the minds of his pupils, remembering that an illustration which is suggestive and illuminating to one man may make no appeal to the intelligence of another. There is always this difficulty, that the illustration or analogy, taken from some other branch of sport or exercise, is never exact. In all cases where a blow is delivered by some instrument held in the hands, be it a golf club, an axe, or what not, the instrument is swung through a considerable distance before it meets the resistance to be overcome. In rowing the full resistance has to be encountered the moment that the instrument starts moving in the direction in which work is to be done. The resistance is fluid; it very easily escapes; it has to be caught and fixed, and the catching of it is a knack, a skilful combination of small manipulations with a big and sudden effort. I know of no other mode of doing work that is exactly like it. It is peculiar to rowing; very baffling to the uninitiated; exceedingly difficult of communication by the coach. The knack is not to be acquired quickly. It is not merely a question of training muscles. The organs of sense, eyes, ears, semicircular canals, touch, and the nerve centres which receive and transmit impulses from them to the muscles, all have to be trained by practice before the movements of body and limbs can be co-ordinated with the necessary degree of exactitude. If the coach thinks of this he will not expect too much at first and will not try to push his men on too fast. Above all things he will not chatter incessantly about the 'beginning' until it becomes an afternoon terror, paralysing the oarsman's will and making that which he seeks to attain unattainable. It may safely be said that nobody ever learned to 'get the beginning' by snatching at it under fear of a too exacting coach's displeasure. The qualities required for getting hold of the beginning are just those required for shooting driven game. In both cases familiarity with the correct handling of the weapon, oar or gun, is a prerequisite; but in addition to this alertness, confidence, coolness, steadiness combined with promptitude and decision, very rapid action when the right moment arrives, are all essential to making a clean job of it. I leave it to coaches to consider how much a young sportsman might be expected to improve if his every miss were punctuated by the harsh criticism of an instructor stationed behind him.

In rowing, as in shooting, the beginner has many times to miss and try again, but in rowing the misses follow one after the other with disconcerting frequency. Every stroke brings with it a consciousness of failure to do what is wanted, and a man may easily be reduced to a state of exasperation by a too importunate and peremptory coach.

It is further to be borne in mind that the highest racing qualities are frequently associated with a highly strung nervous temperament —often enough camouflaged by an assumed carelessness or brusquerie of manner, and therefore apt to pass unnoticed or to be misinterpreted by an inexperienced coach. Such a temperament is always liable to fits of depression ; is often rebellious, and when rebellious, prone to throw down tools and give up the job if unskilfully or unsympathetically handled.

To secure that prompt and firm hold of the water which constitutes a ' beginning ' the oarsman must move very quickly at the critical moment, and this power to move quickly infers a large amount of freedom and liveliness in his preliminary actions. Therefore the rate of stroke must not be artificially slow. As soon as the crew is provisionally made up the coach must insist upon its maintaining a lively rate of stroke. On fixed seats about 28 to the minute is none too fast. For some time a novice has to row rather hard to keep up this rate of stroke, but this is all to the good, for it is while he is working pretty hard at a rate of stroke which does not allow him time to paralyse himself by excessive attention to detail that an oarsman first begins to get that firm hold of the water which constitutes a ' beginning '. Until the beginning, or something that passes muster for it, has been established, it is not possible to differentiate between rowing and paddling. To paddle well is one of the finer arts of oarsmanship and a young crew seldom attains to it. But its paddling may be expected to improve proportionally to its capacity to row hard and well.

At this period the coach may profitably ask himself what he means by ' paddling ', and when he is quite sure of the right answer explain it to the crew. We are now dealing with fixed seats, not with slides, and the answer is not quite so easy as might be supposed. The late Mr. W. B. Woodgate, whose authority on all matters pertaining to fixed-seat oarsmanship was unrivalled, dealt with the question in the first edition of the Badminton volume on Rowing, and it is evident that the views of fixed-seat oarsmen on this subject differed a good deal from those which are current to-day. Mr. Woodgate begins by saying that ' paddling is an art which is of much importance in order to bring a crew to perfection ' ; from which it may be inferred that he considered it, as I do for fixed-seat rowing, as belonging to the concluding rather than to the earlier stages of practice. He tells us that most of his contemporaries were of the opinion that paddling should consist of rowing gently with less force and catch at the beginning and with less reach than when rowing hard, but with the blade fully covered. Mr. Woodgate objected that if men were taught to paddle with less reach and less catch at the beginning they would fail in these two important particulars when ordered to row hard, and recommended a lighter blade but an equal reach and catch in paddling. The argument has something more than an academical interest for those who are training fixed-seat crews. It shows that things are and were recognized to be different on a fixed seat from what they are on a 16-inch slide. On both the catch must be got by a sharp lift back of the body at the beginning. On a fixed seat the momentum of the lift back supplies the energy required at the end of the stroke : if it is checked the work is thrown on the arms, and this is not permissible. On a sliding-seat the amount of work done in the middle and at the finish of the stroke is largely regulated by the action of the legs, and by experienced oarsmen can be adjusted to a nicety. Evidently the fixed-seat oarsman is in a dilemma. If he gets a sharp catch at the beginning he must carry on his body-action to the end of the stroke, and then he is rowing hard. If he ceases to row hard he fails to catch the beginning. The truth I think is that, as the amount of work done per stroke is much less on a fixed than on a sliding-seat, the difference between ‘ paddling ’ and ‘ rowing ’ depends much more on the rate of stroke on a fixed than on a sliding-seat. A fixed-seat crew must at all times move briskly with a good deal of energy in the swing back. At a rate of 28 or 30 strokes to the minute it cannot get much pace on the boat. Owing to the relatively slow pace the resistance to be overcome is less, and the rapidity of movement required to catch the beginning is also less. The oarsmen must move briskly to keep up the rate of 30 strokes in the minute, but they are not working at full power : they are paddling. To increase the pace of the boat the rate of stroke must be raised: the resistance to be overcome by the boat is increased, and the bodies have to spring back quicker to catch the beginning. At 36 strokes to the minute the oarsman is rowing much harder than at 30; when the stroke is raised to over 40 per minute he has to move very quickly and, if he maintains his proper length of swing, to row very hard indeed. In other words, in fixed-seat rowing the energy of the swing back is proportionate to the rate of stroke to a much greater degree than in sliding-seat rowing, and coaches will find that their pupils will learn to row hard by trying to keep up a long body-swing at a fast stroke. It will be found unprofitable to try to teach them to do a great deal of work at a slow stroke. It must not be forgotten that, before the days of sliding-seats, a good crew was expected to keep up an average of 40 strokes a minute over the Henley course, and to be able to command as high a rate as 46 or 48 per minute in spurts or short bursts of speed. When once men have been trained to move at this rate to drop to 30 strokes a minute is as abrupt a change of pace and energy as a drop from a gallop to a trot. If by good fortune a young crew is rowing behind a born stroke who has a very nice judgement of pace and rhythm, and that indefinable power of leadership which enables him to compel the men behind him to do his will, it will, towards the end of its training, unconsciously acquire the art of sending the boat along in a lively manner with a minimum expenditure of effort. That is true paddling, but it is a thing to be hoped for rather than consciously aimed at. If it is made too much of an objective in coaching and, as is generally the case, the stroke is not more than competent, the attempt to 'paddle' is only too likely to degenerate into dull unrhythmical work at an inordinately slow stroke, the monotony and lifelessness of which is much more tiring to the crew than sharper and livelier methods.

Some coaches are very exacting about work, and so constantly impress upon individuals the duty of rowing hard that their pupils, from a very intelligible desire to please their master, exaggerate every movement and make a great exhibition of effort in order to gain credit and promotion. As a rule they exhaust themselves without contributing much to the pace of the boat. To my thinking over-insistence on the merit of hard work is an error when one is dealing with young oarsmen, and is the parent of much bad oarsmanship. Long experience convinces me that the great majority of healthy young men and boys are willing and even eager to work up to the limit of their powers if only they find themselves sufficiently comfortable to let themselves go without fear of the consequences. It is the coach's business to bring them to such a condition of comfort, individually and collectively, that they can let themselves go. There is a lot of awkwardness to be overcome before a novice can lay out his full strength to advantage. Try to get rid of the awkwardness which is balking his efforts—it is generally as much awkwardness of mind as of body—and lead him by degrees to the *enjoyment* of the exercise of his full strength. I italicize the word enjoyment, for that is the final aim. Rowing must be treated as a sport, not as a mortification of the flesh. Enjoyment follows the feeling of mastery over one's instruments—from the sense of accomplishment of well-directed effort. Every stroke well rowed can carry with it the same sense of satisfaction as a good drive at golf, and the oarsman can accumulate a much larger stock of satisfaction than a golf-player, for his strokes are so much more frequent. But for the same reason, if he fumbles them he accumulates a much larger stock of mortification, and is quickly reduced to despair or apathy if scolded and browbeaten till his failures assume the proportion of moral delinquencies. As I have said before, the condition requisite to success in oarsmanship is faith, and faith is not to be compelled by bullying or slave-driving, but by creating and maintaining an ideal which all are willing to strive for. The ideal of work must be a high one, and every man in a crew should be educated to the conviction that it is a point of honour to attain to it.

A coach may get some results, though far from the best results, by being vituperative and tyrannical, but on the other hand he will fail to get the best results if he is too gentle and persuasive. Boat-racing is an energetic and often a grim business, and those who would excel in it must go about it in an energetic and sometimes a grim way, coach and crew alike. When a crew is being selected and trained for a race it is necessary to study individuals very closely and to form accurate judgement of their willingness to work. Some men are gluttons for work, and it may be necessary to check their propensities for a time, lest their too elephantine efforts become a hindrance to the rest of the crew. As Dr. Warre used to say, they are of the most noble order of the bullock, and an eight is altogether too delicate a piece of machinery to let bullocks run riot in it. Most men are just simple honest fellows, happy to do their share of work if only they can find out how it ought to be done. Some of them, no doubt, are a bit timid about exhausting themselves, and dismayed when they are called upon for a fresh effort after they have arrived at what seems to them the extreme limit of exhaustion. On this point the coach must be absolutely firm: they have to become familiar with exhaustion and must be urged on until, by familiarity, exhaustion loses its terrors for them. This is the great act of faith which a man has to perform when he undertakes to win the guerdon of oarsmanship: that if he holds himself together, and concentrates his will on his task, he can go on rowing hard long after the time when, in his inexperience, he thinks that he is rowed to a standstill. It is only when he is confirmed in this faith that he is a reliable oarsman. A coach may sympathize secretly with his men's distress, but he cannot afford to be compassionate until he has brought them into the way of faith.

Finally, there are the lazy, the slack, and the faint-hearted, who are always trying to do a bit less than their share, and will relax their efforts the moment they think that the coach's eye is off them. If it is evident that their failure to do work is due to slackness, and not to inexperience, it is best to get rid of them, even at a sacrifice of apparent skill and strength. But it is not always possible to get rid of them. A faint-hearted man the coach should always get rid of, without compunction. He will let the crew down in the day of battle. But the man who is simply indolent is another proposition. He may be very strong, and there is no other who looks like filling his place with advantage. He may be skilful in the arts of oarsmanship beyond his fellows and contribute to the stability and comfort, though not to the power of the boat. He may be incorrigibly lazy in practice, but a useful and even determined worker in a race. He may be simply lethargic, but so far responsive to objurgations that there is some hope that he may be permanently galvanized into life. It is hard for the coach to decide what to do ; all the harder because in a young crew sufficient data for forming accurate judgements of character are still wanting. The chances are that he must include one or more indolents in the crew, and having included them, how is he to deal with them ? By 'giving them hell' ? Well, that may be tried, but it is not expedient to keep it up too long, for the rest of the crew quickly lose confidence in those who are kept constantly under the lash and with loss of confidence there will be loss of cohesion. The crew will tend to break up. The offender may be a cynical, don't care, take me or leave me sort of character, quite impervious to appeal, but inclined to sulk and still further relax his efforts when abused. If he cannot be dispensed with he must be tolerated, but for the sake of the crew he must be roused up now and again. How and when the coach must decide. With such a one a grim form of humour may be the only effective weapon, but it is not every one who can wield it.

When the coach has now decided upon the composition of his crew, with the inclusion of as few lazy-bones and scrimshankers as may be, he enters on the final stages of preparing them for the race. Such as they are and such as he has been able to make them, he must abandon all further attempts to improve individual form, and must devote all his efforts to bringing them up to concert pitch. He is no longer a private tutor but the conductor of a band. His men may not be very skilled performers on their instruments, but they must learn to play with vigour and to play in time. He has to infuse into them the will to work together; to make them watchful, alert, concentrated on the business in hand; oblivious of everything but the rhythmic energy of their combined movement. If he is successful the crew will find itself, and individual shortcomings will fade into insignificance as the team develops into a compacted whole. But if he thinks to get good team work by scolding individuals he will find his crew much in the condition of a football team in which every man is playing his own game, and defeat is the penalty of lack of co-operation.

Before he embarks upon the final stages of polishing up a young and inexperienced crew a coach should form a very clear mental image of what he really is aiming at. If his image is in the least degree hazy he will not be able to communicate his objective to his crew. Furthermore, he must be quite sure that what he aims at is appropriate to the conditions under which the race is rowed, and within the capacity of his crew. Probably he will have in his mind some ''Varsity' crew, some outstanding and successful College eight or Henley crew, as a pattern for imitation. But none of these are altogether appropriate for present use, for they involve the application to fixed seats and clinker-built boats of methods belonging to sliding-seats and keelless boats. The difference between the two kinds of apparatus is almost as great as that between a golf-club and a hockey-stick, and postulates a considerable difference in style. But where, it may well be asked, is one to turn for a good example of the style appropriate to fixed seats? It must be confessed, nowhere, for unfortunately the art of fixed-seat rowing is extinct. Not, however, irrecoverably, for in 1907 a Balliol Torpid, some few days before the end of their practice, blossomed forth into a style which had not been seen on the Isis for many years, and very easily went head of the river. It was coached by Mr. L. E. Jones. What methods he adopted to recover that long-lost style I do not know, but to oarsmen old enough to remember how veterans of the fixed-seat era used to propel their boats, it seemed as if they had gone back to the fifties of last century. They reminded me of Chitty, Hornby, and Short, oarsmen of bygone days who had never vitiated their fixed-seat style by rowing on sliding-seats as so many of their immediate successors did. In my boyhood I have rowed with all three and have often seen Dr. Hornby propelling a gig pair on the Datchet reach to watch the practice of the Eton eight. I wish that I could give such a description of their style as to create a picture of it in the minds of my readers.

Perhaps the most characteristic thing about it, the feature in which it differed most from modern oarsmanship, was the firmness of their seat. They sat in their boat as a good horseman sits in the saddle, and they used their stretchers as a horseman uses his stirrups, taken up a hole for going across country. With the firmness of seat there was ample flexibility of the thigh-joints, admitting of a long and vigorous swing of an upright but not artificially stiffened body. Both in swing forward and swing back the legs were brought into use as a support and to give impetus to the body-swing, but the action of the legs did not shift the position of the seat. There was no shuffling about or screwing, whether sideways or to and fro, on the seat. I have been told that the coaches of old times, such as Arthur Shadwell, used to chalk a cross on the exact spot on which the oarsman was to sit and instructed him to sit on and not to budge from that spot. Evidently the older oarsmen attached importance to a firm seat, and with reason, for it could not be maintained unless the knees were braced and the feet firmly planted on the stretcher. Given the firm seat, the swing of the old oarsmen, whose action I am trying to describe, was astonishingly vigorous. At the beginning of the stroke they did not attempt to burn all their powder in one concentrated catch. The long carvel-built but keeled boats in which they rowed offered too much resistance to make a mere catch at the beginning effective. The water was caught promptly and firmly enough at the beginning of the stroke, but the effort was extended into a long pull through the water. There was a pronounced swing back of the shoulders and the elbows were carried well past the sides at the finish, which was noticeably hard and clean ; the oar-handle pulled well home to the chest.

The recovery was elastic and the wrist-work smart and accurate, but the hands were not shot away with the velocity that was in vogue at the Universities for many years after the introduction of keelless boats. I have the impression that these oarsmen made the long and hard finish an aid to the recovery, and actually drew the body up a trifle towards the oar-handle as the latter approached the chest. The swing forward had an undefinable appearance of being powerful, vigorous, and business-like. It was steady and well balanced on the feet, but, if my memory serves me right, there was not so great a contrast between the rate of the swing forward and that of the swing back as has prevailed since the introduction of keelless boats. The nearest analogy to the whole cycle of stroke and feather that I can think of is the movement of the crosshead-block of a large horizontal steam-engine, which moves to and fro on its bed with perfect regularity, smoothness, and power, without any stop or jerk at either end of its course. The analogy is not exact, for the crosshead-block moves forward and back at the same pace, whereas the oarsman moves faster back than forward; but the evenness of the motion, the certainty of the pick up at each end of the stroke, the combination of power with elasticity and smoothness of running, are features in the steam-engine which are worthy of study by the oarsman.

This illustration may or may not appeal to the imagination of a coach, but however that may be, I wish by reiteration to conjure up in his mind the idea of a firmly seated body, supported by well-braced knees and feet firmly pressed against the stretcher; a fore and aft swing through a wide angle about the pivot of the thigh-joints; the shoulders and elbows carried well back to ensure a hard finish; throughout the whole cycle of stroke and feather abundant but withal disciplined and rhythmical energy and vigour of movement.

I may seem to modern oarsmen to lay too much stress upon the hard finish. Lest I should be accused of exaggerating this feature in the oarsmanship of the middle of the last century, let me quote what the late Mr. E. D. Brickwood, one of the leading exponents of metropolitan oarsmanship, said about it: 'Care should likewise be taken not to lessen the force applied to the oar as the stroke draws to a conclusion, but to put the whole strength of the arms and shoulders into the finish of the stroke, where it will naturally diminish quite fast enough, as the oar forms an obtuse angle with that portion of the boat before the rowlock.'[1] There can be no doubt about the author's valuation of a hard finish, but the sentence as it stands is objectionable because it seems to justify and even to recommend pulling home with the arms. What Mr. Brickwood really meant is that the upper arms should be pulled back and the arms carried past the sides by the use of the latissimus dorsi muscles, the use of which is fully explained on pp. 330 and 364 of this work. It will do much for the revival of good junior oarsmanship if coaches will be persuaded to attach importance to a hard finish and will make themselves acquainted with the muscles by which it can be obtained. A proper finish will lead to a better recovery. A better recovery will give a longer and better controlled swing forward, and this, in turn, will bring with it a harder, quicker, and more decisive catch of the water at the beginning of the stroke.

Before leaving the subject of fixed-seat oarsmanship it is necessary to say something about the lay-out of the work. A coach should be familiar with the measurements proper to fixed-seat rowing, should understand the reasons for their adoption, and should make sure that every one of his pupils is properly seated, has his stretcher of the right length, and has his work set at the proper distance and at the right height. The rowing space allotted to each oarsman is the distance between the fore-edge (that is, the edge nearest to the bow) of his seat and the fore-edge of the seat of the man next in front of him. This distance is determined by the length of the legs of a tall man when extended at the end of the stroke, and as an oarsman is in much the same position at the end of the stroke whether on a fixed or a sliding-seat, there is not so much difference between the rowing spaces

[1] *Encyclopaedia Britannica,* 9th edition, Article 'Rowing'.

as might be supposed. On a fixed seat the knees should not be pressed down quite flat at the finish and the stretcher should be more upright than is necessary for a sliding-seat, so some little economy of space can be effected. In a boat fitted with 16-inch slides the standard measurement for the rowing space is 4 ft. $2\frac{1}{2}$ in.; with fixed seats it is from 3 ft. 9 in. to 4 feet. The width of the fixed-seat thwart (which also serves as the oarsman's seat) is 7 inches, leaving 3 ft. 5 in. to 3 ft. 2 in. space for his legs. The height of the upper surface of the thwart above the bottom boards on which the oarsman's heels rest should be 7 inches for a fixed seat. In a boat built to be fitted with slides it is something less than this, but the runners and the sliding-seat itself raise the oarsman's seat to as much as $8\frac{1}{2}$ inches above his heels. The most important measurement is that which is commonly known as the distance which an oarsman is from his work. It is the distance from the aft edge of the seat to a thwartship line drawn through the aft edge of the working thowl of the rowlock. For fixed-seat rowing this distance is usually taken as 12 inches, but under special circumstances a coach may vary it. Before sliding-seats were introduced, oarsmen had learned by long experience that a man seated 10 inches away from his work could more easily catch hold of the water at the beginning of the stroke, but was disadvantageously placed for a long and hard finish. Conversely they found that an oarsman seated 14 inches away from his work was in the best position for a hard finish, but had difficulty in catching hold of the water at the beginning. The middle position of twelve inches was generally adopted as giving the best results at both ends of the stroke for an oarsman of average build. The earliest sliding-seats had a travel of only 4 inches, and were adopted, not with any idea of adding to the oarsman's power by the greater use of the muscles of his legs, but to enable him to make the best of both ends of the stroke. From what precedes it is evident that if a coach wishes his crew to concentrate on the beginning of the stroke and to keep up a high rate over the course, he will put them 11 or 10 inches away from their work. But if he has a heavy, rather slow-moving crew, incapable of sustaining a fast rate of stroke but able to swing back hard and long at the finish, he will put them 13 or 14 inches away from their work. As a rule, however, it is inexpedient to depart from the normal measurement of 12 inches.

As the thwarts of a boat are built into her frame and cannot be moved, the distance at which a man sits from his work is regulated, not by shifting the seat, but by altering the shape of the outrigger. The normal measurements and the normal shape of outrigger for a boat built to be used with fixed seats only are shown in fig. 45.

Unfortunately, in these days, eight-oared boats are rarely built for use with fixed seats only. After they have served their turn in such races as Lents or Torpids at the Universities, they are wanted to carry crews who are learning the elements of rowing on sliding-seats. For this purpose the boat-builders fit them with thwarts 22 or 24 inches wide, to carry 14-inch or 16-inch slides, and when the slides are not in use a small fixed seat, about 7 in. × 11 in., is screwed into what is considered the appropriate place on the thwart. In such a boat the coach must make sure that the fixed seat is in the appropriate place, and that the effective rowing space allotted to each man and the set-out of the work are as nearly correct as circumstances allow. It cannot be correct if the outriggers are of the pattern used for sliding-seat boats. If the boat is built primarily for use with sliding-seats, with 24-inch thwarts, and the aft edge of the thwart flush with the working thowl of the rowlock, the outriggers are bound to be of the sliding-seat pattern. A comparison of figs. 45 and 46 shows that the framework of a fixed-seat boat differs materially from that of a sliding-seat boat. It will be observed that in both cases the outriggers are not simply screwed on to the sax-boards, but are fastened by bolts passing through the enlarged upper ends of the main ribs *r*. In a fixed-seat boat the ribs are spaced evenly along the length of the hull, a large rib *r* alternating with a smaller rib *r′* ; the outrigger stays are bolted to the larger ribs and the thwarts occupy every fourth inter-space between a larger and a smaller rib (see fig. 45). In a sliding-seat boat (fig. 46) the main ribs *r* coincide with the fore and aft edges of the thwarts, and as the distance between the aft edge of one thwart and the fore-edge of the next is 26½ inches, and the thwarts themselves measure 24 inches fore and aft, the main ribs are not spaced evenly. Two lesser ribs *r′* are inserted in each of the interspaces between the main ribs (see fig. 46). It is the normal practice to make the aft edge of the thwart of a sliding-seat boat correspond with the line drawn

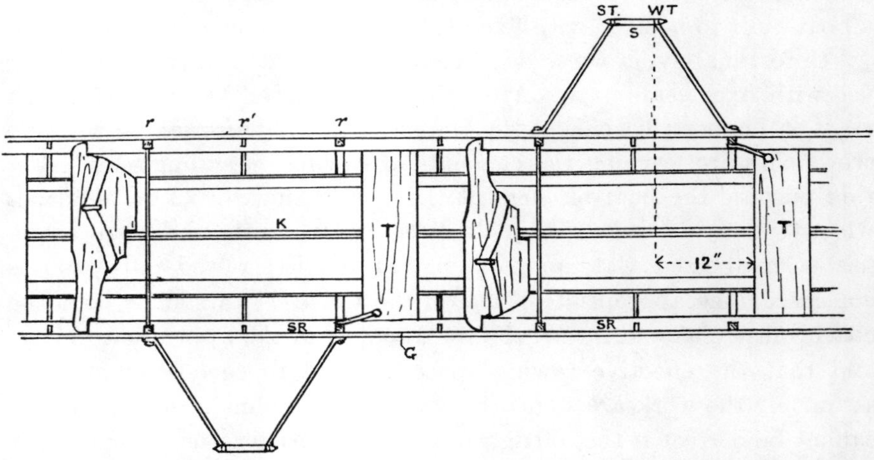

FIG. 45. Two midships compartments of a fixed-seat eight (the ‘Eton *Monarch*’). G, the gunwale or sax-board; K, the kelson; *r*, *r*, the main ribs; *r′*, lesser rib; S, sill of the rowlock; SR, stringer, often called the ‘ribbing’ by boat-builders; ST, stopping thowl of the rowlock; T, thwart or seat; WT, working thowl of rowlock.

athwartship through the aft edge of the working thowl of the rowlock. In boating parlance each oarsman slides up to his work. As a consequence of these differences in build the outrigger of a fixed-seat boat has the form of an isosceles triangle, of which the side of the boat is the base, and the apex is truncated to accommodate the rowlock. But in a sliding-seat boat the outrigger has the form of a right-angled triangle, and to give it extra strength a single additional stay is carried forward and bolted to the sax-board (*a s.* in fig. 46).

If, in a boat designed for use by a sliding-seat or fixed-seat crew as may be required, the working thowl of the rowlock is in a line with the aft edge of the thwart, and the temporary fixed seat is screwed into the thwart at a distance of 12 inches from that edge, the oarsman will be sitting 12 inches away from his work, but the space occupied by his legs will be curtailed by 2½ inches, and if he is long-limbed he will not be able to set his stretcher at the right length. If, on the other

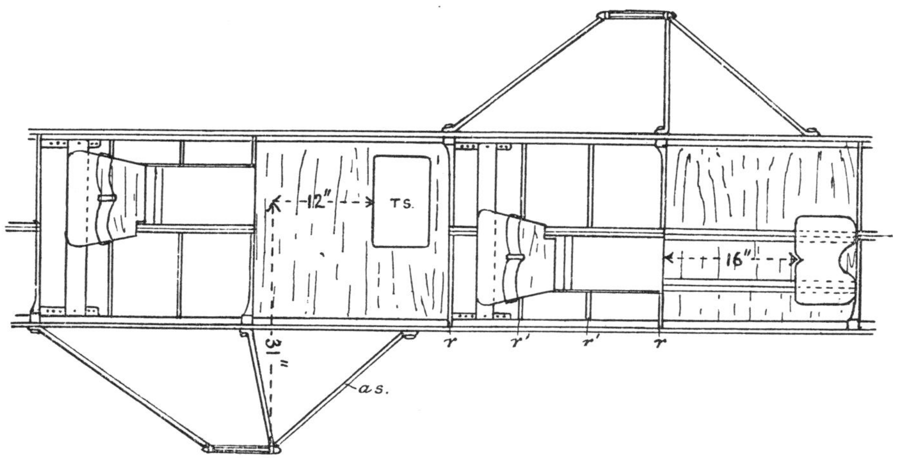

FIG. 46. Two midships compartments of a sliding-seat racing eight. The starboard outrigger is altered to adapt the work for a fixed seat. *a s.*, additional stay to outrigger; *r*, *r*, main ribs; *r′*, *r′*, lesser ribs; TS, temporary seat fixed on thwart.

hand, the temporary seat is fixed so as to give him full room for his legs, the oarsman will be seated 14½ inches away from his work and will experience great difficulty in catching the beginning of the stroke. The only remedy is to alter the shape of the outrigger in such wise that, when the oarsman is seated 12 inches away from his work, he has a space of at least 3 ft. 2 in. between the aft edge of his temporary fixed seat and the fore-edge of the *thwart*—not the temporary fixed seat—of the man in front of him. The alteration required is indicated in the starboard outrigger in fig. 46. When once made the alteration may be permanent, for the only result, when the boat is again fitted with sliding-seats, will be that the oarsmen will be $2\frac{1}{2}$ inches away from their work—rather an advantage than otherwise for early instruction in the art of sliding.

The coach must bear in mind that clinker-built boats are of as many patterns as there are boat-builders, and that fashions change in boat-building as in everything else, so that an old boat may differ considerably from a new one by the same boat-builder. Therefore the dimensions and recommendations given above are only applicable to a particular case and must be varied to suit different cases. The important thing is that a coach should have an exact knowledge of the measurements necessary to fit a man comfortably into a boat, whether on a fixed seat or on a sliding-seat ; and that he should have so much practical acquaintance with the principles of boat-building as to be able to make such alterations in the rig of a boat as occasion may require. I am convinced, from what I saw of the practice of the Oxford Torpids in 1923, that the majority of the boats were so badly rigged that their crews had little opportunity of rowing correctly.

CHAPTER XI

ON COACHING

SLIDING-SEATS

Instruction in the art of sliding follows close upon junior races on fixed seats. A coach cannot give too much thought and trouble to the education of his pupils in this stage of their rowing career. It is necessary to begin all over again ; to give every man long periods of individual attention in a tub-pair ; then to have recourse to a tub-four, and to postpone practice in an eight-oar until such time as his charges have attained to some considerable degree of mastery over their slides. Hitherto the young oarsman has been taught the value of a firm seat. Now he is placed on a very slippery elusive seat which at every movement of his body seems to escape from his control. His difficulties are many and must not be increased by too abrupt a change from familiar conditions. The first lessons will be on short slides, but in a boat fitted for long slides, and the coach must be careful to set the work to the best advantage. On a fixed seat his pupils will have been seated 12 inches from their work. That was a compromise. They would have got a better hold of the beginning if they had been seated 10 inches from their work ; a better finish if they had been seated 14 inches from it. Common sense suggests that they should be 14 inches away from their work at the finish of the stroke, and the back-stops should be adjusted accordingly. The slide may be allowed a travel of 6 inches, so the front-stop should be adjusted to make the front edge of the sliding-seat 8 inches away from the work when the oarsman is full forward. The stretchers should not have as much rake as is usually given for use with long slides ; wedge-shaped pieces may be nailed to them to reduce the rake. Each oarsman should adjust his stretcher to such a length that he can press the slide firmly against the back-stop without quite straightening his knees. Straps should be taboo. It is best to take them off the stretchers and leave them behind on the raft, lest the coach should weakly yield to the importunities of pupils who declare that they cannot manage their slides without them. On this matter of rowing without straps the coach should be adamant. It is true that without them an oarsman will flounder as much in his earliest efforts as does a man who puts on skates for the first time. But the difficulty of preserving the balance of the body is as easily overcome in the one case as in the other, and the advantage gained by learning to row on a slide without straps is incalculable. In dispensing with the use of straps the coach must see that the stretchers are set at the proper distance for each individual. If the stretcher is too long the difficulty of rowing without straps is increased to the verge of impossibility.

When all these adjustments are made and instruction begins, the coach must bear in mind that his men are not seated much nearer to their work than they were on a fixed seat. Therefore they must lift back their bodies at the beginning of the stroke as they did on a fixed seat, and must learn, while they are doing it, to 'hold the slide'. Beginning my rowing as I did in the days when short slides were in use both at school and University, I have no doubt that I am right in recommending this old-fashioned method for beginners. The reason for holding the slide and the manner in which it is held have been fully explained on pp. 137–140. The novice should be thoroughly drilled until he has mastered the art of lifting back his body without simultaneously thrusting back his slide. It is equally important to discipline him in the art of drawing back his elbows and shoulders whilst he is driving back his slide in the latter half of the stroke. The short slide prolongs and strengthens the finish. For that purpose it was originally introduced: for that purpose it should be used as long as its travel does not exceed 8 inches.

When a considerable degree of proficiency has been attained the slides may be lengthened, inch by inch, by moving the front-stop stretcherwards, until finally the oarsmen are sliding up to their work. As the slide lengthens the knees are raised higher and the shins become more nearly vertical in the full forward position. It is more difficult to bend the ankles to the required extent, and more rake must be given to the stretchers. But the less rake a man can manage with the better, so a coach should urge his pupils to perform exercises calculated to give suppleness to the ankles. Heel-traps are of great assistance. Their use is not attended by any of the objectionable features associated with toe-straps, and they should be brought into use as soon as the length of slide exceeds 9 or 10 inches. Straps are necessary in an eight-oar, but oarsmen should be taught to do without them in a tub-pair, even when the slides are of full length. When used they should be drawn tight over the instep, and the coach should see that the staples through which they pass are so fixed that the straps grip the instep and not the toes. It is important to attend to all these minutiae when dealing with young oarsmen. Old oarsmen may be expected to look after them for themselves.

No more need be said here of the principles which a coach should inculcate when his pupils have been promoted to the use of long slides. They are set out in full in Chapters IV and V, and if the preliminary training has been thorough all the foundations of good oarsmanship should have been laid securely. The long slide should not lead to a deterioration in form, but rather to an added grace due to the prolongation of the rhythm and the greater freedom of movement of the lower limbs.

Instruction in the art of sliding will normally occupy the early spring months. With the onset of summer crews have to be prepared for races of various degrees of importance. In principle there is little difference between the preparation of a crew for a more important and a less important race, but in practice the coach's difficulties increase to some unknown power of the magnitude of the object aimed at. Thus, at the Universities, it may require the highest art to gain or retain the headship of the river, but it may be comparatively easy to coach a crew to gain a few places in the second division.

The first process is that of selection, and this involves not only the choice of the eight men who are to row, but also the putting of these into the most suitable positions in the boat. There will almost certainly be an admixture of old and new hands ; either the old or the new may predominate, and it will sometimes happen there are 5 or 6 old stagers, some of them of doubtful quality, and as many young oarsmen of promise, but as yet insufficiently tested in the matter of performance. In such a case it may be very difficult to make a good selection. There is a natural reluctance to discard men who have borne the burden and heat of former days ; an equal reluctance to deny promotion to youngsters who bid fair to render better service than their seniors. Theoretically the coach should allow himself to be influenced by no other consideration than that of making the best use of the best material available. But in so sensitive and intimate an organization as a College boat club this theory will not always work. It may be that the first man the coach would wish to discard on the score of indifferent oarsmanship is the captain of the boat. The next man he would wish to put out may be a very popular and influential member of the club, whose rejection would arouse so much resentment that the morale of the crew would be jeopardized from the very start of practice. In the making up of a crew the spirit of *camaraderie* and good fellowship is almost of as much importance as skilled oarsmanship, and it may well be that the eight best oarsmen will not necessarily make the best crew. More often than not the coach who is undertaking the training of the crew has had nothing to do with the earlier training of the men he has to choose from, and must rely in the first instance on the information supplied to him by the captain, who may have strong prejudices in favour of or against particular individuals. The chances are that the captain has already made up his mind as to who is to row in each place in the boat and will not easily be persuaded to surrender his judgement. Again, the time for practice may be short and the final choice cannot be delayed for more than a few days. The coach can only act as seems best under the circumstances of the case. As the possible combinations of circumstances in different cases are infinite, no rules can be laid down for his guidance, but the following hints may be of service both to coaches and to captains who have to work up the raw material for coaches to deal with :

You must base your selection on three qualities : character, physique, and skill in oarsmanship. The two first are almost unalterable, but given the first two, you may alter the third to a very large extent.

Be mistrustful of men of the genial, expansive, effusively keen type. They may be all right, but their keenness should be put to a pretty severe test before it is accepted as a fact. It is also well to remember that in the course of training effusiveness is apt to pall on other members of the crew.

A pliable character, who submits readily to the will of his coach, is quick to learn and pleasant to deal with ; but his pliability may, and often does, imply a fatal readiness to yield to an adversary's will in the day of battle.

An out and out pessimist may so depress the spirits of his fellow-oarsmen as to bring a crew to shipwreck. But many an Englishman, and more often, a Scot of the dour type, puts on pessimism as a sort of defensive armour against such (in his estimation) deplorable weakness as a display of enthusiasm. It is from among such shell-backs that one may collect the hardest and most reliable workers, and when they are known to be such, their pessimism, by some law of contradiction, keeps the rest of the crew in good humour.

If possible, exclude from the crew a man of intriguing disposition ; particularly one who, not being the captain, tries to gain the ear of the coach and influence his judgement of individuals. Such a one may insidiously undermine the whole morale of the crew.

One can seldom afford to discard a born and tried fighter on the score of indifferent oarsmanship.

Before you make your final selection make sure that every man is sound in wind and limb. The most important points are a good action of the heart ; elastic arteries ; a good chest development and expansion. These should be vouched for by competent medical opinion.

Do not attach too much importance to weight and excessive muscular development. In boat-racing the capacity to move quickly is of more importance than great power slowly applied. Big heavy men of a lethargic temperament are of little use in a light boat. Men of great muscular development are often bad stayers. They can do a prodigious amount of work for 3 or 4 minutes, but after that their bolt is shot and they are little better than passengers. Sometimes, however, a big heavy man is simply a slow starter, who only warms up to his work after half a mile or so of hard rowing. He is of a more useful sort, for it is generally possible to improve his capacity for getting under way quickly. Finally, it should be remembered that, as explained more fully on p. 24, medium-sized and small men are, on the average, stronger than big ones. There are a few big, muscular, heavy men who can move as quickly and stay as long as lighter men. Their presence in a crew is invaluable, but it should never be forgotten that they are exceptions to the general rule.

The chances are very much against your putting the right men in the right places in a racing eight at the first time of asking. If the men have had little or no previous experience of light boats your first selection is nearly sure to be wrong. The best arrangement is a subject for experiment, and you should not hesitate to change the order of the boat as frequently as you may think necessary in the earlier stages of practice. But your experiments should be well thought out and not made at random, and you must not lose time in coming to a final decision. The time available for getting the crew together is probably only too short, and the period soon arrives when change is in the highest degree undesirable, if not impossible.

From what precedes it follows that, however inexperienced they may be, crews should not be kept too long in heavy boats, and that they should be given a sufficient amount of hard work in early stages of practice to enable the coach to judge of the working value and staying power of individuals.

The business of selecting and placing men in a crew is a very large part of a coach's art and, if one may judge from the large number of crews to be seen in any year in which the men are obviously wrongly placed, the faculty of choosing and arranging is given to very few. It requires not only insight but foresight, almost a gift of prophecy, to put men into the places which they will ultimately occupy to the best advantage. For one should not judge by what men are doing now, but by what one thinks one can get them to do three or four weeks hence. Obviously the first thing to be done is to get the three or four stern oars settled in their places. The question of paramount importance is, Who is to row stroke? Born strokes are so rare that it may be assumed that no such treasure is available. The chances are that some one oarsman is indicated as stroke by the preference of the captain and senior members of the crew. One or two others may be indicated as possibilities. A choice has to be made, and in the making of it the coach will find it useful to take into account the following considerations.

The man whom the crew finds it most easy to follow is not necessarily the best stroke for racing purposes. Some of the most famous and successful strokes have been far from easy to follow. A comfortable stroke is one whose cadence is so uniform and invariable that the crew can follow it without any strain on the attention. Behind such a one all may seem to go well at a slow rate in the earlier stages of practice. But when the time comes for increasing the pace, it will often be found that the crew has grown indolent, and that the stroke cannot vary his well-worn theme sufficiently to shake them out of their indolence.

It is often good policy to utilize a comfortable stroke for the first week or ten days of practice, while the prospective racing stroke is acquiring some of the niceties of oarsmanship in another seat in the boat.

An old stager, whose only qualification is that he has occupied the stroke thwart with very moderate success for the last season or two, may be a veritable old man of the sea about the neck of the crew. He should by all means be got rid of, if a better can be found. He may, however, be quite useful if placed well back in the crew.

It is a common, but on a long slide nearly always a mistaken, policy to choose a small man for the stroke seat. A stroke need not be heavy but, for a sliding-seat, he should be fairly tall. A man of short stature is almost invariably short in the thighs, and this is a great disadvantage to him on a long slide, involving undue effort to maintain the required length of swing. On a fixed seat it is otherwise : a man with a long but strong back and relatively short legs is rather at an advantage. Hence it often happens that a stroke who has shown great promise on a fixed seat in junior races proves a failure on a sliding-seat. He may be lively and may be able to keep up the effort of managing his slide at a slow stroke, but when he attempts to raise it the effort is too great : he gets short and his liveliness degenerates into a bucket.

Though a stroke need not be heavy, his weight should be at least reasonably commensurate with his inches : otherwise he will not have the strength to lead his crew. There is no greater mistake than to suppose that a stroke need only set length and rhythm and that his work is a matter of little consequence. To get the best out of his crew he must do his full share, and on occasion a bit more than his share, of the work. It is always advisable to ease a hard-working stroke of slight physique by reducing the width of his blade.

The first requisite in a stroke is energy and the desire and will to impart his energy to others. Another and equally important requisite is courage. Given these two it will generally be possible to impart a sufficient sense of rhythm, length of swing, and precision in marking the two ends of the stroke, to make an oarsman into at least a tolerable leader of a crew. But as he is the leader, it is a *sine qua non* that he must have some power of initiative.

Excitability must not be mistaken for energy. An excitable man at the stroke thwart is pretty sure to land the crew in disaster. He will be energetic to the point of wildness while his excitement lasts: when it evaporates he will collapse.

A coach will find that his judgement is materially assisted by rowing for some distance behind each of the candidates for the stroke seat in a tub-pair. If he is young and in sufficiently good condition a coach should take no. 6's or no. 7's seat and row for a journey in the eight behind each candidate. A good sculler may always be regarded as a possible candidate for the stroke seat.

In the last resort a coach will do well to follow the old-fashioned plan of putting the best and most experienced oarsman in the stroke seat, giving him as good a backing as possible at no. 6 and no. 7 and leaving him to do his best.

Next in importance to stroke is no. 7. His qualities should in many ways be the obverse of stroke's, for he should not want to lead but to follow. He must, however, do something more than follow; he must appreciate, interpret, and emphasize the qualities of his stroke. It is well to have a stylish and polished oarsman at no. 7, for he will communicate polish to the remainder of the crew; curiously enough, to a greater extent than stroke is able to communicate it. But a rough oarsman who rows with character and decision is to be preferred to a stylist whose rowing lacks the necessary quality of emphasis. It is well to have a powerful oarsman at no. 7, but a less powerful man who rows with precision is to be preferred to a more powerful one whose oarsmanship is indecisive. A good no. 7 will go far to compensate for the shortcomings of a moderate stroke. A bad no. 7 can smother even a good stroke. On what principle oarsmen are usually selected to fill the place of no. 7 it is hard to say, but it is the fact that, in the majority of College crews, the choice seems to have fallen upon the man least suited to the position. A coach cannot be too particular in his choice of a no. 7, and he may find it necessary to try man after man until he hits upon one who can fill the place to his satisfaction.

No. 6 should be a strong, steady, hard-working oarsman who can be relied upon to keep length of swing and to get into the water with a thump in accurate time behind his stroke. There is nothing more helpful to a stroke than the knowledge that, whate'er betides, his no. 6 will be in, there, behind him, to support him. Many a race has been won, and as many lost, from no. 6.

Nos. 4 and 5 are traditionally the heavy-weights of a crew, but it is not a good thing to put into these places men who have no other recommendation than their avoirdupois. Good hard-working middle-weights should be preferred to men who add weight but not propulsive force to the boat. None the less good heavy-weights are a great asset. No. 5 is especially responsible for keeping the length of swing going in the middle of the boat. No. 4 should be a good stayer : if he gives way the whole of the forward half of the crew is sure to follow suit. Nos. 3 and 2 should be honest, capable, hard-working oarsmen. Bow should be sturdy, strong, and active, but should not by much exceed 11 stones in weight. There is a tendency to underrate the importance of the bow oarsman and yet, at the same time, paradoxically to overrate it by putting in a 12-stone man who would be more suitably placed at no. 2 or no. 3. A bow should get a very quick and firm hold of the water at the beginning, for any failure in this respect may lead to the boat being pulled round. He should have a neat and quick recovery, for, if he moves sluggishly at this end of the stroke, he will retard the forward shoot of the boat. The bow oarsman is nearly always cramped for room and if he is oversized for the place he is likely to lose both form and efficiency.

After a few days' study and experiment a coach may be supposed to have arranged the best men at his disposal in the places best suited to their several capacities. Let us imagine that his crew is composed half of old, half of new hands ; that the former are very unequal in experience and proficiency, one or perhaps two of them having reached a high standard of oarsmanship : that a competent stroke has been discovered and that he is efficiently backed up by no. 6 or no. 7, possibly by both. This may be taken as fairly typical of the composition of a College crew in the first division either at Oxford or Cambridge, or of a metropolitan or school crew intending to compete at the Henley Regatta. It would take at least a month's steady preliminary practice, with frequent long rows, to inculcate style and uniformity, and another two or three weeks' more intensive practice to bring such a crew up to racing pitch. But the opportunity of keeping the same crew together for such a long period of time is usually denied even to metropolitan and school clubs, and at the Universities the shortness of the term and the exigencies of examinations put all thought of long preparation out of the question. The time for practice is short; some part of it has already been consumed in selecting and arranging the crew, and the races are imminent before the men have really settled down to their places. The conditions are not favourable for striving after an ideal standard of perfection, and the coach must realize, from the outset, that his business is to make the best of such material as he has got in the limited time at his disposal. The time is too short and the material may be very patchy, but both coach and crew must work in the faith and hope that much may be achieved if only there is the will to achieve it. It will be the first care of the coach to give his men a sufficiently good conceit of themselves. He must dispel the idea, so often present in their minds, that they are only second-rate kind of fellows from whom only a second-rate kind of performance can be expected. This is a most exasperating attitude of mind, often unsuspected by an inexperienced coach, but very commonly adopted by several members of a College crew. They excuse themselves by saying that they are not So-and-so—mentioning the name of some prominent oarsman whom they have probably been told to take as a pattern. They are really trying to excuse themselves from the trouble of attaining to a satisfactory standard of proficiency, and no real progress is possible until every member of the crew acquires enough faith in himself to believe that, by taking sufficient trouble, he can make himself a class better than he now is.

It is all-important to get a crew, both individually and collectively, to have confidence in its power to row hard, at a fast stroke, and to stay the course. Modern oarsmen are apt to be terrified at the idea of rowing a fast stroke. This is largely attributable to their having been allowed to paddle at an absurdly slow rate of stroke from the beginning of practice, and the coach has only himself to blame if, when he sets his pupils to row a time test, they fall far short of the standard through inability to put any life into their work.

Here it may be said that the first time a crew is asked the question over the whole course it will generally give a pretty clear indication of what it is going to be ; fast, medium, or slow. If the watch says ‘ fast ’, all is well and the coach will have an easy time. The crew will be in good spirits and may be relied upon to try to better its performance every time that it rows the whole or any substantial part of the course. If the watch says ‘ medium ’, a great deal may be done to improve the pace before the day of the race. On the other hand, it may make no further improvement and the crew may even take a turn for the worse through over-anxiety and inability to keep steady when rowing a fast stroke. To bring such a crew through its difficulties, to send it to the post resolute and confident in its capacity to reproduce the best that it has done in practice, requires much tact and judgement on the part of the coach. He will probably find it pays best to set his men to row frequent bursts of about a minute's duration at the highest rate of stroke they can command, and to set them to row longer pieces at a reduced rate of stroke, but none the less at an average rate of not less than 35 to the minute. He will be careful not to hustle his men. He will certainly do no good by upbraiding them. His task is to get them to believe that what they are asked to do can be done with a little determination : that difficulties which seem insuperable can be overcome by practice. Success will depend on the collective temper of the crew and on the tact and temper of the coach himself, factors that are so infinitely variable and so easily upset by trifling and unforeseen circumstances, that no rules can be laid down for the guidance of the parties concerned. Save this rule perhaps: Whatever methods a coach may think fit to adopt he must be his own natural self and not try overmuch to work according to the book. If he is not naturally tactful he will only make himself ridiculous by an excessive display of what he hopes will pass muster for tactfulness. If he is not naturally cheerful he will exasperate his men by an attitude of forced cheerfulness. Towards the end of training a crew becomes curiously sensitive and irritable and is ready to withdraw its confidence on the least provocation. It will have formed a pretty sound judgement of its coach in the earlier stages of practice and at the end of it will prefer him to remain as they have known him. If, as sometimes happens, a coach finds that he has lost the confidence of his crew, he had better find somebody else to finish his job for him.

If the watch says ‘ slow ’, it is a bad case both for crew and coach. If the lack of pace is due to a bad stroke and a better cannot be found, or if it is due to a general inertia on the part of the crew, there is nothing for it but to go doggedly on and to keep up hope as long as possible. It is bad policy to set a slow crew to row constant trials over conventional distances against the watch. Nothing is more detrimental to the morale of a crew than the knowledge that day after day they have failed to cover a given distance in respectable time. It is better to start them from some unaccustomed landmark and to set them to row for a given time. The coach must form his own opinion of whether the pace is improving or not. It is often the case that a crew is slow because of some obvious fault—a bucket forward, or want of leg-work, or a bad beginning. The coach will then concentrate on this fault and hold out the hope that when it is cured pace will follow. But he must be quite sure that he is concentrating upon the fault to which the lack of pace was due. It must be confessed that, as a rule, a crew that is slow is incurable. There is nothing to be done but to make its existence as tolerable as circumstances allow until the race comes and puts it out of its misery. But if the men are strong and willing there is always some hope, for I have known a few crews, whom I had regarded as doomed to defeat, suddenly become inspired and snatch victory on the day of battle. In almost every case it was because they found the use of their legs at the critical moment.

Of the higher arts of coaching—of preparing a 'Varsity crew for the Boatrace, or some combination of first-class oarsmen for the Grand Challenge Cup at Henley, I will not write. Such tasks are undertaken by men more fitted to give than to receive instruction and it would be an impertinence to offer advice to their experience. Moreover all that there is to be said on such matters is contained in Mr. Harcourt Gold's little brochure to which I referred at the beginning of Chapter X.

But there are two things I should like to say in conclusion. Firstly, I would say to all but the most experienced coaches, never copy another man's methods. Much may be learned by accompanying a master of the craft and observing how he handles a crew. But his methods cannot be your methods, because you are not he. What you learn must be passed through the alembic of your own understanding and transmuted into your own metal before you attempt to pass it off on a crew.

Finally—and this is a point not sufficiently considered—success in coaching depends on complete reciprocity between the teacher and the taught—the coach and the crew. Much has been written and said of the duty of a coach towards his crew, but singularly little of the duty of a crew towards its coach. The qualities of tact and forbearance in the crew are every whit as important as they are in the coach, and results would often be happier for all concerned if the crew would realize that one half of the coach's success depends on themselves.

CHAPTER XII

ON MUSCULAR ACTION IN ROWING

Nobody would undertake to run a motor-car without previously making himself acquainted with its structure and mechanism. Yet there are scores of persons who confidently undertake the management of a crew without any knowledge of the infinitely more complicated mechanism of the human body. It is true that there is all the difference in the world between a machine and a living being which sets itself in motion, functions, and brings itself to a stop, without any external aid or interference. Nevertheless, as far as mere bodily movement is concerned, an oarsman may be regarded as a machine, but differing from any ordinary machine in this, among many other respects : that whereas a machine is designed to do a certain thing in a certain way and can only do it in that way, the human organism is not primarily designed for rowing, and when set to do it can accomplish the task in a good many different ways, most of which are, from the point of view of efficiency, the wrong ways. Surely the difference is not of a kind which absolves the manager from the necessity of acquiring some little knowledge of the mechanism which he undertakes to direct.

The trouble is that the living mechanism is not only very capricious in its action, but is complex beyond any machine that was ever invented. Even if we leave out of account the nervous, respiratory, circulatory, and other systems on which the functioning of the whole depends, and confine ourselves to the consideration of the muscular system as the motive power of the oarsman, it would take a large treatise to deal thoroughly with all its details. I make no pretence to write any such treatise. It would involve the description of a vast amount of minute and repellent detail, the very bulk of which would make it unacceptable to those for whose instruction it was written. Therefore, as I am bound to make my treatment of the subject as brief, and at the same time as intelligible as possible, I must omit much, and for the rest must presuppose some acquaintance with anatomical and physiological fact on the part of my readers.

To begin with, there is the skeleton, which for present purposes may be regarded as a system of levers set in motion by the muscles attached to them.

The principal bones of the skeleton with their joints or articulations are illustrated and named in figs. 47, 49, and 55. We distinguish at first sight the skeleton of the head and trunk, which anatomists call the axial skeleton ; and the skeleton of the limbs, which anatomists call the appendicular skeleton.

In the axial skeleton we need not concern ourselves with the skull further than to bear in mind that it is rather loosely articulated to the top of the vertebral column, and that in the living subject the head is heavy and is kept in balance and position by muscular action.

Of the backbone or vertebral column it is important to remember that it is neither a single piece, nor straight, nor rigid. It is, in fact, made up of some thirty-three separate pieces, the vertebrae, all but five of which are within certain limits movable on one another. A single vertebra is a disk-shaped piece of bone, called the body of the vertebra, to the posterior side of which is attached an irregularly shaped bony arch. Posteriorly each arch bears a more or less long projecting piece called the dorsal spine, and either the arch or the body bears on each side a more or less prominent projection known as the transverse process. These projections, the nature and various shapes of which may be studied in figs. 49 and 55, serve for the attachment of muscles. The disk-shaped bodies of the vertebrae are joined together by thickish layers of elastic material known as the intervertebral disks, and the successive vertebral arches are connected by joints which admit of a certain amount of movement between successive vertebrae.

The vertebral column is obviously divisible into four regions, to which may be added a fifth very short tail region. It is important to notice that each region is curved in such a way that the curvature of any one region is opposite to that of the region next below it (fig. 68 A). The uppermost region is that of the neck : it comprises seven vertebrae which do not bear any obvious ribs and its curvature is convex forwards. Next below it is the thoracic region, comprising twelve vertebrae, each of which bears a pair of ribs. The curvature of the thoracic region is concave forwards. The lumbar region, corresponding to what are known in popular language as the loins, comprises five vertebrae which do not bear ribs, but have stout and conspicuous transverse processes. When the body is upright the curvature of the lumbar region is convex forwards. In adult life the five sacral vertebrae are fused together to form a solid mass known as the sacral bone, in which, however, the elements of the component vertebrae are readily recognizable. The transverse processes of the sacral vertebrae are large, and their outer ends are expanded and fused together to form what is known in human anatomy as the lateral mass. The outer aspect of the upper part of the lateral mass on each side presents a large uneven surface for the articulation of the hip-bone. The sacrum is deeply concave forwards. The caudal or tail vertebrae, four or five in number, are rudimentary and of little importance, except that an oarsman who slouches at the finish of the stroke is apt to bring them into contact with his seat and to get a sore tail. Without going into elaborate details, it should be noted that the articulations between the vertebrae of these several regions of the backbone are such that the greatest amount of bending backwards is permitted in the neck region ; the greatest amount of bending forward in the lumbar region ; but the thoracic region can be bent forwards or backwards only to a limited degree. The thoracic vertebrae, however, are so constructed as to permit of a certain amount of rotation one upon another. Thus the upper part of the body can be twisted round over the lower part, a movement which is very convenient when we wish to look behind us, and not infrequently indulged in by oarsmen who allow their bodies to follow the arc described by the handle of the oar during the swing forward. The greatest amount of lateral bending of the vertebral column takes place in the lumbar region. By a combination of lateral

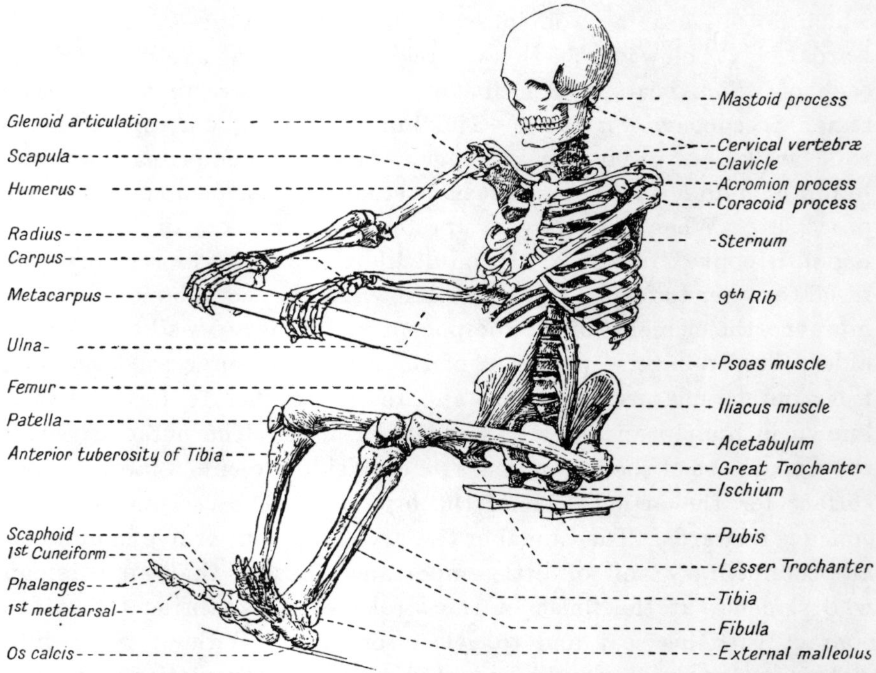

Fig. 47. The skeleton in a rowing position (note, in posing the skeleton the seat has inadvertently been placed too high above the heels).

and anterior flexure of the lumbar region with rotation of the dorsal region, indifferent oarsmen contrive to 'swing over the inside leg' and exhibit a 'screwing' action of the body.

Of the ribs it is sufficient to say that the first seven pairs are articulated to the thoracic vertebrae behind, and joined by elastic bands of cartilage to the breast-bone in front; the next three pairs are joined by cartilage to the ribs next in front of them, and the last two pairs have no anterior attachments and are called floating ribs. The general shape of the breast-bone and ribs and of the thoracic cavity enclosed by them is shown in fig. 47. It should be noted that the first pair of ribs are short, and the eighth or ninth pair the longest, so the thorax is pear-shaped with the narrow end uppermost. The breadth of the shoulders is not due to the ribs, but to the shoulder-

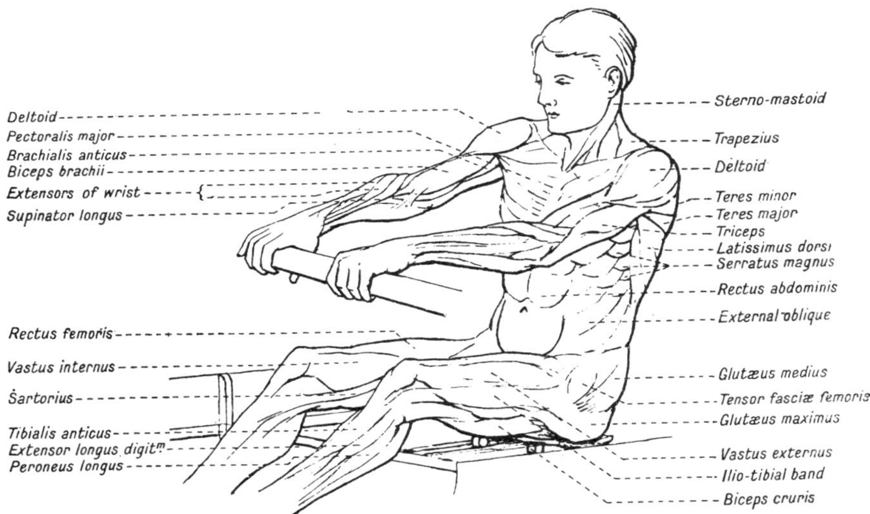

Fig. 48. Illustrates the superficial muscles. Except that the position of the legs has been corrected, the attitude is exactly the same as that of the skeleton in fig. 47.

blades and collar-bones, and the muscles attached to them. It should also be noted that the ribs (which have double articulations with the bodies and transverse processes of the thoracic vertebrae) in the first part of their course bend backwards, and then sweep round to enclose the sides and front of the thoracic cavity. As a consequence there is, on either side of the back, a broad furrow between the dorsal spines of the thoracic vertebrae and the posterior ends of the ribs in which the great erector spinae muscles of the back are lodged.

The principal bones of the limbs are sufficiently well shown, in the positions which they occupy during the stroke, in fig. 47. As they are fully named it will not be necessary to give a detailed description of them, but there are several features relating to the joints, and more particularly to the attachments of the limbs to the trunk, which require special attention.

In both the upper limb and the lower limb the attachment to the trunk is not direct, but by the intervention of special skeletal elements known respectively as the shoulder-girdle and the hip or pelvic girdle. It must be clearly understood at the outset that, whereas the pelvic girdle is firmly and immoveably attached to the sacral portion of the vertebral column, the shoulder-girdle has no such attachment, but is capable of a considerable range of movement and is only articulated by a movable joint to the breast-bone. The shoulder-girdle is made up of the shoulder-blade or scapula and the collar-bone or clavicle. The scapula, the shape of which is best illustrated in fig. 49, is a triangular plate of bone, slightly concave internally, with its apex directed downwards and its base uppermost. Its outer angle is thickened and truncated to form a shallow cavity called the glenoid cavity, for the articulation of the rounded head of the upper arm or humerus. The upper third of the posterior surface of the scapula is traversed by a diagonal ridge of bone known as the spine of the scapula. This ridge becomes deeper as it approaches the outer border of the scapula, and finally is produced into a stout curved process which overhangs the glenoid cavity, and is known as the acromion process. The glenoid cavity is also overhung by a short, stout, beak-shaped projection from the upper and outer border of the scapula, known as the coracoid process. The scapula is attached to the backbone and ribs only by muscles, and is not even bound down to the adjacent parts by ligaments, so it can be moved freely towards or away from the backbone and its lower angle can be tilted upwards and forwards, or backwards and downwards, by muscular action. The collar-bone, or clavicle, is a fairly long and rather slender bone, shaped somewhat like the italic letter *f*, and jointed at one end to the acromion process of the scapula, at the other end of the upper segment of the breast-bone. As the acromion process overhangs the glenoid cavity, the shoulder-joint does not occupy a fixed position with regard to the trunk, but can be rotated through the arc of a circle, of which the articulation of the

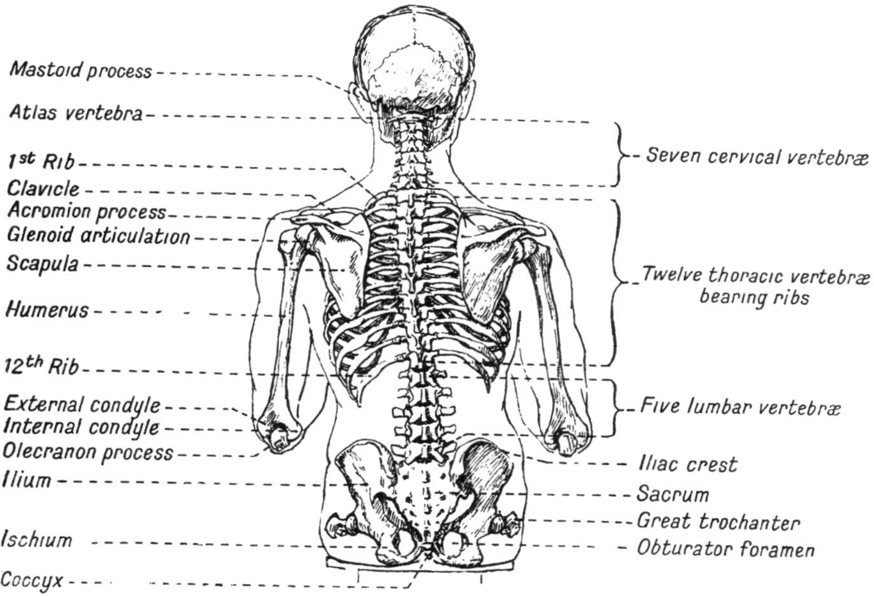

FIG. 49. Hind view of the skeleton of the trunk and upper limb in the position of the finish of the stroke.

collar-bone to the breast-bone is the centre. This mobility of the shoulder is of great importance in rowing, and in order that the use and misuse of the shoulders may be thoroughly appreciated, a coach should make himself fully acquainted with the structure and movements of this part of the skeleton. In fig. 50 the shoulder-girdles and their relation to the ribs, vertebral column, and breast-bone are represented semi-diagrammatically, the right shoulder being somewhat thrust forward and the left shoulder slightly drawn back, as would be the case with a bow-side oarsman in the act of swinging forward.

The upper arm has a large hemispherical surface for articulation with the glenoid cavity of the humerus, and the arm is capable of movement in any direction at the shoulder-joint. This great liberty of movement is exemplified in round-arm and over-arm bowling, but in correct rowing the upper arm simply moves in a plane which is but slightly inclined to the median plane of the body. Oarsmen who square their elbows at the finish of the stroke are making an illegitimate use of the liberty of action afforded by the shoulder-joint. Of the two bones of the forearm it should be noticed that one, the ulna, makes practically the whole of the articulation with the upper arm at the elbow. The other, the radius, makes the whole of the articulation at the wrist. When the palm of the hand is held upwards the radius and ulna are parallel to one another, and the hand and forearm are said to be supinated. When the palm of the hand is turned downwards, as it is to grasp the oar in rowing, the radius crosses over the ulna and the hand and forearm are said to be pronated. Whether the forearm be pronated or supinated, the elbow is a simple hinge-joint, admitting of movement only in one plane.

The wrist is made up of eight short and variously shaped bones, the flexibility of the wrist-joint being due to the manner in which these eight bones are articulated with one another, and with the radius and the five metacarpal bones of the hand. The general arrangement of the bones of the wrist, the hand, the fingers, and the thumb can be sufficiently well understood by an inspection of fig. 47. The reader should observe, by trial of his own wrist, that when the forearm is pronated, the wrist-joint can be bent downwards till the hand is at right angles with the forearm ; that it can be bent upwards to about half this extent ; and that it is capable of a considerable degree of lateral movement.

The shape and relations of the hip-bones or pelvis are shown in three-quarter front view in fig. 47 ; in hind view in fig. 49 ; and in profile in fig. 55. In fig. 49 we see the central mass of the sacrum, which is a direct continuation of the vertebral column and, as has been explained, is formed of five vertebrae fused together. It terminates below in the rudimentary tail or coccyx. To each side of the upper part of the sacrum are firmly attached the broad expanded and curved iliac bones, each having a prominent curved upper margin, known as the iliac crest. In its lower half each iliac bone becomes

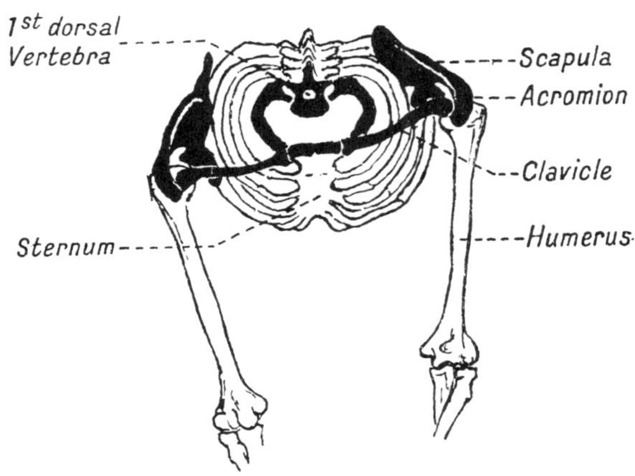

Fig. 50. Semi-diagrammatic view from above the thorax and shoulder girdles, the upper arms extended as in rowing. The first pair of ribs, the collar-bones, and the shoulder-blades are represented in black.

narrower from front to back, but thicker from side to side, and forms the upper moiety of a deep cup-shaped cavity, the acetabulum, which is the socket into which the rounded head of the thigh-bone fits. Below and in front of the acetabulum, a rather narrow bone, the pubis, projects forwards and inwards towards the middle line. Here it expands somewhat, is united to its fellow of the opposite side by a fibro-cartilaginous articulation known as the symphysis pubis, and thence turns at a sharp angle backwards and outwards to be continued into the ischium. The last-named bone runs backwards and downwards from the acetabulum, at first curving inwards, but in its lower half outwards, from the middle line. Behind and below it is enlarged to form a projecting mass known as the ischial tuberosity : from this point it turns sharply forward and inward to be continued into the pubis. In childhood the ilium, ischium, and pubis are separate bones which meet in the acetabulum, and each contributes its share to the formation of that cavity, but in adult life the three bones are completely fused together. In the sitting position the ischial bones support the weight of the trunk (fig. 49), and it should be observed that they are curved somewhat like the rockers of a rocking-chair, in such a manner that the body can be rocked to and fro upon them.

The thigh-bone or femur is the longest and largest bone in the body. It is also the most variable in length relatively to the whole height. A short man usually has a relatively short femur and a tall man a relatively long femur. It is the length of thigh relatively to the trunk that gives a tall man an advantage on a long slide. The femur is described as having a head, a shaft, and a lower extremity. Observe (fig. 47) that the shaft is slightly curved and enlarged towards each extremity. The head does not lie in a line with the shaft, but is borne on the end of a short neck, which is set upon the upper extremity of the shaft at an angle of about 125° to 130°. The angle and also the length of the neck are subject to some degree of variation in different individuals. The longer the neck and the wider the angle at which it is set on the shaft, the easier it is to flex the hip-joint and to obtain a long reach forward in rowing. Coaches should note that men who are narrow across the hips cannot well be taught to get a long swing forward, and are to that extent debarred from attaining the highest standard of oarsmanship. Above and to the outside of the neck the upper extremity of the shaft of the femur ends in a thick roughened process, the great trochanter, which serves for the attachment of important muscles. Below the neck and to the inner and hinder side of the upper end of the shaft is another prominent projection known as the trochanter minor. It is connected with the trochanter major by a ridge, and serves for the attachment of the ilio-psoas muscles (fig. 47). The head of the femur is an articular surface covered with smooth cartilage, in shape nearly three-quarters of a sphere. It fits into the acetabulum, and the hip-joint thus formed, being a ball-and-socket joint, admits of movement in every direction, but in certain directions the movements are limited, partly by ligaments, partly by the projecting rim of the acetabular cavity. The action of the hip-joint is of prime importance in rowing: everybody who undertakes to give instruction in oarsmanship should make himself acquainted with at least the outlines of the anatomy of the joint. The hip-joint is said to be *flexed* when the thigh is bent up towards the trunk; *extended* when the thigh is straightened in line with the trunk; *abducted* when the limb is moved outwards away from the middle line; *adducted* when the limb is drawn towards the middle line. Some of these movements may be combined. Thus when an oarsman slides forward the thigh is both flexed on the trunk and drawn outwards to separate the knees from one another, the combined movement being known as *circumduction*.

The lower end of the femur presents two rounded eminences for articulation with the lower leg, known respectively as the internal and external condyles. They are united in front, but separated by a deep groove behind. The knee-cap, or patella, slides in the broad groove between the anterior aspects of the internal and external condyles.

The lower leg or crus, like the forearm, comprises two bones: the tibia or shin-bone and the fibula. Of these the tibia is much the larger, being, next to the femur, the longest bone in the skeleton. Its upper end presents two shallow concave surfaces for articulation with the condyles of the femur; its lower end takes by far the larger share of the articulation of the leg with the ankle. The fibula is a slender bone on the outside of the leg. It takes no share in the formation of the knee-joint, its upper end being articulated with a prominence on the outer side of the upper end of the tibia. Its lower extremity shares with the tibia in the formation of the ankle-joint.

The ankle, which corresponds to the wrist of the upper limb, but has nothing like the same mobility, is made up of seven bones, most of them squarish in outline, but two of them are of irregular shape and much larger than the rest. The uppermost of the two, the astragalus, presents above a convex pulley-shaped surface for articulation with the tibia ; below it articulates with the calcaneum or heel-bone. The last named is the largest bone of the foot, and its large backward projection forms the heel. To it is attached the strong tendo Achillis of the calf muscle. The remaining bones of the foot and toes do not call for special description.

The knee-joint is a very complicated structure, in the composition of which the patella forms an important part. It is sufficient to point out here that the knee acts, for the most part, as a simple hinge-joint. When it is straight no rotation of the joint is possible, but when it is flexed a considerable amount of rotation is allowed, and this renders possible the attitude assumed by the legs when the slide is drawn forwards to its fullest extent at the beginning of the stroke. The ankle is also mostly a hinge-joint, but, in addition to the movements of flexion and extension, the foot can be rotated to some extent outwards and to a lesser degree inwards, as when we turn out or turn in our toes. The reader will understand that at every joint the bones entering into its composition are tied together by strong fibrous ligaments, the arrangement of which is often curious and very complicated. Being inelastic the ligaments not only prevent the bones from falling or being pulled apart, but by their disposition set a limit to the extent to which any joint can be bent. In youth, however, the ligaments are not so inelastic, but they can be stretched to a certain extent by practice. In rowing this is notably the case with the thigh- and ankle-joints, the ligaments of which may be so far stretched by constant exercise as to allow of greater freedom of play than is normal.

Before entering upon a discussion of the muscles chiefly used in rowing it will be advisable to consider the action of certain muscles selected as examples of muscular action in general. The simplest form of joint is a hinge-joint, and the best example of a hinge-joint in the body is the elbow. The articulation of the ulna with the humerus admits only of simple movements of flexion and extension. For present purposes we can leave out of consideration the radius and its special and somewhat complicated action in pronating and supinating the forearm : in any case it does not affect the movement of the ulna on the humerus. The muscle which simply bends the elbow and does nothing else is not, as is commonly supposed, the biceps of the upper arm, but a smaller, flatter, and rather broad muscle, the brachialis anticus, lying between the biceps and the humerus. Its position and action are illustrated in quite a diagrammatic way in figs. 51 and 52. In descriptive anatomy we speak of the ‘ origin ’ and the ‘ insertion ’ of a muscle. The origin is the attachment to that bone which is supposed to be unmoved ; the insertion is the attachment to the bone which is moved when the muscle in question contracts. The brachialis anticus takes its origin, by a large number of fibres of attachment, from a rough surface covering the lower half of the front side of the humerus. It is inserted, by a short tendon, on the beak-shaped process, known as the coronoid process, on the front of the upper end of the ulna. When the muscle contracts its fibres become shorter and thicker ; the tendon pulls on the coronoid process and the ulna is raised, or, as we say, the joint is flexed. This is the usual way of stating what happens, but as reaction is always equal and opposite, if the humerus were not held fast by muscles acting in a contrary direction to the pull of the brachialis anticus, it would be drawn towards the ulna as much as the latter bone is drawn towards the humerus. On relaxation of the brachialis muscle the hand or forearm drop down of their own weight if the upper arm is hanging down by the side of the body, but if the upper arm is held out horizontally the elbow must be straightened by the extensor muscles of the joint. The extensor muscles of the elbow are the triceps, a large composite muscle which will be described farther on, and a small triangular muscle called the *anconeus* situated to the outside of the elbow-joint. The anconeus arises from the back of the external condyle of the humerus and is inserted on the outer side of the olecranon and the upper fourth of the back of the shaft of the ulna. When it contracts the anconeus pulls on the olecranon and brings the ulna into line with the humerus. Small as it is, this

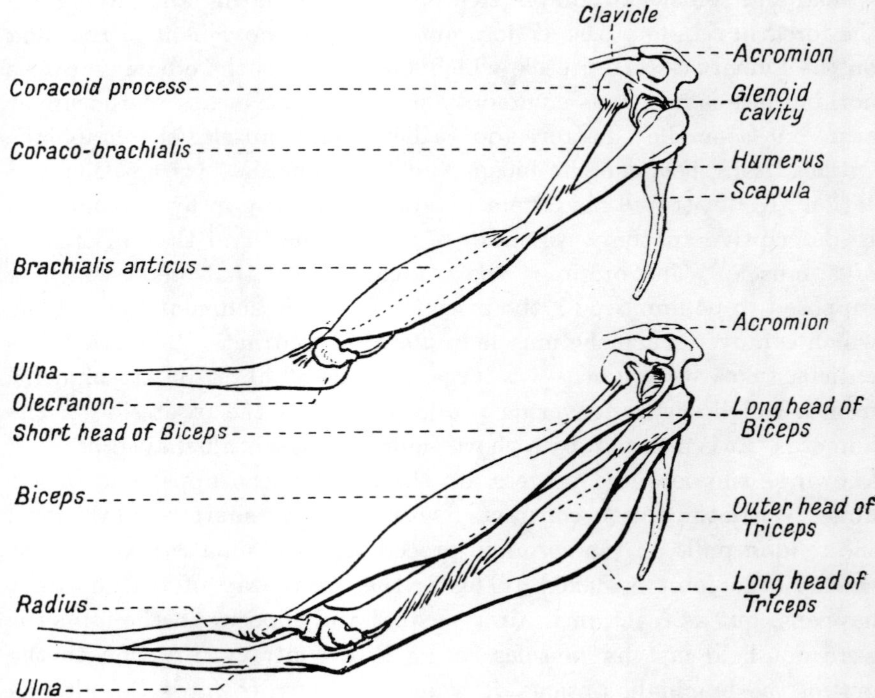

Fig. 51. Flexor and extensor muscles of the elbow : the arm partly extended.

muscle plays a not unimportant part in the action of ' shooting away the hands ' in rowing, and becomes more than ordinarily well developed in oarsmen.

Whilst the brachialis anticus and anconeus are examples of simple flexors and extensors of a single joint, the biceps and triceps muscles of the upper arm are examples of muscles which pass over more than one joint, and therefore produce greater variety of action. The fleshy part, or belly, of the biceps muscle divides above into two heads, the inner of which is attached by a tendon to the coracoid process of the scapula. The outer or long head ends in a long rounded tendon which is lodged in a groove in front of the upper end of the humerus, passes over the head of the humerus, and curving inwards and backwards is attached to the upper part of the glenoid cavity of the scapula.

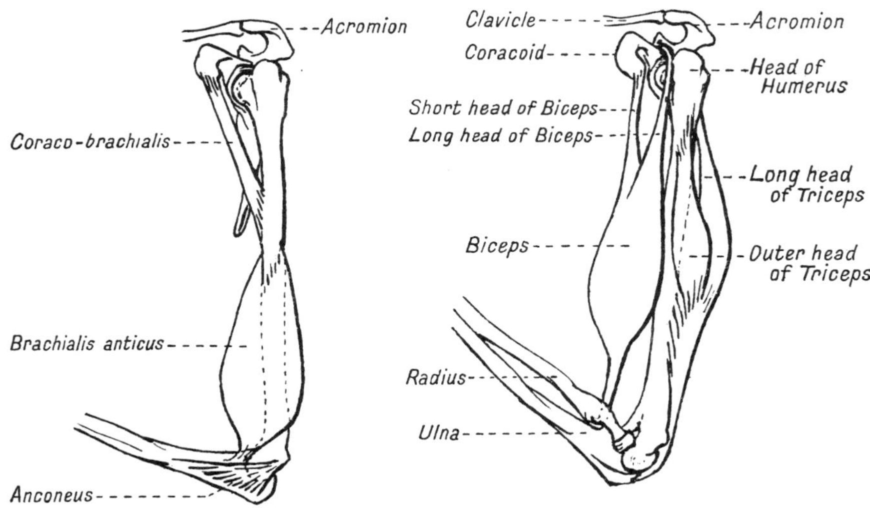

FIG. 52. Flexor and extensor muscles of the elbow: the arm flexed.

The lower end of the biceps ends in a flat tendon which is inserted on a prominent tubercle about an inch below the head of the radius. In considering the action of the biceps the position of the bicipital tubercle requires attention. When the forearm is supinated and the radius lies parallel to the ulna, the bicipital tubercle is slightly to the inside of the front of the radius, and when the biceps contracts its tendon pulls directly on the radius and flexes the elbow-joint. But when, as in rowing, the forearm is pronated, the head of the radius is rotated through a half-circle and the bicipital tubercle is shifted to a position below and rather to the outside of it. The biceps tendon is therefore twisted underneath the bone, and the first effect of contraction of the muscle is to supinate the forearm. But an oarsman must retain the grasp of his oar with his hand pronated. Therefore, if he brings the biceps into action to bend the elbow in the latter half of the stroke, he has to take a very firm grip with his fingers to resist its supinating action. When considerable resistance, such as is offered by the handle of the oar, is encountered, the flexor muscles of the wrist and fingers assist in bending the arm at the elbow. Hence the oarsman, who has begun by relying on the biceps to bring his arms home, soon acquires the habit of simultaneously contracting the muscles of the under side of the forearm and is ‘ pulling home with his arms ’. Further consequences follow from the undue use of the biceps. As its upper tendons are fastened to the shoulder-blade, when resistance is met with, its contraction tends to pull the shoulder forward and also to raise the arm at the shoulder at the time when it should be depressed and drawn back. This brings the biceps into opposition to other muscles, among them the triceps. The last named is a composite muscle situated at the back of the upper arm. It is inserted below by a broad, flat tendon into the olecranon process of the ulna. Above it is divided into three parts, known as the middle or long head, the outer head, and the inner head. The long head arises from the scapula immediately below the glenoid cavity. The outer and inner heads arise from the humerus ; the former from the upper and outer part of the back of the bone ; the latter from a long surface of attachment extending along the back of the humerus for three-quarters of its length. The outer and inner heads are simple extensors of the elbow-joint, but the long head, while it assists in extension, also tends to pull down the arm from the horizontal position, thus acting in direct opposition to the biceps, which tends to elevate it.

From the above consideration of the actions of a few comparatively simple muscles we can learn something about the nature of muscular movement in general. For one thing we learn that, because a muscle is described by a single name, its fibres do not necessarily act all together or all in the same direction. One of its parts may be in action at one time and another part at another time. Thus, in the action of drawing back the upper arm and simultaneously bending the elbow, the long head of the triceps helps to depress the upper arm, but its inner and outer heads must be relaxed, for if they were contracted, they would prevent the elbow from being bent. Conversely, when the upper arm is elevated and the elbow straightened, as in the recovery in rowing, the inner and outer heads of the triceps contract to assist in straightening the elbow, but the long head must relax, for if it did not, it would pull in opposition to the muscles elevating the arm at the shoulder-joint. It will be seen that, for the proper performance of many of an oarsman's movements, it is necessary that some parts of large muscles should be relaxed whilst others are in a state of contraction.

At the same time it must be understood that in most movements not involving much more resistance than that of the weight of the limbs and body, contraction of any given group of flexor muscles is generally accompanied by a slight contraction of the opposing group of extensor muscles and vice versa. The slight opposition thus offered serves to steady the limb and to give precision to the action of the joint. Indeed, the equilibrium of the whole body when at rest is maintained by the constant but slight tension of opposing groups of muscles, and even in vigorous exercise it is generally necessary that a joint, or a limb, or a segment of a limb should be fixed, it may be only for a moment, to afford a *point d'appui* for the muscles producing the movement in question. Such fixation involves the use of opposing muscles, and, generally speaking, the ease and efficiency of any bodily movement depend on the appropriate muscles being contracted to exactly the right amount, at exactly the right moment, and only for just so long as is required. It will be my endeavour, in the following pages, to point out the muscles that are appropriate to the proper performance of the various movements of the recovery, swing forward, and stroke.

CHAPTER XIII

ON MUSCULAR ACTION DURING THE RECOVERY, SWING FORWARD, AND STROKE

Distinction must be made between movements that involve little or no resistance beyond moving the weight of the body and limbs, and those which meet with and have to overcome great resistance, such as the movements of the body and limbs during the stroke through the water. We may speak of the internal resistance of the weight of the body and limbs and the external resistance due to the weight of the oar and the boat.

In the recovery and swing forward the external resistance to be overcome is small. Such as it is, it consists chiefly in feathering and starting the oar on its backward sweep outboard. There is also the friction of the slide, but this is so small as to be almost negligible.

In the recovery of the oar, what is commonly called 'the drop of the hands' means a quick and partial extension of the elbow-joint. The 'turn of the wrists' means that these joints, which are flexed to nearly their full extent at the finish of the stroke, are suddenly over-extended.[1] The 'shoot away of the hands' means that the elbow-joints are still farther extended, and, simultaneously, the upper arm is elevated at the shoulder-joint. These movements follow in rapid succession, and if skilfully performed, are blended into one continuous movement.

The first sharp and partial extension of the elbow is effected by the triceps muscle of the upper arm, and all its three heads are brought into action, for while the wrists are 'dropping', the upper arm is still

[1] The wrist is said to be 'extended' when the back of the hand is in a line with the forearm; 'over-extended' when the hand is bent back and the knuckles are above the wrists.

drawn back and the long head serves to hold and steady it in that position as well as to assist in the extension of the elbow. The over-extension of the wrists is effected by certain of the extensor muscles which, when the hand and forearm are supinated, are conventionally described as being situated at the back and outer side of the forearm, but in pronation these muscles come to lie on the upper side of the upper part of the forearm and their tendons pass more or less diagonally towards the inner side of the wrist. The extensor muscles of the wrist and fingers are illustrated and named in fig. 53, but only three out of the whole group are brought into action in the extension of the wrist.

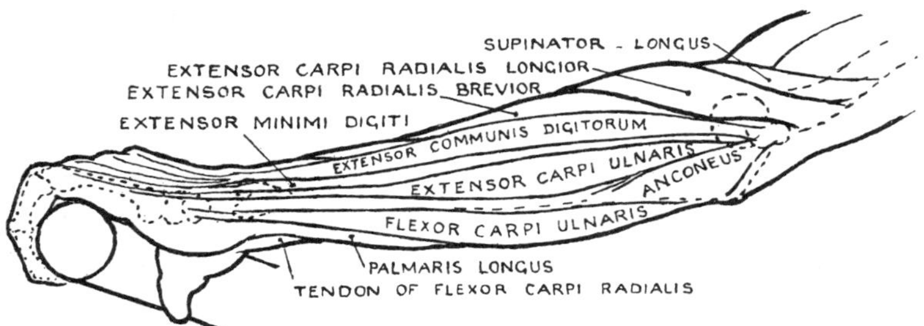

FIG. 53. The muscles of the outer side of the forearm: the hand grasping the oar.

As the thumb and fingers must retain their grasp of the handle of the oar in the act of feathering, their extensors are necessarily relaxed and their flexors remain in contraction. The three extensor muscles of the wrist are the long extensor and the short extensor of the radial side, and the extensor of the ulnar side of the wrist. The first named becomes largely developed and forms a prominent feature in the oarsman's arm. It arises from the ridge above the outer condyle of the humerus, curves round towards the radial or thumb side of the forearm, and at the end of the upper third of the forearm terminates in a long, flat tendon which passes under the extensors of the thumb and is inserted on the base of the metacarpal bone of the first or index finger. The shorter radial and ulnar extensors of the wrist arise from the external condyle of the humerus and are inserted on the bases of the metacarpal bones of the middle and little fingers respectively. At the wrist the tendons of the extensor muscles pass under, and are held down by, a broad strong bracelet of ligament known as the posterior annular ligament.

As the elbow straightens the extensors of the wrist assist in extending the elbow, but the main agents in thrusting the handle of the oar away from the body (' shooting out the hands ') are the anconeus and the inner and outer heads of the triceps. As the elbow straightens the upper arm is elevated at the shoulder-joint by the coraco-brachialis and the anterior fibres of the deltoid muscle of the shoulder, and it is obvious that the long head of the triceps must relax to allow the humerus to swing upwards. In these days it is rare to see the successive movements of dropping, turning, and shooting away the handle of the oar neatly and accurately performed. From what precedes it is evident that the triceps is the main agent in extracting the blade of the oar from the water and afterwards thrusting the handle of the oar away from the body. Young oarsmen should take special pains to understand its action and learn to use it in the right way. It must not be contracted too violently, for it is inexpedient to straighten the arms with a jerk or to set the elbow rigid during the swing forward. As the elbow straightens the action of the triceps is moderated by a very slight contraction of the biceps, the short head of which assists in raising the arm at the shoulder-joint. But the chief agents in elevating the upper arm and sustaining it in a raised position during the swing forwards, thus ensuring what is known as ' lightness of the hands ', are the clavicular fibres of the deltoid and the coraco-brachialis muscles. After long consideration I am convinced that for good and easy oarsmanship the latter is much the more important of the two. The coraco-brachialis (figs. 51 and 52) is a strap-shaped muscle arising from the coracoid process along with the short head of the biceps. It is inserted into the middle of the inner surface of the shaft of the humerus. Its action is to lift the upper arm and at the same time to draw it inwards. When contracted it suspends the upper arm from the shoulder-blade as if by a strap and, being perfectly simple in its action, allows the arm to swing freely in the shoulder-socket while maintaining it in the elevated position. Being covered by the short head of the biceps, only a small portion of it appears on the surface on the inner side of the arm, near the armpit.

The deltoid muscle will be described farther on.

The recovery of the body takes place simultaneously with, but is quite independent of, the recovery of the oar. In fig. 68 the body is represented as swung back nearly 30° past the perpendicular. A vertical line drawn through its centre of gravity, which is rather high up because of the weight of the head, falls some inches behind the back of the seat, and the body would topple over backwards but for the tension of the walls of the abdomen and of the muscles indicated by thick lines in the diagram. The action of these muscles cannot well be explained without reference to the positions occupied by the skeleton of the trunk and lower limbs when the oarsman is in this attitude. The lean back of the body is partly due to the backward concavity of the lumbar region of the vertebral column, but much more to the pelvis, which is inclined so far backwards that the coccyx or tail-bone is nearly in contact with the hind edge of the seat. The weight of the body rests on the hinder part of the tuberosity of the ischium and the pubis is directed upwards and forwards. The knee-joints are extended, though not quite to the fullest extent possible, but the thigh, of course, is far from being in a straight line with the body, and the thigh-joint is about half-way between its full limits of extension and flexion. The tendons and muscles which support the trunk at the end of the swing back, and afterwards pull it forward in the recovery, belong to three groups. The first are the abdominal muscles, with their strong tendinous expansions, the latter known to anatomists by the awkward name of aponeuroses. They pass from the breast-bone and ribs to the projecting anterior end of the pubic bone ; to the anterior half of the iliac crest ; and to a strong band of tendon called Poupart's ligament, which passes from the anterior angle of the iliac crest to the spine of the pubis, and forms the lower limit of the abdomen.

Considering these in a little more detail: the lateral walls of the abdomen are formed by a triple sheet of muscle. Externally the obliquus externus muscle, arising from the external surfaces of the eight lowest ribs by separate slips, the uppermost of which interdigitate with the slips of the serratus magnus, and the lowermost with the origins of the latissimus dorsi muscle. The upper fibres of the obliquus externus run diagonally from above downwards towards the mid-line of the abdomen (but do not reach it); the fibres from the lowest ribs pass more vertically downwards to their insertions on the anterior half of the iliac crest. Beneath the external oblique is the internal oblique, the fibres of which pass diagonally from behind and below, forwards and upwards, crossing those of the external oblique nearly at right angles. The innermost layer of the muscular wall is the transversus abdominis, the fibres of which are horizontal. None of the fibres of these three sheets of muscle reach the middle line of the abdomen, but end some distance from it in strong tendinous fibres which co-operate to form a strong, broad, oval sheet of tissue covering and protecting the front of the abdomen. Anatomists describe it as made up of the aponeuroses of the three above-mentioned layers of the lateral abdominal muscles. Where the aponeuroses of the two sides of the body meet in the mid-ventral line they unite to form a strong cord, the linea alba, extending from the lowest part of the breast-bone to the pubis. The linea alba forms a well-marked longitudinal furrow in muscular subjects. On either side of it is a broad band of muscle, the rectus abdominis (figs. 59 and 68 A), originating below from the pubic crest, and inserted above into the sternal cartilages of the fifth, sixth, and seventh ribs. The fibres of the rectus abdominis are not continuous, but are interrupted at fairly regular intervals by transverse narrow bands of tendon, one of which is on a level with the navel, and generally two above and one below the navel. The upper two-thirds of the rectus abdominis is imbedded in the great tendinous sheet forming the anterior wall of the abdomen: its lower third lies behind it. The two recti abdominis are the 'belly-muscles', much talked of, and often strained, by oarsmen. But, as I hope to show, there is no reason why they should have any undue strain put upon them, and they certainly should never be exercised so violently as to rupture their fibres. Outside all these, below the skin, is the superficial fascia of the abdomen, the deeper part of which is an elastic membrane, of some strength but not so thick and strong as its representative, the tunica abdominalis, in four-footed animals. It is, however, fairly well developed in some individuals, and probably is made stronger by use in most oarsmen. When the body is swung back past the perpendicular at the end of the stroke the abdominal fascia, the recti abdominis, the linea alba, the great abdominal aponeurosis, and the fibres of the external oblique muscle, are put on the stretch and by their mere tension prevent the body from falling backwards. It is obvious that if the oarsman 'lies back' the strain is much greater and may become excessive. Of course, when muscles are put on the stretch, their fibres contract to the amount required to support the strain thrown upon them. Thus the balance of the body is maintained without any conscious effort, but it requires a definite act of volition to contract the muscles sufficiently to produce movement. The muscles and tendons so far described are superficial and connect the breast-bone and ribs with the pelvis. They have no power to pull the hip-bones forward, and do not act directly on the vertebral column. But when forcibly contracted they pull the ribs and breast-bone down towards the pubis, thus acting indirectly on the vertebral column, to which they stand somewhat in the relation of the string to a bow that is being bent. Contracted to their full extent, they pull down the upper part of the body, and the thoracic and lumbar regions of the vertebral column are bent as far forward as they will go. In the action of climbing the abdominal muscles are of great importance. The hands grasp a branch above the head; by contracting the abdominal muscles the back is arched; the pelvis and lower limbs are pulled up ; a new foothold is obtained ; the arms are again extended for another grasp ; and so on. But an oarsman is not expected to pull himself forward to his oar-handle like a monkey climbing up a tree, and he should remember that undue use of the abdominal muscles leads to exactly that kind of movement, with the disadvantage that the oar-handle affords no fixed support for him to hold on to.

The hip-bones and the lower part of the vertebral column are directly supported, and in the recovery of the body pulled forward, by the rectus femoris and the psoas and iliacus muscles (fig. 54). The rectus femoris is one of the extensor muscles of the knee, and as such has played its part in flattening down the knee at the end of the stroke. It arises by two tendons attached, the one to the anterior inferior spine of the iliac bone, the other to the outer side of the iliac bone just above the acetabulum. It is the first of these that is put on the stretch when the knee is extended. Below the rectus femoris is prolonged into a flat tendon, inserted into the upper surface of the knee-cap. The knee-cap, in turn, is fastened by a strong tendon to the front of the upper end of the shin-bone. When the body leans back and the legs are stretched out, as at the finish of the stroke, the upper tendon of the rectus femoris can be felt and seen as a prominent ridge on the upper part of the thigh near its junction with the body, but it becomes slack when the body is brought forward to the perpendicular. The ilio-psoas group of muscles (psoas and iliacus in fig. 54 : see also fig. 47) are the most important flexors of the hip-joint. Situated at the back of the abdominal cavity behind the viscera, they hardly appear on the surface and can only be demonstrated by deep dissection. The psoas muscle originates by fleshy slips from the transverse processes and the bodies of the last dorsal and all the lumbar vertebrae. Its fibres converge downwards to form a thick elongated muscle, which emerges from the abdomen below Poupart's ligament, passes over the pubis, and ends in a tendon which passes round the inside of the femur and is inserted into the small trochanter. The iliacus muscle arises from the base of the sacrum and from the anterior surface and crest of the iliac bone. Its fibres converge downwards and are inserted, partly on the tendon of the psoas, partly on the femur a little beyond the small trochanter. The ilio-psoas is put on the stretch at the finish of the stroke. In conjunction with the rectus femoris it is the proper agent in the recovery of the body. The oarsman is instructed not to bend his knees during the recovery of the body. The rectus femoris, being an extensor of the knee as well as a flexor of the thigh-

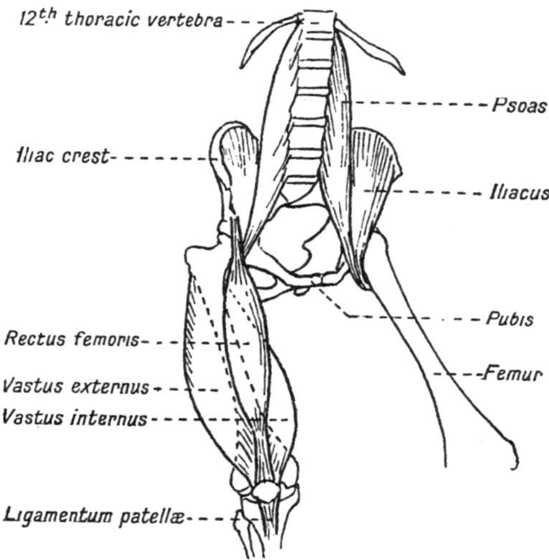

Fig. 54. The ilio-psoas and quadriceps extensor groups of muscles.

joint, by its contraction keeps the knee down at the same time that it pulls the hip-bone forward. The iliacus muscle simply pulls the hip-bone forward, rotating it about the acetabulum as a centre. The psoas draws the whole lumbar region of the vertebral column forward to the perpendicular position, and in so doing necessarily brings forward the upper part of the trunk.

What has to be realized is that the really important thing in the recovery is to bring the hips and loins forward. This can be done by the ilio-psoas, but cannot be done by the use of the abdominal muscles.

Indeed, as may be seen by inspection of fig. 68 A, the recti abdominis being attached to the forward projection of the pubis tend to rotate the hip-bone backwards, and oarsmen who suffer, as so many do, from strained 'belly-muscles' must often have set them in violent opposition to the only muscles they need to use in the recovery—those which rotate the hip-bone forwards. A word here about 'sitting up at the finish'. There is a middle course and two extremes. One extreme, which mistakenly passes for good form, is to carry back the head and upper part of the body by hollowing the small of the back as much as possible. This involves extra strain on the abdominal walls, and the extra effort of the erector spinae muscles to bend back the lumbar curvature to its fullest extent is wasted, for it is a pull in opposition to the strain on the abdominal muscles, and has little, if any, effect in propelling the boat. The other extreme is the slouched finish with the small of the back and shoulders rounded, the chin down, and the neck inclined forward. This seems a restful position to the oarsman, as it relieves the tension on the abdominal walls, but he has to sit on his tail-bones to get any length of swing back. He is then in a position in which the ilio-psoas muscle cannot be used to advantage, and he inevitably tries to recover his body by the use of the recti abdominis muscles, which, among other disadvantages, impedes his respiration in a manner to be described farther on. The middle course is a tolerably upright sitting posture, the small of the back curved neither inwards nor outwards, the tail-bones not quite in contact with the hind edge of the seat, the head and neck carried as shown in fig. 34. From this position the proper recovery muscles, the rectus femoris and ilio-psoas, can be used to the greatest advantage.

When the recovery is completed the body is upright, the knees very slightly bent, the tail-bones so far lifted from the back of the seat that the pelvis is nearly upright, but probably still inclined a trifle backwards. The movements of the recovery pass without a break into those of the swing forwards. This involves continued flexion of the thigh-joints ; steady flexion of the knee-joints ; a certain amount of circumduction of the thighs to ‘ open the knees ’; bending the ankles; and in the upper part of the body movements of the shoulders to allow the arms to follow the arc described by the handle of the oar. Also, as the body bends forward, the neck has to be bent back to keep the head in an upright position. There is little or no external resistance. So much impetus has been given to the oar that it has to be checked rather than pushed forward, unless a strong wind is blowing against the boat. The friction of the slide is very slight and is overcome by the momentum of the body moving forward. Practically all the work to be done is that of overcoming the internal resistance of the body and limbs. To this end forcible and abrupt contractions of the muscles are not necessary. In order that the movements may be uniform and balanced, the operative muscles should contract gradually, and the poise of the body and limbs should be maintained by just the required amount of contraction of their opponents and no more.

When the body has arrived at the perpendicular and the knees begin to bend, the rectus femoris will go out of action. It has done its duty in pulling the hip-bone forward and any farther tension on its part would offer too much resistance to the bending of the knee. All tension is removed from the abdominal muscles, and they should relax to allow the abdomen to bulge forwards as the diaphragm descends in the act of inspiration, of which more hereafter. Practically the whole work of swinging the body forwards and simultaneously raising the knees falls on the ilio-psoas muscle. The iliac portion continues to pull the crest of the ilium towards the thigh, but its action in this respect is limited. Even when the oarsman has swung forward as far as in fig. 21, the pelvis, on a 14- or 16-inch slide, is only slightly inclined forward. It cannot go far forward because the thigh is bent upwards to the extreme limit of flexion allowed by the structure of the hip-joint and farther movement is prevented by the neck of the femur coming in contact with the projecting rim of the acetabulum. The iliacus at one and the same time draws the crest of the ilium down towards the thigh-bone and pulls the thigh up towards the ilium, just as an elastic band wrapped round the handles of an open pair of nut-crackers pulls them together when both handles are let go. On a fixed seat, the thighs being raised to a much less extent, the pelvis can be, and should be, inclined much farther forwards, and reference to fig. 19 shows that the older generation of oarsmen made full use of this circumstance. But the degree to which the pelvis can be inclined forward is limited. Even on a fixed seat, some considerable part of the swing forward must be accomplished by bending the backbone. In fig. 55 the eight lowest thoracic and the lumbar, sacral, and coccygeal vertebrae are shown in their relation to the pelvis. When the body is upright the lumbar curvature is markedly concave backward. This is due to the fact that the lumbar intervertebral disks are somewhat wedge-shaped in section, being thicker in front than behind, and the vertebral bodies themselves are slightly wedge-shaped, being rather thicker behind than in front. As the slips of origin of the psoas are attached to the contiguous margins of the vertebral bodies as well as to the intervertebral disks the pull of the whole muscle compresses the elastic intervertebral disks, straightens out the lumbar curvature, and brings forward the vertebral column as far and farther than the position shown by the dotted lines in fig. 55. It should be observed that more movement is possible between the last lumbar and the sacral vertebral than between any of the others : in the drawing the forward inclination of the vertebral column is mostly due to the movement between these two. Farther bending forward will be produced by approximating the upper lumbar vertebrae and to some small extent by still farther arching the thoracic region of the spine. It is important to notice that the action of the psoas draws the whole of the lumbar region forwards and downwards, thus ensuring that very desirable accomplishment, a swing forward with a straight back ; and this without any forced effort, but by the use of the muscles intended by nature to produce this movement. The insertion of the ilio-psoas into the small trochanter at the back of the femur causes this bone to be rotated outwards when the muscle contracts, and thus starts the gradual opening of the knees necessary to make room for the stomach as the body swings down.

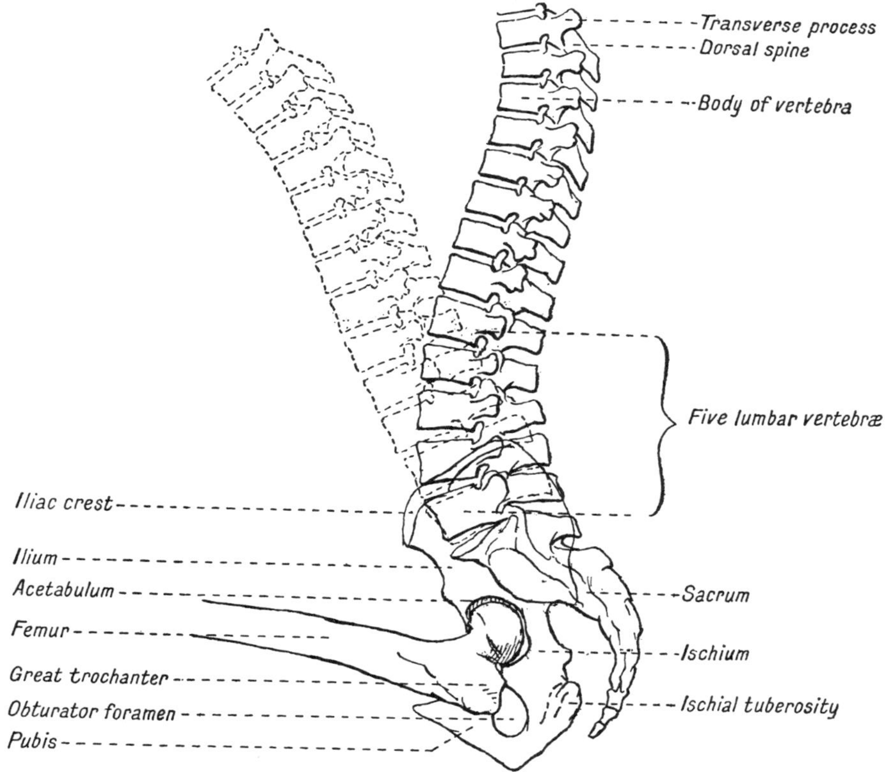

Fig. 55. Illustrates the flexion of the lumbar region of the vertebral column.

As the thigh rises the knee is necessarily bent, but without any great muscular effort. The principal flexors of the knee are the hamstring muscles, but of these only the short head of the biceps cruris need be used in the swing forward. The others tend to rotate the pelvis backwards, in a direction contrary to that in which it should be moving, and their action should be reserved to a later period in the cycle of the stroke. The sartorius muscle, which arises from the anterior superior iliac spine and passes diagonally across the front of the thigh to be inserted on the upper part of the inner surface of the tibia, both flexes the knee and abducts it, that is to say draws it outwards from the middle line. In conjunction with the ilio-psoas, it is instrumental in 'opening the knees' as the oarsman swings and slides forward. The gastrocnemius, or calf muscle, is also a flexor of the knee when the heel is fixed, and is undoubtedly used as such by oarsmen: usefully when they are provided with heel-traps, but in the absence of heel-traps contraction of the gastrocnemius tends to pull the heel away from the stretcher. Many oarsmen do pull their heels away from the stretcher, probably in the effort to use the gastrocnemius as a flexor of the knee. But the gastrocnemius, pulling up the heel-bone, prevents the foot being bent up towards the shin,[1] as it must be when the knees rise and the slide comes forward. This leads to cramped and awkward movement, and, on the whole, the use of the calf muscles is undesirable in rowing. To bend the ankle the muscles on the front of the shin, notably the tibialis anticus, are brought into play. These and other muscles of the leg will be described farther on.

Whilst the lower part of the trunk is being drawn downwards and forwards, the upper part is more or less passively carried forward by it, but the change of position of the trunk involves changes and adjustments in the upper part of the body, chiefly in the shoulders and neck. As the hands and extended arms have to follow the arc described by the handle of the oar the shoulders have to accommodate themselves to the ever-varying positions of the arms, and in addition, in order that the feather may be kept at an even height above the water, the arms have to be elevated at the shoulder-joint exactly in

[1] For reasons too remote to be explained here, anatomists speak of the ankle as being 'flexed' when it is straightened out, as when standing on tiptoe; 'extended', when the toes are lifted up towards the shin. Following the popular usage I shall speak of the ankle as 'straightened' in the former, as 'bent' in the latter position.

proportion to the downward movement of the shoulders as the body swings forward.

The chin is raised and pushed a little forwards by the action of the sterno-mastoid muscles passing from the mastoid process of the skull behind and below the ear to the inner end of the collar-bone. The upper vertebrae of the neck are sufficiently bent back, as I think, by a slight contraction of the upper fibres of the trapezius muscle. I doubt whether the splenii and trachelo-mastoid muscles are of much importance in keeping the head up. No doubt they must contract slightly to sustain the weight of the head and to draw back the upper part of the neck as the body inclines forward, but after a study of a series of film photographs I am satisfied that they are only brought into vigorous use by oarsmen who commit the error of boring their shoulders forward.

In the description of the skeleton it has been explained that the shoulder is attached to the body only by muscles, save for the somewhat precarious articulation of the collar-bone with the sternum. The shoulder can be moved backwards and forwards, elevated and depressed, and in any of these movements the muscles producing action in one direction must be opposed to the required extent by muscles acting in the contrary direction, in order that the shoulder may be steadied and kept in a proper position. These muscles are numerous, and the way in which they co-operate to produce the movements of the shoulder permissible in rowing is difficult to explain. To understand their action it is necessary to remember that, when the body is reached forward to its full extent, and the blade of the oar immersed, the arms are in the same position relatively to the body that they are when, the body being erect, the extended arms are raised until the hands are level with the eyes. Therefore the whole arm is gradually raised at the shoulder as the body swings forward, and gradually depressed at the shoulder as the body swings back. Again, as the hands move first outwards and then inwards on an arc as the body swings forward, and as these movements are reversed as the body swings back, there is a large amount of movement at the shoulder-joint, which must be controlled and directed by appropriate, but not cramped by excessive, muscular action.

Let us first consider the muscles that connect the shoulder-blade and collar-bone with the ribs and vertebral column, and first of all those at the back of the shoulder-blade whose general function it is to draw it back towards the middle line. The deeper muscles, as seen from behind, are illustrated in fig. 56 ; the superficial muscles in fig. 57. The levator anguli scapulae arises from the transverse processes of the four upper cervical vertebrae and is inserted into the upper part of the vertebral border of the scapula. Its action is to elevate the upper angle of the scapula. The rhomboidei, minor and major, arise from the dorsal spines of the seventh cervical and first four or five thoracic vertebrae and are inserted into the vertebral border of the scapula below the levator. Their action is to draw the scapula upwards and towards the middle line. The trapezius (fig. 57) arises from the occipital region of the skull, from the ligamentum nuchae, and from the dorsal spines of the seventh cervical and all the thoracic vertebrae. Its fibres converge towards the shoulder and are inserted into the spine of the scapula and also into the outer third of the collar-bone. It is obvious that the action of the trapezius will differ according as its upper, middle, or lower fibres are contracted. The general direction of the pull is towards the middle line of the back, but the upper fibres act powerfully in pulling the whole shoulder-girdle upwards. On the other side of the scapula, lying between it and the ribs, is the serratus magnus muscle (fig. 65 A). It arises from the sides of the first eight ribs by nine fleshy slips, two of them being attached to the second rib. The uppermost fibres pass nearly horizontally to be inserted into the upper part of the vertebral border of the scapula. The lower slips, from the fourth to the eighth ribs, converge like the sticks of a half-opened fan to be inserted into a rough surface on the inside of, and just above, the lower angle of the scapula. The serratus withdraws the shoulder-blade from the vertebral column, and when the arm is raised from the shoulder enables it to be farther outstretched. On the front of the body the pectoralis minor arises from the sternal ends of the third, fourth, and fifth ribs and is inserted on the coracoid process of the scapula. As it draws the upper end of the scapula forwards and downwards it tends to tilt its lower angle in the opposite direction.

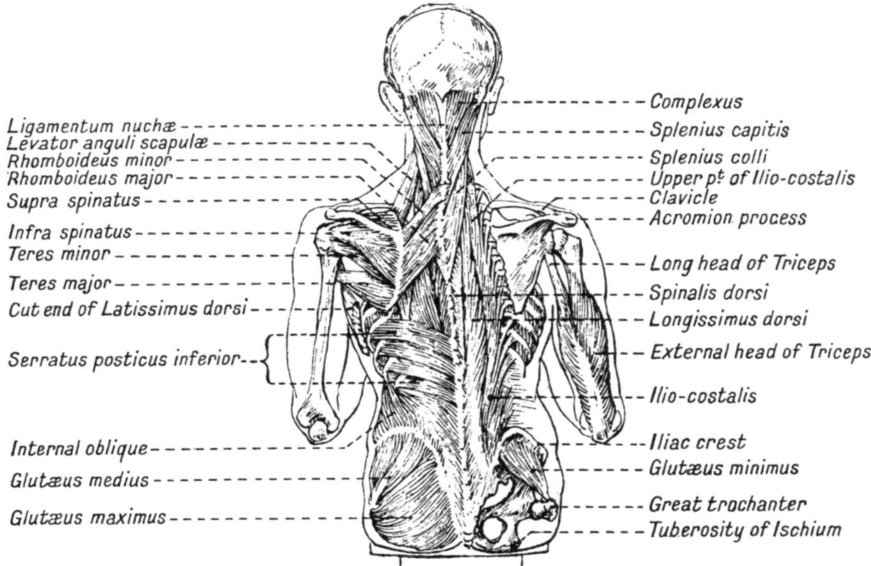

FIG. 56. A deep dissection of the muscles of the back and shoulder. The deeper muscles are shown on the right side, and the vertebral border of the scapula is cut away to show the insertions of the ilio-costalis.

Except for the anterior and upper fibres of the trapezius, already mentioned, the clavicle has few direct muscular attachments to the trunk. There is a small subclavius muscle connecting its lower edge with the junction of the first rib with the breast-bone. Above there is the sterno-mastoid, a prominent muscle of the neck, connecting the breast-bone and the inner end of the clavicle with the mastoid process of the skull.

The muscles connecting the shoulder-girdle and trunk with the upper arm are more numerous, and perhaps, from the oarsman's point of view, more important. Behind the shoulder-blade we find (fig. 56) the supra-spinatus, the infra-spinatus, and the teres minor converging to be inserted into the great tuberosity on the outer side of the top of the humerus. The teres major, arising from near the inferior angle of the scapula, is inserted lower down on the humerus into the inner border of the bicipital groove and therefore towards its front side. The supra-spinatus simply elevates the arm. The infra-spinatus and teres minor pull the arm back, and, at the same time, rotate the humerus outwards. The teres major, being inserted farther from the shoulder-joint, is more efficient in pulling back the arm and tends to rotate it outwards. The subscapularis muscle arises from the inner surface of the shoulder-blade and therefore lies between it and the serratus magnus. Its fibres converge to form a broad tendon inserted into the small tuberosity in front of the humerus. The subscapularis carries the raised arm forwards, but rotates it inwards when brought past the side as at the finish of the stroke.

Here may be mentioned the latissimus dorsi, one of the most important muscles in rowing. It has a very extensive origin, arising from the spines of the four or five lowest thoracic vertebrae, from all the lumbar and the upper two or three sacral vertebrae, from the posterior third of the iliac crest of the pelvis, and from the two or three lowest ribs. The whole muscle is triangular in shape, the fibres converging upwards as they pass round the side of the body and ending at the armpit in a short, flat tendon, inserted into the humerus just above the teres major. The latissimus dorsi pulls the upper arm downwards and backwards, and is, or should be, the chief agent in bringing home the arms at the end of the stroke.

In front of the shoulder we have, in addition to the biceps brachii, the relations of which to the shoulder-joint have already been sufficiently described, the coraco-brachialis and the pectoralis major. The coraco-brachialis, as has been explained on p. 316, elevates the upper arm and comes into action as the hands are shot away and the arm swings upward during the forward movement of the body. The pectoralis major (fig. 59) covers the breast: it arises from the inner third of the clavicle, from the sternum, and from sternal cartilages of the second to sixth ribs; also from the upper part of the aponeurosis

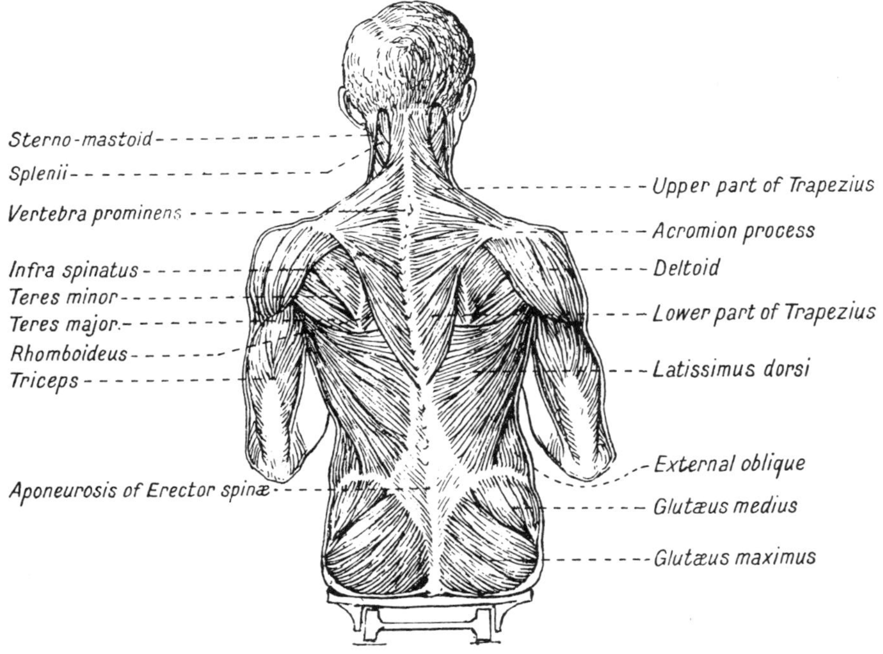

FIG. 57. Superficial muscles of the back and shoulders.

of the external oblique muscle. The fibres, converging like the sticks of a fan, are inserted into the humerus at the outer margin of the bicipital groove. The clavicular fibres of the pectoral tend to raise the upper arm; the lower fibres tend to depress it. Generally, the pectoral tends to draw the upper arm forward, thus acting in opposition to the latissimus dorsi.

The deltoid (fig. 57), a large triangular mass of muscle, covers the shoulder like a cap. It arises from the spine and acromion process of the scapula and from the outer third of the collar-bone. From this extensive origin the fibres converge downwards over the head of the humerus to be inserted into a well-marked *V*-shaped depression about half-way down and rather to the outer side of the front surface of that bone. The fibres of the deltoid are divisible into a posterior group, arising from the spine of the scapula ; a middle group, arising from the acromion process ; and an anterior group, arising from the tip of the acromion and the clavicle. The two latter groups assist the coraco-brachialis in elevating and sustaining the upper arm in front of the body. Contraction of the whole muscle, one of the commonest causes of bad oarsmanship, stiffens the shoulder and prevents any freedom of movement of the upper arm.

With all the muscles operating in their several ways on the shoulder-joint and interacting with one another, an analysis of what happens, or ought to happen, during the swing forward is far from easy. But we may save ourselves the trouble of too minute an inquiry, for there is, or ought to be, very little muscular effort of the shoulders at this phase, unless the oarsman is rowing against a strong wind. The arms are largely supported on the oar, their weight being just about sufficient to balance its outboard weight. The impetus given to the oar by the wrists at the recovery needs no further acceleration, but rather the reverse. None the less, the arms are not simply passive, but have to guide and keep control over the movement of the oar. The most important thing is the adjustment of the shoulders as the hands follow the arc described by the handle of the oar. The amount of adjustment required and the constantly changing position of the arms relative to the body are not, I think, generally or sufficiently clearly recognized. To avoid a tediously long description I have given in fig. 58 drawings of three different positions during the swing forward. Though the figures are diagrammatic they are carefully drawn to scale, and one of them is based upon a photograph taken vertically above an oarsman posed for this purpose. In *A* the oarsman has just completed the recovery: the body is vertical and the oar is at right angles to the side of the boat. The shoulders are nearly parallel with the thwartship plane. The left, or inside, hand is opposite the right breast, and it should be noted that the measurement between the inside hand and shoulder-joint is greater than the corresponding measurement in the outside arm. Consequently the outside elbow is somewhat bent, a feature which can be recognized in any crew that has been snapshotted in the act of recovering. Here it is clear that the inside arm has been drawn across the front of the body, an action very appropriately performed by the coraco-brachialis muscle. But the outer arm is drawn away from the body, for which purpose the outer fibres of the deltoid, viz. those attached to the spine of the scapula, must come into play; perhaps also the supra-spinatus muscle. In *B* the oarsman is about half-way through the swing and slide forward. The oar is at an angle of 35° to the thwartship plane and the hands are just about equidistant from the median line drawn through the body of the oarsman. The position of the arms is such that they are naturally slung from the shoulders by the coraco-brachiales muscles, but now the outside arm has to reach a considerably greater distance than the inside arm. It is just about at this time that the oarsman

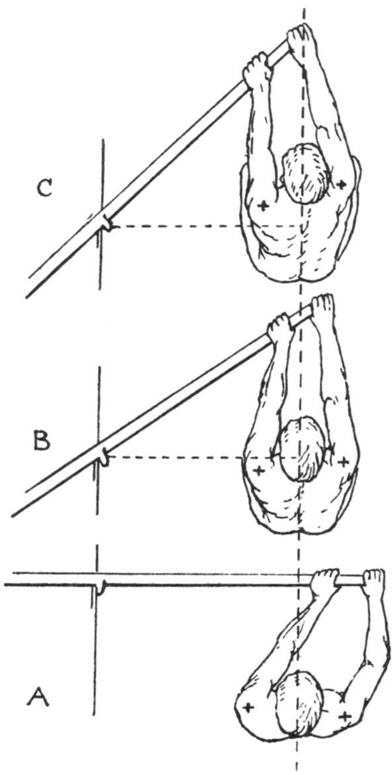

FIG. 58. Three positions in the swing forward as seen from above, showing the changing attitudes of the arms and shoulders.

turns his oar off the feather by raising the inside wrist. This does something to compensate for the extra distance to be bridged over by the outside arm ; but not all that is necessary, if the outside fingers are to retain their hold on the oar. The outside shoulder must come a little forward. In *C* the oarsman has arrived at nearly, if not quite, his full reach forward. The oar is at an angle of 45° to the thwartship plane ; many reach out still farther up to 48° or even 50°. The outside hand is now to the inside of the median line, the inside arm stretched out nearly straight from the shoulder. The difference between the distances to be reached across by the outside and inside arms is still farther increased, and this difference can only be compensated by still farther advancing the outside shoulder. In this drawing the positions of the shoulder-joints, marked by crosses, were accurately determined in a photograph taken from the living model. He was not overreaching, but the angle at which the shoulders are inclined to the thwartship plane is considerable, amounting in this case to 20°. It should be observed that, in comparison with *B*, the inside shoulder in *C* is relatively thrust back. The necessary advancement of the outside shoulder should be effected, and by a finished and shapely oarsman is effected, mainly by the action of the serratus magnus. This muscle, illustrated in fig. 65 A, draws forward without unduly elevating the shoulder, and incidentally, by raising and expanding the eight upper ribs to which it is attached, assists in dilating the chest during the inspiratory act that accompanies the swing forward. But, as is shown in fig. 65 A, the lower elements of the serratus pull the shoulder-blade downwards, and it is evident that the action of the whole muscle is such that, if it were not counterbalanced by other muscles, the shoulder-blade would be dragged out of place. The two rhomboidei and the levator anguli scapulae (fig. 56) take their share in steadying the shoulder-blade, but by far the most important muscle, whether it be rightly or wrongly used, is the trapezius. If we sit erect with the arms extended in front of the body in the attitude of an oarsman, we can raise the arms as high as the shoulder by the use of the deltoid muscles. But no farther. If we want to raise the arms above the shoulder the upper fibres of the trapezii must be brought into action, and anybody can assure himself of this by feeling the slope of his shoulder with the hand of the opposite side as he raises the extended arm above the horizontal. But, it may be objected, no oarsman wants to raise his arms above the horizontal. Wait a moment. Extend both arms horizontally in front of the body and, keeping them exactly in that position, bend forward the body as in the swing forward. Down go the arms and hands, and if one were in a boat and holding an oar, up would go the feather sky high. As the body swings down in rowing the arms have to swing upwards, well beyond the limit to which they can be lifted by the deltoids. This extra elevation is given by the use of the upper fibres of the trapezii. As the body swings down gradually, so should the trapezii contract gradually; so proportioning their effort to the downward movement of the body as to maintain the collar-bone and shoulder-blade (for the fibres of the trapezius are attached to both) in a position which allows the arm to swing without constraint from the shoulder-joint, and to maintain just that amount of pressure on the oar which is required to keep the blade level on the feather. When we come to work it out we find that 'light hands' really mean a nicely graduated action of the trapezii: muscles situated in the shoulder and the back. At two points, one during the swing forward, the other at the end of it, the trapezii are called upon to do just a little more. When the oar is turned off the feather, an operation performed mainly by the inside wrist, the wrist and forearm should be slightly raised as the appropriate flexor muscles[1] bend the wrist and so turn the oar off the feather. We say the wrist and forearm should be raised: really the whole arm has to be raised from the

[1] The appropriate muscles are the flexores carpi radialis and carpi ulnaris and the palmaris longus. The flexors of the digits are already in contraction to keep the fingers hooked round the handle of the oar. The flexor of the thumb is brought into use to slightly tighten the grasp as the oar is turned off the feather. I do not propose to go farther into detail about these muscles.

shoulder. In the position that the arm is already in this can only be done by a little extra lift of the trapezius. Similarly 'raising the hands over the stretcher' means that the whole weight of the arms

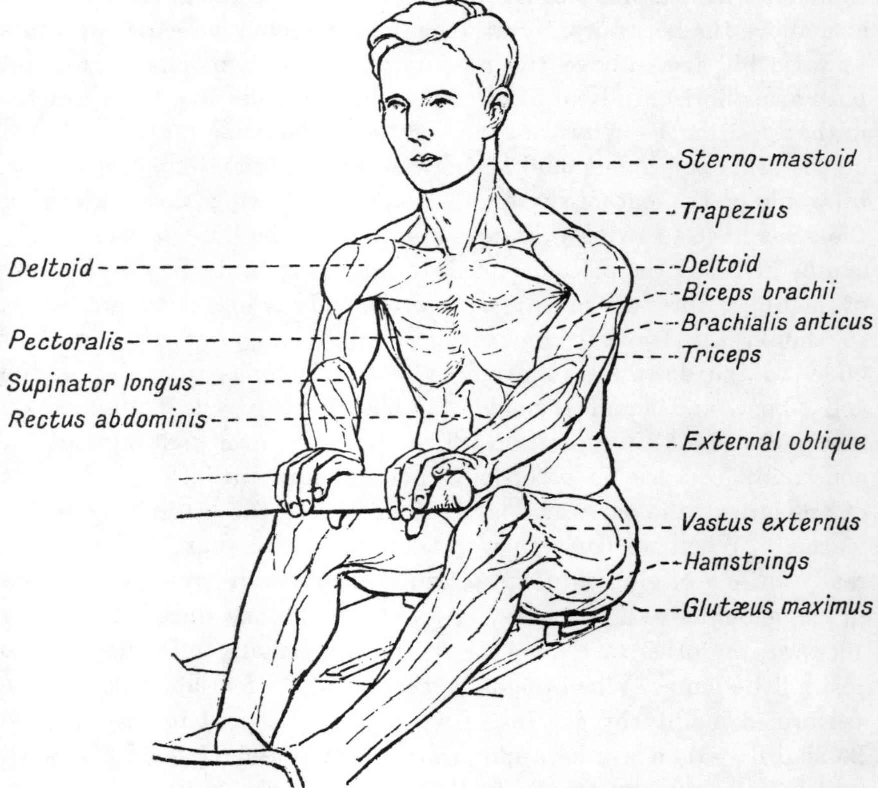

Fig. 59. The swing forward.

is taken off the handle of the oar. In other words, they must be still farther elevated, and this, again, involves a little extra effort on the part of the trapezii. It must not be forgotten, in this connexion, that whilst the trapezius is supporting and lifting the elements of the shoulder-girdle, viz. the collar-bone and shoulder-bone, the deltoid, the coraco-brachialis, and to a certain extent the biceps, are holding up the arm from the shoulder-girdle. Many oarsmen, I think, use the biceps too much for this purpose and therefore come forward with crooked arms. Many oarsmen, and very good oarsmen too, make use of the clavicular fibres of the pectoralis major to advance the outer shoulder at the beginning of the swing forward, as illustrated in figs.

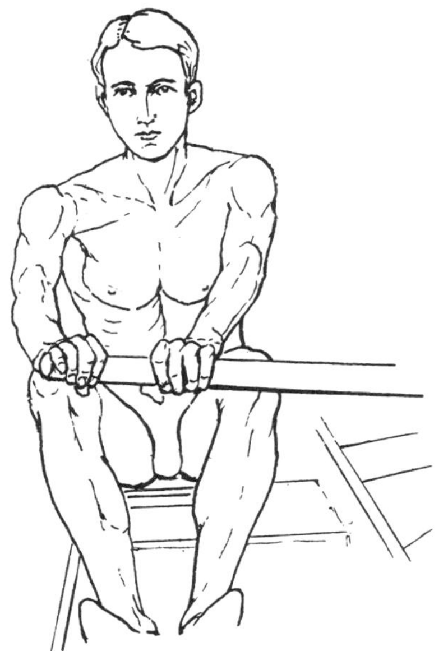

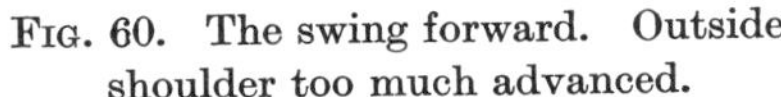

FIG. 60. The swing forward. Outside shoulder too much advanced.

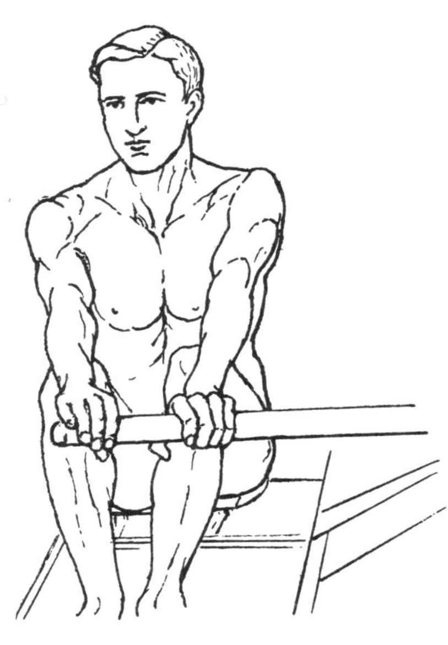

FIG. 61. The swing forward. Arms straight, shoulders square.

59 and 60, but I cannot think this action is desirable. It is always associated with a bent outer elbow and, as in both the models who sat for these figures the trapezius of the outer shoulder is obviously in a state of contraction, I suspect that the pectoral is called into use to counteract the too great elevating action of the former muscle. Fig. 61, a photograph of an old-fashioned oarsman who has shot his

arms out straight in a manner seldom seen nowadays, shows that the use of the pectoralis major is quite superfluous. The outer arm in this case is held up from the shoulder by the coraco-brachialis, and the clavicular fibres of the deltoid and the pectorals are lax.

I have elsewhere warned oarsmen against exaggerated action. Fig. 31 D, taken from a cinema film of a prominent contemporary heavy-weight oarsman, is a good example of the exaggerated use of the trapezius muscles during the swing forward. The crew was only paddling at 22 strokes a minute, so the attitude may be taken as normal for the oarsman in question and is not due to exhaustion or to more than an ordinary effort during a hard row. The oarsman is about half-way forward, and exhibits a number of lapses of form common to powerfully built men who have not learned their rowing in boyhood. The stomach is hollowed by the contraction of the rectus abdominis muscles which have been used to bring the body forward. Consequently the chest has been dragged down, and the dorsum of the back is greatly arched. As the ilio-psoas group of muscles has not been used to recover the body, the line of the lower part of the back is vertical, and it is evident that the body is not being swung forward from the hip-joints. In order to secure his reach forward the oarsman is pushing forward with both shoulders, contracting the trapezii to such an extent that the shoulders are lifted towards the ears, and the neck is buried between them. The attitude is that of a typical round-backed oarsman and is faulty in almost every respect. Among other disadvantages the indrawn abdomen prevents the free descent of the diaphragm and is a hindrance to a full intake of air into the lungs during the recovery. All these deficiencies may be compensated by a magnificent physique, great muscular power, and great length of limb. But an oarsman who comes forward in this position can never get a really quick hold at the beginning of the stroke, can never properly couple up his leg-work with his body-swing, and is bound to exhaust himself unduly in a hard race. By way of contrast I have given in fig. 31 A a drawing of a fellow-oarsman taken from the same picture on the film and therefore at exactly the same point of the stroke. This individual enjoys, and deservedly enjoys, the reputation of being one of the most accomplished of present-day oarsmen. The back, by no means rigidly straight, shows an even curve from the seat. The hips have been brought forward by the action of the ilio-psoas muscles. The recti abdominis are relaxed and the stomach bulges forward as the diaphragm descends. Note that the oarsman has his mouth wide open to take in a deep breath during the forward swing. The outside shoulder is advanced, but not excessively, and it is elevated just to the required extent. The whole attitude is easy and restful, as it should be during the phase of the stroke in which there is no hard work to be done.

Fig. 20 is drawn from a photograph of a famous pre-war oarsman not distinguished for the elegance of his movements. It has caught him at the extreme forward limit of his swing, and I think it may stand for the longest swing forward possible on a sixteen-inch slide. Here we have the typical overreach characteristic of many oarsmen of that period. The head and neck are thrust forward in order that the outside shoulder may be advanced as far as possible by the action of the trapezius. It is probable, though it is impossible to determine the point, that the shoulder-blade is being pulled forward as far as it will go by the action of the pectoralis minor on the coracoid process. Note that the hands are on a level with the nose and that in a moment they must be elevated still farther, for the photograph shows that the blades have not yet entered the water. Without a doubt the thrust forward of the shoulders is exaggerated and entails an extra effort on the part of the oarsman without any sufficient degree of compensation in the little extra length of stroke obtained. Yet this is what may be called a legitimate overreach (if any exaggeration in oarsmanship is legitimate), for it is not a substitute for a deficient swing forward of the body from the hip-joints, but only an extension—a needless extension perhaps—of a very long body-swing. Cover the upper part of the figure with the hand and it will be seen that the hips are well inclined forwards and the small of the back is flat and pressed far down towards the thighs. The greater part of a very long reach has been obtained, as it should be, by the powerful and continued use of the ilio-psoas muscles. They are the true recovery muscles, and reference to fig. 65 A should sufficiently convince any one who may entertain a doubt on the subject how efficient they are in bringing the lower part of the backbone as near to the thighs as the conformation of the body permits.

The muscles that bring the oarsman forward and enable him to maintain the required degree of guidance and control over the oar have been sufficiently described. We now come to the all-important part of the stroke when great rapidity of movement is necessary; a large amount of resistance has to be overcome; and every available muscle suitable to the performance of the required work must be brought into action. The muscles of the legs, of the back, of the shoulders, but only to a very minor degree those of the arms, are all involved. It is required to straighten the back; to forcibly extend the hip- and knee-joints; to draw back the shoulders; and finally to bend the elbows and draw back the upper arm.

The muscles that straighten and lift up the back are known collectively as the erector spinae group. Those of the right side of the body are shown in fig. 56. They are segmental muscles; that is to say, they are related to, and to a large extent act separately on, each of the segments of which the trunk is primarily composed; these segments being represented by the vertebrae and, in the thoracic region, by the ribs attached to them. Being attached to so many separate bones, the erector spinae muscles are exceedingly complicated, and several component parts are recognized and named by anatomists. For present purposes it is only necessary to distinguish the large mass of muscle lying on each side of the back, in the groove between the dorsal spines of the vertebrae and the angles of the ribs, and extending from the sacrum and hip-bones up to the neck and head (fig. 56, p. 329). It begins below in a broad strong tendon arising from the back part of the iliac bone, from the sacrum, and from the dorsal spines of the sacral and lumbar vertebrae. An external group of muscular fibres originates from the posterior fifth of the iliac crest. In the lumbar region the muscular mass divides into two longitudinal columns. The outer, called the ilio-costalis (also known as the sacro-lumbalis), runs up the back of the ribs towards the neck. In its course, on the one hand, it sends out external offshoots which are inserted on the ribs ; on the other hand, it is reinforced by additions in the form of muscular slips arising from the ribs. The general plan is that the muscular slips arising from the lower ribs are inserted into the upper ribs, and the slips arising from the upper ribs are inserted into the transverse processes of the lower vertebrae of the neck. The inner column of muscle is known as the longissimus dorsi. Starting from the broad tendon in the sacral region it gives off a series of offshoots both inwardly and outwardly. The former are inserted in regular series into the lumbar vertebrae, and into the transverse processes of the thoracic vertebrae : the latter into the transverse processes of the lumbar vertebrae and the inner ends of the nine or ten lowest ribs. In the neck the longissimus dorsi is continued into the transversalis cervicis and trachelo-mastoid muscles, both built on the same plan as the upper continuation of the ilio-costalis ; that is to say, they are formed of a number of muscular bands which unite vertebrae lower down in the series with vertebrae higher up in the series. The slips of the trachelo-mastoid pass from the lower neck vertebrae to the mastoid process of the skull. A third element of the erector spinae group, the spinalis dorsi, connects the dorsal spines of the two uppermost lumbar and the two lowest thoracic vertebrae with a number of the higher thoracic spines. The united action of all these muscular bands contracting together on both sides of the back is very powerful. It has been stated that the pull of the erector spinae in straightening the back from the bent position, as measured by the muscular dynamometer, varies in persons of medium strength from 200 to 400 lb. This, I think, is an over-estimate, for in my laboratory at Oxford, out of some 1,500 undergraduates who submitted themselves to measurement, the average strength of pull was 220 lb. and the strongest pull recorded 385 lb. The instrument measured the strength of pull exerted by a man stooping down as if to lift a weight placed between his feet, and from this position he could bring into action several groups of muscles in addition to the spinal erectors.

Fig. 57 shows sufficiently clearly how the spinal erectors in the neck are overlaid by the splenius capitis and splenius colli muscles, which, in conjunction with the trachelo-mastoid, bend back the head and neck : but if the muscles of one side only are used, bend the neck laterally, and cause rotation of the head on the axis vertebra.

Space and the fear of wearying the reader by a too great profusion of anatomical description prevent more than the bare mention of the extremely complicated, deeply seated muscles underlying the spinal erectors. Generally speaking, they may be described as groups of muscular bundles passing from vertebra to vertebra ; some of the most important of them connecting the transverse processes with the neural spines, not of adjacent vertebrae, but of vertebrae some four or five places higher up in the series. The united action of all these muscular bundles, when those of both sides of the back are contracted, is to hold the vertebrae together and to give a certain figure and rigidity to the back. As they receive a nerve supply somewhat different from that of the spinal erectors, they presumably act independently of them and are probably important agents in maintaining the proper poise of the body during the swing forward. During this movement the oarsman is exhorted to relax the muscles of his back, but at the same time is told to sit up and not to slouch. The explanation of these apparently contradictory orders is, that the function of the spinal erectors is to straighten the bent back, and therefore they must be relaxed to allow the back to be bent forward to the extent shown in figs. 20 and 34. But the deeper-seated muscles, such as the semispinalis and the multifidus spinae, are normally concerned in the maintenance of the erect posture when there is no external work to be done, and, as the body bends forward, they are subjected to a certain amount of strain and resist it to just the extent required to maintain the proper poise and balance of the trunk.

The great extensors of the hip-joint are the buttock muscles, or glutaei, passing from the iliac bone and sacrum to the thigh. They are three in number on each side : the glutaeus maximus, the glutaeus medius, and the glutaeus minimus. Their general arrangements are best seen from behind as in figs. 56 and 57. The glutaeus minimus, the most deeply seated of the three, arises from a broad curved surface on the outer and hinder side of the iliac bone, its fibres converging to form a tendon inserted on the anterior border of the great trochanter of the thigh-bone. The glutaeus medius arises from the anterior three-fourths of the iliac crest and part of the outer surface of the ilium above the glutaeus minimus. Its fibres converge as they descend and terminate in a fan-shaped tendon inserted on the outer surface of the great trochanter. The glutaeus maximus, a thick, broad band of muscle forming the greater part of the buttock, arises from the posterior fourth of the iliac crest ; from the aponeurosis of the erector spinae muscles ; from the sacrum and coccyx and from the great sacro-sciatic ligament which runs from the sacrum and coccyx to the tuberosity of the ischium. The deeper layer of fibres of the lower half of the muscle are inserted into a rough surface on the lower and outer side of the thigh-bone, below the great trochanter. The more superficial fibres of the lower half, and all the fibres of the upper half, are inserted into a strong band of tendon which covers the great trochanter and is continued down the outside of the thigh as a tough sheet of tendon known as the fascia lata. The ilio-tibial band, conspicuous against the contracted muscles of the thigh in figs. 65 and 66, is a specially strong tendinous portion of the fascia lata which runs down the side of the thigh, across the knee-joint, and is inserted into the outside of the anterior tuberosity on the upper front surface of the tibia or shin-bone. When the extensor muscles of the thigh are in action the ilio-tibial band is pulled tight by the action of a special muscle, the tensor fasciae femoris, which arises from the anterior angle of the iliac crest and is inserted into the ilio-tibial band just below—in the sitting position just in front of —the glutaeus medius.

The glutaeus maximus is the chief extensor of the hip-joint, its action being to bring the bent-up thigh into a line with the body. It is of the utmost importance to oarsmen because on the full use of it depends the powerful lift back of the hips which couples up the work of the erector spinae and thigh muscles. But its action, when the thigh-joint is flexed to the extreme degree that it is in the full forward position in rowing, is by no means easy to understand, and I have made a special drawing (fig. 62), which I hope will make its action comprehensible. When the thighs are so much flexed that the knees are in the armpits, the glutaeus maximus is stretched to its fullest extent : in this position it must tend to act as an abductor as well as an external rotator of the thigh. If the thigh-bone is fixed by the action of other muscles, contraction of the lower fibres of the glutaeus maximus must pull the sacrum forcibly in the direction of the upper part of the thigh and therefore extends the hip. But if the knee is allowed to bend and the thigh-bone is allowed free play, contraction of these fibres must aid in pulling down the thigh, with the result that the sliding-seat is driven backwards. The oarsman will ‘ shoot his slide ’. Therefore there is a right way and a wrong way of using the glutaeus maximus, the right way depending on the simultaneous contraction of other muscles whose use and relations must be described farther on.

Photographs show that the glutaeus medius is strongly contracted throughout the greater part of the stroke. No doubt its action is assisted by the glutaeus minimus. Both these muscles are powerful abductors of the thigh, and in walking or running come principally into action in supporting the body on the limb which is at the moment in contact with the ground. In rowing I imagine that their principal use is to steady and fix the upper end of the thigh-bone ; their abducting action being balanced by the adductor muscles of the thigh. The posterior fibres of both muscles probably also aid in extending the hip-joint at the beginning of the stroke, for, as may be seen in side view in fig. 66 A, when the thigh is bent upwards the great trochanter, into which these two muscles are inserted, is depressed well below the level of the acetabulum. I leave out of account the consideration of a number of muscles, the pyriformis, obturator internus, gemelli, and quadratus femoris, which originate mostly from the inner surface of the pelvis and are inserted into the great trochanter. Their arrangement is too complicated to make clear to any but a skilled anatomist, and they are subsidiary muscles whose chief function is to support

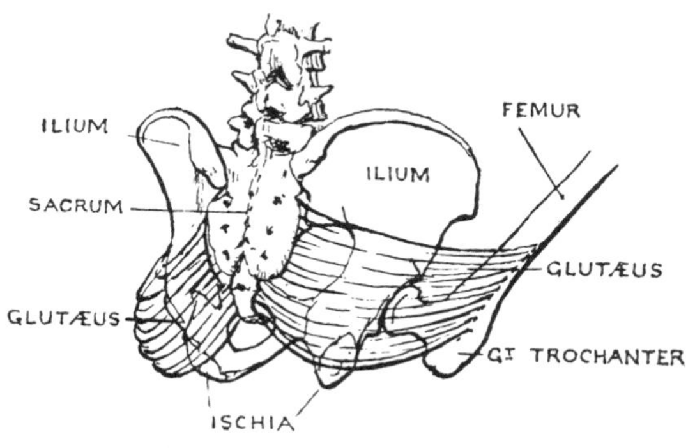

FIG. 62. Shows the deeper fibres of the glutaeus maximus muscle when the hip-joint is strongly flexed and the thighs abducted.

and steady the hip-joint. They also assist in lifting back the hip-bones when the thigh is strongly flexed at the beginning of the stroke. The obturator externus is a flexor and adductor of the thigh, and is probably brought into use in the swing forward.

The muscles of the thigh fall naturally into three groups: the extensors, mostly on the front and outside; the flexors at the back, and the adductors on the inside of the thigh.

The extensor muscles are collectively known by the name of the quadriceps extensor femoris (fig. 54). Three of its subdivisions, the vastus externus, the vastus internus, and the crureus (the last named is really only a deeper portion of the vastus internus), take their origin from the rough line extending for nearly the whole length of the back of the thigh-bone and from almost the whole length of its front and inner side. They form prominent muscular masses; the vastus externus on the whole length of the upper and outer side, the vastus internus on the lower half of the inside of the thigh. Their tendons unite below with that of the rectus femoris and are inserted into the knee-cap, beyond which they are continued into the ligamentum patellae, a short thick tendon inserted into the prominent anterior tubercle at the upper end of the shin-bone. The rectus femoris muscle arises by two tendons from the hip-bone and passes straight down the front of the thigh to the knee-cap. It is obvious that the two vasti, with the crureus, simply straighten out the knee-joint. The rectus femoris, when the pelvis is fixed, also straightens out the knee-joint, but when the thigh is fixed it pulls the hip forward, as has been explained on p. 320. The flexor muscles or hamstrings on the back of the leg are three in number. On the outer side the biceps cruris; on the inner side a group of two known as the semitendinosus and semimembranosus. Their arrangement is sufficiently well shown in fig. 63. Arising close together from the tuberosity of the ischium, they diverge below: the biceps cruris to be inserted into the head of the fibula: the two others to be inserted into the upper part of the inner side of the tibia. That part of the biceps arising from the ischium is known as its long head: its short head arises from the lower half of the rough line on the back of the thigh-bone, and joins the tendon of the long head. The short head of the biceps simply bends the knee: it is of importance, not only in bringing the slide forward, but more especially in fixing the knee at the moment that the hips are lifted back at the beginning of the stroke. The long head of the biceps and the two other hamstring muscles bend the knee when the hip is fixed, but extend the hip when the knee is fixed. The action of the hamstrings varies a good deal in different bodily movements. For example, in landing on the feet after a jump, the hamstrings bend the knees to reduce the shock of landing and simultaneously extend the hip to assist the body in recovering its balance. But in the act of springing up after stooping down to make a jump, the hamstrings forcibly extend the hips while the knees are being extended, and this is their action throughout the stroke in rowing. The reader should refer to figs. 66 A, 67 A, and 68 A, noting the increasing degree to which the pelvis is

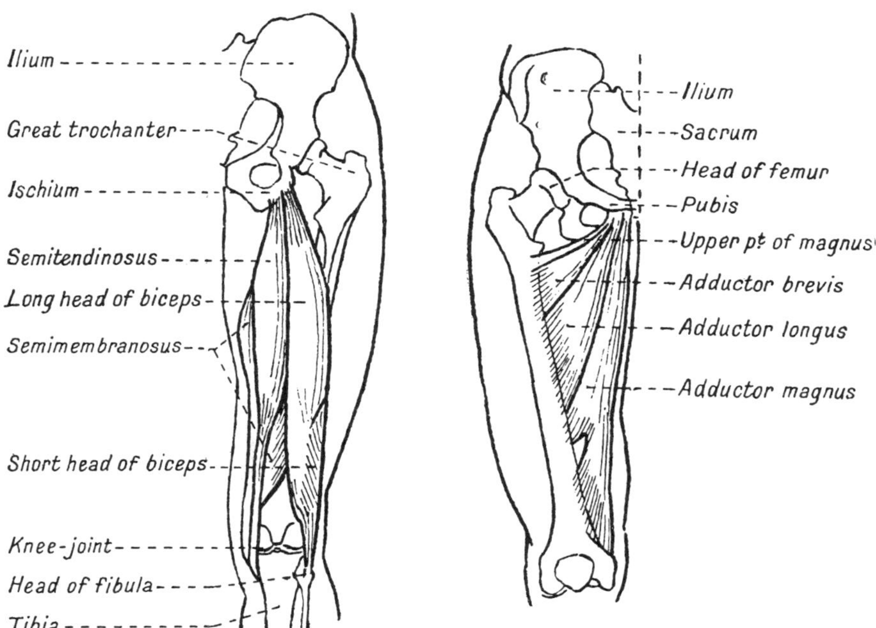

FIG. 63. The hamstring muscles.

FIG. 64. The adductor muscles of the thigh.

tilted back (' extended ') and how largely this is effected by the pull of the hamstrings (of which only the biceps cruris can be shown in the figures) on the tuberosity of the ischium. Their action will be considered in greater detail when the co-operation of the various groups of muscles used during the stroke is described.

Of the adductor muscles of the thigh, the pectineus, the adductor brevis, and the adductor longus pass from the pubic bone of the pelvis to the back of the thigh-bone. The adductor magnus takes its origin from the ischium as well as from the pubis, and is inserted along the whole length of the rough line at the back of the thigh-bone, its more internal portion, originating from the ischium, being continued into a tendon which is inserted into a prominence on the inner condyle of the thigh-bone. The gracilis is a more slender muscle, arising from near the union of the two pubic bones, and tapering to a long tendon which passes down the inside of the thigh and is inserted, in close proximity to the tendons of the sartorius and semitendinosus muscles, into the inner surface of the upper part of the tibia. The exact relations of the adductor muscles are not easily explained or illustrated, as some are overlaid by others, and the fibres of the adductor magnus twist round from their origin to their insertion in a manner requiring a longer description than can be given here. For present purposes fig. 64 shows sufficiently well the arrangement of the chief adductors. They draw the thigh inwards and thus oppose the abducting action of the glutaei. The two opposing groups of muscles contracting together serve to steady the thigh. When the thighs are bent up at the beginning of the stroke, the adductors, and particularly the ischial fibres of the adductor magnus, must act powerfully in assisting to extend the hips and, if I may judge from their great development in some individuals, are largely used for this purpose by many oarsmen. Some use them to such an extent that they clap their knees together at the beginning of the stroke, but to do this they must relax the more important and powerful glutaei, and such oarsmen never attain to a high degree of efficiency in the use of their legs. It should be observed, however, that as the thighs are drawn inwards during the stroke the adductors must in all cases take some, and that not an unimportant, share in the leg-work.

In photographs taken of oarsmen in action one cannot fail to be struck by the strongly contracted state of the muscles on the front and outer side of the lower leg. They are concerned in bending the ankle-joint and in maintaining the pressure of the foot upon the stretcher, but their precise action in an oarsman who is rowing, as he should row, without undue reliance on his toe-straps, is rather baffling. From the very beginning of the stroke the oarsman should 'drive his heels into the stretcher'. Now there is no muscle which acts directly on the heel in such a manner as to drive it into the stretcher. The oarsman can only keep the heel down by bending the foot up towards the shin by the use of the extensor muscles situated on the front and outer side of the shin (see fig. 65 A). Of these the most important is the tibialis anticus, which arises from the outer tuberosity and outer surface of the shaft of the tibia, and from the strong membrane connecting the tibia with the fibula. As it descends towards the ankle its tendon crosses over from the outside to the inside of the leg, passes under the tendinous anklet known as the anterior annular ligament, and is inserted into the innermost of the distal row of ankle-bones (the inner cuneiform bone) and the base of the metatarsal bone of the great toe. Its function is simply to bend the ankle-joint, and by itself it does not bend up the toes. Alongside, and to the outer side of it, are the extensors of the toes. The great toe has its own extensor arising from the front surface of the fibula and the interosseous membrane between it and the tibia. Its tendon, passing between that of the tibialis anticus and the long extensor of the toes, is held down to the ankle by the annular ligament, and runs along the upper side of the great toe to be inserted into its last or ungual phalanx. The long extensor of the toes arises from the outer tuberosity of the tibia and the upper three-fourths of the shaft of the fibula. Its tendon, after passing under the annular ligament, divides into four slips which are inserted into the phalanges of the four outer toes. The long extensors co-operate with the tibialis anticus in bending up the foot. When there are straps to offer resistance they aid materially in bending the ankle, but if straps are dispensed with, they pull the toes away from the stretcher and the work of bending the ankle is thrown exclusively, as in any case it should be mainly, on the tibialis anticus. There are short extensor muscles of the toes taking their origin from the outer surface of the anterior part of the heel-bone. They are brought into active use by oarsmen who pull unduly hard at their toe-straps and, as they are detrimental to good rowing, I neither figure nor describe them.

Photographs show that the peroneal group of muscles on the outside of the leg are also strongly contracted for the greater part of the stroke. The peroneus longus and peroneus brevis are illustrated semi-diagrammatically in fig. 66 A. The former arises from the head and upper two-thirds of the shaft of the fibula. About half-way down the leg it ends in a long tendon which passes behind the projecting lower extremity of the fibula known as the external malleolus, turns forwards and downwards to the outer border of the foot, where it enters a groove on the under surface of the cuboid bone of the ankle. Thence it passes across the sole of the foot and is inserted into the lower side of the inner cuneiform bone and the base of the metatarsal bone of the great toe. The peroneus brevis arises from the lower two-thirds of the shaft of the fibula. Its tendon passes, along with that of the peroneus longus, behind the external malleolus, turns forward along the outer side of the foot, and is inserted into the base of the metatarsal bone of the little toe. The peroneus tertius (fig. 65 A) is a small muscle, anatomically belonging to the extensor group. It originates from the lower fourth of the shaft of the fibula, and its tendon, after passing under the annular ligament, is inserted on the upper surface of the metatarsal bone of the little toe. The peroneus tertius partly aids in bending up the ankle, but it also raises the outer border of the foot and draws it outwards. The peroneus longus and brevis straighten out the ankle-joint, but also act along with the peroneus tertius in raising and drawing outwards the outer border of the foot, an action which is greatly assisted by the tendon of the peroneus longus passing underneath the sole of the foot and pulling down the base of the great toe. The peronei are of great importance in keeping the feet in their proper position on the stretcher, and in so doing they act in opposition to the tibialis anticus, which raises and draws inwards the inner border of the foot. Many oarsmen, by failing to balance this action of the tibialis anticus by the use of the peronei, turn in the toes and lift the inside of the foot from the stretcher during the swing forward and during the first half of the stroke, thereby greatly weakening their drive from the stretcher. It is one of the advantages of learning to row without straps that it compels the oarsman to bring the peronei into use. As is so often the case, it is extremely difficult, if not impossible, to make him realize the existence and use of these muscles by a direct effort of will.

As the knees are flattened and the slide driven back during the stroke the ankles, which were bent up towards the shins (but not nearly to so great an extent as is generally supposed), are gradually straightened out until, at the end of the stroke, the feet are as nearly in a straight line with the shins as they will go. This straightening out of the ankle-joint, accompanied by pressure of the soles of the feet against the stretcher, should be effected mainly by the deeply seated flexor muscles, which, being covered over and concealed by the great muscles of the calf, are ignored and seldom properly used. These flexors are the opposites and almost the counterparts of the extensors. The tibialis posticus arises from nearly the whole of the interosseous membrane between the tibia and fibula, and from the adjacent surfaces of those two bones. Its muscular fibres end in a strong flat tendon which turns forward in a groove below the internal malleolus of the tibia, and is inserted into a prominent tubercle on the lower and inner surface of the scaphoid bone of the ankle. The tibialis posticus presses the sole of the foot against the stretcher without raising the heel, and therefore does exactly what is required in rowing ; but it also, in conjunction with the tibialis anticus, raises and draws inwards the inner border of the foot, so its action in this respect has to be neutralized by the peronei. The long flexors of the four smaller toes and of the great toe, arising respectively from the posterior face of the tibia and from the posterior face of the fibula, repeat to a large extent on the inner side of the ankle and on the sole of the foot the arrangement of the long extensors on the outer side of the ankle and instep of the foot. They also press down the toes and sole of the foot against the stretcher without raising the heel, and are much more useful to oarsmen than the larger and more superficial muscles of the calf. These last, the gastrocnemius and the soleus (fig. 68 A), terminate below in the strong tendo Achillis, which is inserted into the posterior projection of the heel-bone. The gastrocnemius arises from the lower end of the thigh-bone by two heads, one above each of the condyles. The soleus, a broad flat muscle underlying the gastrocnemius, arises from the posterior surface of the upper part of the tibia and fibula, its tendon uniting with that of the gastrocnemius to form the tendo Achillis. Acting together these two muscles lift the heel from the ground and raise the body on the toes. They may possibly come into use at the very end of the stroke, when the foot is straightened out to the same extent as it is when, in a standing position, the body s raised on tiptoe. But at the beginning and in the middle of the stroke they should on no account be used, as they pull the heel away from the stretcher, and weaken the straight drive down from the knee to the stretcher along the axis of the tibia. Many, probably the majority of oarsmen, do use the calf muscles and fail to keep their heels in contact with the stretcher. It is a fault only to be cured by persevering practice without straps, and the oarsman who has acquired the habit of using his calf muscles betrays himself by floundering terribly when he is first deprived of the artificial means of tying his feet down to the surface he is to get his purchase from. The gastrocnemius, used by itself, acts as a flexor of the knee when the ankle-joint is fixed by the anterior muscles of the leg ; this is an additional reason for not bringing this muscle into use at the beginning of the stroke, for it counteracts the thrust down of the knee produced by the action of the extensor muscles of the thigh. Even during the slide forward the gastrocnemius should not be used, as it tends to pull the heel away from the stretcher. The only possible use of this powerful and conspicuous muscle is to momentarily assist in fixing the knee at the very beginning of the stroke, and even that, I think, is best left to the short head of the biceps cruris.

We have now considered in detail all the muscles that can be used by the oarsman to overcome the resistance offered by the boat during the stroke through the water. We have still to consider how they may be used in combination, or in sequence, to the greatest possible advantage. Let it be clearly understood at the outset, in combination rather than in sequence, simultaneously rather than in succession. The time during which the blade of the oar is immersed and doing work in the water is short even at a slow rate of stroke. At forty strokes per minute it is less than half a second, and there is not time to deliberately shift the burden from one group of muscles to another, even if it were desirable to do so. In order to appreciate what follows the reader should first examine carefully the four drawings, figs. 65 to 68, illustrating four successive positions during the stroke in which the muscular prominences, as shown in the photographs from which the drawings were made, are purposely over-emphasized. He should compare with these figs. 65 A to 68 A, in which some of the most important muscles brought into action during the stroke and their attachments and relations to the skeleton are indicated by thick black lines. To begin with he should take particular notice of the following: (1) The different degrees to which the hip-bones or pelvis are inclined to the vertical in the four successive positions. (2) The variations in the curvature of the vertebral column, particularly in the lumbar region. (3) The successive positions of the shoulder-blade and its relation to the ribs. (4) The extent to which the knee, and (5) the extent to which the ankle is bent in the four successive positions.

In fig. 65 the oarsman is not in the full forward position but has already caught hold of the water. He has already begun to lift his body back from his thighs, and in doing so has pushed back his slide some two inches. It is a good representation of the initial effort of the stroke as it should be made. The knees, although they must have descended a trifle to push back the slide two inches, are relatively fixed, as also are the ankle-joints. To fix the ankle, the tibialis anticus and long extensor of the toes are in conspicuous contraction on the shin, and the peroneal group on the outside of the leg. The knee is being kept flexed by the obvious contraction of the short head of the biceps, and I think that my model is also using the gastrocnemius for the same purpose. The knee being thus kept bent, and the lower leg fixed, the thigh-bone is being thrust into the socket of the aceta-

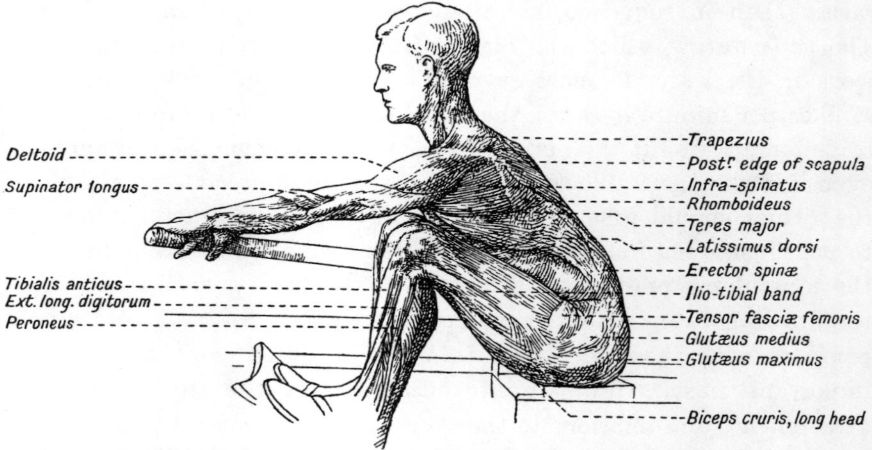

Fig. 65. The beginning caught. The body is lifted back from the thighs and the slide has been moved back about two inches. The chief muscular prominences are labelled.

bulum much as a ship's mast is boosted down upon her keel by the tension of a forestay (the quadriceps extensor), a backstay (the hamstrings), and side stays (the adductors on the inside and the ilio-tibial band on the outside of the leg). The tensor fasciae femoris muscle is strongly contracted, thus making tense the ilio-tibial band : consequently the outer side of the thigh is flattened and does not exhibit any marked muscular prominences, for the quadriceps extensor has not yet begun to contract forcibly enough to flatten down the knees. The glutaeus medius and the superficial fibres of the glutaeus maximus are strongly contracted, rendering tense the fascia lata over the great trochanter, and thus keeping the head of the thigh-bone firm in the acetabulum. On the lower side of the thigh the long head of the biceps cruris (the outer hamstring) is prominent. In conjunction with the inner hamstrings, it is pulling on the tuberosity of the ischium, the united action of these muscles tending to rotate the pelvis about the acetabulum as a centre. The action of the legs at this period is deserving of close attention. Propped firmly against the stretcher, they

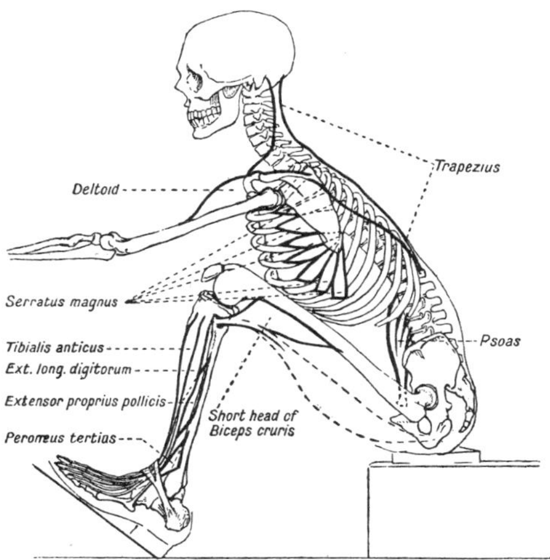

Fig. 65 a. Corresponds to Fig. 65. The thick black lines show the relation to the skeleton of some of the principal muscles used in the swing forward.

are withstanding the whole resistance encountered by the blade of the oar at the moment of its impact with the water. But, for the moment, they are passive rather than active agents in withstanding that resistance. When only slightly bent, as on a fixed seat, they have been described by an eminent anatomist as 'firm, inflexible pillars, pressing the feet immovably against the stretcher and forming, as it were, a fulcrum by which the body is enabled to retain its exact position on its seat during the powerful action of the glutaei'. For a sliding-seat this description is hardly applicable, the limb being bent at such an angle that it can scarcely be likened to a pillar. The seat is movable, and has already begun to move backwards as a result of the muscular action of the legs. None the less the leg, when properly used at the beginning of the stroke, is momentarily immobilized by its own muscular action. The feet are planted immovably on the stretcher ; the knee is fixed ; the head of the thigh-bone is kept steady in the socket of the hip-joint and forms the pivot about which the trunk (including the hip-bones) rotates. The essential thing is the steadying of the hip-joints whilst the trunk is being lifted back from the thighs. Returning to fig. 65, we see that the vertebral column is still bent forward in the lumbar region, but the erector spinae muscles are in vigorous action and are prominent at the small of the back. At the upper extremity of the trunk the outside shoulder is well advanced, but not overreached, nor elevated. The upper fibres of the trapezius, though taut, are not unduly contracted. The middle and lower fibres of the trapezius and the rhomboids are sufficiently contracted to keep the vertebral border of the scapula in position and to prevent the shoulder from yielding to the strain of the oar. Of the muscles which connect the upper arm with the shoulder and trunk, the deltoid, the infra-spinatus, the teres minor and major, and the latissimus dorsi are seen stretched to their fullest extent. We say stretched, but they are not passively stretched : they are in a state of incipient contraction, preparatory to the more powerful action which, in a later phase of the stroke, will pull back the shoulder and upper arm.

In the arm itself, the biceps, the triceps, and the extensors on the upper side of the forearm are stretched taut by the pull on the oar, but the only muscles in an active state of contraction are the flexors on the lower side of the forearm, whose function it is to keep the fingers firmly hooked round the handle of the oar.

The head is naturally poised on the neck and not thrown back, nor yet allowed to droop forward. The poise is maintained by the action of the sterno-mastoids and a slight contraction of the muscles at the back of the neck.

In general, the muscles of the arms and upper half of the body are braced to take the strain of the oar. The muscles of loins, the buttocks, and the hamstrings in the leg are doing the work at the beginning of the stroke. The question arises, Which of the three does the chief share of the work at this critical moment ? Or do all three take an equal or nearly equal share ?

On a fixed seat there is no doubt about the answer. The work falls almost entirely on the buttock muscles, the glutaei. The anatomical authority[1] quoted above (p. 355) writes :

> ' The first of these movements ' (the drawing back of the trunk) ' is generally referred to the muscles of the back. But this is an error. The muscles of the back, under the general name of erector spinae, act upon a nearly inflexible pillar and nothing more. The sum of their action cannot exceed in its range a greater length than from one to two inches, while the trunk has to move through a space equal to 45°, or one-eighth of a circle. We must look, therefore, to some other agency that can directly influence the relations between the trunk and lower extremities, and operate in drawing backwards the entire trunk from an angle of 45° to an angle of 90°, and of restoring the body to its upright position and somewhat beyond it. This can only be effected by the great muscles of the buttock, attached between the trunk and the thigh.'

This is perfectly true for straight-backed, fixed-seat oarsmen whose forward position is well illustrated in fig. 19. The object of the rigidly straight back was to make of it ' a nearly inflexible pillar ', which could be swung back by the action of the glutaei. In such a back the erectors of the spine do little more than keep the pillar firm and prevent it from bending forwards. But on a long slide, in the full forward position, the hip-joint being flexed to the fullest possible extent by the raising of the knees towards the armpits, the pelvis cannot be rotated forwards to nearly the same extent that it can be on a fixed seat. The vertebral column is by no means the

[1] ' Muscular Action in Rowing ', by F. C. Skey, C.B., F.R.C.S., in the *Lancet*, 2 Oct. 1869. This is the only memoir I have been able to discover which deals adequately with the subject.

'nearly inflexible pillar' described by Mr. Skey (see p. 141 and fig. 55, p. 325), and in ninety-nine cases out of a hundred the oarsman, in order to get the utmost possible length of reach forward, bends the lumbar region of the backbone, and doubles the body over the knees. The attitude of such an oarsman, when full forward, is well illustrated by fig. 34, traced from a cinematograph record of the Cambridge crew of 1924. The individual portrayed was, by common consent, the most graceful and polished oarsman in a highly polished crew, yet the photograph shows him in a constrained and ungraceful position at the moment when he is raising his hands to lower his blade into the water. He is overreaching, and it was the one fault of an otherwise remarkably good crew that all its members overreached in this manner. It was a waste of effort, for, as a consequence of the overreach, the blades descended obliquely into the water and the first part of the stroke was rowed in the air. What concerns us here is, that the unnecessary length of reach forward is clearly obtained by bending the lumbar region of the vertebral column. The only muscles capable of bringing the upper part of the trunk back from this to the erect position are the erectors of the spinal column. Fig. 34, 'got it', four pictures farther on in the film, show the same oarsman when he has fairly got hold of the water. When the two figures are superimposed it can be seen that the pelvis has hardly been moved through any angle at all, but the upper three-fourths of the body, from the level of the lowest lumbar vertebra upwards, have been moved through an angle of 14°. The slide has been pushed back two or three inches, but, relatively to the seat, the pelvis has been held in a fixed position, whilst the erector spinae has been lifting back the upper part of the body. The glutaei must have shared in fixing the pelvis, though their action cannot be seen owing to the oarsman's shorts and the gunwale of the boat. But the large share taken by the hamstrings in fixing the pelvis is clearly shown by the prominence of the long head of the biceps cruris in fig. 34. Without this use of the hamstrings the oarsman would 'shoot his slide'.

The great majority of oarsmen who slide correctly use their muscles in this manner at the beginning of the stroke. They fix the pelvis, and rely mainly on the powerful erector spinae group to straighten up the body and get the required pull on the handle of the oar. Photographs leave no room for doubt on this matter. Since the erector spinae muscles form the strongest group in the whole body, if they are well and truly used there can be no objection to this style of rowing. I have my doubts whether it is the best style. A few oarsmen, in virtue of a special conformation of the hip-joints, are able to swing forward the pelvis, even on a 16-inch slide, quite as far as is possible on a fixed seat. Fig. 20, taken from a photograph of an eminent pre-war oarsman, stands in contrast to fig. 34, though in both the oarsmen exhibit too great an overreach of the shoulders. In fig. 20 the whole trunk has been swung forward from the hip-joints. The lumbar region of the back is not humped as in fig. 34, but is, if anything, slightly concave. Here the back forms the ' nearly inflexible pillar ' described by Mr. Skey. The spinal erectors can do little more than maintain that inflexibility, and the lift back of the trunk must be effected by the powerful action of the glutaei. On the whole I think this is the better way, as the firm pillar is lifted back more rapidly than the bent column is straightened out, and the momentum of the body-weight is more effective. But, as has been pointed out, there are only a few individuals who can bring their hips forward to this extent on a long slide. It is further to be remarked that the oarsman depicted in fig. 20 never brought his slide quite up to the front-stop. If he had he would not have been able to get the same length of swing from the hip-joints. He preferred length of body-swing with the use of only fourteen inches of slide to a curtailed body-swing with the use of the full sixteen inches. An examination of the runners of a sliding-seat eight shows that most oarsmen of 5 ft. 10 in. or less stature unconsciously adopt the same method. The wheel-marks on the runners show that they bring up the slide one or two inches short of the front-stop.

We may now turn to fig. 66 and compare with it fig. 34, in which the oarsman is seen at the same phase of the stroke, but nearly in three-quarter view instead of in profile. Fig. 34 is the more natural of the two, as it is taken from a film of a crew in motion, whereas the model for fig. 65 was posed in a laboratory. He was, however, pulling

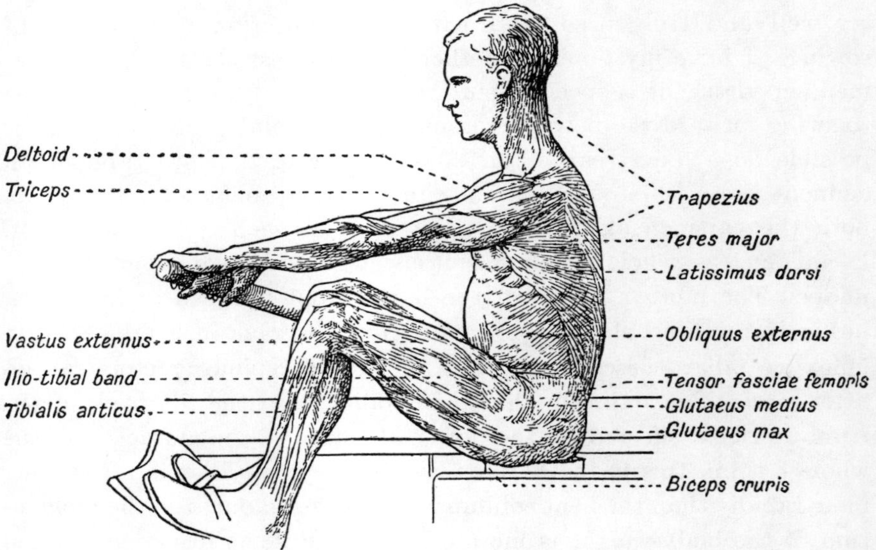

FIG. 66. The early middle of the stroke. The trunk is upright and the muscles of the thighs are contracting forcibly to drive back the slide. Observe the position of the left shoulder as compared with Fig. 65.

hard, and being stripped of his clothes, the muscular prominences of his body and limbs are clearly visible.

The trunk is upright, and the head and neck naturally poised on the shoulders. The slide has been driven back five inches (rather more in fig. 34) ; the knees are still bent and so much raised that the arms clear them by little more than two inches. The arms are still quite straight, pulled taut by the resistance of the oar. In the leg, the tibialis anticus and the peroneal group of muscles are still strongly

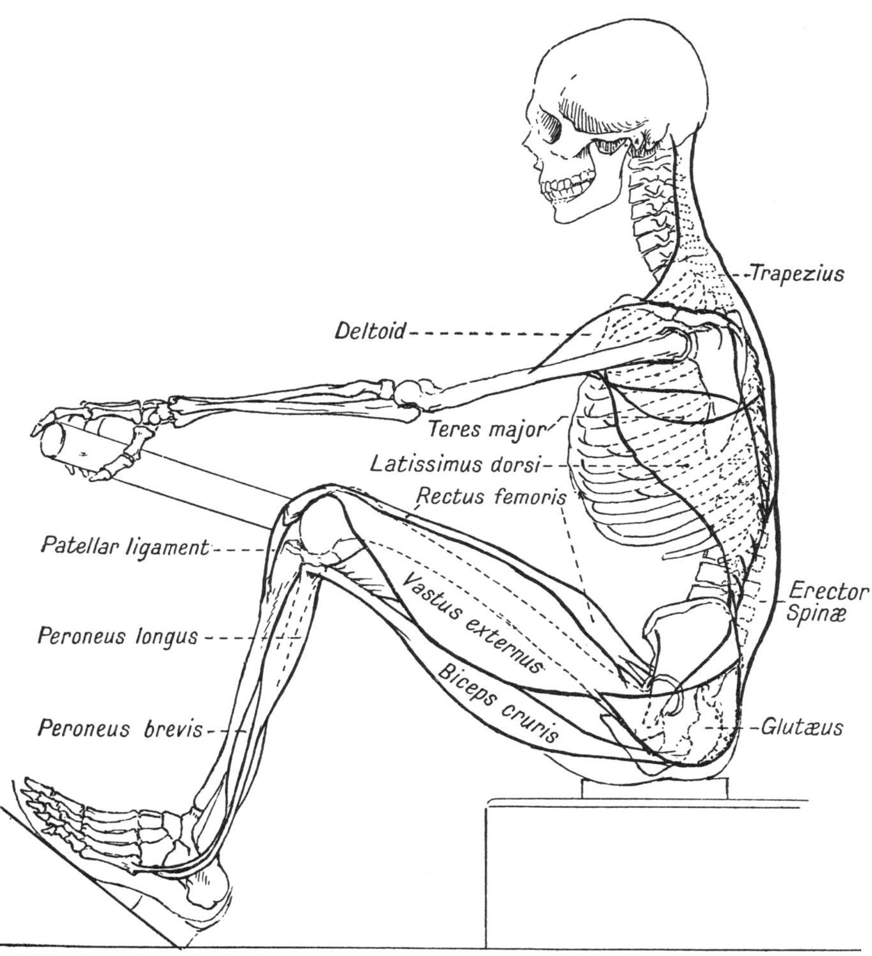

FIG. 66 A. Corresponds to Fig. 66. The thick lines show the relation to the skeleton of some of the most important muscles used during the stroke. Note the inclination of the pelvis.

contracted to keep the heel down on the stretcher. In the thigh the quadriceps extensor is in full action, to flatten down the knees and drive back the slide. Therefore the rectus femoris and vastus externus are prominent on the upper and outer surfaces of the thigh. The short head of the biceps cruris is out of action, but the long head is still contracted, though not so prominent as in fig. 65. The tensor

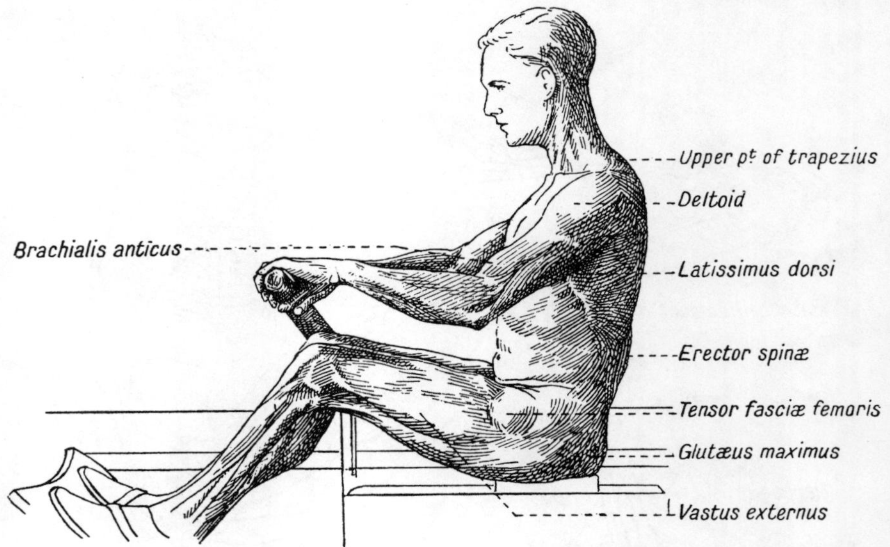

FIG. 67. The slide has been driven back about 12 inches and the arms are bending. The head and neck are dropped too much forward. Note the contracted state of the latissimus dorsi muscle.

fasciae femoris remains contracted to tighten the ilio-tibial band. The glutaeus medius is still prominent, but hardly to the same extent as in fig. 65 : it is keeping the fascia lata tense over the great trochanter. The glutaeus maximus is strongly contracted. It has lifted the trunk to the upright position and has still much work to do in pulling back the pelvis and straightening out the flexed hip-joint. In the trunk the erector spinae is strongly contracted, but now its function is rather to maintain the upright position of the back than to bend back the vertebral column. The shoulders are still forward, but the outside shoulder in particular has been drawn back some way from the position it occupied at the beginning of the stroke. The shoulder-blade has been drawn back towards the vertebral column by the trapezius and

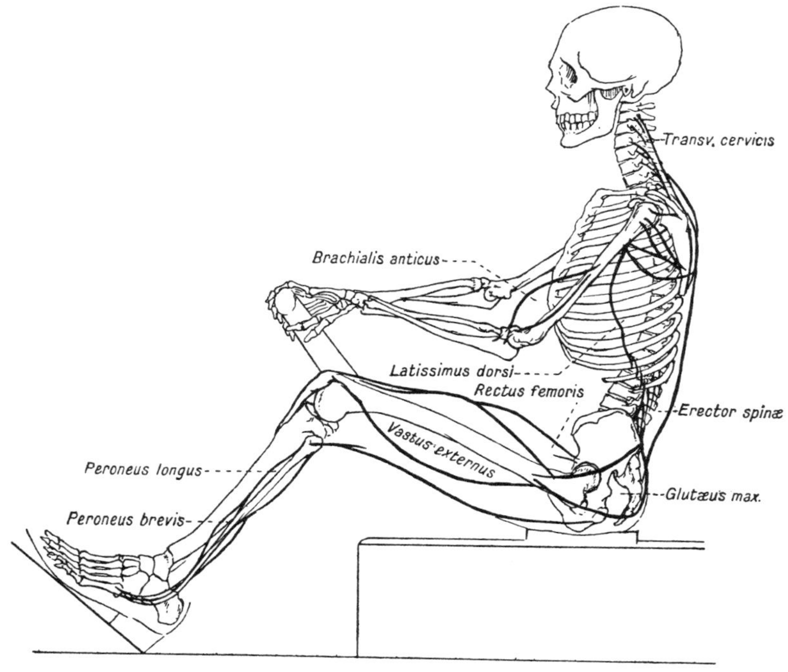

Fig. 67 A. Corresponds to Fig. 67. The muscles indicated as in the two previous figures. Note the increasing backward inclination of the pelvis.

the rhomboids. The middle and lower fibres of the former are seen in active contraction, and in a side view no part of the latter is now visible on the surface. The deltoid, the teres major, and the latissimus dorsi are conspicuous. They, as also the teres minor and infra-spinatus, which are not so clearly seen, are contracted in opposition to the pull of the arms on the handle of the oar. The muscles of the upper arm and forearm are in the same state of tension as at the beginning of the stroke. It should be observed that the lips are tightly closed, and the abdominal walls tense and slightly distended owing to the descent of the diaphragm. This is due to the respiratory effort, to be described in detail farther on.

Fig 66 A is intended to demonstrate the relation of the skeleton to the chief muscles in active use at this phase of the stroke. Attention should be specially directed to the curvatures of the vertebral column, the position of the shoulder-blade, and the backward inclination of the pelvis. The reader should also note how the muscles of the trunk and thigh are coupled up by the intervening glutaei.

In the third phase of the stroke, figs. 67 and 67 A, the upright trunk is inclined only a little farther backwards than in fig. 66. The model has allowed his head to droop a little forward, which somewhat spoils the look of the picture, but the position of the head and neck has been corrected in fig. 67 A. The slide has been driven back nearly thirteen inches by the steady extension of the legs. The shoulders are being drawn back, the elbows are bending, and the hands are just passing over the knees.

Though the position of the lower limb has changed to a considerable extent the same muscles are in action as before, with the exception of the biceps cruris, which has apparently slackened its effort. In the region of the hips the glutaeus maximus is strongly contracted and is continuing the work of straightening out the angle between the legs and the body. The glutaeus medius is not so prominent, but the tensor fasciae femoris rather more prominent than before. The back is being maintained in its firm upright position by the action of the erector spinae. The greatest change is in the position of the shoulder. The continued action of the trapezius and rhomboids has drawn the scapula much farther round the ribs towards the backbone. The upper arm is being pulled back past the side of the body, partly by the teres major and other muscles passing from it to the shoulder-blade, but chiefly by the powerful action of the latissimus dorsi. This muscle, instead of appearing as a thin triangular sheet as in figs. 65 and 66, is now contracted to a thick mass below and behind the armpit. On the upper surface of the upper arm the muscular swelling nearer to the elbow than to the shoulder indicates that it is the brachialis anticus, not the biceps, that is taking the chief share in bending the elbow.

Figs. 68 and 68 A illustrate the position of the oarsman at the moment when the hands come home to the body at the end of the stroke. The lower limbs are fully extended and the slide is driven out against the back-stop. There are no muscular prominences in the lower leg, as no further effort of the tibialis and peronei is required to keep the heels against the stretcher. In the thigh, the final flattening down of the knees and the last push home of the slide seem to have been effected by the rectus femoris, the remainder of the quadriceps remaining, however, in a state of contraction. This final effort of the rectus, which is associated with the backward inclination of the pelvis to which it is attached, can be felt by any one who grasps the upper part of the front of the thigh while going through the motions of the finish. The vigorous use of the rectus femoris at this juncture is a material aid to the recovery of the body. The glutaei, by a final effort of contraction, have inclined the hip-bone well back past the perpendicular (fig. 68 A), and a simultaneous final effort of the erector spinae has fully restored the anterior convexity of the lumbar region of the vertebral column. In other words, the small of the back is curved inwards rather than outwards. Chiefly by the action of the lower part of the trapezius, the shoulder-blade has been drawn well back towards the middle line. A simultaneous and final contraction of the latissimus dorsi has drawn the upper arm well back past the side, and at the same time has kept the shoulder down. The operative muscles of the back and shoulders are not clearly visible in a profile view, but are well illustrated in figs. 56 and 57.

On the anterior aspect of the body, the abdominal wall is put on the stretch. When the blade of the oar leaves the water and the body loses the support afforded by the resistance of the water to the oar, the recti abdominis muscles are largely instrumental in supporting the trunk, the centre of gravity of which is now so far behind a line drawn perpendicularly through the hip-joint that it would topple over backwards if unsupported. But a good oarsman will not rely on the

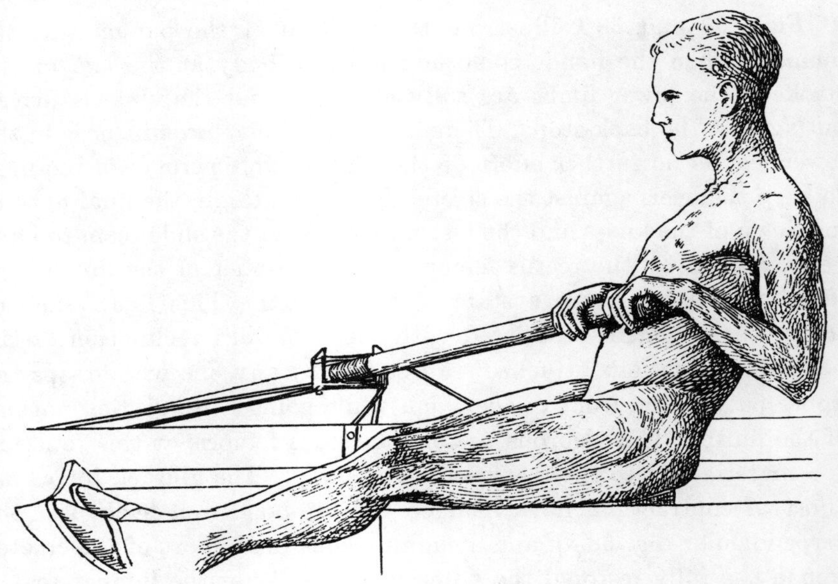

Fig. 68. The finish of the stroke. The shoulders are drawn well back and kept down; the elbows are carried well to the rear and the wrists are arched; the thumbs are just touching the body. The legs are fully extended. In this position there are no conspicuous muscular prominences on the legs and the front of the body.

recti abdominis. As he finishes the stroke he will bring the iliopsoas group into action: first, to steady and set a limit to the backward swing of the trunk; eventually, after the body has been brought to a standstill, to draw forward the hips and loins in the recovery.

Fig. 68 A represents the position of the oarsman at the finish of the stroke. The blade of the oar is still in the water. Mainly by the action of the brachialis anticus and the latissimus dorsi the hands have been drawn home until the thumbs just touch the body. Though it has nothing to do with the action of bending the elbow and drawing in the hands, I have figured the triceps brachii of the upper arm. At this instant the brachialis anticus and the biceps must relax and

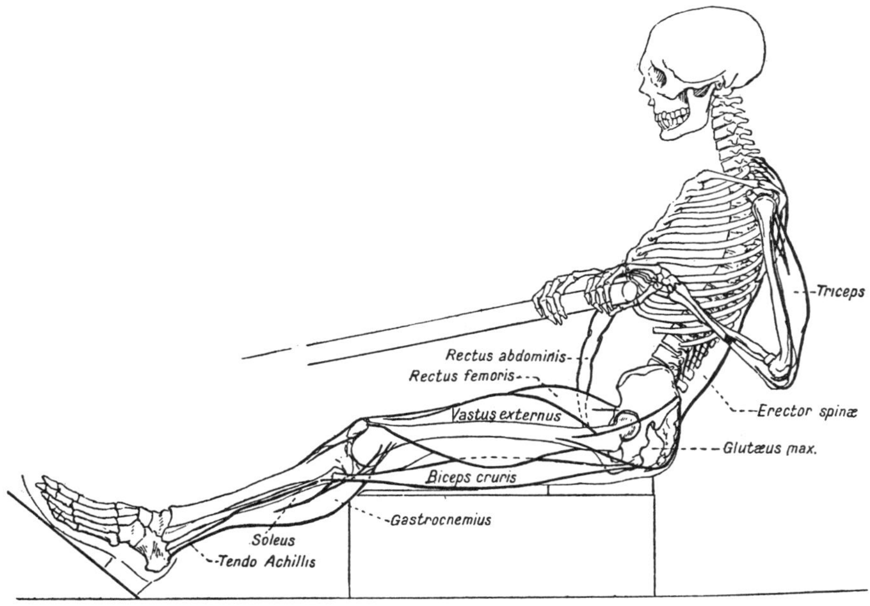

FIG. 68 A. Corresponds to Fig. 68. The muscles indicated as before. Note the angle to which the pelvis is tilted back at the finish of the stroke, bringing the coccyx down to the hind margin of the seat.

the triceps must come smartly into action, to depress the forearm and lift the blade clean out of the water. It is the only muscular movement required to produce this result. No drop of the shoulder or dip of the body is necessary. Indeed, if the oarsman has finished in the position shown in figs. 68 and 68 A no drop of the shoulders is possible. They are already kept down as low as they will go. The dip of the body resorted to by so many oarsmen who have not mastered the use of the triceps is a complex muscular movement in which the abdominal muscles, and probably also the quadratus lumborum, play the chief part. It is a detrimental movement, because it starts the abdominal muscles into activity, and once started, they will continue to contract and will take an improper share in the recovery of the body. It cannot be too strongly insisted on that the only legitimate function of the abdominal muscles is to keep firm the walls and steady the contents of the abdominal cavity. This function they have to perform throughout the stroke and the swing forward, but especially when the movements of the trunk are suddenly reversed at the beginning of the stroke and at the recovery. Hence a good deal of work is thrown upon the abdominal muscles, on the obliques as well as on the rectus abdominis. They become highly developed by the exercise, and the muscular fold, where the external oblique muscle is attached to the iliac crest, is usually as conspicuous in oarsmen as in a Greek statue. I sometimes wonder whether the great prominence given to this feature by ancient sculptors was due to the fact that the Greeks were eminently a nation of oarsmen, and that the best models were chosen from those who had developed themselves by the exercise of the oar.

We have now dealt with the action of the principal muscles brought into use in the whole cycle of the stroke and swing forward. It should be borne in mind that many of the muscles enumerated have somewhat different parts to play at different times. In the stroke their function may be either dynamic or, so to speak, static or holdfast. In the former case the muscle contracts forcibly to set the limbs or trunk in motion. In the latter case it contracts, usually in opposition to other muscles, just sufficiently to hold fast a limb or the shoulder, or it may be the hip, for the purpose of affording a *point d'appui* for parts set in motion by other muscles. Thus at the beginning of the stroke the muscles of the legs act mainly as holdfasts, while the trunk is being set in motion by the dynamic action of the erector spinae, the glutaeus maximus, and the hamstrings, these last acting most powerfully when used in combination. When the trunk has been lifted back, the extensor muscles of the thigh function dynamically, straightening out the knee-joint and driving back the slide. As soon as they begin to function in this way, their opponents, which were helping to hold the limb fast, must relax and go out of action. Similarly in the shoulder, during the first part of the stroke, the trapezius, the latissimus dorsi, the rhomboidei, the deltoid, not to mention many others, act chiefly as holdfasts. As the oar sweeps round towards the thwartship plane, these muscles begin to contract more vigorously and draw back the shoulder and upper arm. The effective length of the stroke in the water depends largely on the due observance of the proper sequence of the dynamic action of the muscles of the trunk, legs, and shoulders. Groups of muscles are used in combination, but there is a proper sequence for the activation of each group. Much of the bungling of beginners and of bad oarsmen is due to their attempting to bring all the appropriate muscles of the trunk and limbs into use at once. Sometimes experienced oarsmen, in the excitement of a close race, try to bring all their muscular power to bear by a single concentrated effort and begin to 'tear at it'. Inevitably they shorten the stroke in the water, diminish rather than increase the pace of the boat, and quickly exhaust themselves.

Much might be written on the subject of false sequences in bringing powerful groups of muscles into action: still more on the manner in which various muscles can be, but should not be, used in rowing. As the possibilities of wrongdoing are almost infinite, it would be a waste of time and space to try to enumerate them here. It is sufficient to have indicated the correct action, and I may conclude by reminding the reader that, in the stroke as in the swing forward, there must be no abrupt transference of the effort from one group of muscles to another. At any part of the stroke, the muscles (e. g. those of the legs and shoulders) that are to take up and reinforce the initial effort (of the loins and buttocks) must have begun their work before their fullest power is thrown into the scale.

A final word about breathing movements in rowing. In 'inspiration' the cavity of the chest is enlarged, and air is taken into the lungs, partly by raising the breast-bone and elevating the ribs ; partly by the flattening of the arched muscular partition, the midriff or diaphragm, which separates the thoracic from the abdominal cavity. In 'expiration' the cavity of the chest is diminished, and air is expelled from the lungs, partly by lowering the breast-bone and ribs, partly by the ascent of the diaphragm, which resumes its arched shape. The movements of the arms and shoulders are influential in raising or depressing the ribs and breast-bone. The contractions and relaxations of the abdominal walls are influential in assisting—or impeding—the ascent and descent of the diaphragm. When the arms are raised from the shoulder the ribs and breast-bone are elevated, and inspiration is facilitated. When the shoulders are drawn backwards and downwards and the arms are drawn back close past the sides, the breast-bone and ribs are depressed and expiration is promoted. When the abdominal walls are strongly contracted the contents of the abdominal cavity are pressed up against the diaphragm and expiration is facilitated. When the abdominal walls are relaxed, the diaphragm is free to descend in inspiration. In any form of prolonged exercise deep and regular breathing postpones the period of exhaustion. Distress follows hard upon shallow and spasmodic respiration.

The movements of rowing, when properly executed, facilitate deep and regular respiration. During the swing forward the arms are raised from the shoulder ; the breast-bone is drawn upwards ; the pull of the serratus magnus dilates the chest by raising and expanding the ribs. If the oarsman is coming forward in the correct manner, with the abdominal walls relaxed and the stomach well pressed forward between the thighs, there is no hindrance to the descent of the diaphragm. All the conditions are favourable for taking a long and deep inspiration. But if the stomach is hollowed by the contraction of the abdominal walls, the viscera will be pressed up against the diaphragm and the conditions will only be favourable for a shallow inspiration. Perhaps the oarsman will hold his breath and take no air at all into his lungs when the opportunity is most favourable.

At the beginning of the stroke the oarsman instinctively closes his lips and holds his breath during the big effort of the swing back of the body and drive with the legs. If the lungs have been filled with air, as they should have been during the swing forward, the diaphragm is flattened down and the abdomen somewhat protuberant, as shown in fig. 66. At the same time, the shoulder-blade being fixed by the muscles which attach it posteriorly to the trunk, the chest is kept expanded by the pull of the serratus magnus on the ribs. This temporary inhibition of the respiratory movements, when the lungs are filled with air, is a usual accompaniment of violent exertion. A hundred-yards runner will fill his lungs at the start and hold his breath until the end of the course. The act of respiration would seem to detract something from the intensity of his effort. The oarsman is under no such compulsion to restrain his breath for a long period. Towards the end of the stroke, as his elbows come past his sides and the abdominal muscles contract to steady the swing back of the body, the conditions are favourable for expiration. Usually it is delayed until the hands drop and the effort of the pull is over. Then there is a somewhat forced expiratory effort, coinciding in time with the first movement of the recovery of the body. It is often accompanied by a slight dip of the body, due to the depression of the ribs and breast-bone, and perhaps to the contraction of the serratus posticus inferior. When not exaggerated it is not ungraceful. Following the expiratory effort, there is a pause. Inspiration does not begin until the body has been recovered to the perpendicular.

This is the natural and proper mode of breathing at slow and medium rates of stroke. At a high rate there is less time for the inspiratory action during the swing forward and the breathing movements tend to become short and laboured. Even at a slow rate many oarsmen, especially those who elevate the shoulders towards the finish of the stroke, take short and laboured breaths. The respiratory movements are inhibited during the swing forward and in the first half of the stroke. The act of raising the shoulders at the finish raises the ribs and breast-bone. The chest is expanded, the lips are opened, and there is a short and violent inspiratory effort as the oar is coming home, followed by an almost explosive expiration during the recovery. I call to mind a very powerful and successful oarsman who lifted his shoulders very high at the finish and forced them down with a big effort at the recovery. During these movements he seemed to pump air into and out of his lungs like a pair of bellows, and his forced respiration was audible at quite a considerable distance. It need hardly be said that laboured respiratory movements of this kind are very exhausting. A coach should notice whether his pupils are breathing correctly, and if they are not, should direct their attention to movements which, when correctly performed, will go far to ensure an easy and natural mode of breathing. But he must remember that the respiratory movements are peculiarly liable to be affected by the nervous system. A man who is worried about his breathing movements may easily be made to fall out of Scylla into Charybdis. If things are well in this matter, let well alone.

I have been interested in a peculiar trick of the most polished of present-day oarsmen. He in some measure spoils an almost faultless elegance of action by making a fearful grimace at the beginning of the stroke ; dropping his lower jaw as far as it will go and closing his mouth with a snap when he feels that he has fairly got hold of the water. In concentrating his attention on the proper timing of his effort at the beginning, this oarsman inhibits his respiration by forcibly closing not the lips but the glottis. The trick is of no consequence. The cinematograph shows that most oarsmen make a grimace of some kind when restraining their breath during the stroke, but I have never seen any to compare with this. Our movements are so curiously co-ordinated by habit that the oarsman in question, if he tried to abolish his grimace, would probably lose irrecoverably his characteristic precision at the beginning of the stroke.

CHAPTER XIV

CONCLUSION

I HAD proposed to write an account of nearly half a century's more or less intimate experience of rowing and to tack on to it the fruits of my experience in the shape of some practical hints for the guidance of present and future oarsmen. But, after several false starts, I have been impelled to row a much longer and very different course from what was originally intended. The book has grown to a size which leaves no room for reminiscences. Nor are they wanted, for the chronicles of Henley, of Putney, and of the Universities are so complete that any addition to them is uncalled for. I do not feel called upon to give a list of the individual oarsmen and crews who, in my estimation, were the best I have seen and known. For one thing, such a list is invidious. For another thing, my opinion coincides so nearly with the oft-expressed opinions of the best judges of the subject that, were I to offer it, it would be merely a repetition of a tale many times told.

I may, however, say this much. That when I attempt to conjure up out of my memory an ideal oarsman, I think in the first place of my old friend and fellow-oarsman, at school and at the University, the late Mr. Leonard West. Surely a prince among strokes, for he combined superb leadership with a faultless style. His name is not writ so large in aquatic annals as those of many who preceded or succeeded him, for he was the most modest and retiring of men, and, after his last victory at Putney in 1883, he left the river for the sea and thenceforth was rarely seen outside yachting circles. In the second place I think of the late Mr. J. Hastie of the Thames Rowing Club, whose vigorous and perfectly balanced action, free from all affectation of unnecessary ornament, has rarely been equalled and never surpassed. In the third place I think of Lt.-Col. C. D. Burnell, as he rowed in the

Leander Olympic eight of 1908; for, after preaching for some years in the wilderness, I was able to point to him and say, 'There, that is how I ask you to row'. Whereupon many, who had been unbelievers, saw and were converted.

When I similarly try to form a mental image of an ideal crew my memory invariably harks back to Mr. Muttlebury's Cambridge crew of 1888, conspicuous for its great power, its fine length of swing, its perfect sliding, and above all, for the entire absence of any unnecessary display of effort. I could call to mind many other fine crews; from the London and Thames Rowing Clubs in the eighties of last century; from the Leander Club; from the Universities; and a few conspicuously good College crews from Oxford and Cambridge. But the names are scarcely worth recording without a critical appreciation of each, which space forbids. In more recent years the Leander crew of 1913, stroked by Mr. Geoffrey Tower, was, in my opinion, as good a crew as any that preceded it, and the Cambridge crew of 1924 was a fine example of accurate, well-drilled, and lively oarsmanship.

In a retrospect of nearly fifty years the vicissitudes of English oarsmanship stand out in strong relief. There are cycles of fat years and cycles of lean years which, like trade booms and depressions, follow one another with monotonous regularity. I fancy for somewhat analogous reasons. In rowing, as in so many other human affairs, some theory or principle, generally excellent in itself, is claimed by the expert opinion of the day as the one sure key to success. Its importance is extolled beyond all measure until it leads to wanton exaggeration in some particular direction and other things of equal—perhaps of greater—importance are allowed to fall into neglect. Though the evil effects of exaggeration are soon manifest, the enthusiasts continue to apply their favourite nostrum with so little discretion that the final result is incompetence. For example, at one of the Universities—it is many years ago now and I will not say at which—the theory of discarding all superfluity of adornment in rowing and of concentrating on essentials was for a while conspicuously successful. Presently the desire to avoid exaggeration became itself an exaggeration. It was said that to win races all that was required was ‘ to sit in heaps and plug ’. It was fatally easy to sit in heaps. In course of time the ‘ plugging ’ became ineffective. Drastic remedies and a long and severe course of discipline were required to stop the rot. Throughout this volume I have tried to stress the importance of attaching due value to each of the various phases and incidents of the stroke. Where one part depends so largely on the proper performance of another part, nothing but harm can result from relying too exclusively on the strength of one or two links in the chain.

A further conclusion is forced on me by the retrospect: that while the standard of oarsmanship is, on the average, much higher than it was forty years ago, the number of first-class oarsmen is, if anything, diminished. At Henley the standard of the Thames Cup is higher; the standard of the Grand Challenge Cup is somewhat lower than it was. I do not think it was ever lower than in 1914, when we had the humiliation of seeing two visiting crews fight out the final heat of the Grand Challenge Cup. Curiously enough, this deplorable lapse of form and efficiency followed hard on the heels of a period of good performance.

It was natural and inevitable that oarsmanship should have been at a low ebb for some years after the great war. But the ebb did not run so low, nor did it last as long as was anticipated. In the last two or three years there have been encouraging signs of a return to the high-water marks of pre-war days. The most encouraging sign is the wonderful development of Public School rowing. For more than fifty years before the war Eton held undisputed sway among schools at Henley, with Radley a plucky second. Others put in an occasional and as a rule unimpressive appearance. Now Shrewsbury, under the able tuition of Mr. A. E. Kitchen, has won the Ladies' Plate with a crew which might well have won the Grand Challenge Cup if only it had been entered for it. ‘ Water ’ has been revived at Westminster, and since Mr. M. H. Ellis has taken charge of it, bids fair to regain its supremacy of a century ago. Five other schools are added to the number of those who enter annually for the Ladies' Plate, and it may be hoped that before long Cheltenham will be again represented at Henley. Eight-oared rowing is hardly possible on the Itchen, but Winchester has recently sent four-oared crews of much merit to Marlow. There are several schools at which rowing is possible, but has hitherto been discouraged by the authorities. Is it too much to hope that the example of Cheltenham, situated $8\frac{1}{2}$ miles from the Severn at Tewkesbury, may be followed by others whose opportunities are greater than theirs? The influence of this new enthusiasm for rowing in Public Schools on the fortunes of English oarsmanship should be enormous. The Metropolitan and Provincial Clubs, no less than the Universities, should glean from the harvest ripened in the schools.

For the public in general, rowing, regarded as a branch of Eurhythmics, may be made a very pleasurable and health-giving form of exercise, both for men and women. But to derive real pleasure from it the art must be cultivated with at least as much assiduity as that of dancing. Boat-racing is a more strenuous and in many of its aspects a grim form of amusement. The pleasure to be derived from eurhythmic exercise is there and ought not to be neglected, but other and sterner qualities than those associated with dancing are required. Great energy and determination; a complete disregard of discomfort and fatigue; a real joy in fighting, are all necessary to ensure success. Boat-racing is a very masculine recreation and offers no rewards to the weak, the faint-hearted, or the idler. Withal it is an art, and the race does not go simply to the strong, but to those who have taken the trouble to learn how to use their strength to the best advantage.